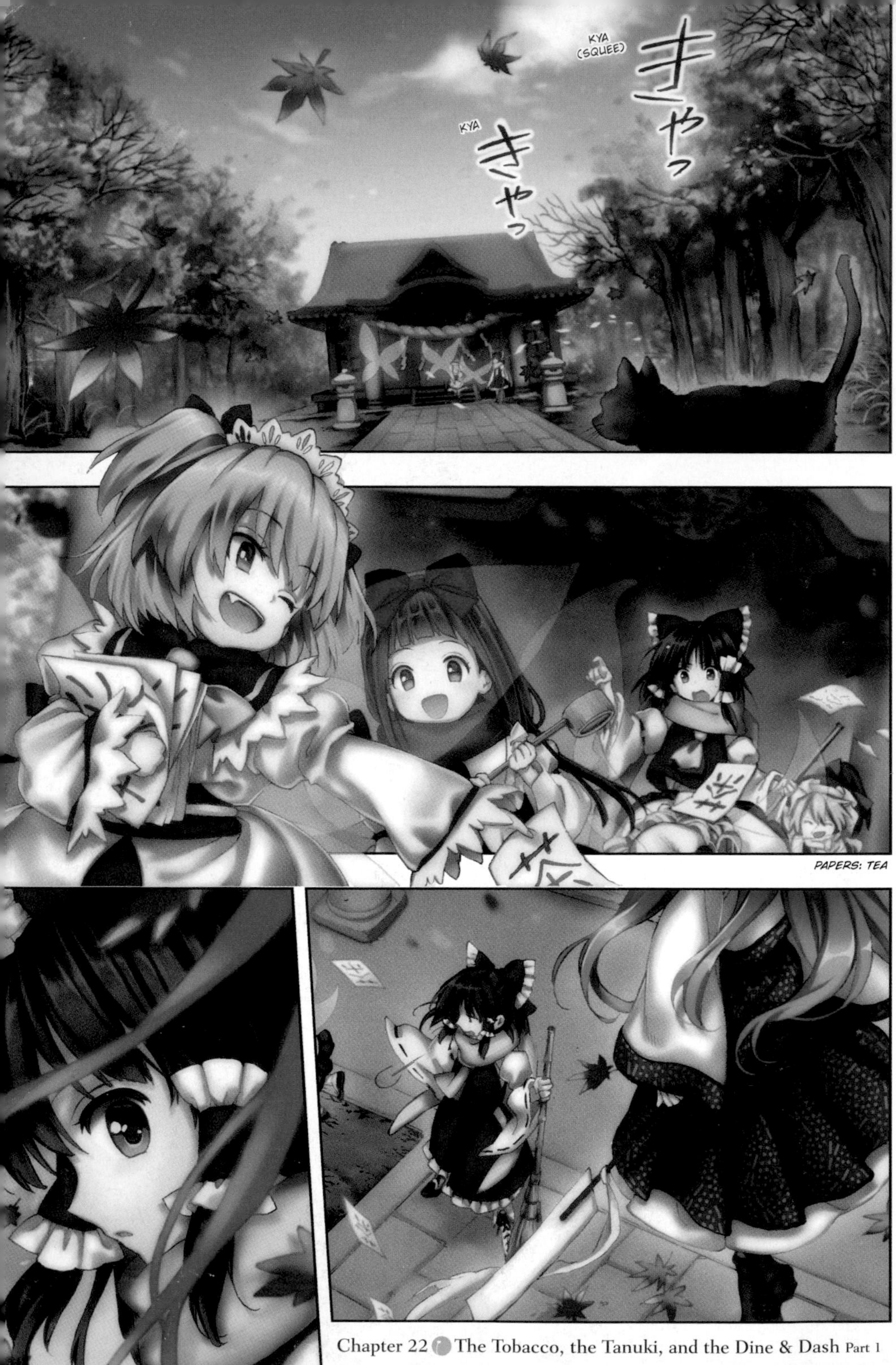
KYA (SQUEE)
KYA
PAPERS: TEA

Chapter 22 The Tobacco, the Tanuki, and the Dine & Dash Part 1

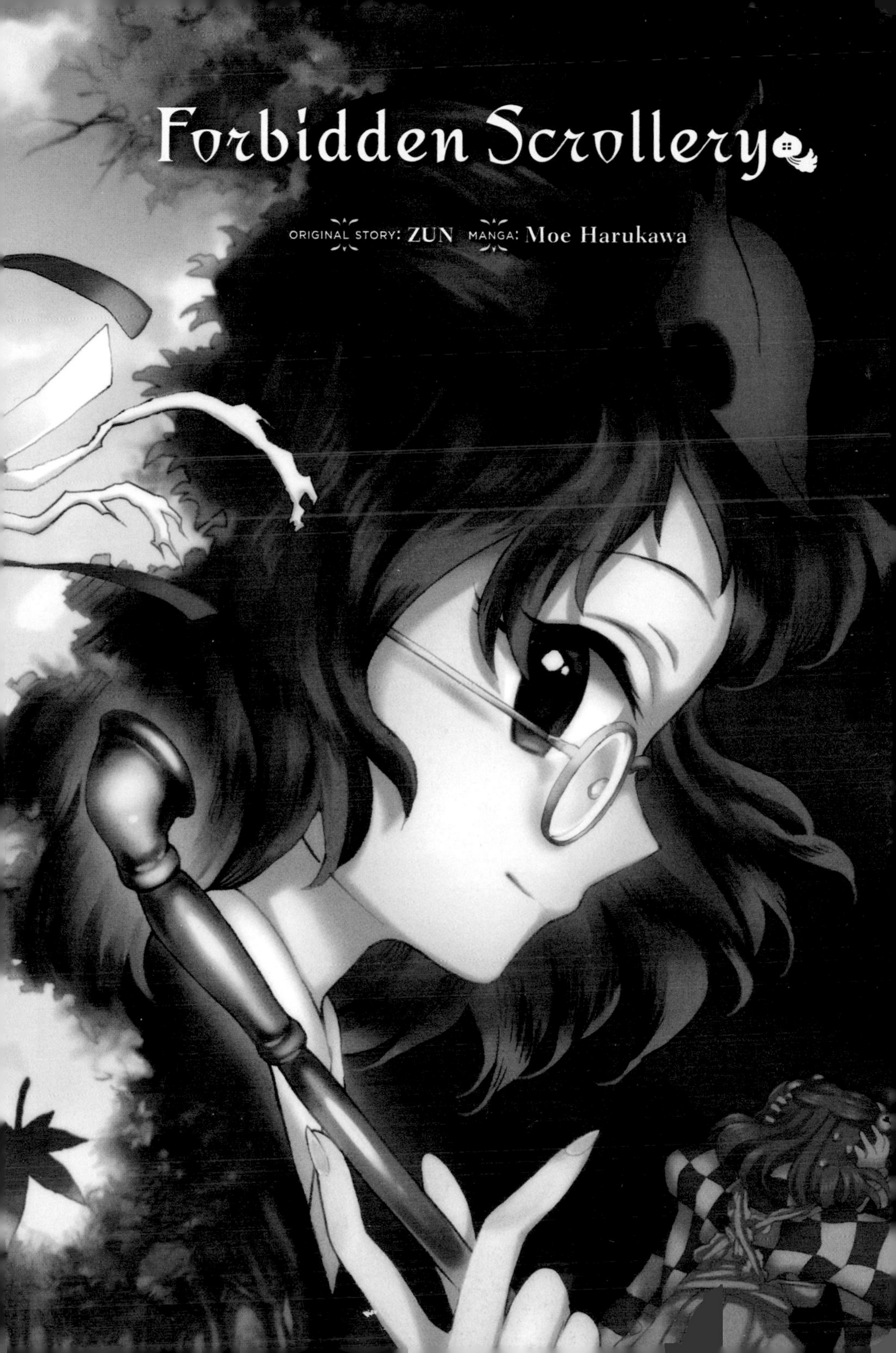
Forbidden Scrollery
ORIGINAL STORY: ZUN MANGA: Moe Harukawa

Chapter 22 The Tobacco, the Tanuki, and the Dine & Dash Part 1

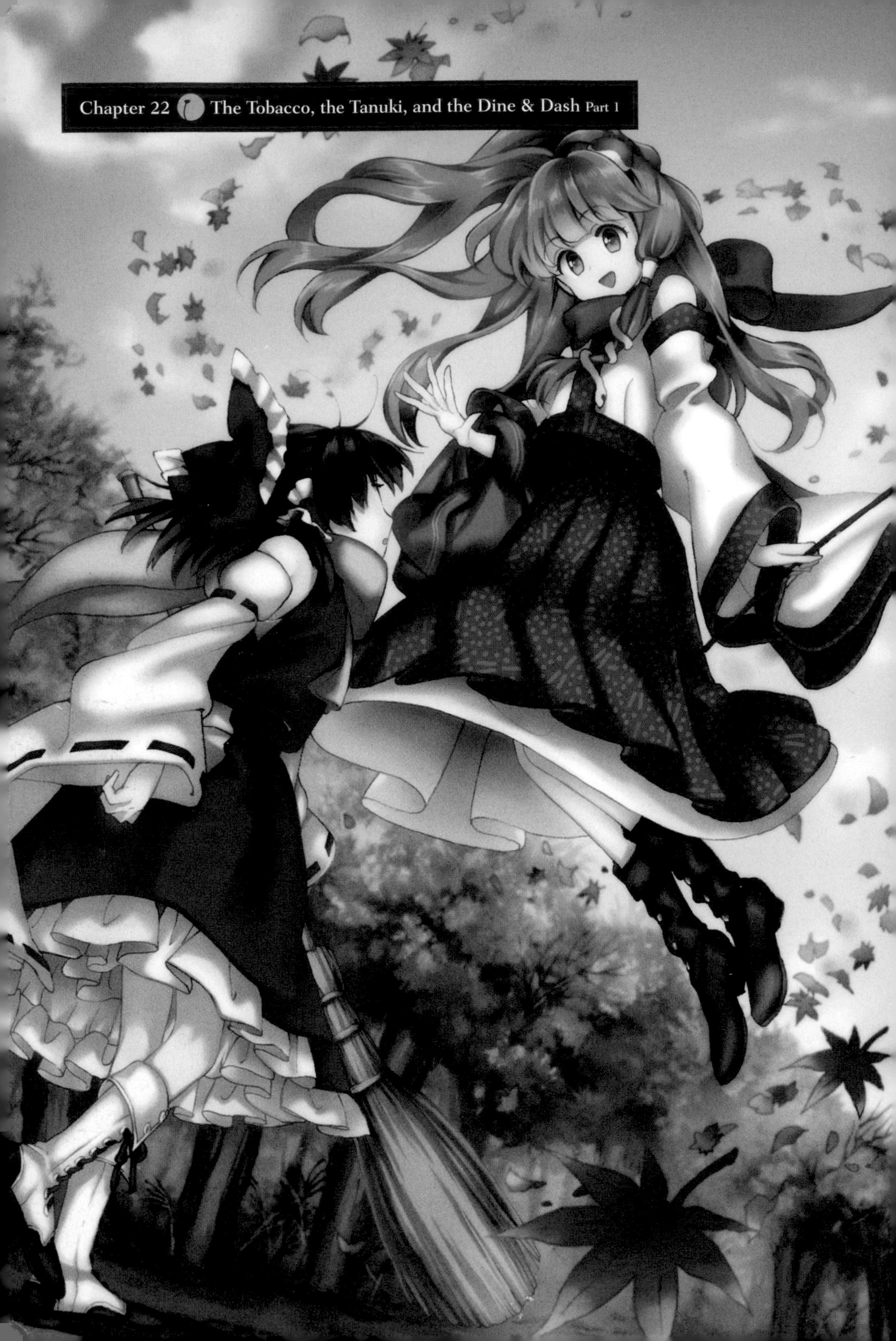

CONTENTS

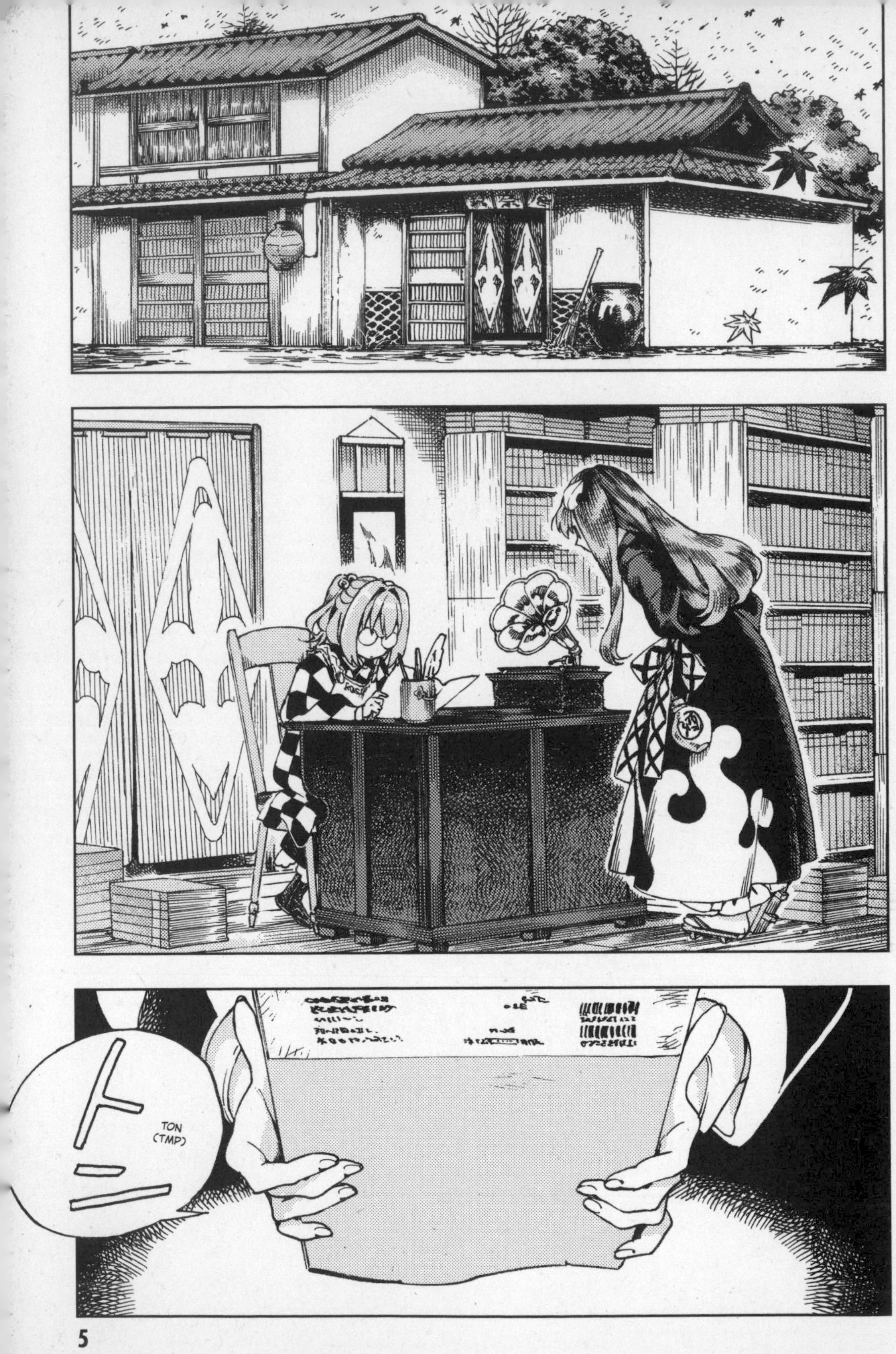
トン
TON (TMP)

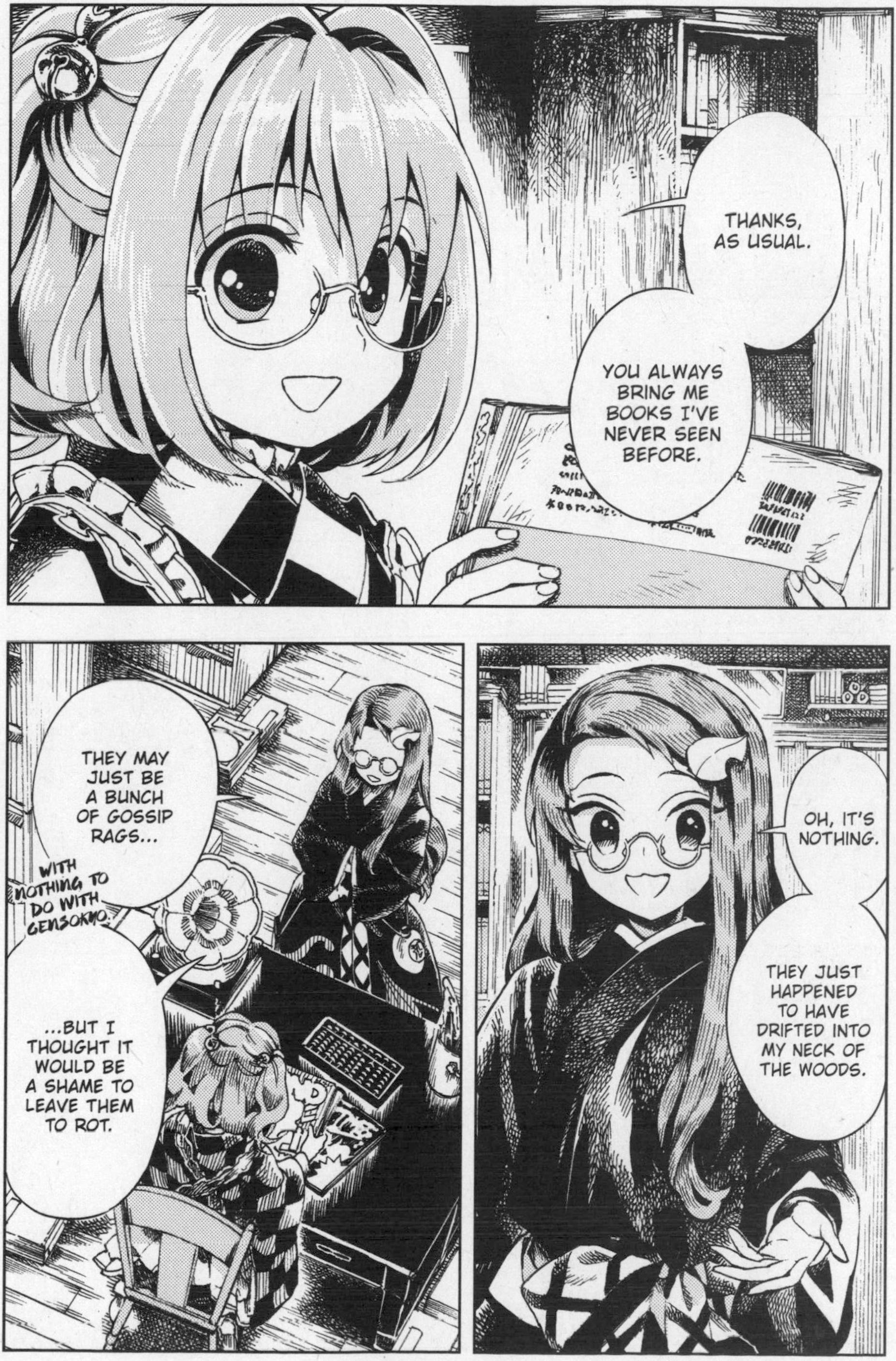
THANKS, AS USUAL.
YOU ALWAYS BRING ME BOOKS I'VE NEVER SEEN BEFORE.
OH, IT'S NOTHING.
THEY JUST HAPPENED TO HAVE DRIFTED INTO MY NECK OF THE WOODS.
THEY MAY JUST BE A BUNCH OF GOSSIP RAGS...
WITH NOTHING TO DO WITH GENSOKYO.
...BUT I THOUGHT IT WOULD BE A SHAME TO LEAVE THEM TO ROT.

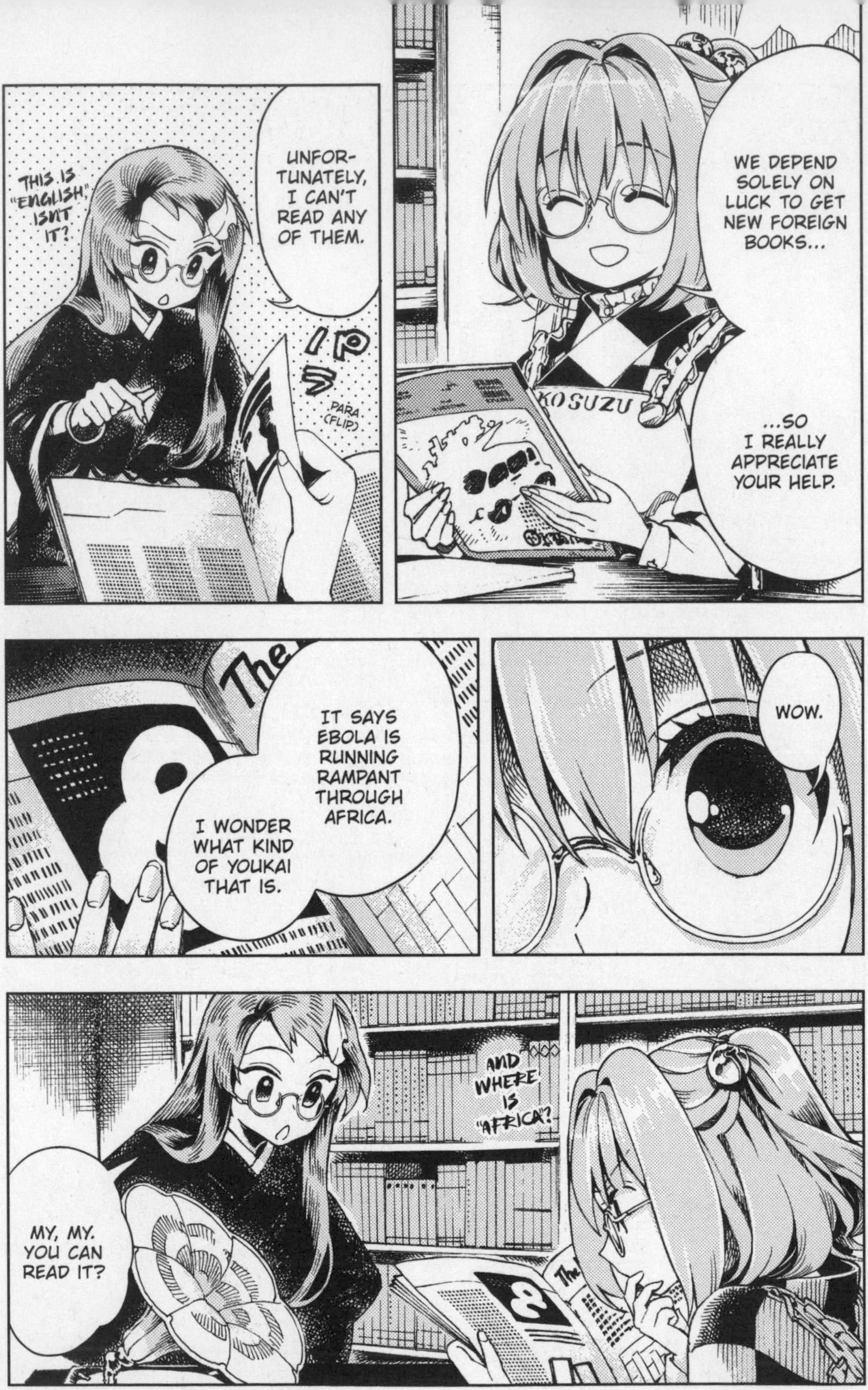
WE DEPEND SOLELY ON LUCK TO GET NEW FOREIGN BOOKS...
KOSUZU
...SO I REALLY APPRECIATE YOUR HELP.
UNFORTUNATELY, I CAN'T READ ANY OF THEM.
THIS IS "ENGLISH," ISN'T IT?
PARA (FLIP)
WOW.
IT SAYS EBOLA IS RUNNING RAMPANT THROUGH AFRICA.
I WONDER WHAT KIND OF YOUKAI THAT IS.
The
AND WHERE IS "AFRICA"?
MY, MY. YOU CAN READ IT?

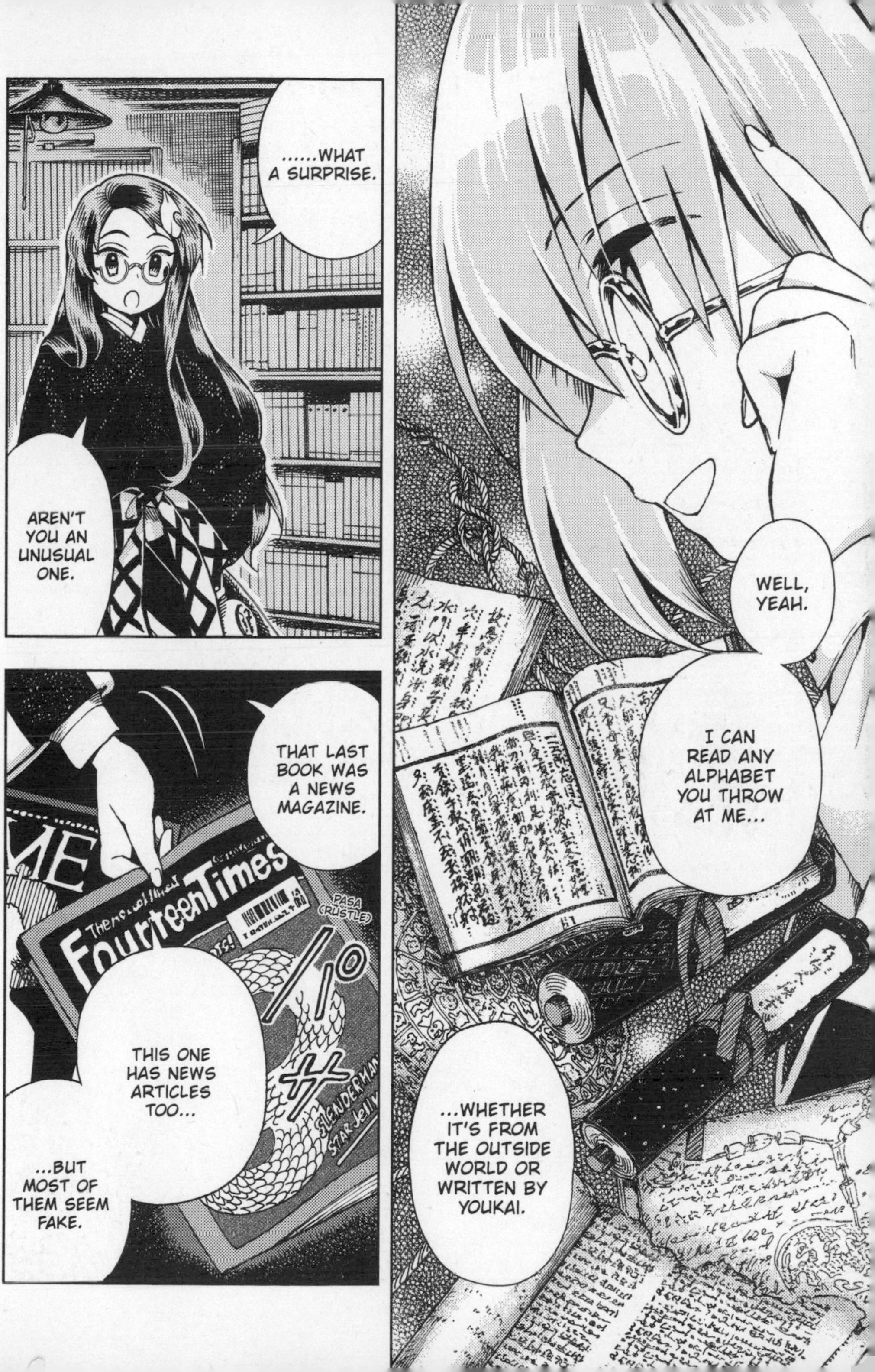
WELL, YEAH.
I CAN READ ANY ALPHABET YOU THROW AT ME...
...WHETHER IT'S FROM THE OUTSIDE WORLD OR WRITTEN BY YOUKAI.
......WHAT A SURPRISE.
AREN'T YOU AN UNUSUAL ONE.
THAT LAST BOOK WAS A NEWS MAGAZINE.
FourteenTimes
PASA (RUSTLE)
THIS ONE HAS NEWS ARTICLES TOO...
...BUT MOST OF THEM SEEM FAKE.

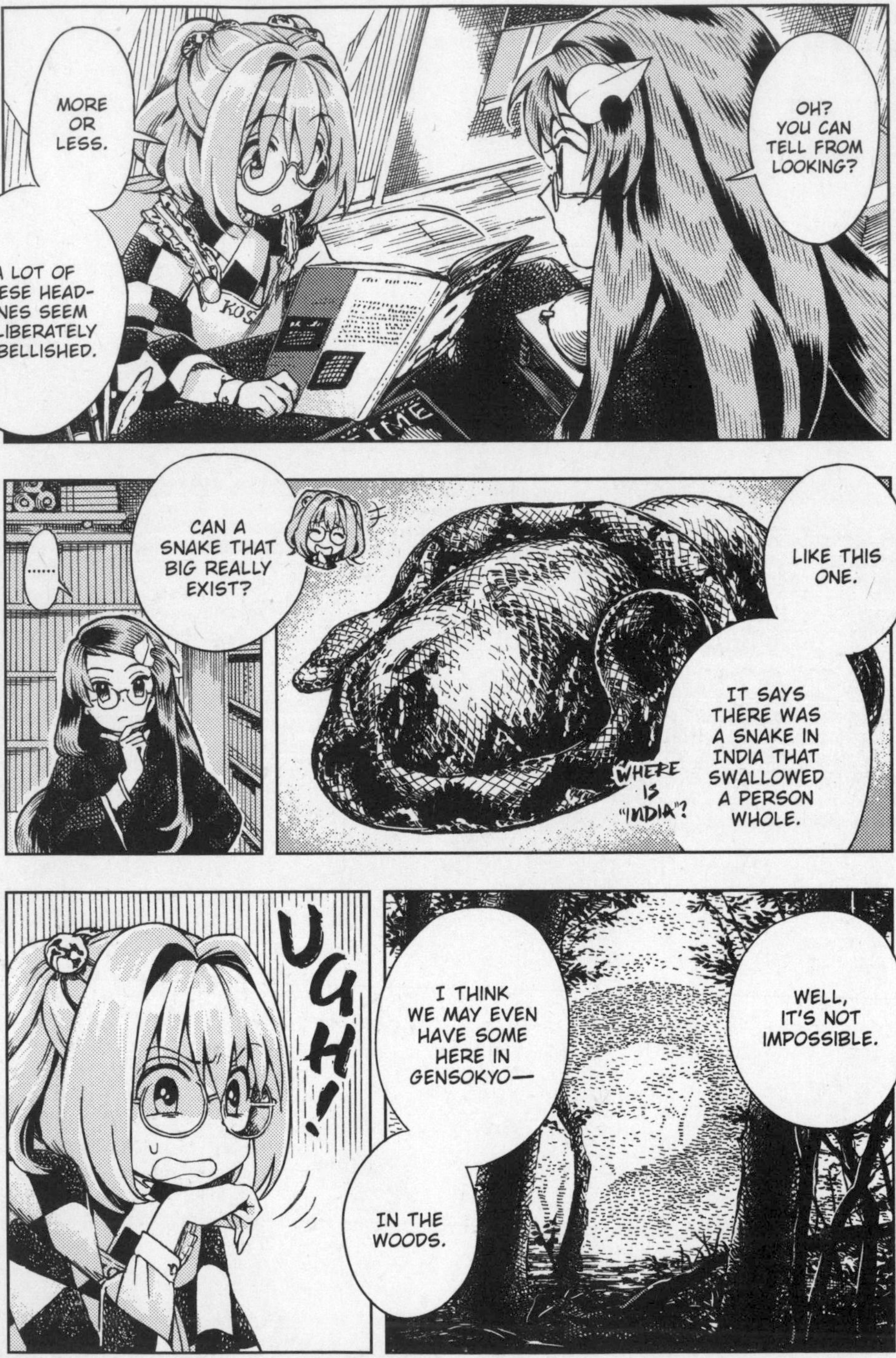
OH? YOU CAN TELL FROM LOOKING?
MORE OR LESS.
A LOT OF THESE HEAD-LINES SEEM DELIBERATELY EMBELLISHED.
LIKE THIS ONE.
IT SAYS THERE WAS A SNAKE IN INDIA THAT SWALLOWED A PERSON WHOLE.
WHERE IS "INDIA"?
CAN A SNAKE THAT BIG REALLY EXIST?
......
WELL, IT'S NOT IMPOSSIBLE.
I THINK WE MAY EVEN HAVE SOME HERE IN GENSOKYO—
IN THE WOODS.
UGH!

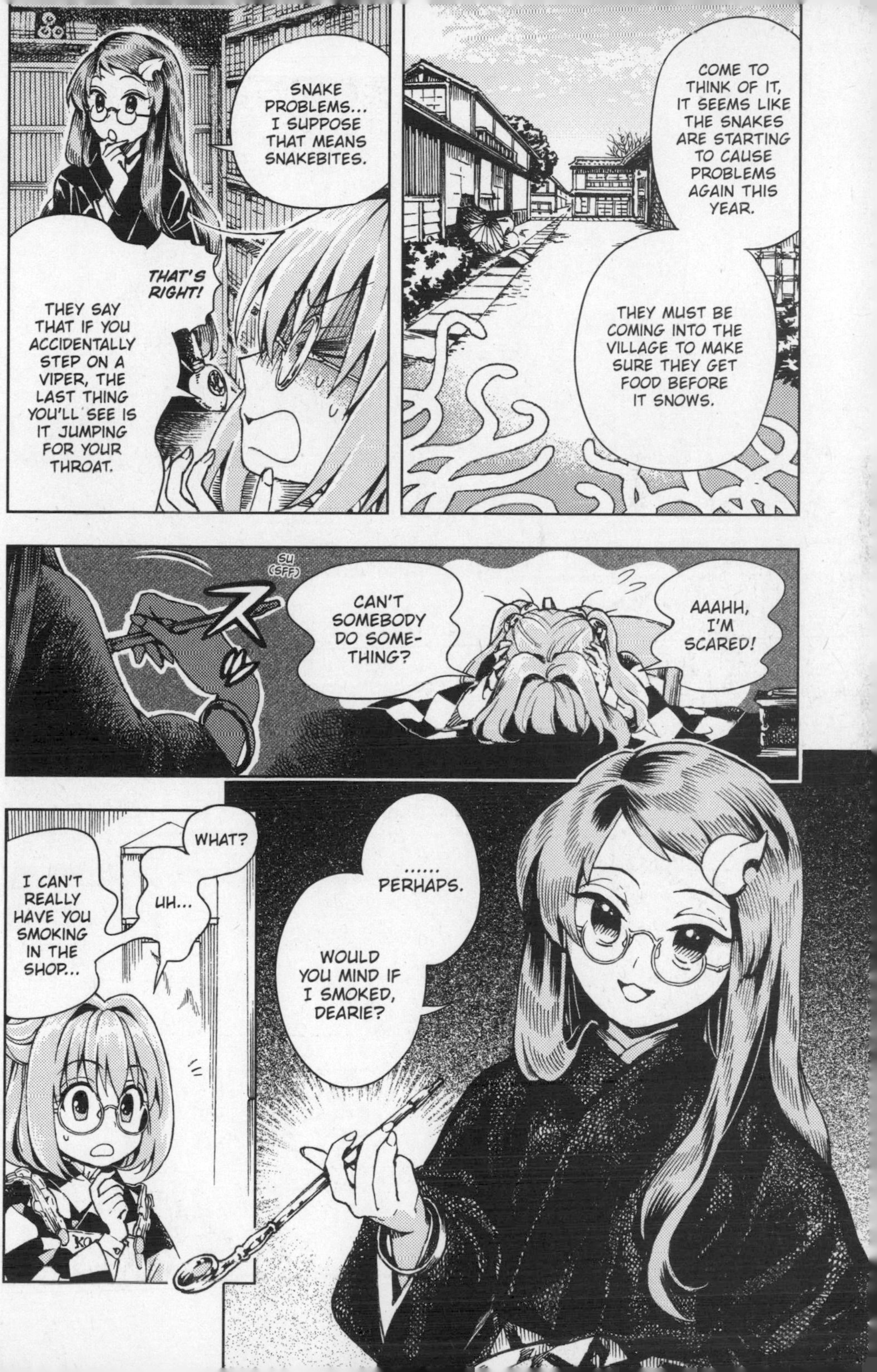
COME TO THINK OF IT, IT SEEMS LIKE THE SNAKES ARE STARTING TO CAUSE PROBLEMS AGAIN THIS YEAR.
THEY MUST BE COMING INTO THE VILLAGE TO MAKE SURE THEY GET FOOD BEFORE IT SNOWS.
SNAKE PROBLEMS... I SUPPOSE THAT MEANS SNAKEBITES.
THAT'S RIGHT!
THEY SAY THAT IF YOU ACCIDENTALLY STEP ON A VIPER, THE LAST THING YOU'LL SEE IS IT JUMPING FOR YOUR THROAT.
AAAHH, I'M SCARED!
CAN'T SOMEBODY DO SOME-THING?
SU (SFF)
...... PERHAPS.
WOULD YOU MIND IF I SMOKED, DEARIE?
WHAT?
UH...
I CAN'T REALLY HAVE YOU SMOKING IN THE SHOP...

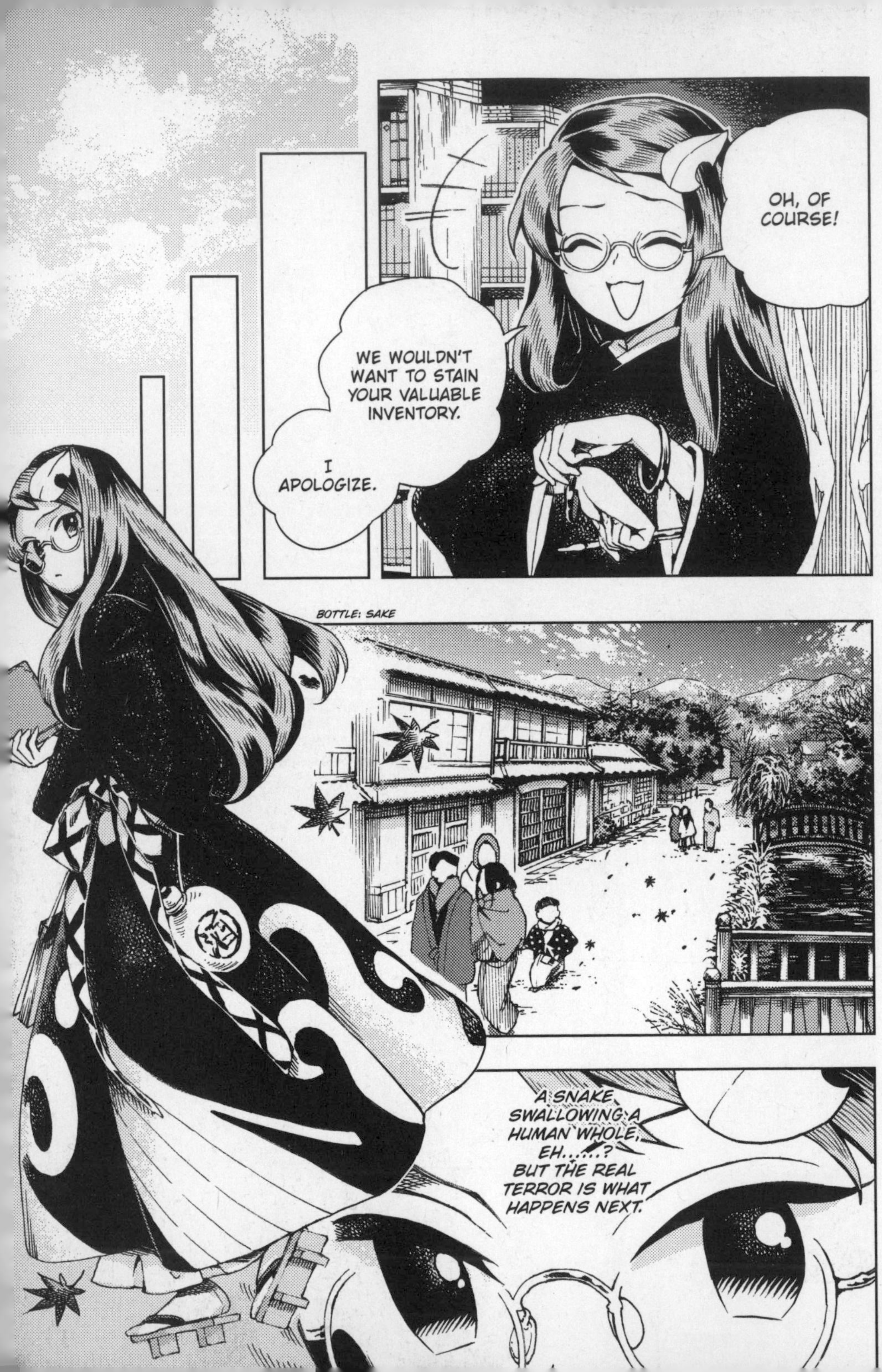
OH, OF COURSE!
WE WOULDN'T WANT TO STAIN YOUR VALUABLE INVENTORY.
I APOLOGIZE.
BOTTLE: SAKE
A SNAKE SWALLOWING A HUMAN WHOLE, EH......? BUT THE REAL TERROR IS WHAT HAPPENS NEXT.

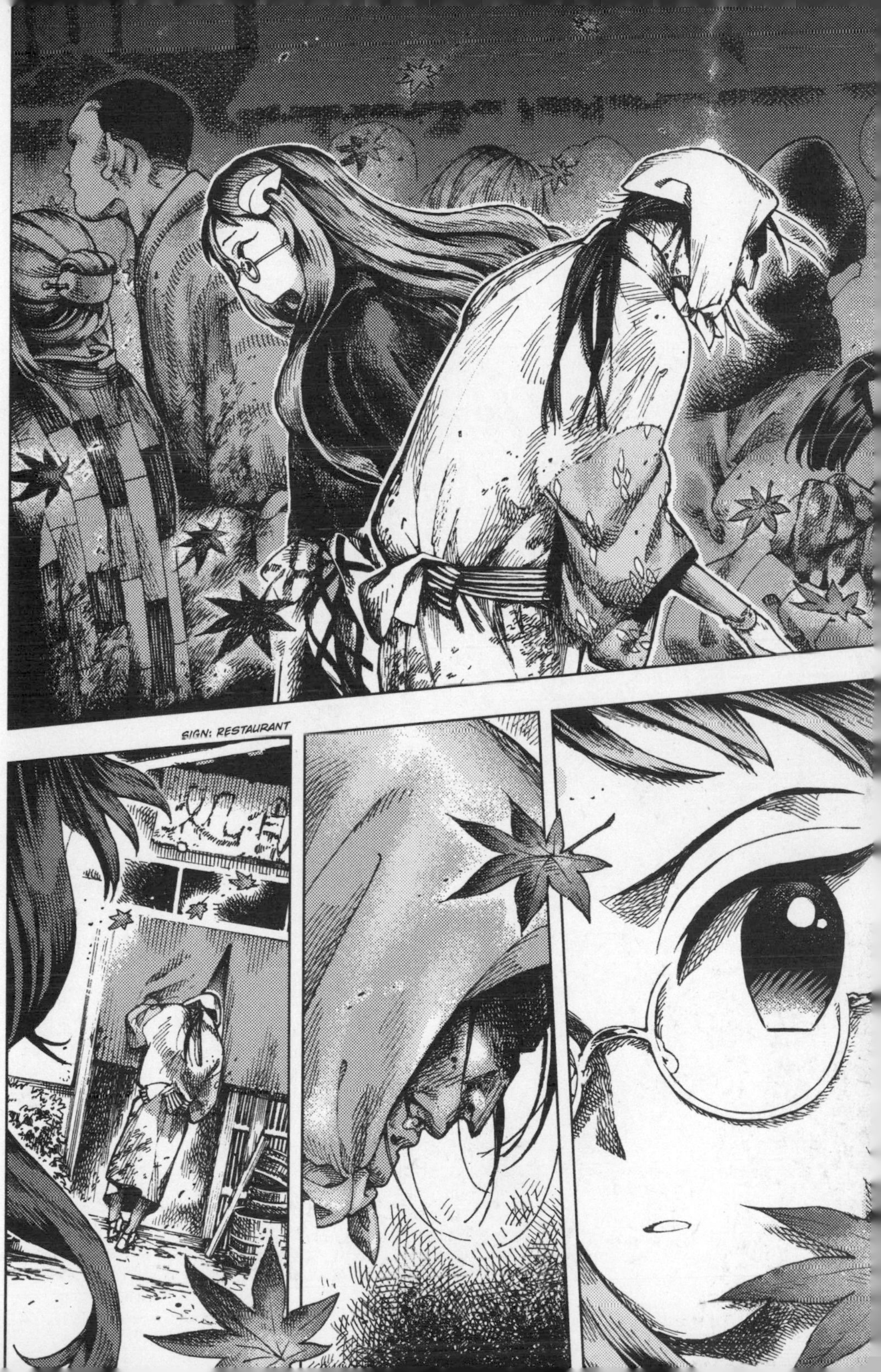
SIGN: RESTAURANT

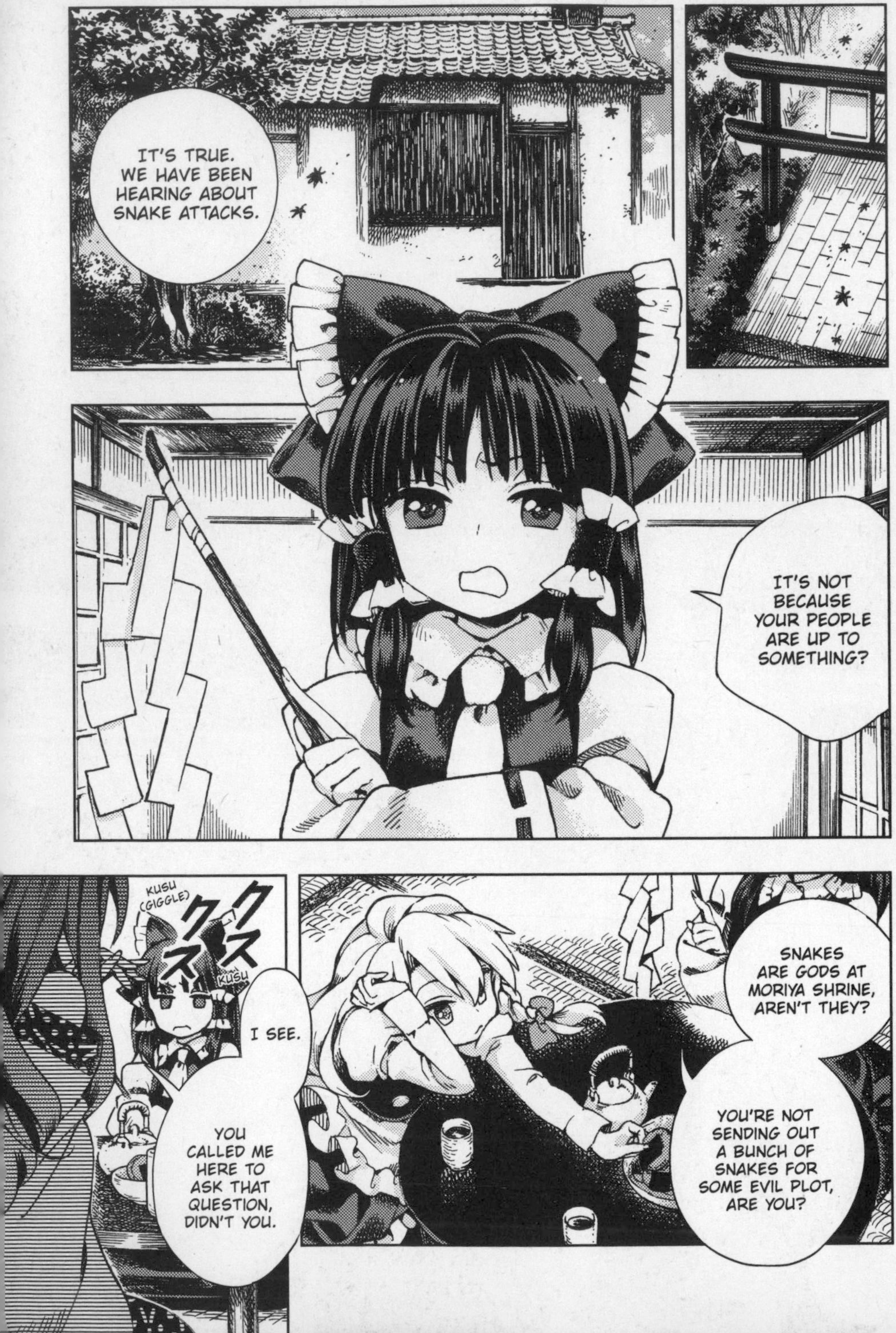
IT'S TRUE. WE HAVE BEEN HEARING ABOUT SNAKE ATTACKS.
IT'S NOT BECAUSE YOUR PEOPLE ARE UP TO SOMETHING?
SNAKES ARE GODS AT MORIYA SHRINE, AREN'T THEY?
YOU'RE NOT SENDING OUT A BUNCH OF SNAKES FOR SOME EVIL PLOT, ARE YOU?
クスクス
KUSU (GIGGLE)
KUSU
I SEE.
YOU CALLED ME HERE TO ASK THAT QUESTION, DIDN'T YOU.

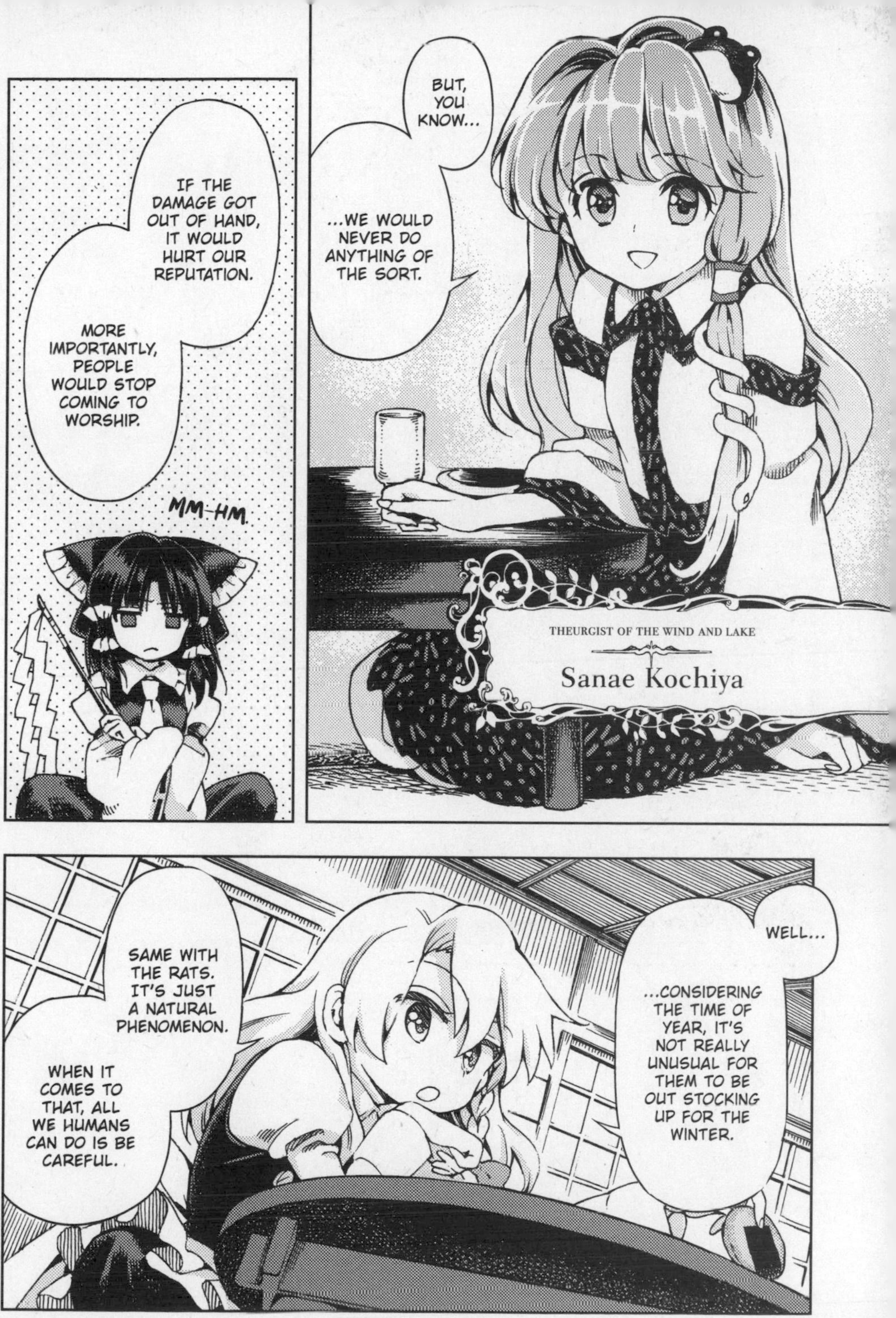
BUT, YOU KNOW...
...WE WOULD NEVER DO ANYTHING OF THE SORT.
THEURGIST OF THE WIND AND LAKE
Sanae Kochiya
IF THE DAMAGE GOT OUT OF HAND, IT WOULD HURT OUR REPUTATION.
MORE IMPORTANTLY, PEOPLE WOULD STOP COMING TO WORSHIP.
MM-HM.
WELL...
...CONSIDERING THE TIME OF YEAR, IT'S NOT REALLY UNUSUAL FOR THEM TO BE OUT STOCKING UP FOR THE WINTER.
SAME WITH THE RATS. IT'S JUST A NATURAL PHENOMENON.
WHEN IT COMES TO THAT, ALL WE HUMANS CAN DO IS BE CAREFUL.

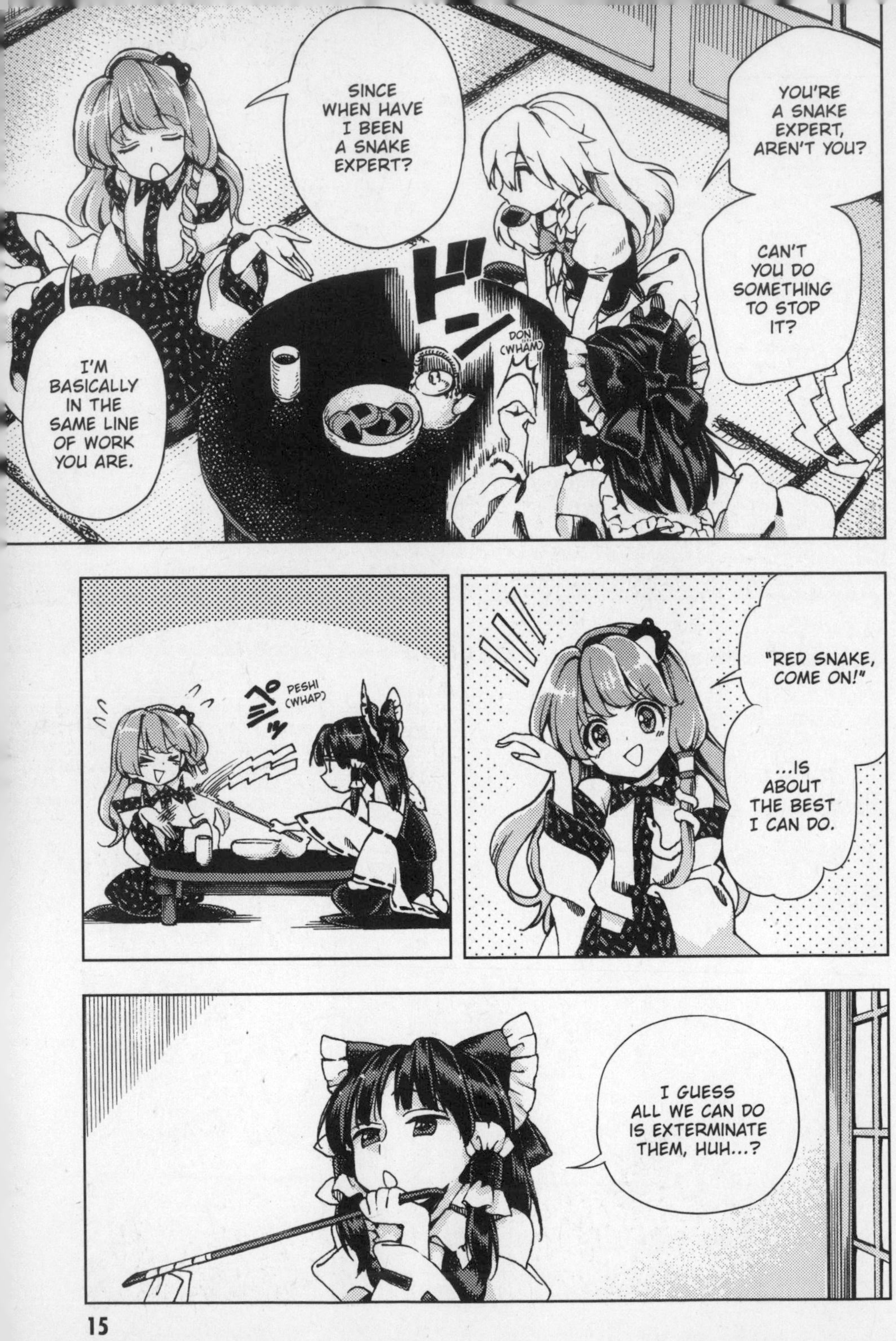
YOU'RE A SNAKE EXPERT, AREN'T YOU?
CAN'T YOU DO SOMETHING TO STOP IT?
DON (WHAM)
SINCE WHEN HAVE I BEEN A SNAKE EXPERT?
I'M BASICALLY IN THE SAME LINE OF WORK YOU ARE.
"RED SNAKE, COME ON!"
...IS ABOUT THE BEST I CAN DO.
PESHI (WHAP)
I GUESS ALL WE CAN DO IS EXTERMINATE THEM, HUH...?

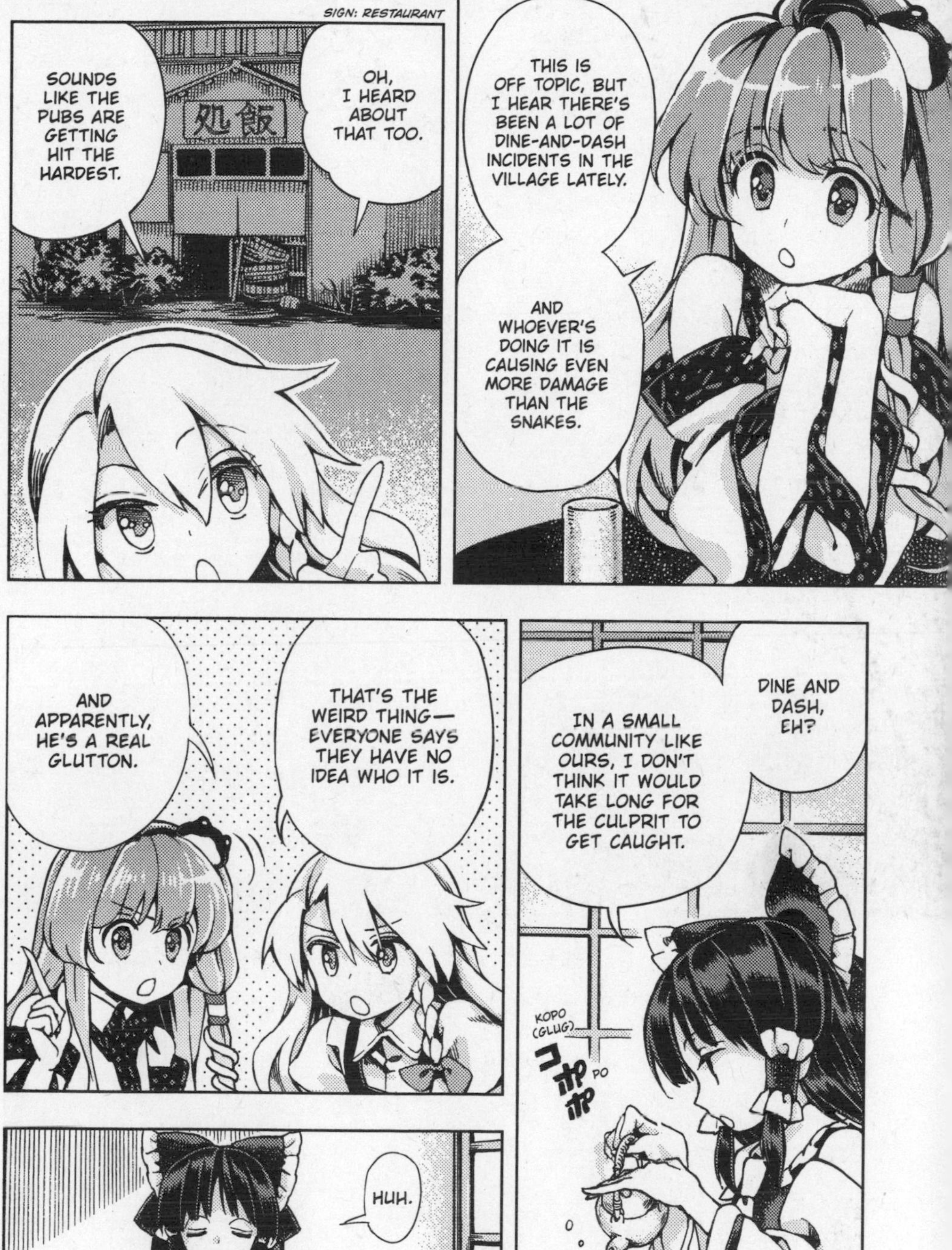
THIS IS OFF TOPIC, BUT I HEAR THERE'S BEEN A LOT OF DINE-AND-DASH INCIDENTS IN THE VILLAGE LATELY.
AND WHOEVER'S DOING IT IS CAUSING EVEN MORE DAMAGE THAN THE SNAKES.
SIGN: RESTAURANT
飯処
OH, I HEARD ABOUT THAT TOO.
SOUNDS LIKE THE PUBS ARE GETTING HIT THE HARDEST.
DINE AND DASH, EH?
IN A SMALL COMMUNITY LIKE OURS, I DON'T THINK IT WOULD TAKE LONG FOR THE CULPRIT TO GET CAUGHT.
KOPO (GLUG)
PO
THAT'S THE WEIRD THING—EVERYONE SAYS THEY HAVE NO IDEA WHO IT IS.
AND APPARENTLY, HE'S A REAL GLUTTON.
HUH.

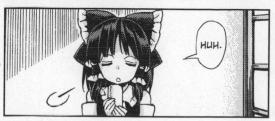

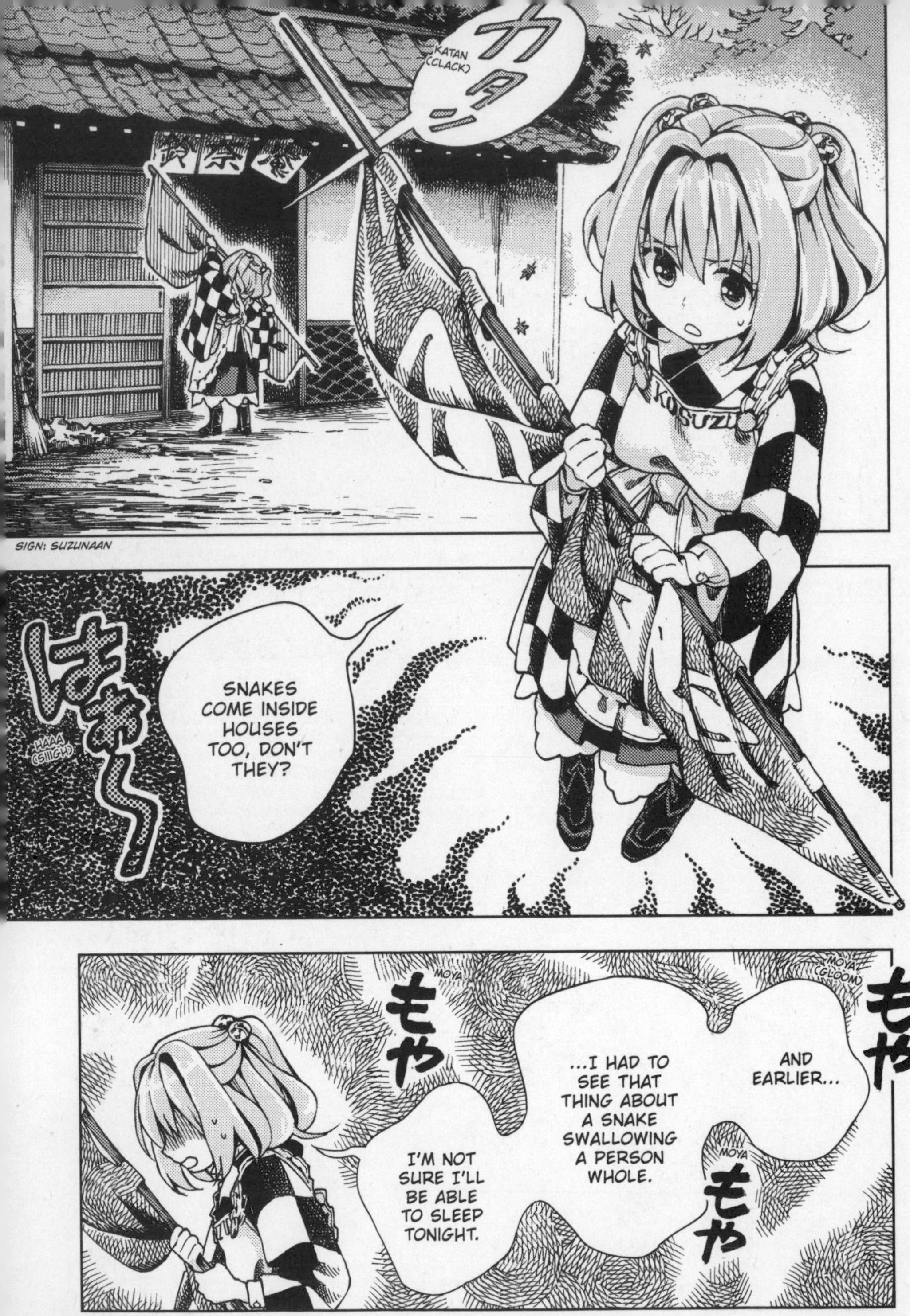
カタン
KATAN (CLACK)
鈴奈庵
はぁ〜
HAAA (SIIIGH)
SNAKES COME INSIDE HOUSES TOO, DON'T THEY?
もや
MOYA (GLOOM)
もや
MOYA
もや
MOYA
AND EARLIER...
...I HAD TO SEE THAT THING ABOUT A SNAKE SWALLOWING A PERSON WHOLE.
I'M NOT SURE I'LL BE ABLE TO SLEEP TONIGHT.

SIGN: SUZUNAAN

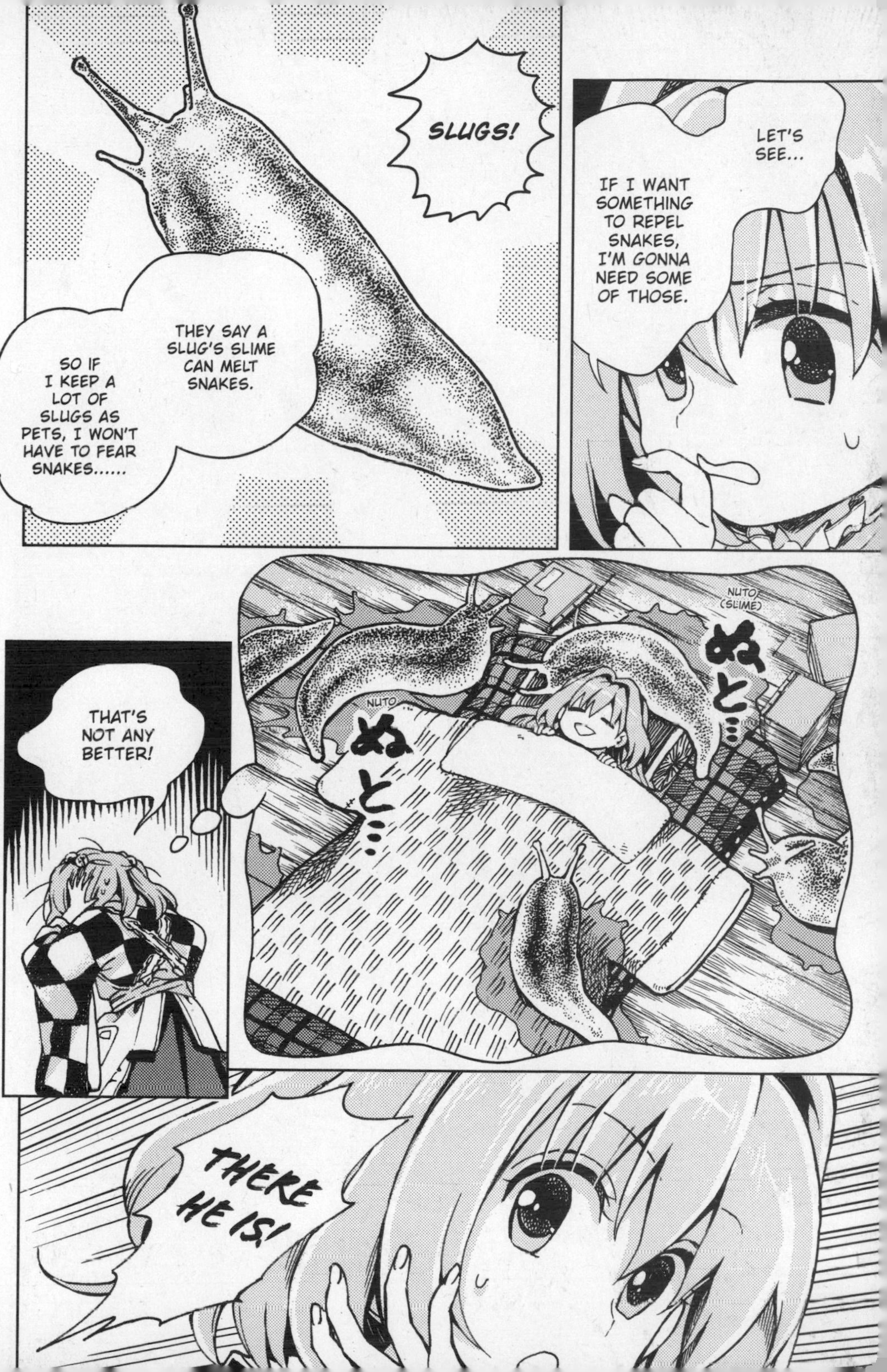
LET'S SEE...
IF I WANT SOMETHING TO REPEL SNAKES, I'M GONNA NEED SOME OF THOSE.
SLUGS!
THEY SAY A SLUG'S SLIME CAN MELT SNAKES.
SO IF I KEEP A LOT OF SLUGS AS PETS, I WON'T HAVE TO FEAR SNAKES......
NUTO (SLIME)
ぬと…
NUTO
ぬと…
THAT'S NOT ANY BETTER!
THERE HE IS!

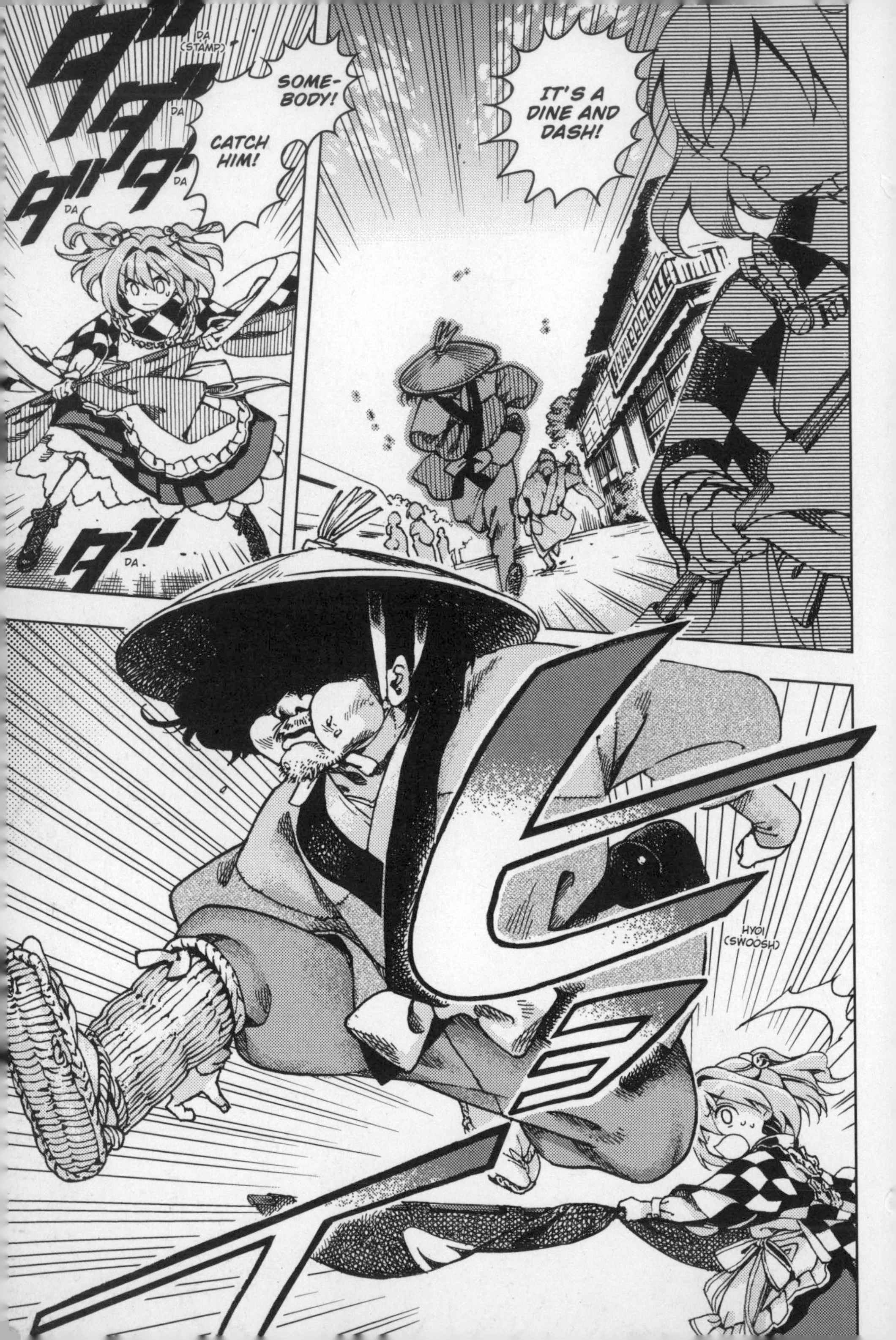
IT'S A DINE AND DASH!
SOMEBODY!
CATCH HIM!
DA (STAMP)
DA
DA
DA
DA
HYOI (SWOOSH)

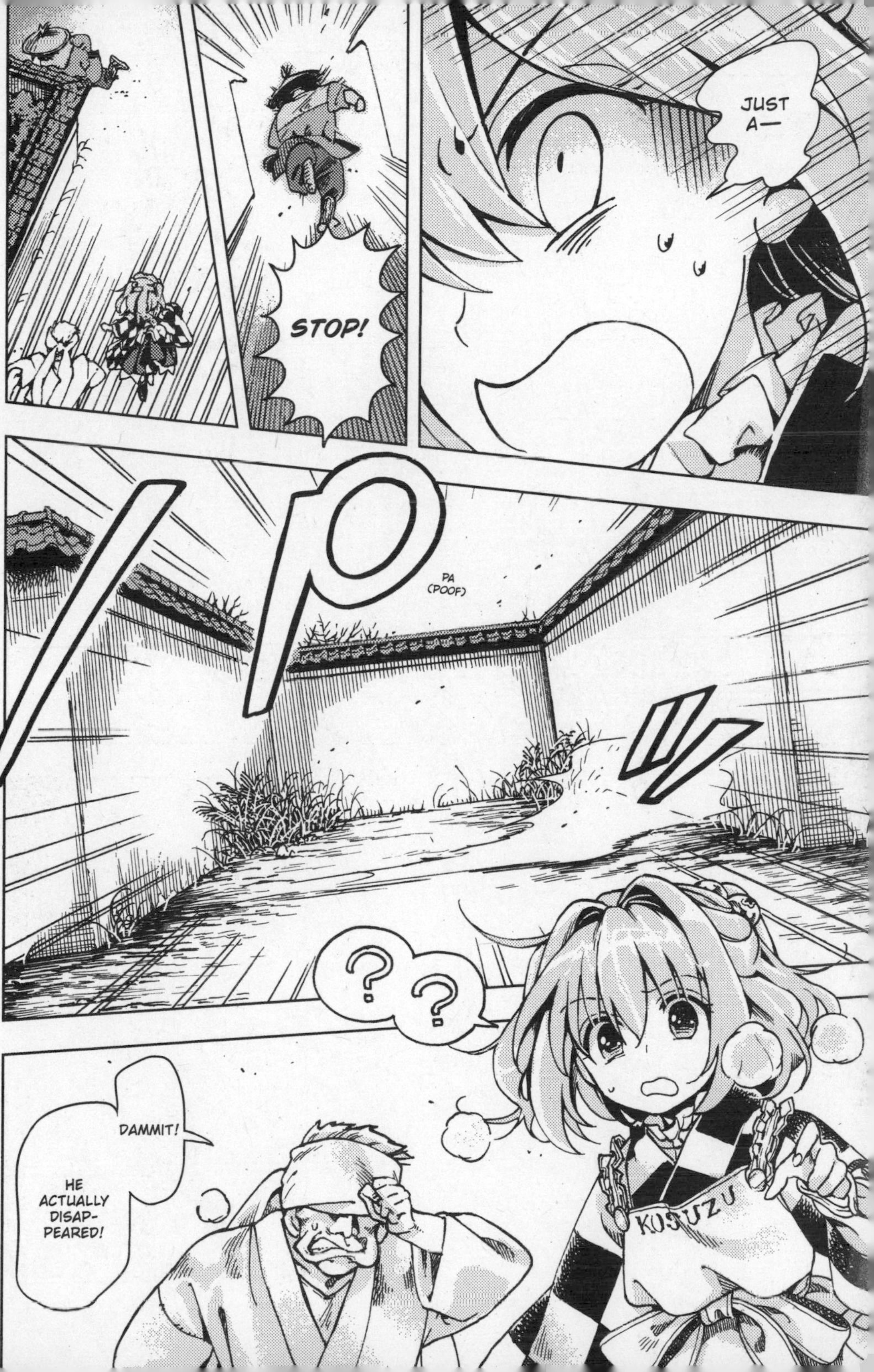
JUST A—
STOP!
PA (POOF)
??
DAMMIT!
HE ACTUALLY DISAP-PEARED!
KOSUZU

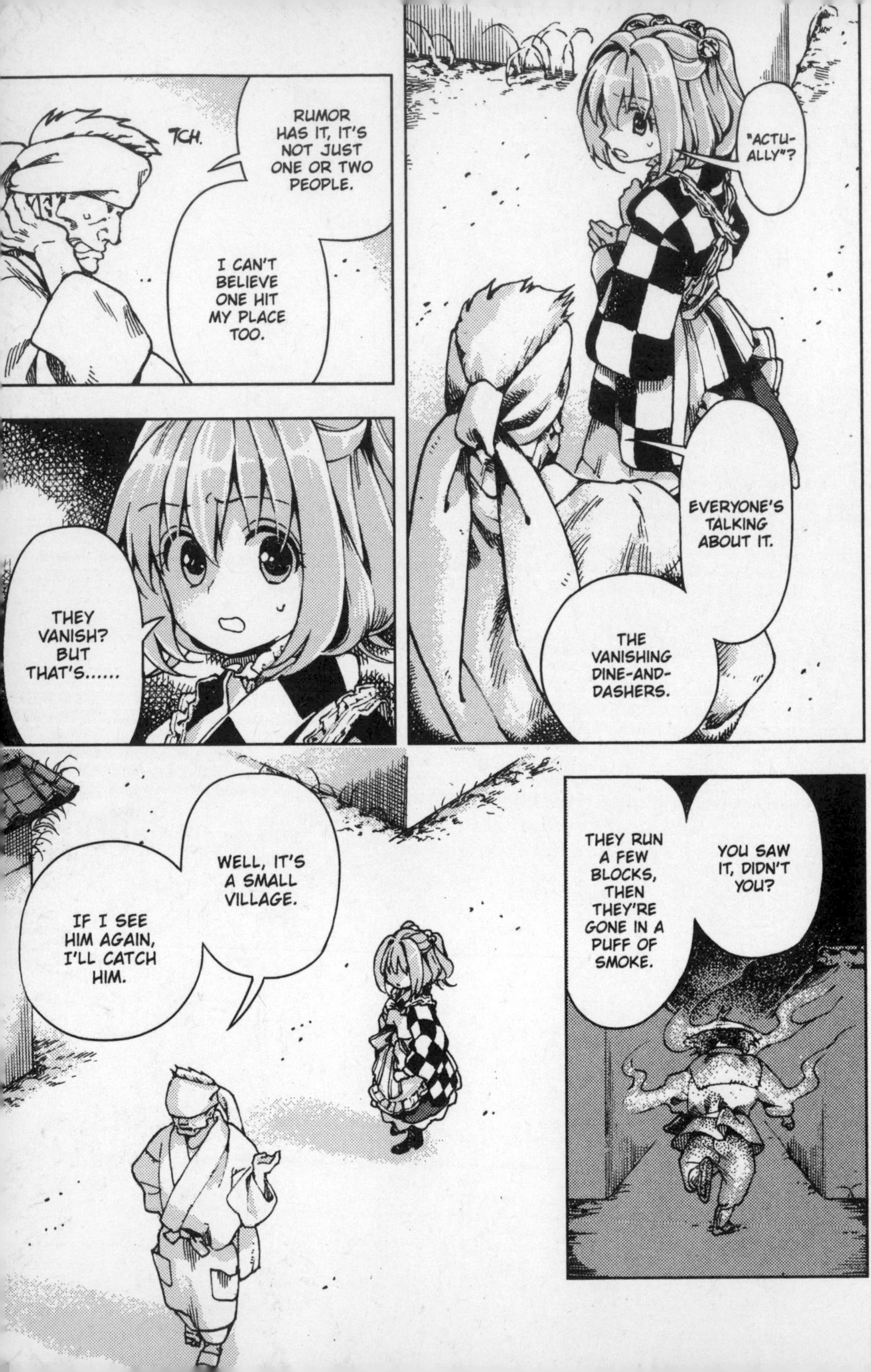

"ACTU-ALLY"?
EVERYONE'S TALKING ABOUT IT.
THE VANISHING DINE-AND-DASHERS.
RUMOR HAS IT, IT'S NOT JUST ONE OR TWO PEOPLE.
TCH.
I CAN'T BELIEVE ONE HIT MY PLACE TOO.
THEY VANISH? BUT THAT'S......
YOU SAW IT, DIDN'T YOU?
THEY RUN A FEW BLOCKS, THEN THEY'RE GONE IN A PUFF OF SMOKE.
WELL, IT'S A SMALL VILLAGE.
IF I SEE HIM AGAIN, I'LL CATCH HIM.

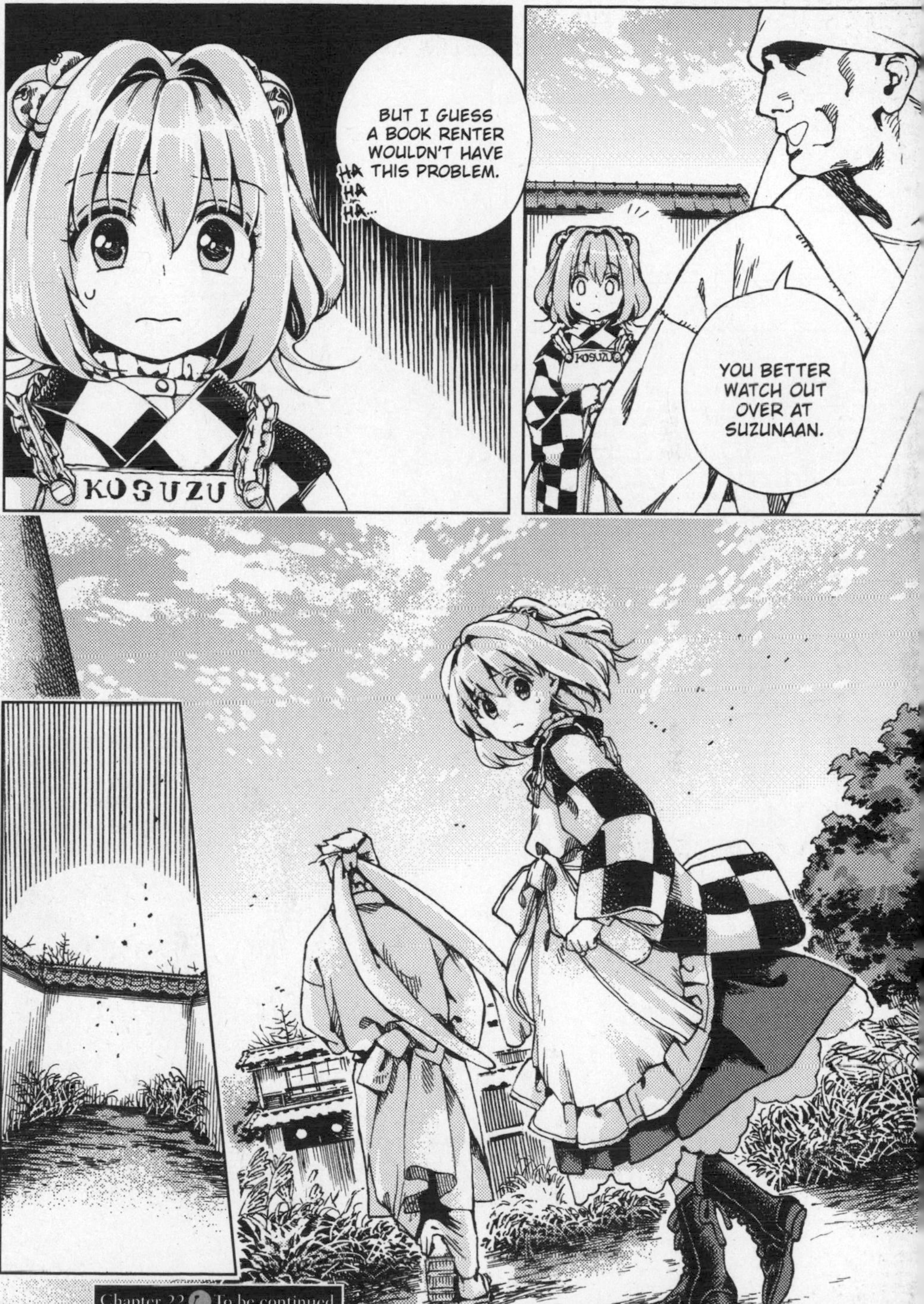
YOU BETTER WATCH OUT OVER AT SUZUNAAN.
KOSUZU
BUT I GUESS A BOOK RENTER WOULDN'T HAVE THIS PROBLEM.
HA HA HA...
KOSUZU

Chapter 22 To be continued

Chapter 23 The Tobacco, the Tanuki, and the Dine & Dash Part 2

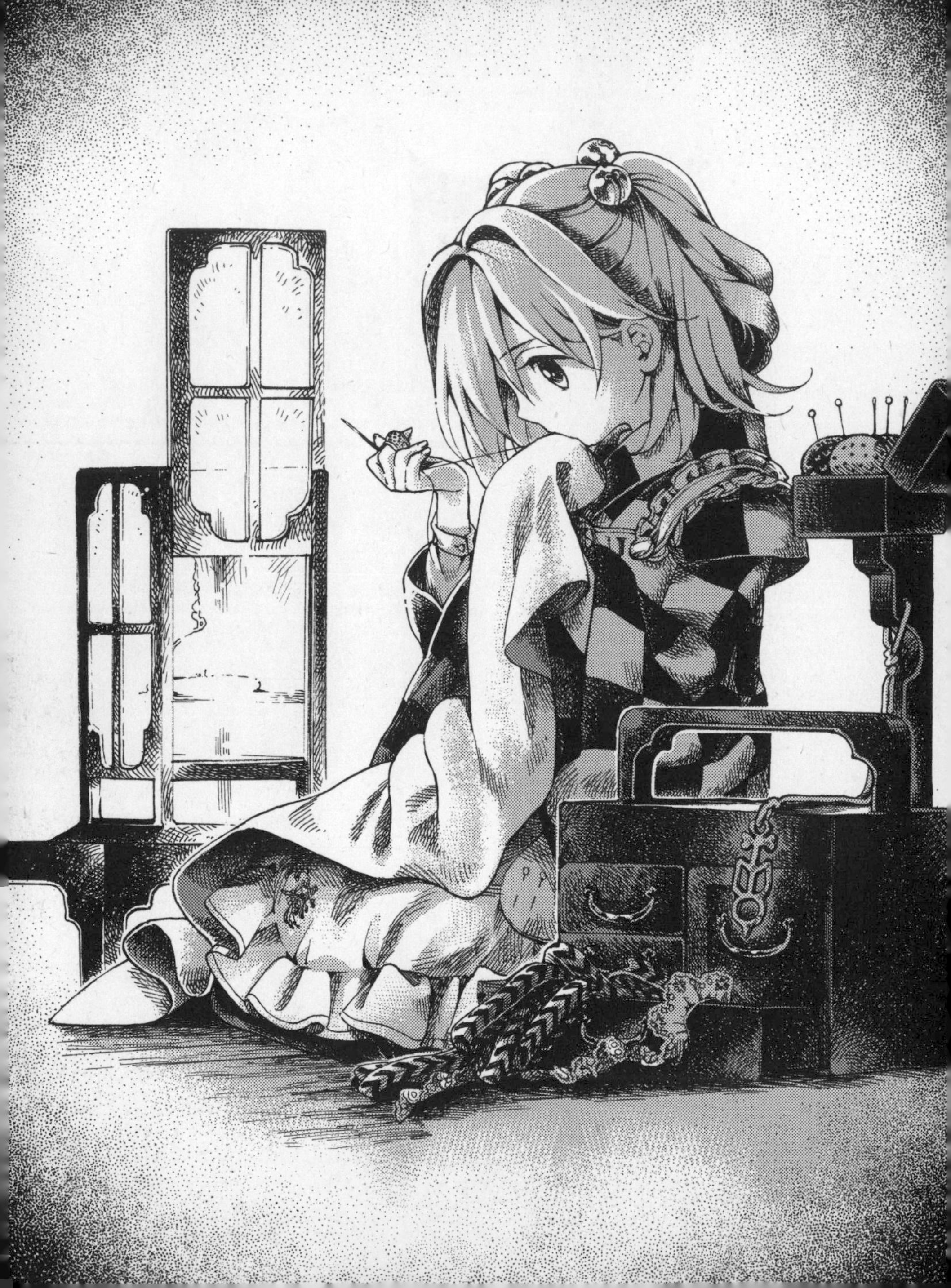

SIGN: MORIYA SHRINE

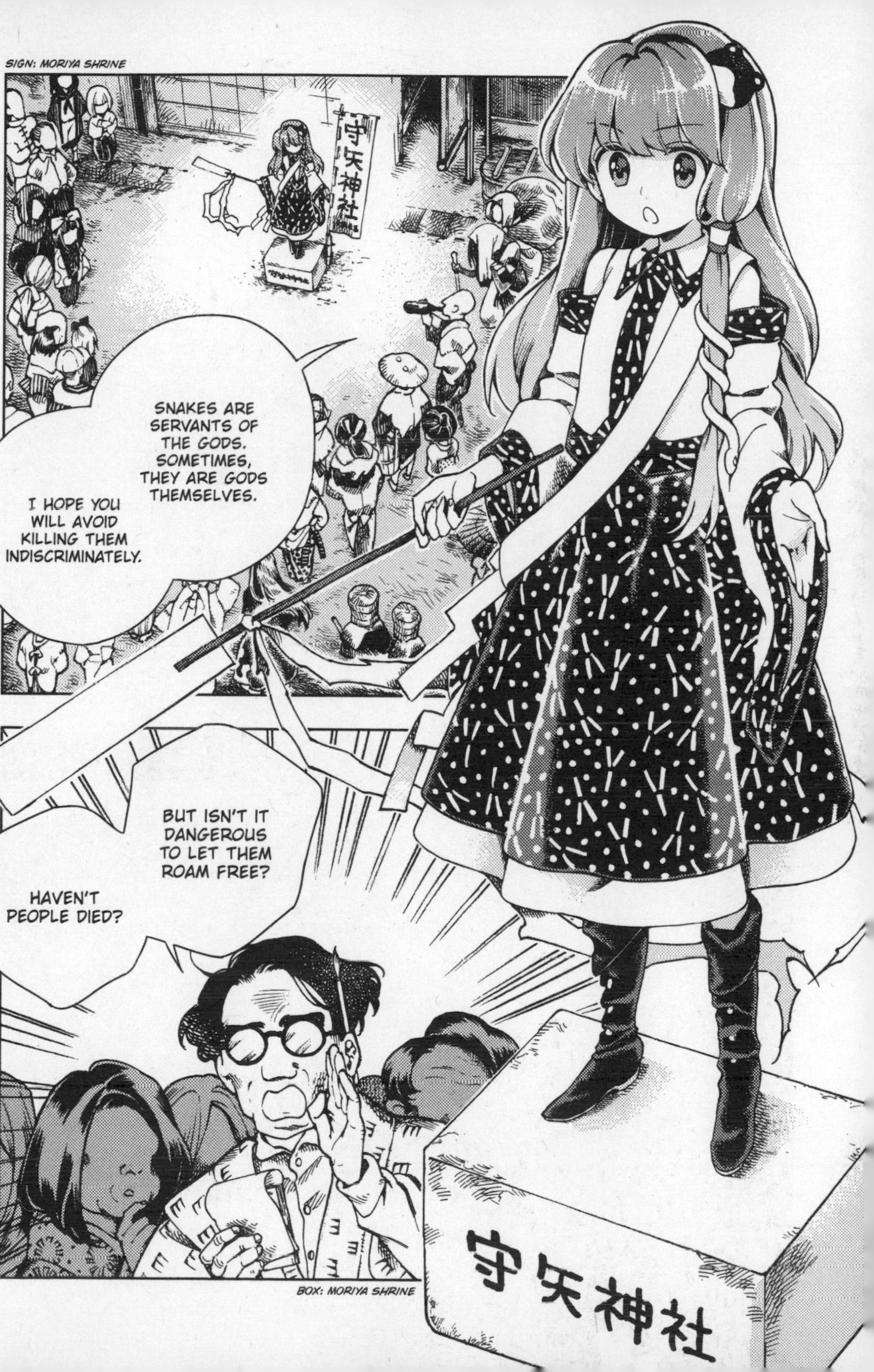
守矢神社
SNAKES ARE SERVANTS OF THE GODS. SOMETIMES, THEY ARE GODS THEMSELVES.
I HOPE YOU WILL AVOID KILLING THEM INDISCRIMINATELY.
BUT ISN'T IT DANGEROUS TO LET THEM ROAM FREE?
HAVEN'T PEOPLE DIED?
守矢神社

BOX: MORIYA SHRINE

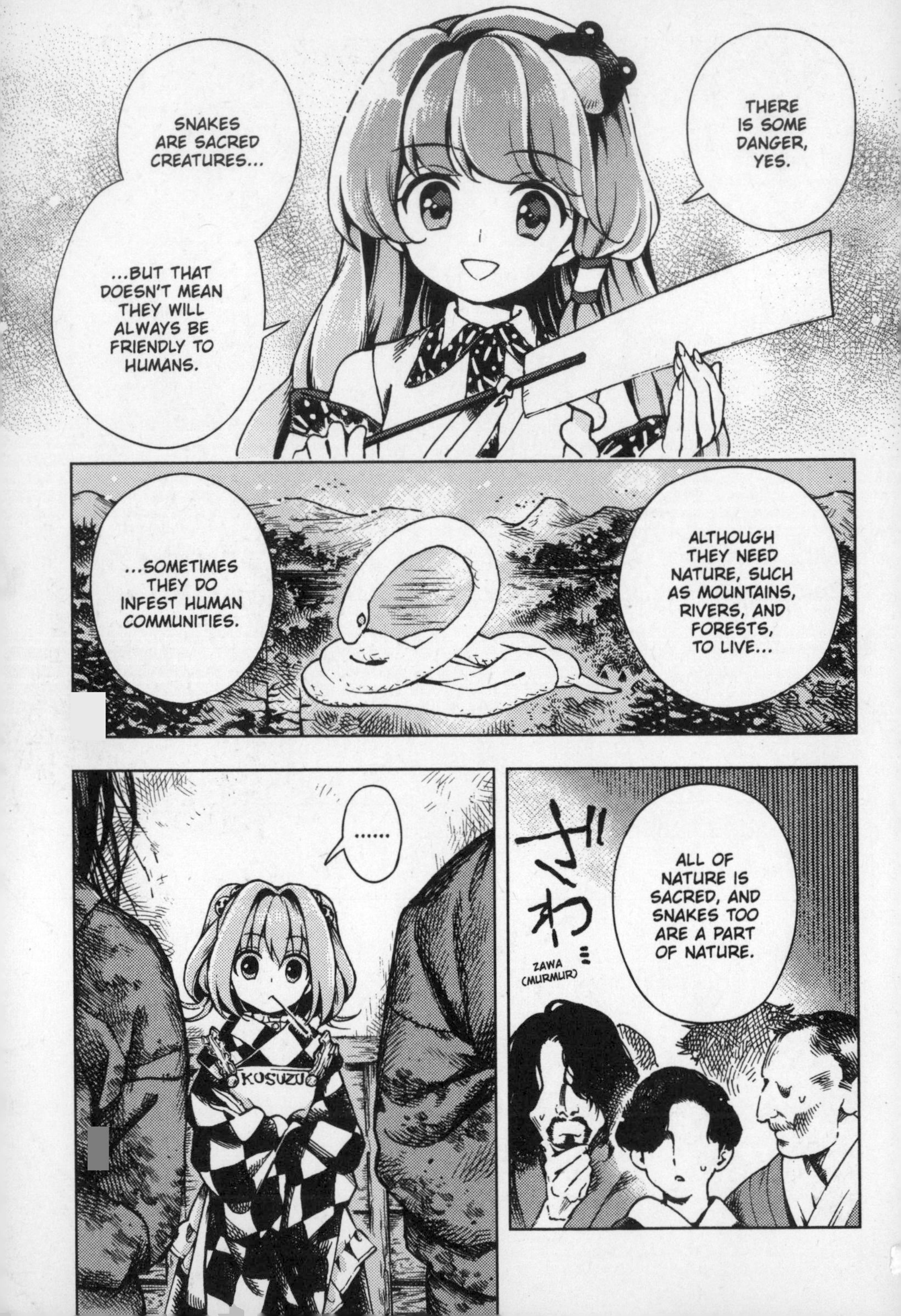
THERE IS SOME DANGER, YES.
SNAKES ARE SACRED CREATURES...
...BUT THAT DOESN'T MEAN THEY WILL ALWAYS BE FRIENDLY TO HUMANS.
ALTHOUGH THEY NEED NATURE, SUCH AS MOUNTAINS, RIVERS, AND FORESTS, TO LIVE...
...SOMETIMES THEY DO INFEST HUMAN COMMUNITIES.
ALL OF NATURE IS SACRED, AND SNAKES TOO ARE A PART OF NATURE.
ざわ
ZAWA (MURMUR)
......

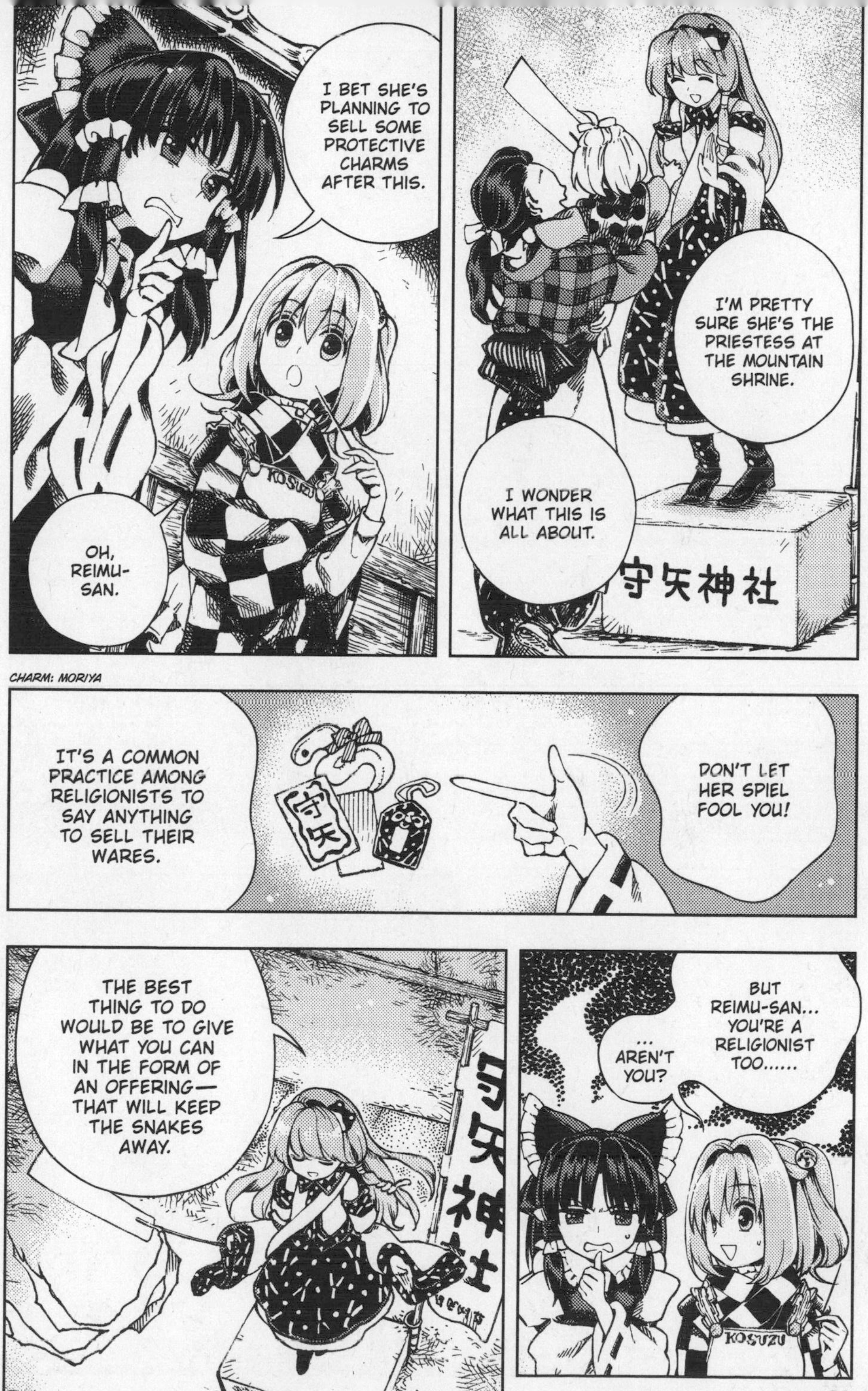
I'M PRETTY SURE SHE'S THE PRIESTESS AT THE MOUNTAIN SHRINE.
I WONDER WHAT THIS IS ALL ABOUT.
守矢神社
I BET SHE'S PLANNING TO SELL SOME PROTECTIVE CHARMS AFTER THIS.
OH, REIMU-SAN.
KOSUZU
DON'T LET HER SPIEL FOOL YOU!
守矢
IT'S A COMMON PRACTICE AMONG RELIGIONISTS TO SAY ANYTHING TO SELL THEIR WARES.
BUT REIMU-SAN... YOU'RE A RELIGIONIST TOO......
... AREN'T YOU?
KOSUZU
THE BEST THING TO DO WOULD BE TO GIVE WHAT YOU CAN IN THE FORM OF AN OFFERING—THAT WILL KEEP THE SNAKES AWAY.

CHARM: MORIYA

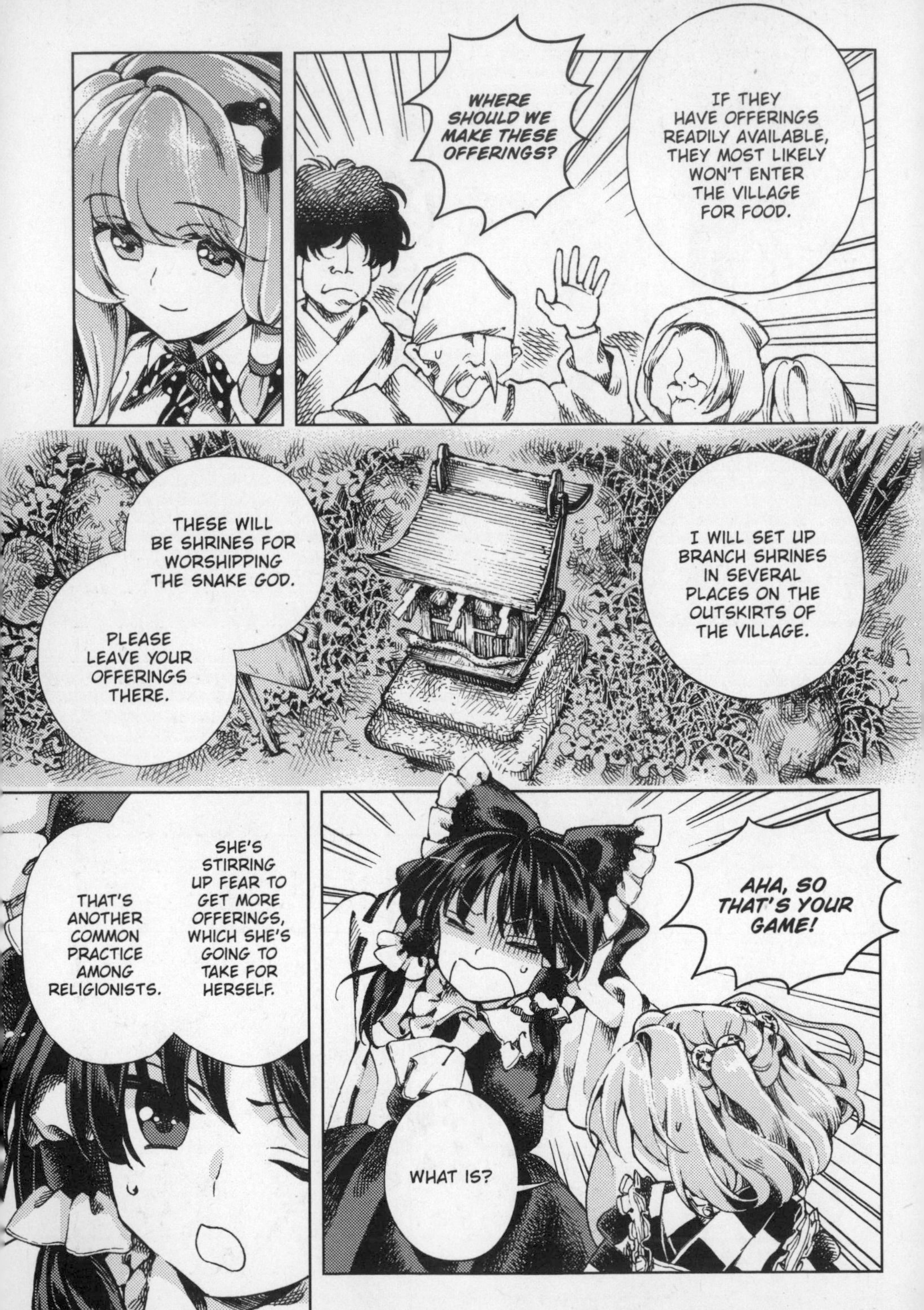
IF THEY HAVE OFFERINGS READILY AVAILABLE, THEY MOST LIKELY WON'T ENTER THE VILLAGE FOR FOOD.
WHERE SHOULD WE MAKE THESE OFFERINGS?
I WILL SET UP BRANCH SHRINES IN SEVERAL PLACES ON THE OUTSKIRTS OF THE VILLAGE.
THESE WILL BE SHRINES FOR WORSHIPPING THE SNAKE GOD.
PLEASE LEAVE YOUR OFFERINGS THERE.
AHA, SO THAT'S YOUR GAME!
WHAT IS?
SHE'S STIRRING UP FEAR TO GET MORE OFFERINGS, WHICH SHE'S GOING TO TAKE FOR HERSELF.
THAT'S ANOTHER COMMON PRACTICE AMONG RELIGIONISTS.

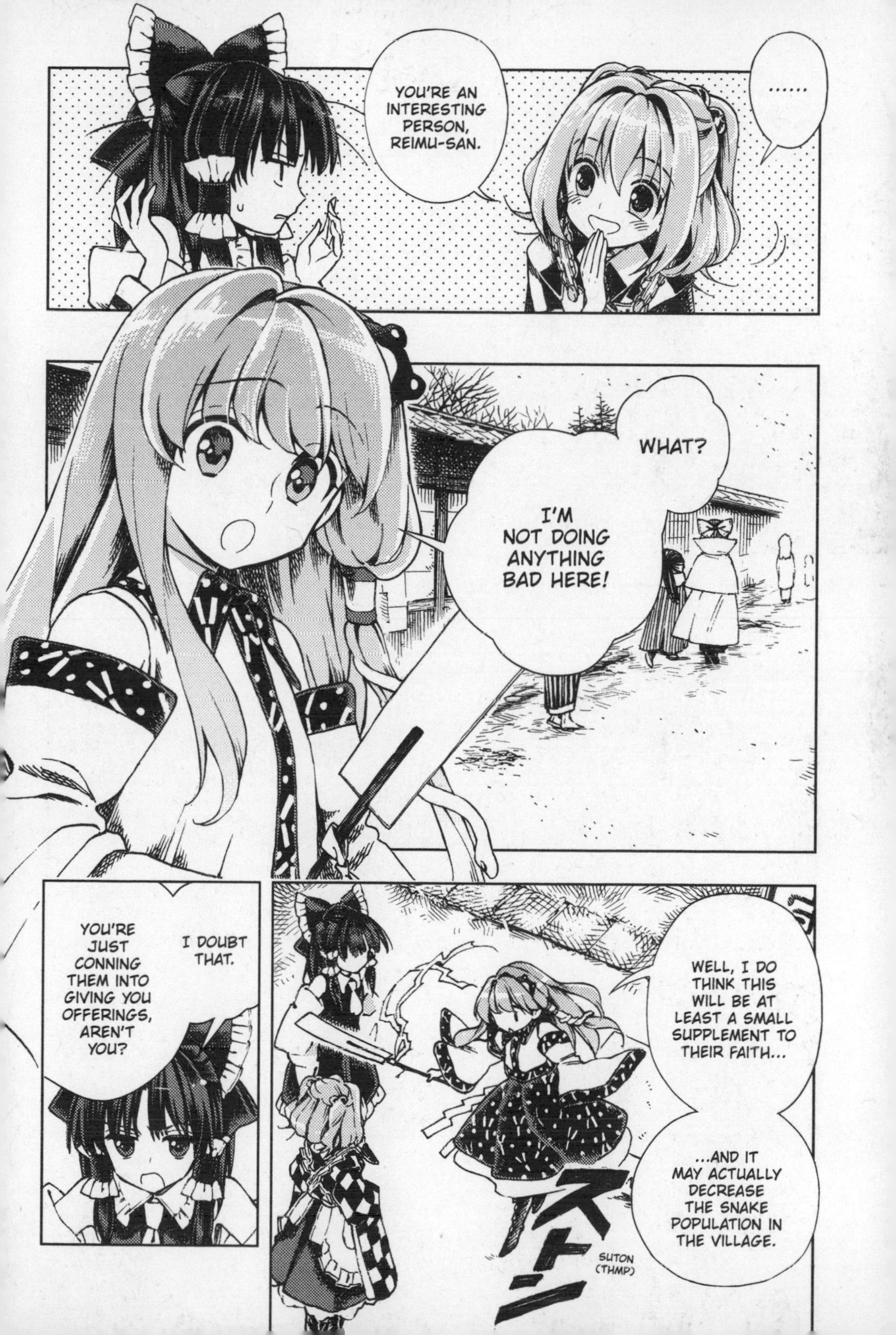
......
YOU'RE AN INTERESTING PERSON, REIMU-SAN.
WHAT?
I'M NOT DOING ANYTHING BAD HERE!
WELL, I DO THINK THIS WILL BE AT LEAST A SMALL SUPPLEMENT TO THEIR FAITH...
...AND IT MAY ACTUALLY DECREASE THE SNAKE POPULATION IN THE VILLAGE.
SUTON (THMP)
I DOUBT THAT.
YOU'RE JUST CONNING THEM INTO GIVING YOU OFFERINGS, AREN'T YOU?

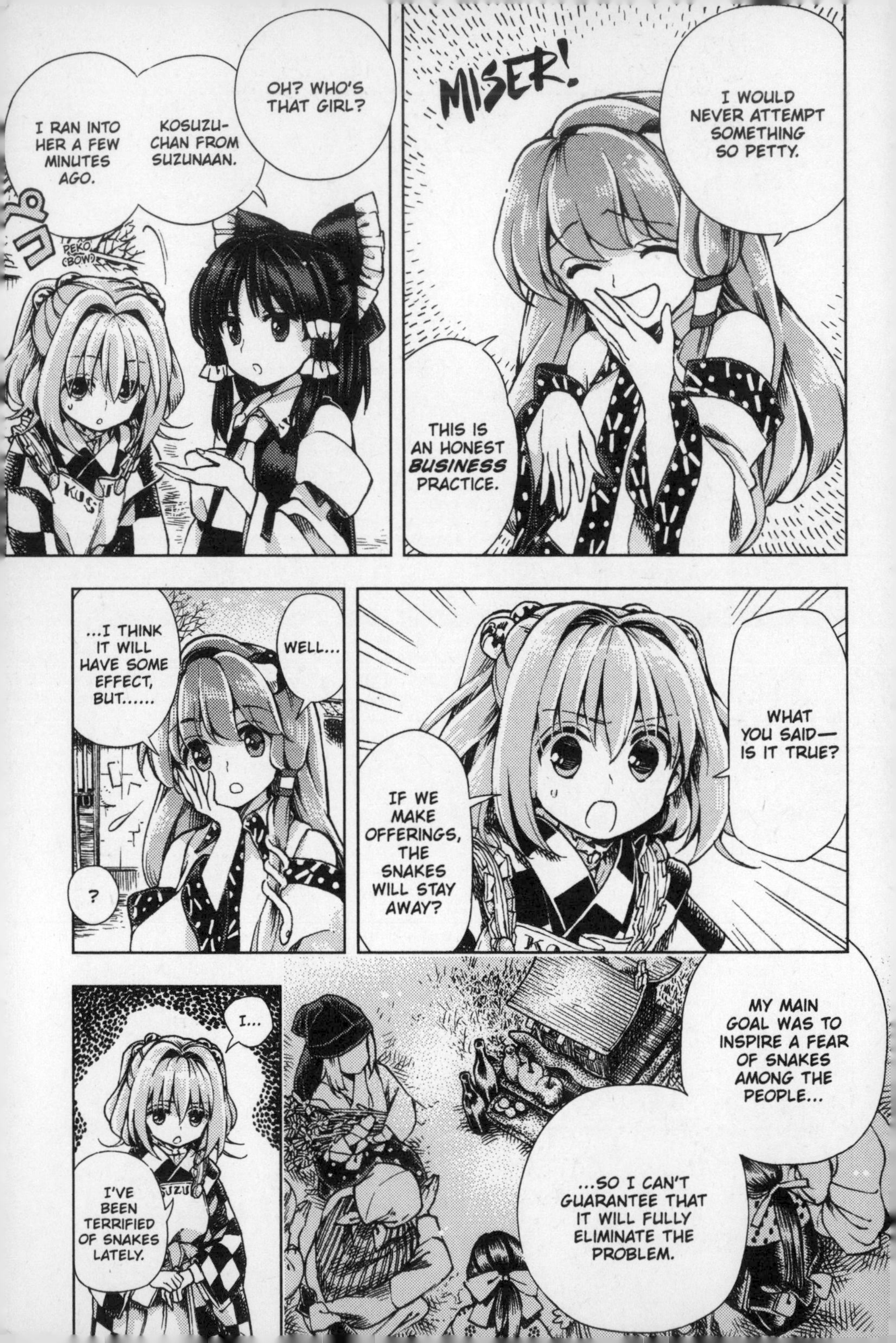
MISER!
I WOULD NEVER ATTEMPT SOMETHING SO PETTY.
THIS IS AN HONEST BUSINESS PRACTICE.
OH? WHO'S THAT GIRL?
KOSUZU-CHAN FROM SUZUNAAN.
I RAN INTO HER A FEW MINUTES AGO.
PEKO (BOW)
WHAT YOU SAID— IS IT TRUE?
IF WE MAKE OFFERINGS, THE SNAKES WILL STAY AWAY?
WELL...
...I THINK IT WILL HAVE SOME EFFECT, BUT......
?
MY MAIN GOAL WAS TO INSPIRE A FEAR OF SNAKES AMONG THE PEOPLE...
...SO I CAN'T GUARANTEE THAT IT WILL FULLY ELIMINATE THE PROBLEM.
I...
I'VE BEEN TERRIFIED OF SNAKES LATELY.

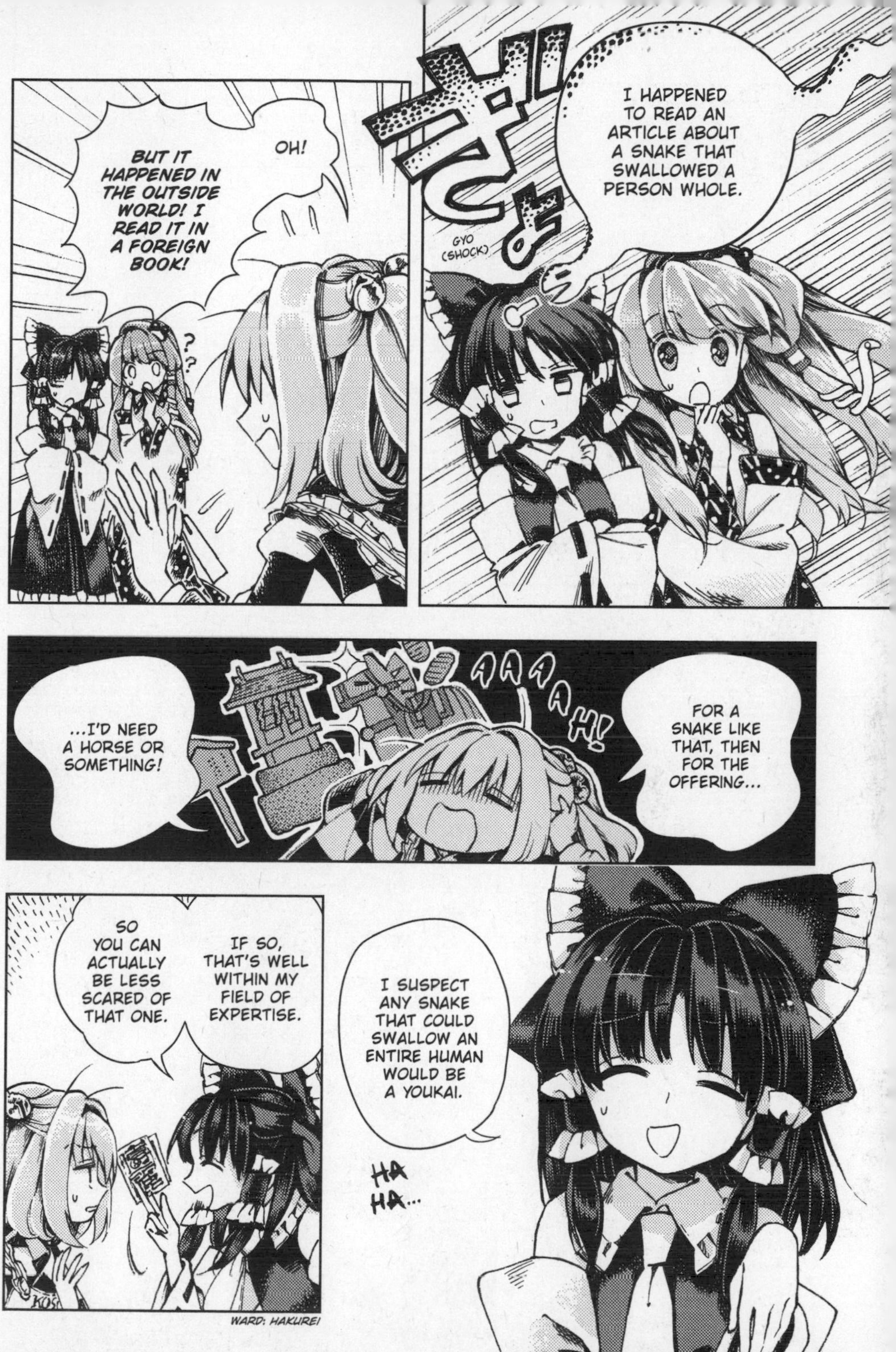
I HAPPENED TO READ AN ARTICLE ABOUT A SNAKE THAT SWALLOWED A PERSON WHOLE.
GYO (SHOCK)
OH!
BUT IT HAPPENED IN THE OUTSIDE WORLD! I READ IT IN A FOREIGN BOOK!
??
FOR A SNAKE LIKE THAT, THEN FOR THE OFFERING...
AAAAAH!
...I'D NEED A HORSE OR SOMETHING!
I SUSPECT ANY SNAKE THAT COULD SWALLOW AN ENTIRE HUMAN WOULD BE A YOUKAI.
HA HA...
IF SO, THAT'S WELL WITHIN MY FIELD OF EXPERTISE.
SO YOU CAN ACTUALLY BE LESS SCARED OF THAT ONE.
WARD: HAKUREI

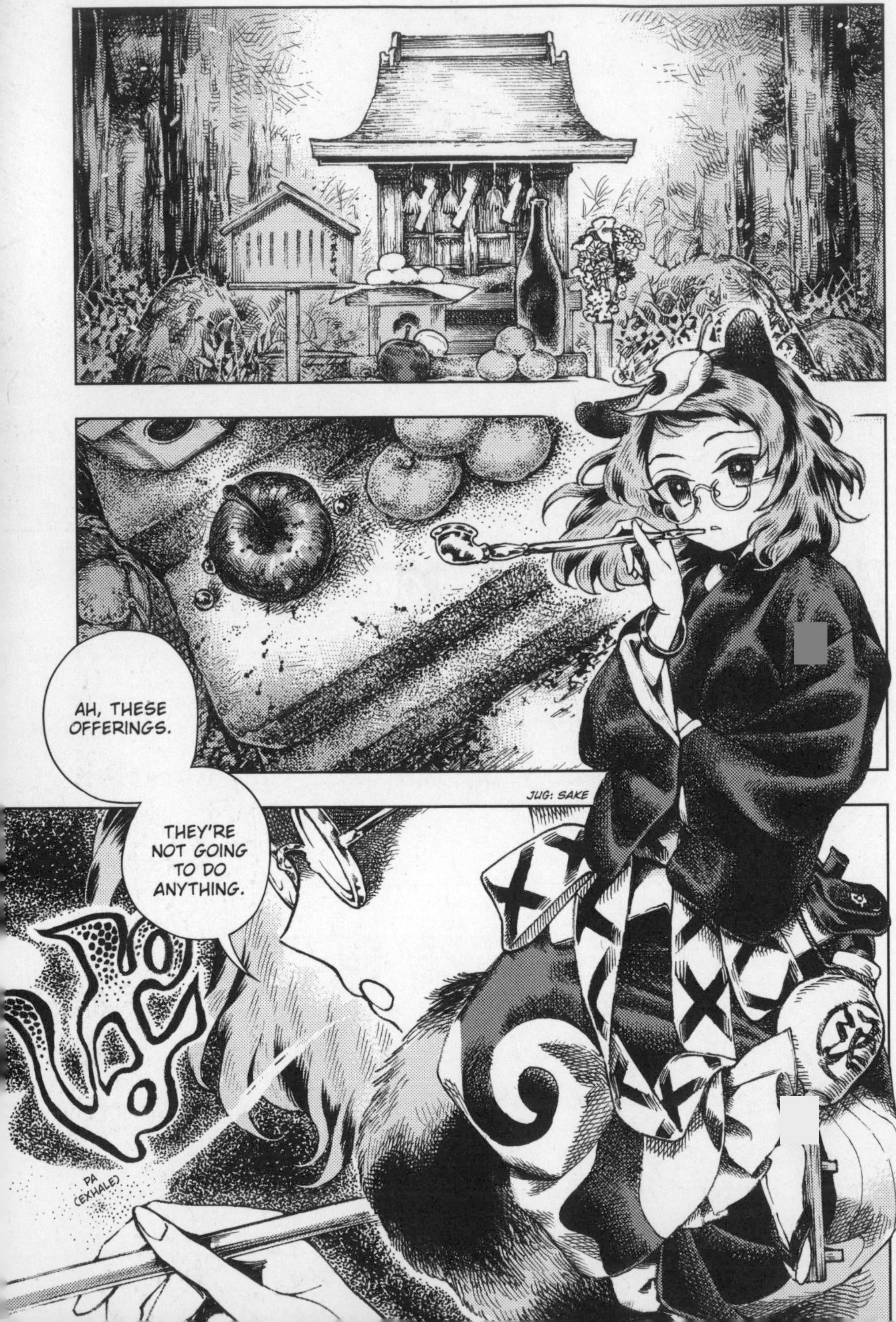
AH, THESE OFFERINGS.
THEY'RE NOT GOING TO DO ANYTHING.
JUG: SAKE
PA (EXHALE)

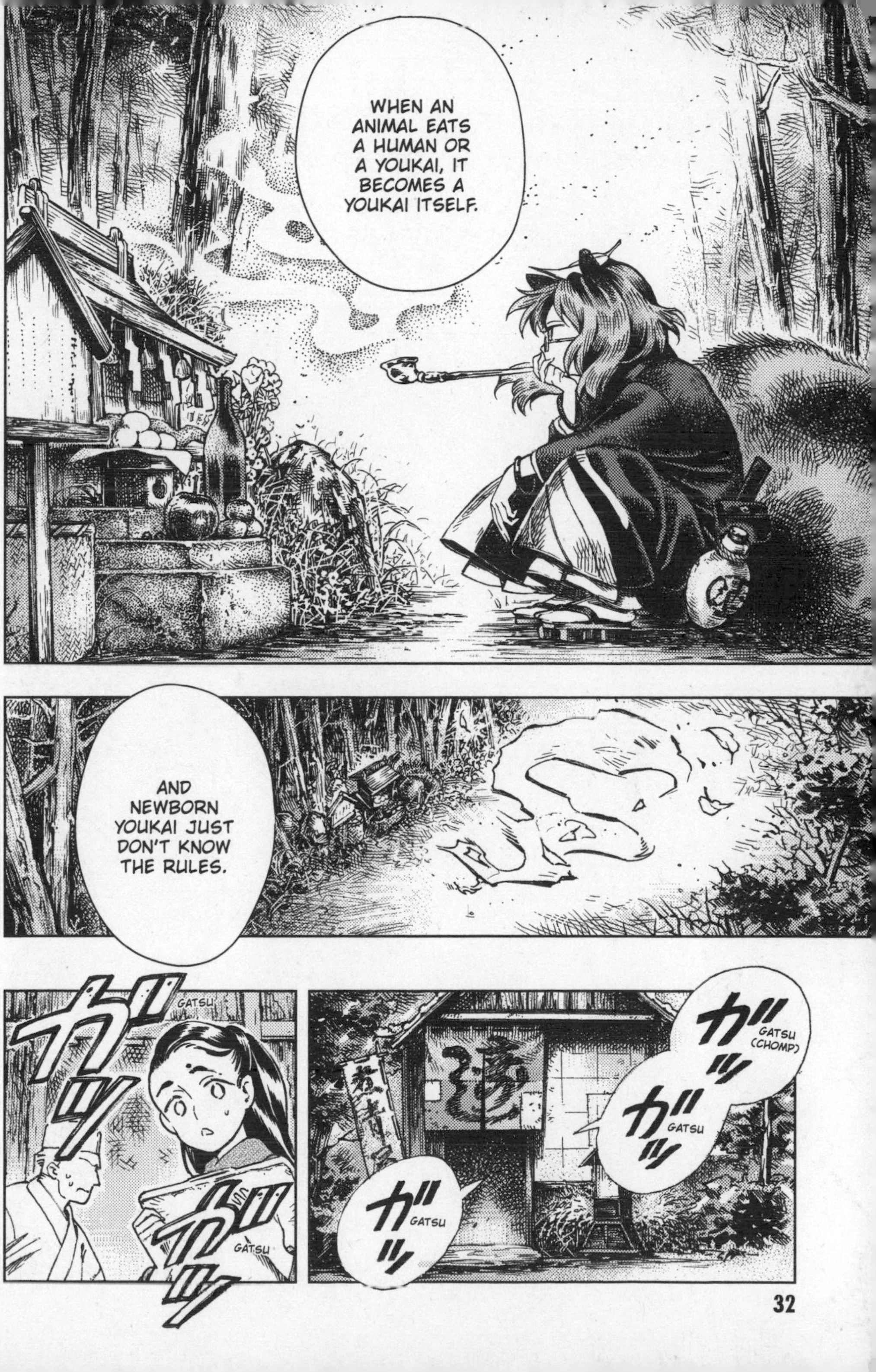
WHEN AN ANIMAL EATS A HUMAN OR A YOUKAI, IT BECOMES A YOUKAI ITSELF.
AND NEWBORN YOUKAI JUST DON'T KNOW THE RULES.
GATSU (CHOMP)
GATSU
GATSU
GATSU
GATSU

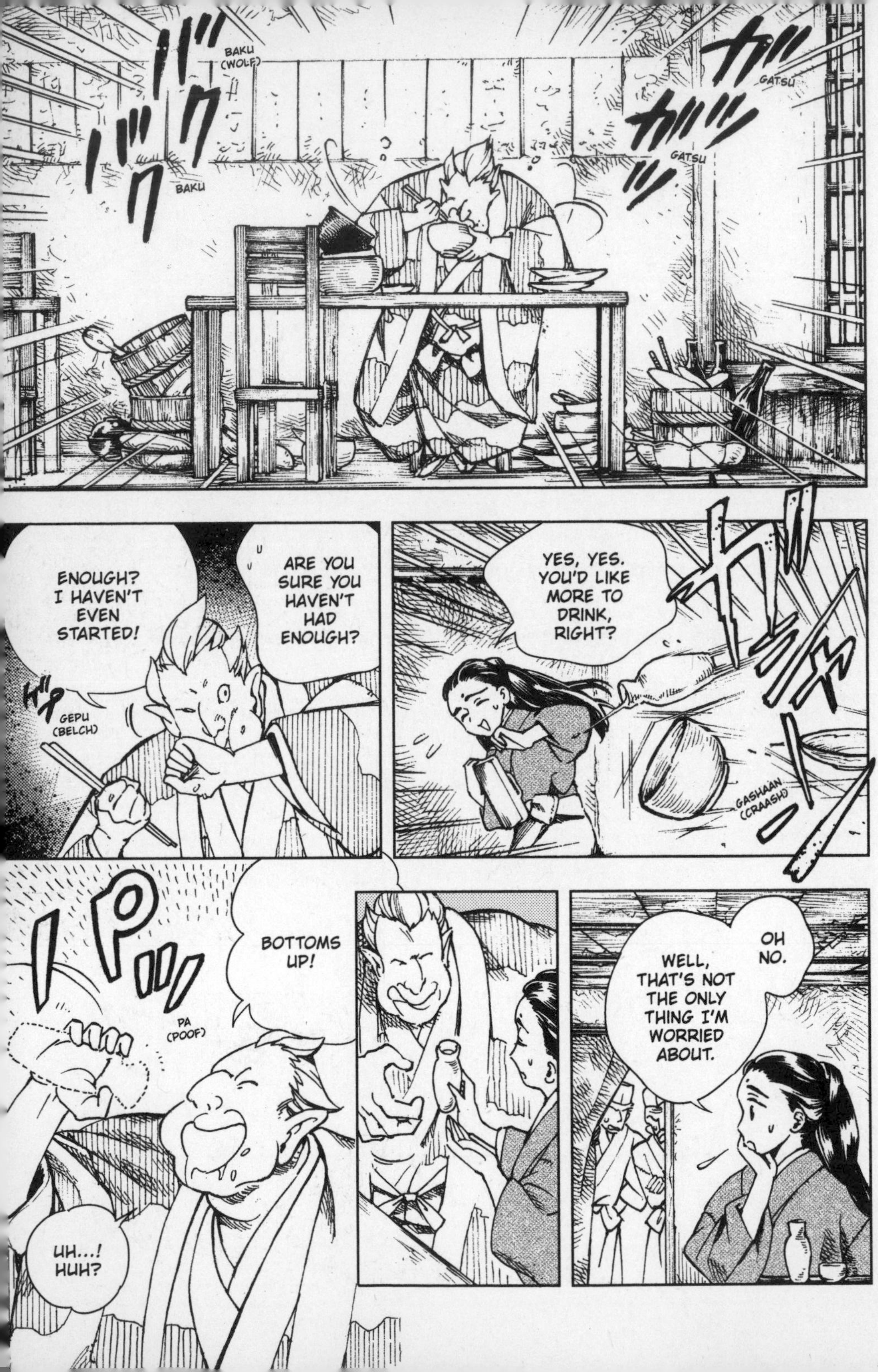
GATSU
GATSU
BAKU (WOLF)
BAKU
YES, YES. YOU'D LIKE MORE TO DRINK, RIGHT?
GASHAAN (CRAASH)
ARE YOU SURE YOU HAVEN'T HAD ENOUGH?
ENOUGH? I HAVEN'T EVEN STARTED!
GEPU (BELCH)
OH NO.
WELL, THAT'S NOT THE ONLY THING I'M WORRIED ABOUT.
BOTTOMS UP!
PA (POOF)
UH...! HUH?

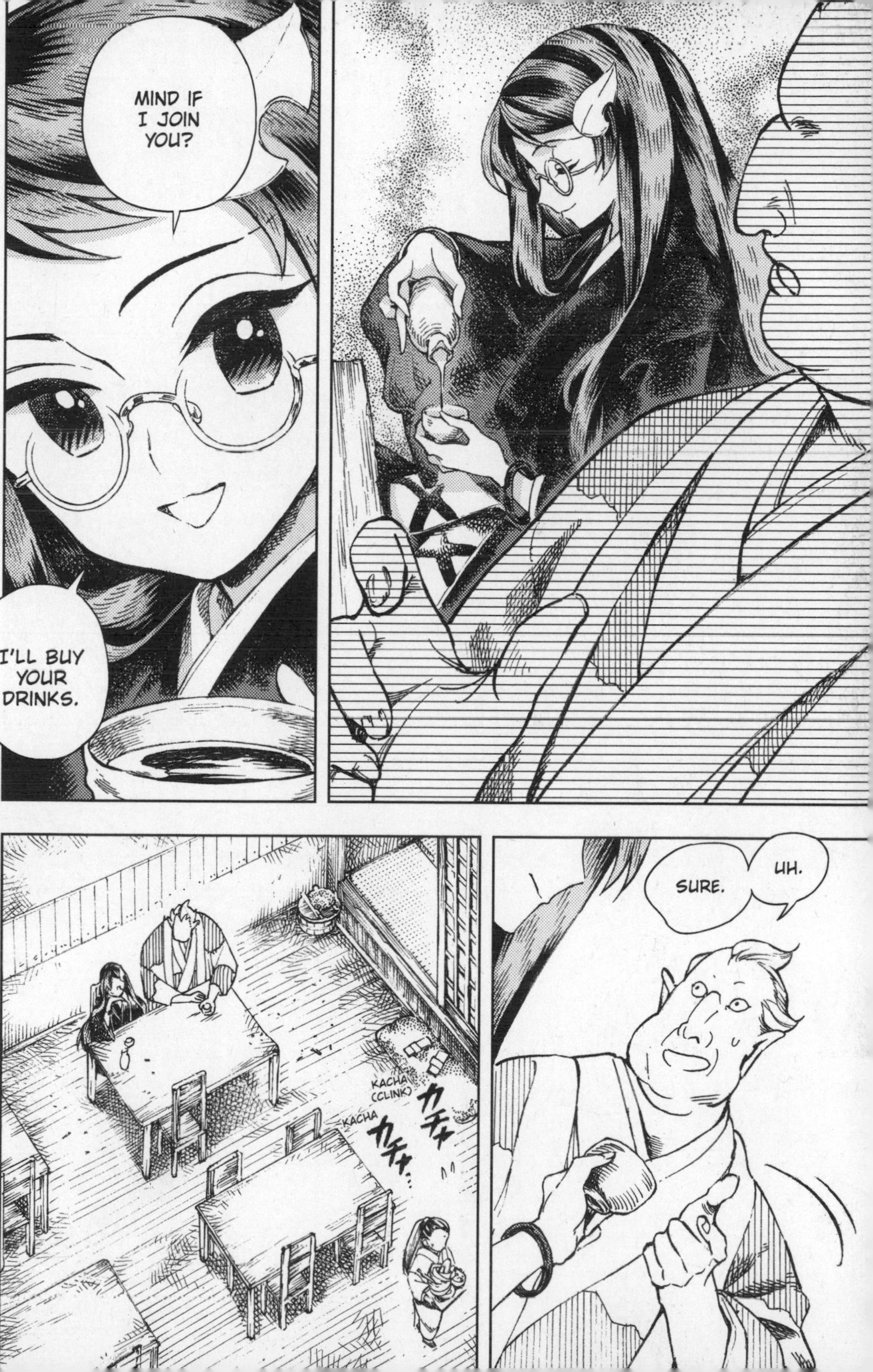
MIND IF I JOIN YOU?
I'LL BUY YOUR DRINKS.
UH.
SURE.
KACHA (CLINK)
カチャ
KACHA
カチャ…

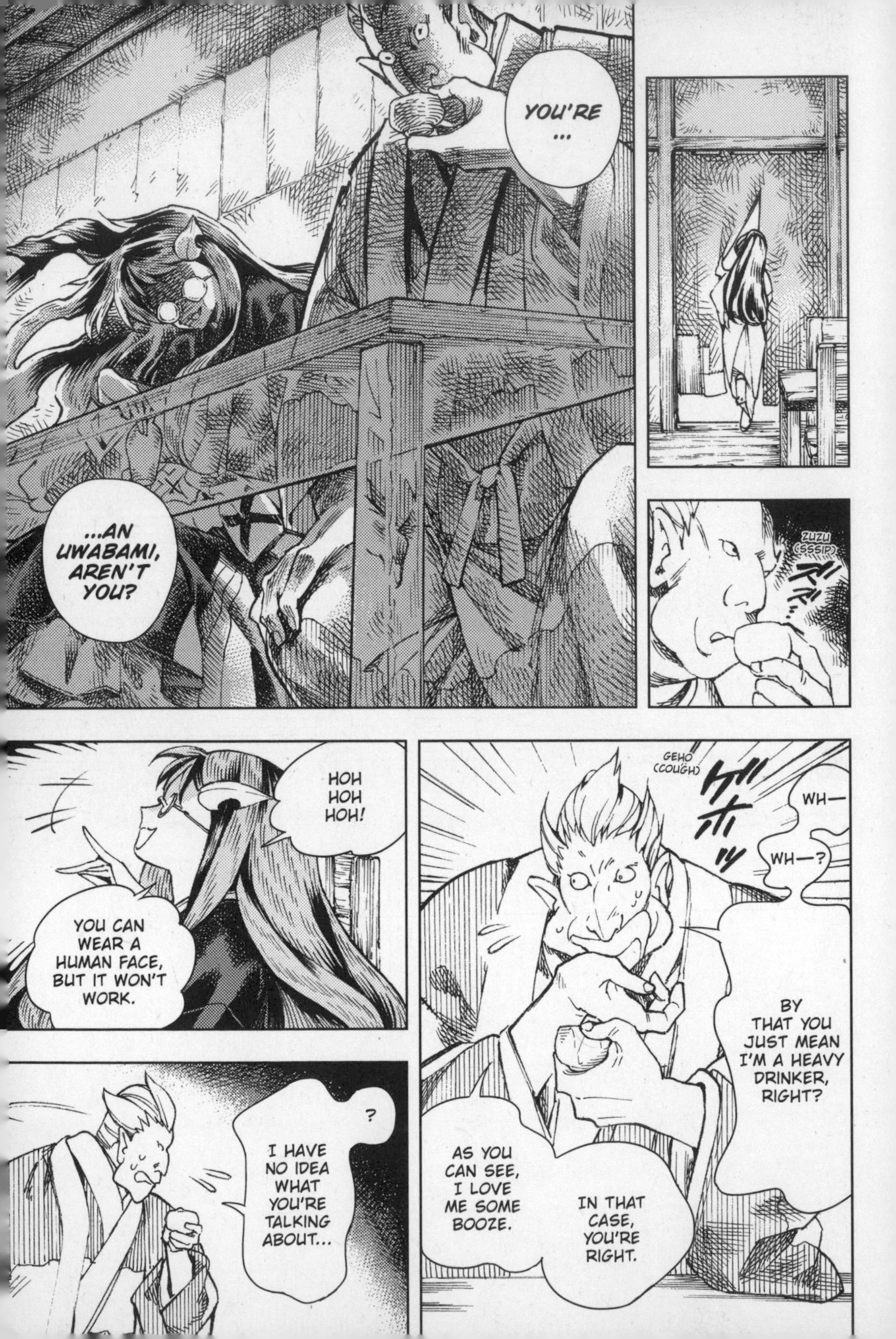
ZUZU (SSSIP)
YOU'RE ...
...AN UWABAMI, AREN'T YOU?
GEHO (COUGH)
WH—
WH—?
BY THAT YOU JUST MEAN I'M A HEAVY DRINKER, RIGHT?
AS YOU CAN SEE, I LOVE ME SOME BOOZE.
IN THAT CASE, YOU'RE RIGHT.
HOH HOH HOH!
YOU CAN WEAR A HUMAN FACE, BUT IT WON'T WORK.
?
I HAVE NO IDEA WHAT YOU'RE TALKING ABOUT...

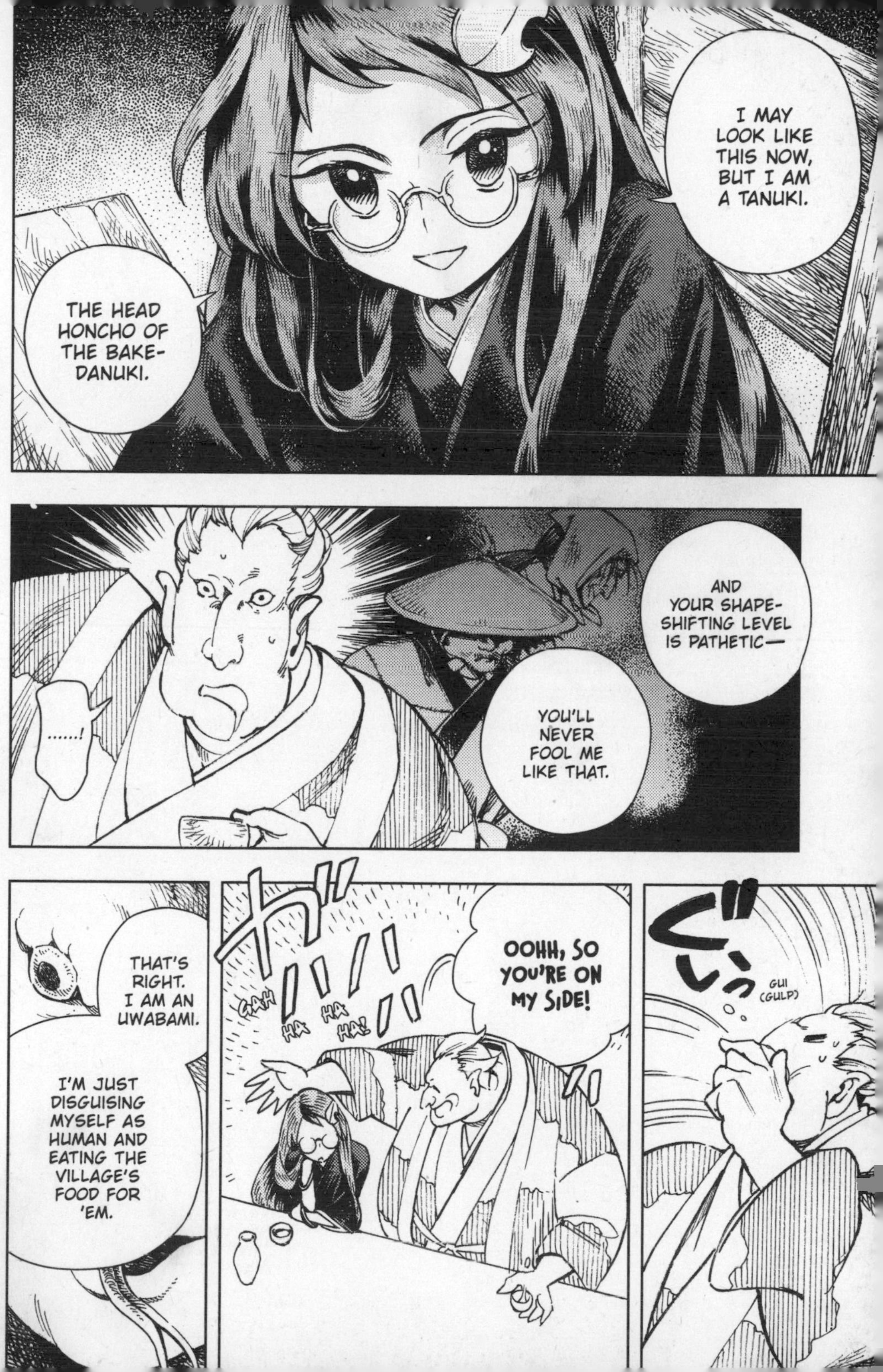
I MAY LOOK LIKE THIS NOW, BUT I AM A TANUKI.
THE HEAD HONCHO OF THE BAKE-DANUKI.
AND YOUR SHAPE-SHIFTING LEVEL IS PATHETIC—
YOU'LL NEVER FOOL ME LIKE THAT.
......!
ぐいっ
GUI (GULP)
OOHH, SO YOU'RE ON MY SIDE!
GAH HA HA HA!
THAT'S RIGHT. I AM AN UWABAMI.
I'M JUST DISGUISING MYSELF AS HUMAN AND EATING THE VILLAGE'S FOOD FOR 'EM.

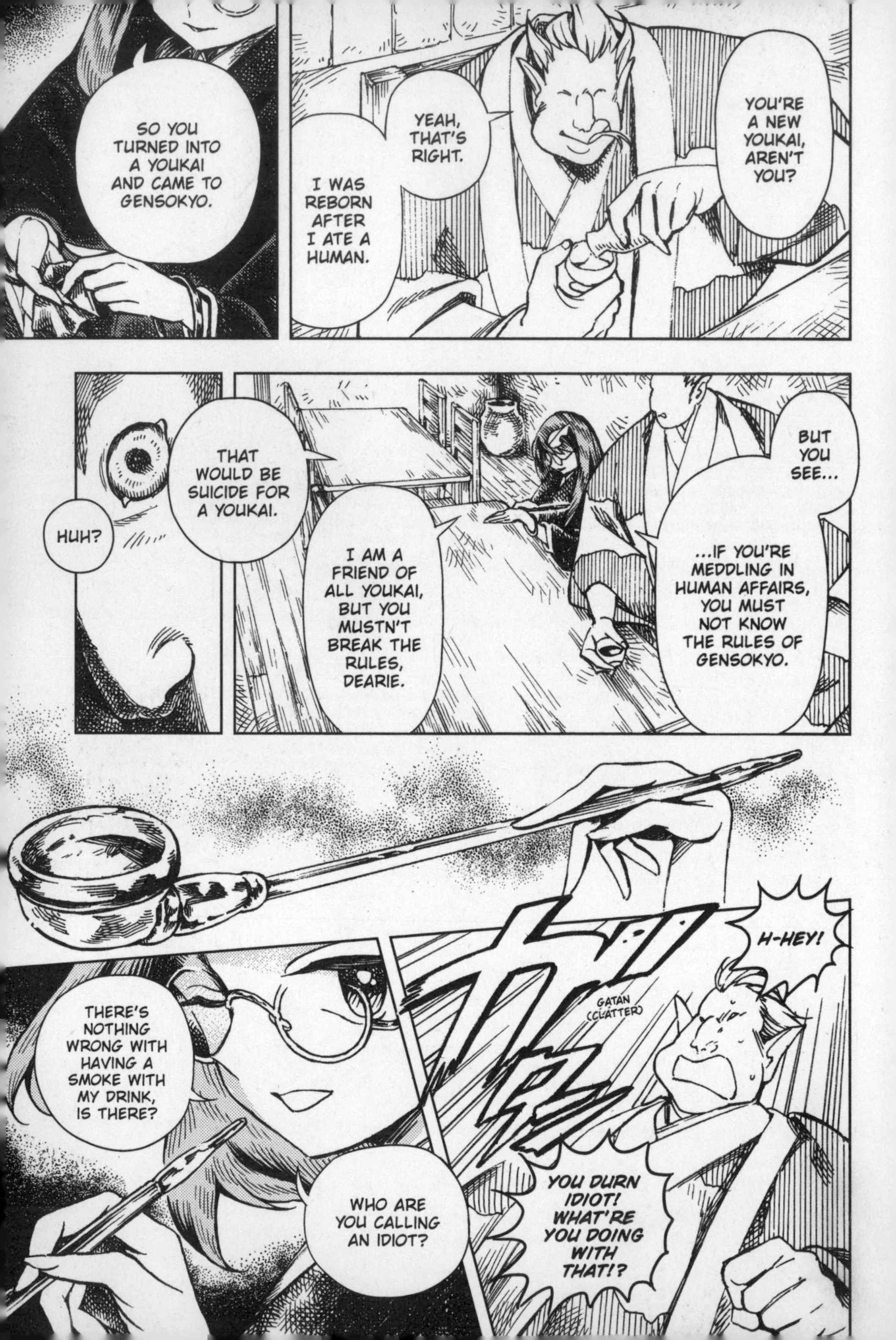
YOU'RE A NEW YOUKAI, AREN'T YOU?
YEAH, THAT'S RIGHT.
I WAS REBORN AFTER I ATE A HUMAN.
SO YOU TURNED INTO A YOUKAI AND CAME TO GENSOKYO.
BUT YOU SEE...
...IF YOU'RE MEDDLING IN HUMAN AFFAIRS, YOU MUST NOT KNOW THE RULES OF GENSOKYO.
I AM A FRIEND OF ALL YOUKAI, BUT YOU MUSTN'T BREAK THE RULES, DEARIE.
THAT WOULD BE SUICIDE FOR A YOUKAI.
HUH?
H-HEY!
GATAN (CLATTER)
YOU DURN IDIOT! WHAT'RE YOU DOING WITH THAT!?
THERE'S NOTHING WRONG WITH HAVING A SMOKE WITH MY DRINK, IS THERE?
WHO ARE YOU CALLING AN IDIOT?

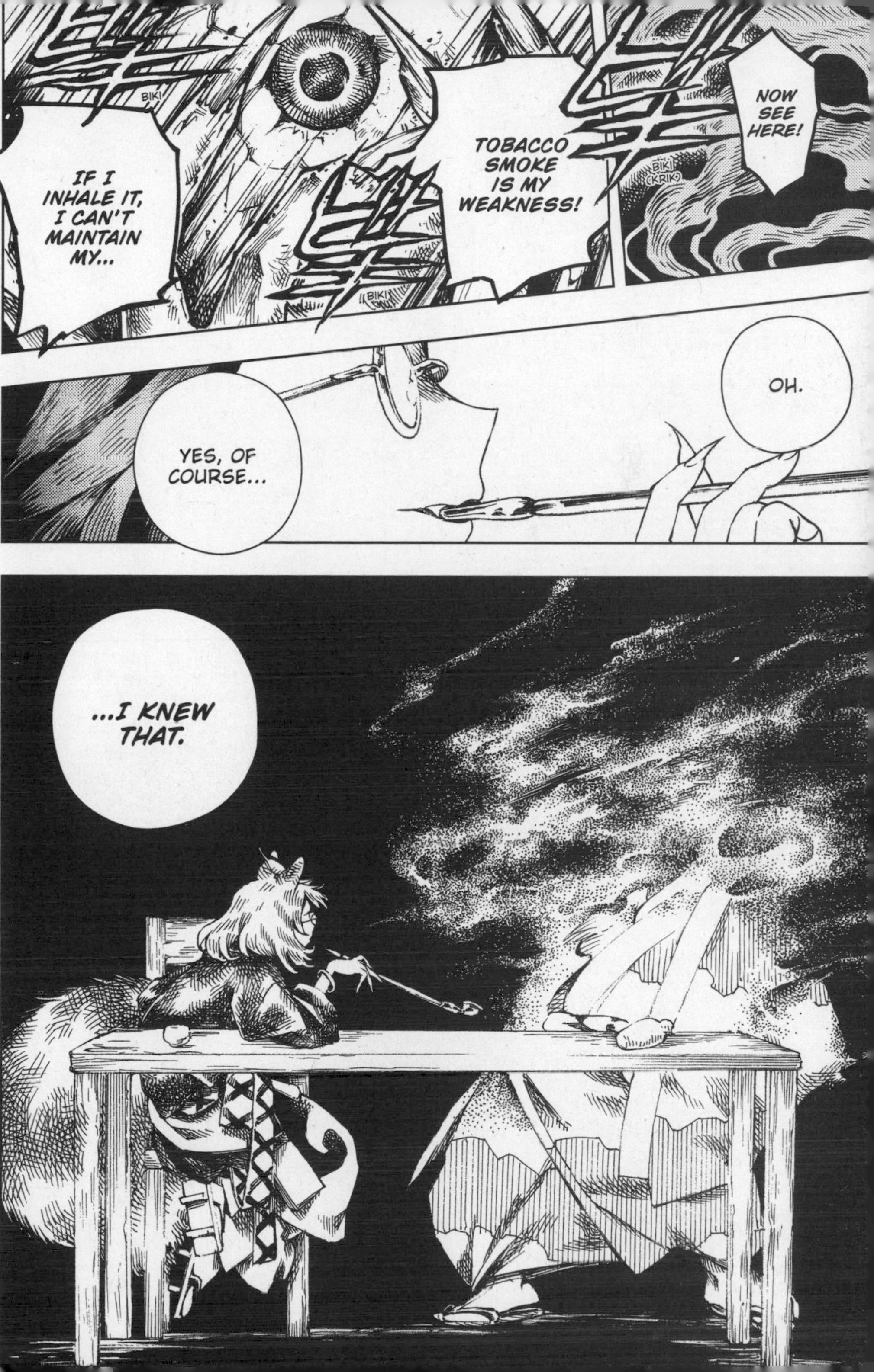
NOW SEE HERE!
TOBACCO SMOKE IS MY WEAKNESS!
BIKI (KRIK)
BIKI
BIKI
IF I INHALE IT, I CAN'T MAINTAIN MY...
OH.
YES, OF COURSE...
...I KNEW THAT.

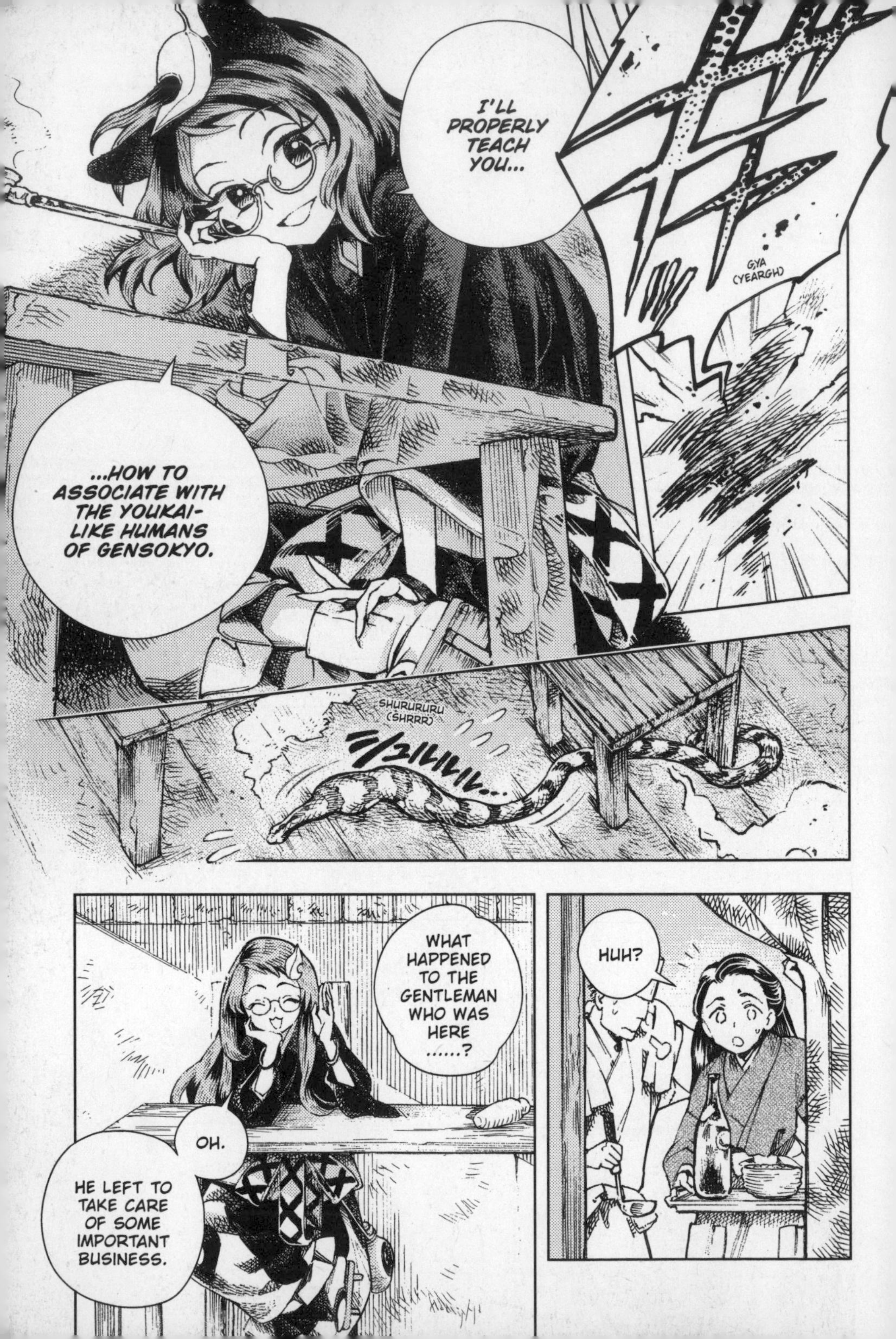
GYA (YEARGH)
I'LL PROPERLY TEACH YOU...
...HOW TO ASSOCIATE WITH THE YOUKAI-LIKE HUMANS OF GENSOKYO.
SHURURURU (SHRRR)
HUH?
WHAT HAPPENED TO THE GENTLEMAN WHO WAS HERE ......?
OH.
HE LEFT TO TAKE CARE OF SOME IMPORTANT BUSINESS.

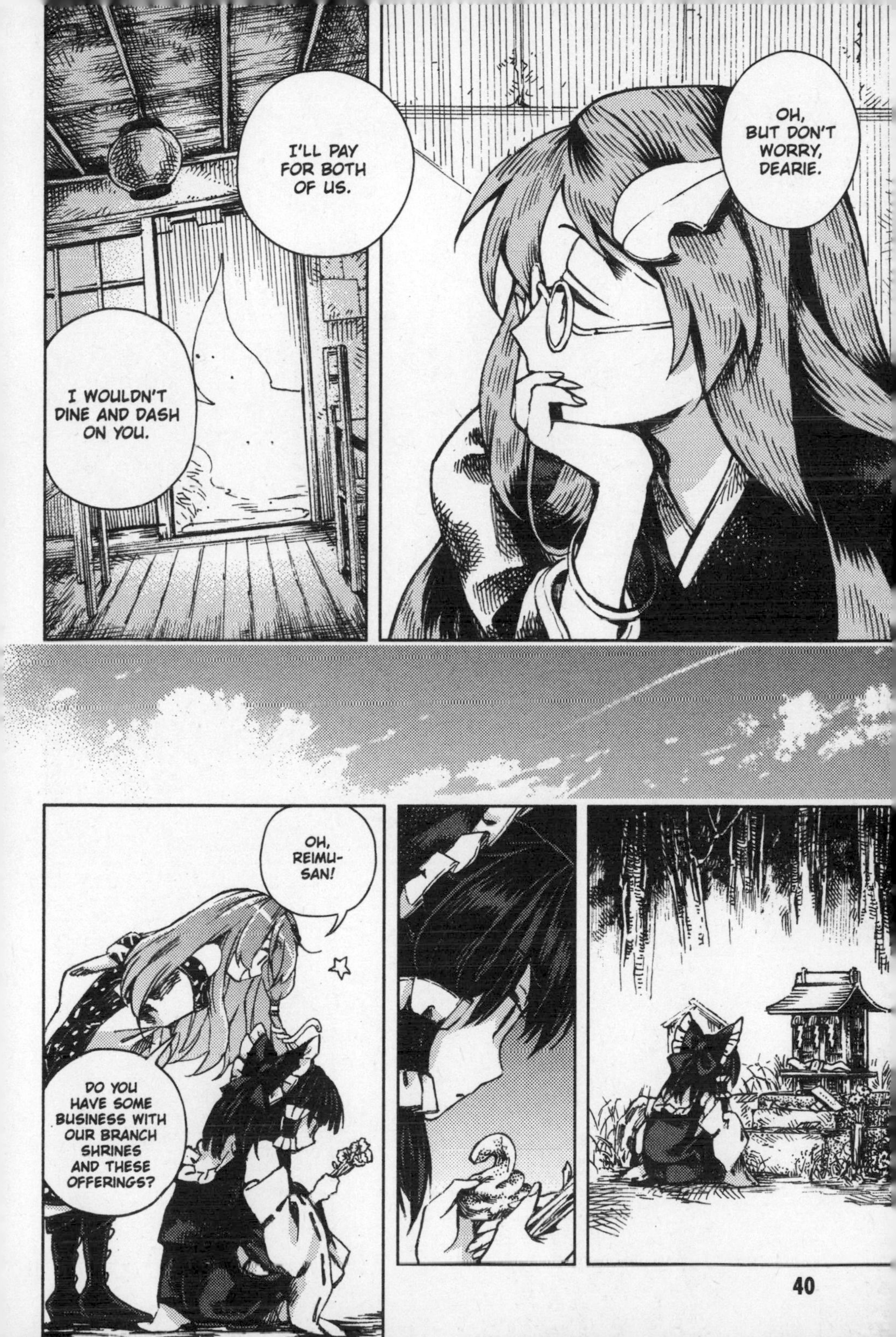
OH, BUT DON'T WORRY, DEARIE.
I'LL PAY FOR BOTH OF US.
I WOULDN'T DINE AND DASH ON YOU.
OH, REIMU-SAN!
DO YOU HAVE SOME BUSINESS WITH OUR BRANCH SHRINES AND THESE OFFERINGS?

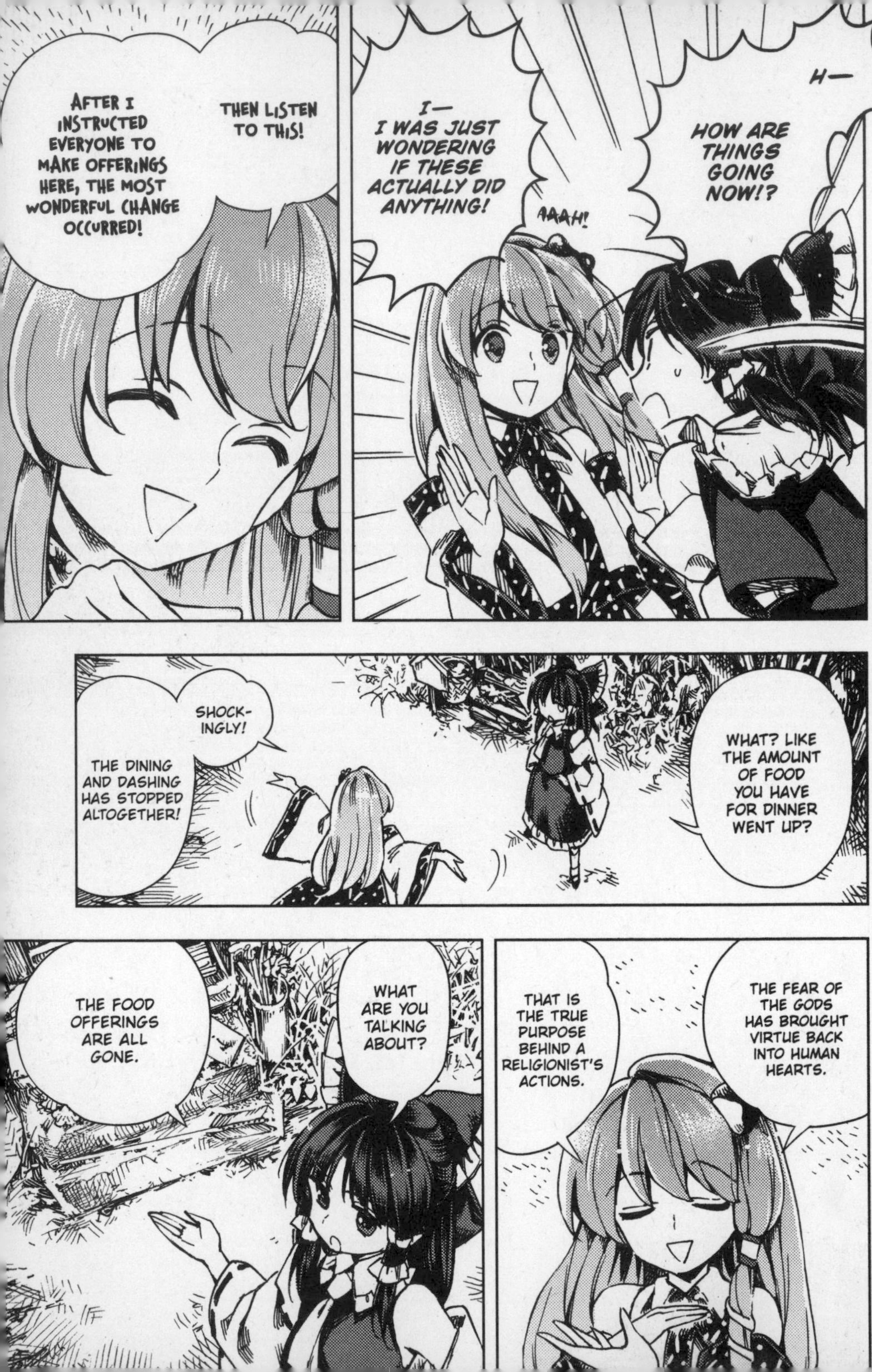
H—
HOW ARE THINGS GOING NOW!?
AAAH!
I— I WAS JUST WONDERING IF THESE ACTUALLY DID ANYTHING!
THEN LISTEN TO THIS!
AFTER I INSTRUCTED EVERYONE TO MAKE OFFERINGS HERE, THE MOST WONDERFUL CHANGE OCCURRED!
WHAT? LIKE THE AMOUNT OF FOOD YOU HAVE FOR DINNER WENT UP?
SHOCK-INGLY!
THE DINING AND DASHING HAS STOPPED ALTOGETHER!
THE FEAR OF THE GODS HAS BROUGHT VIRTUE BACK INTO HUMAN HEARTS.
THAT IS THE TRUE PURPOSE BEHIND A RELIGIONIST'S ACTIONS.
WHAT ARE YOU TALKING ABOUT?
THE FOOD OFFERINGS ARE ALL GONE.

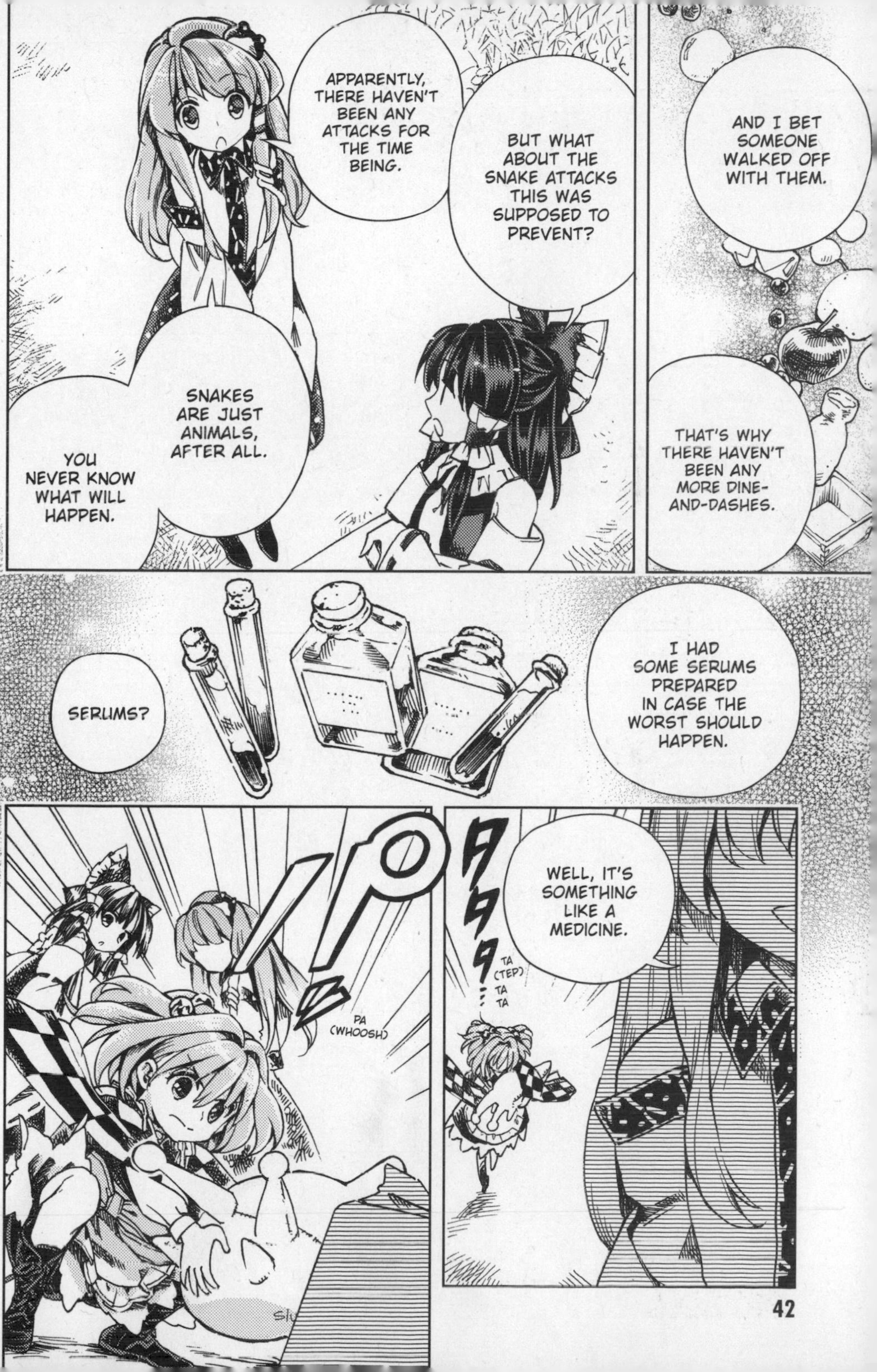
AND I BET SOMEONE WALKED OFF WITH THEM.
THAT'S WHY THERE HAVEN'T BEEN ANY MORE DINE-AND-DASHES.
BUT WHAT ABOUT THE SNAKE ATTACKS THIS WAS SUPPOSED TO PREVENT?
APPARENTLY, THERE HAVEN'T BEEN ANY ATTACKS FOR THE TIME BEING.
SNAKES ARE JUST ANIMALS, AFTER ALL.
YOU NEVER KNOW WHAT WILL HAPPEN.
I HAD SOME SERUMS PREPARED IN CASE THE WORST SHOULD HAPPEN.
SERUMS?
WELL, IT'S SOMETHING LIKE A MEDICINE.
TA (TEP) TA TA
PA (WHOOSH)

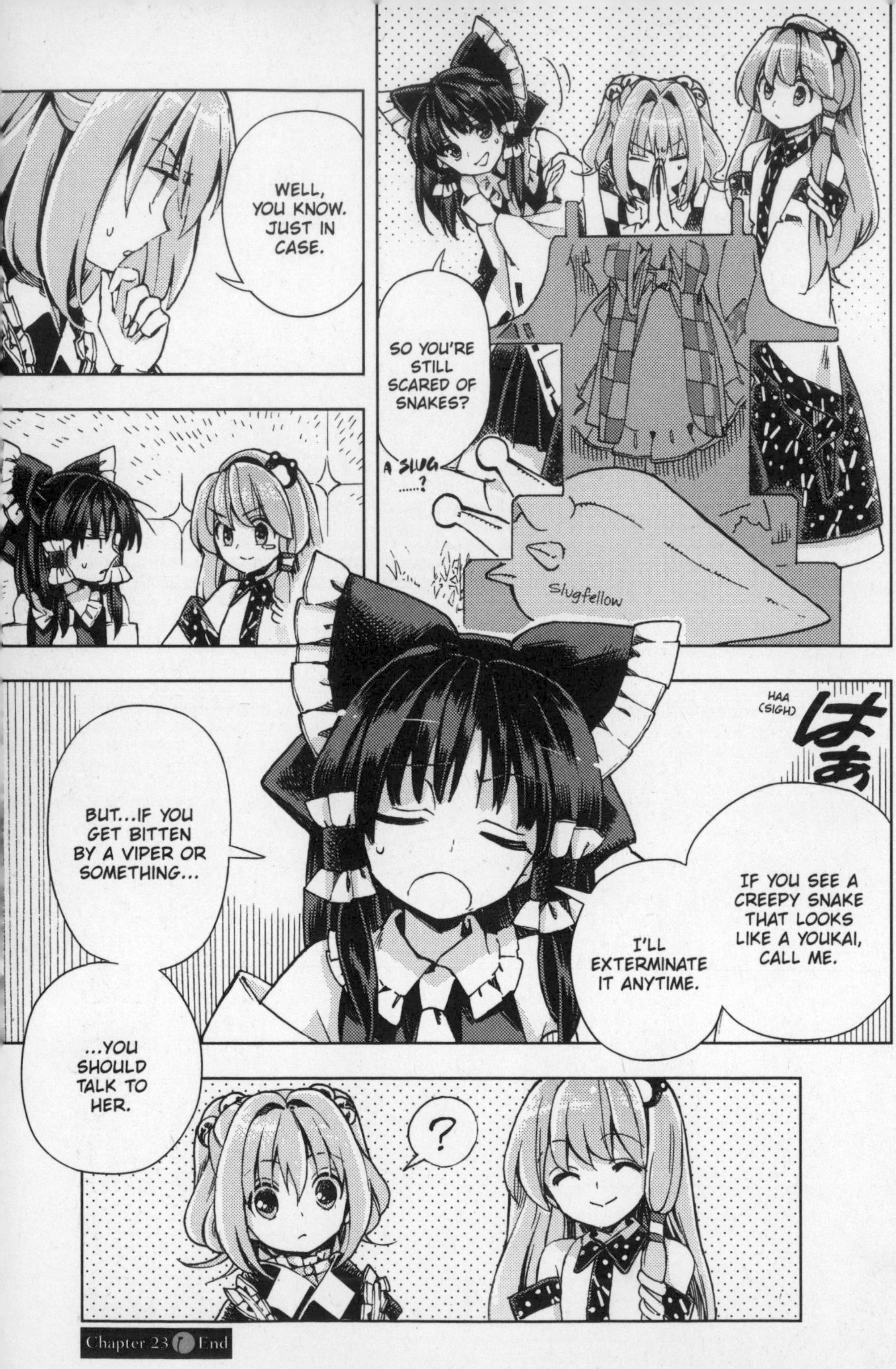
SO YOU'RE STILL SCARED OF SNAKES?
A SLUG ......?
Slugfellow
WELL, YOU KNOW. JUST IN CASE.
HAA (SIGH)
はぁ
IF YOU SEE A CREEPY SNAKE THAT LOOKS LIKE A YOUKAI, CALL ME.
I'LL EXTERMINATE IT ANYTIME.
BUT...IF YOU GET BITTEN BY A VIPER OR SOMETHING...
...YOU SHOULD TALK TO HER.
?

Chapter 23 End

Forbidden Scrollery

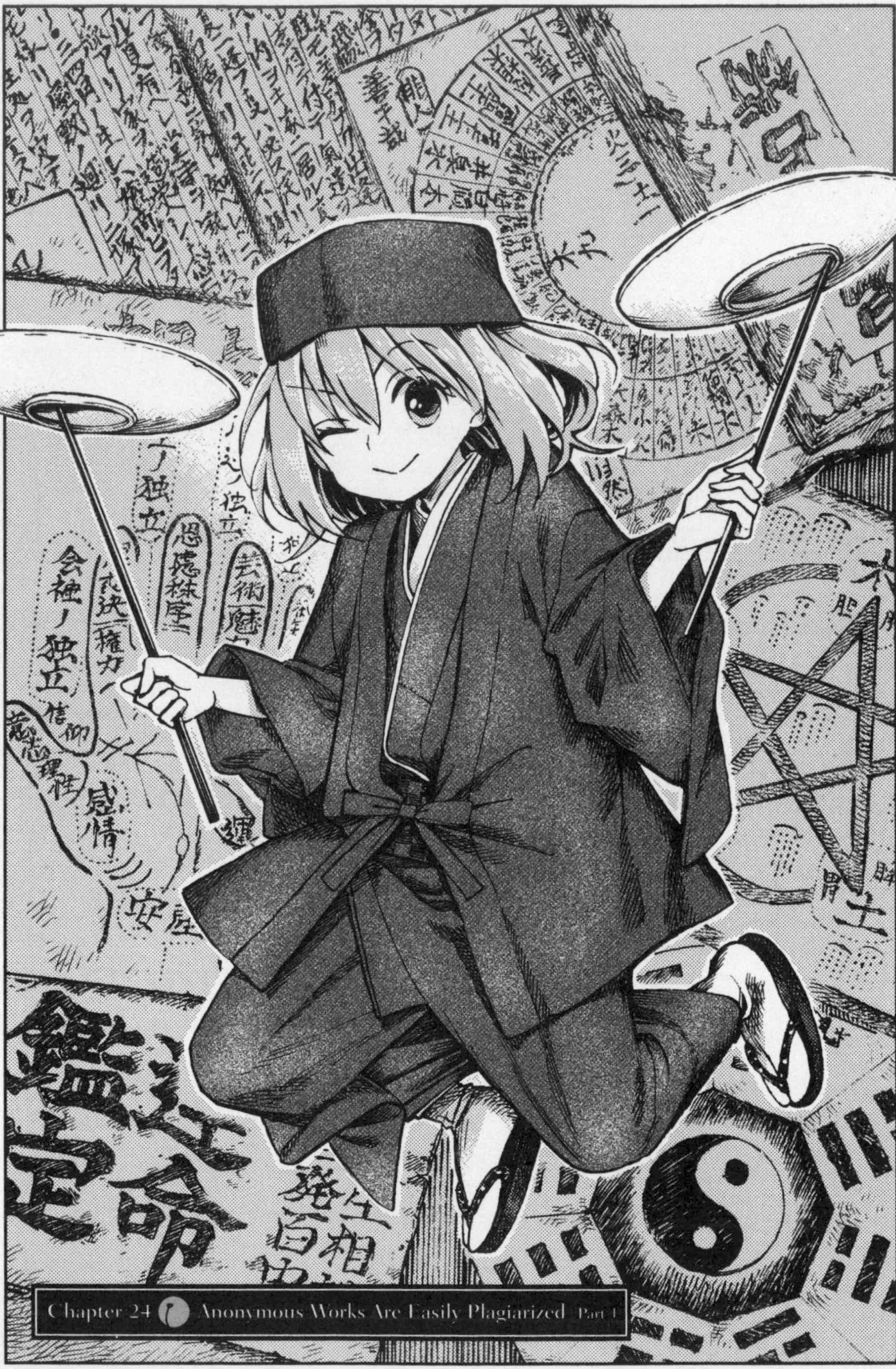
Chapter 24 Anonymous Works Are Easily Plagiarized Part 1

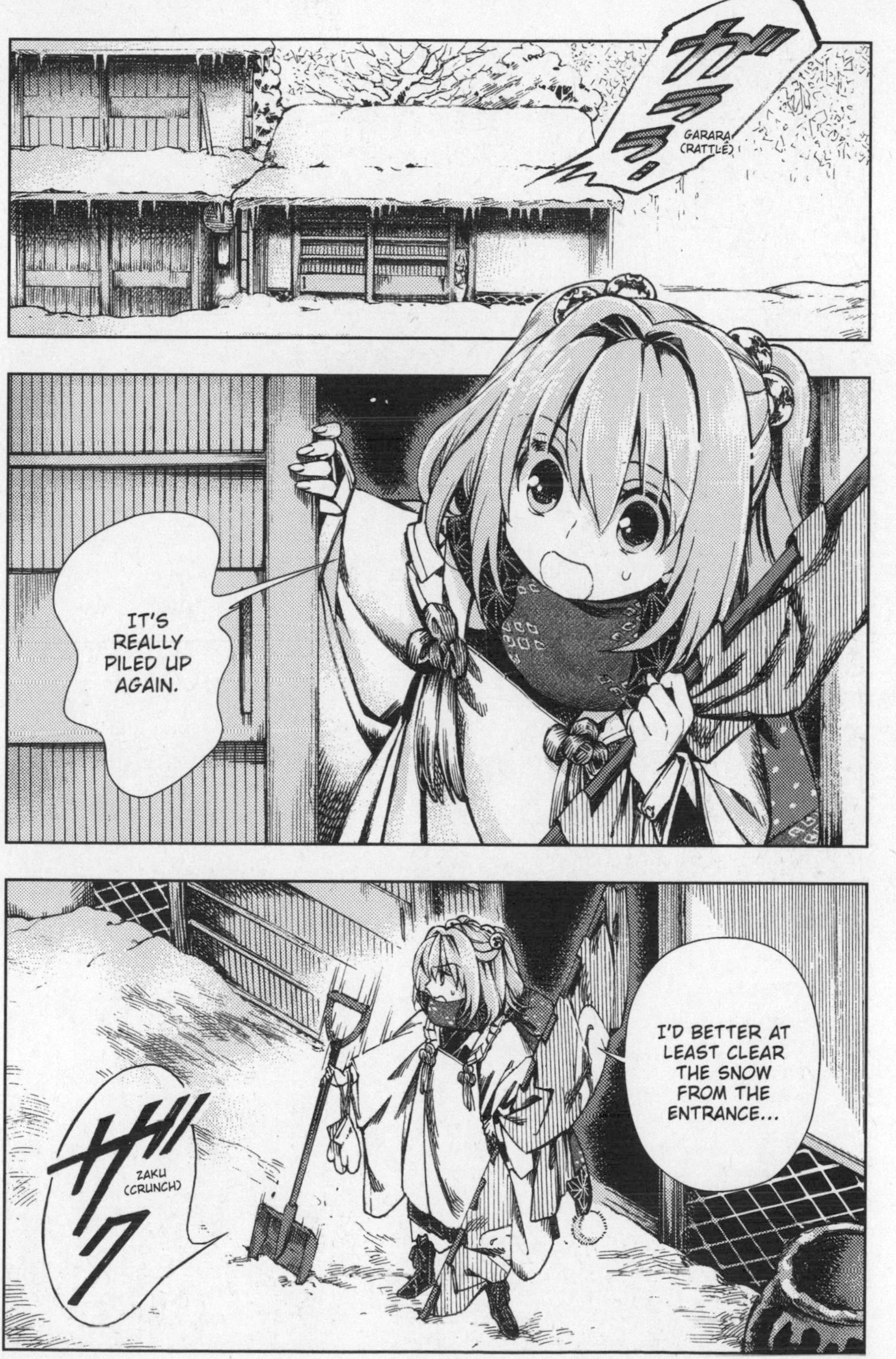
ガララ
GARARA (RATTLE)
IT'S REALLY PILED UP AGAIN.
I'D BETTER AT LEAST CLEAR THE SNOW FROM THE ENTRANCE...
ザク
ZAKU (CRUNCH)

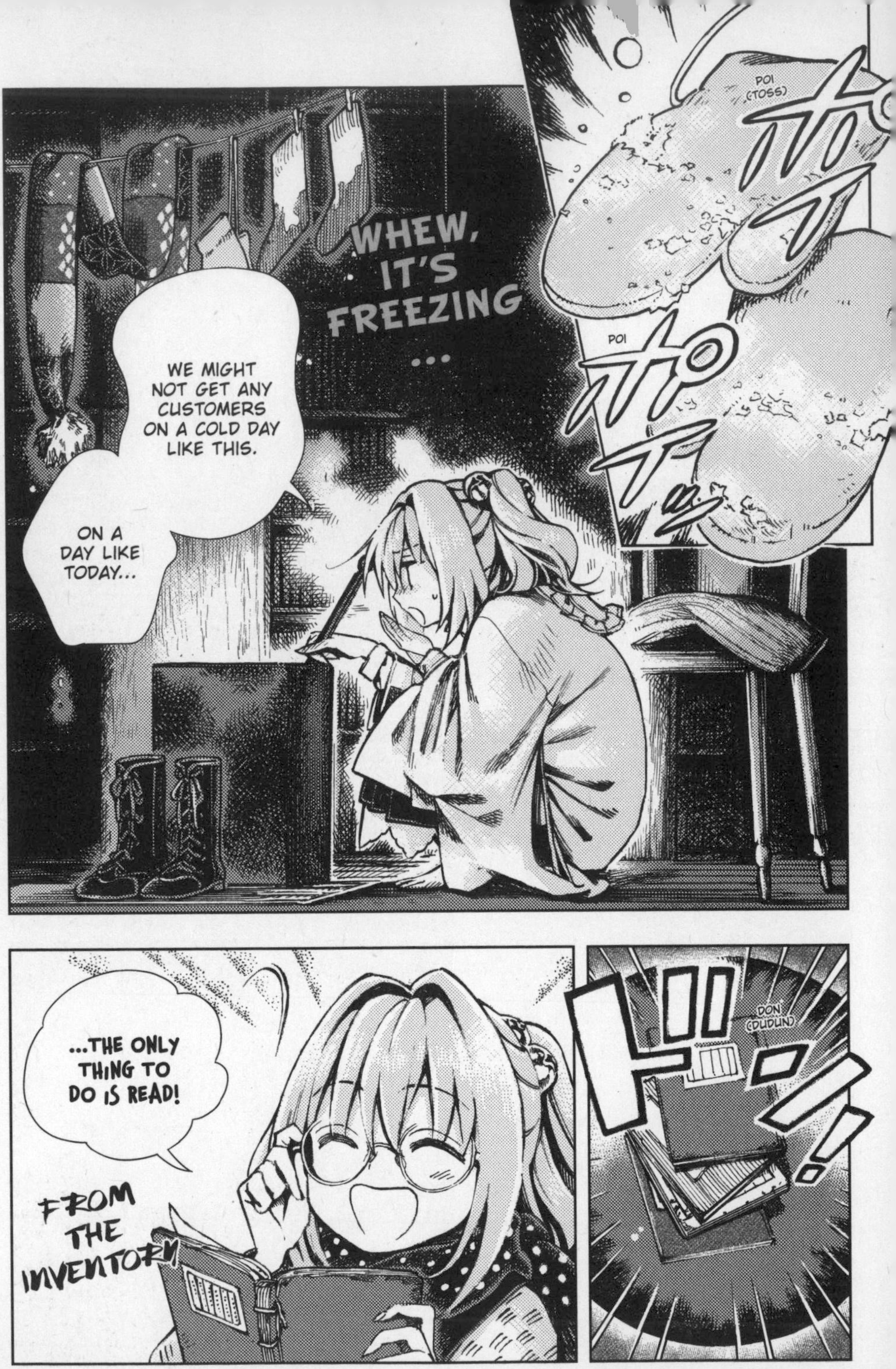
POI (TOSS)
POI
WHEW, IT'S FREEZING...
WE MIGHT NOT GET ANY CUSTOMERS ON A COLD DAY LIKE THIS.
ON A DAY LIKE TODAY...
DON (DUDUN)
...THE ONLY THING TO DO IS READ!
FROM THE INVENTORY

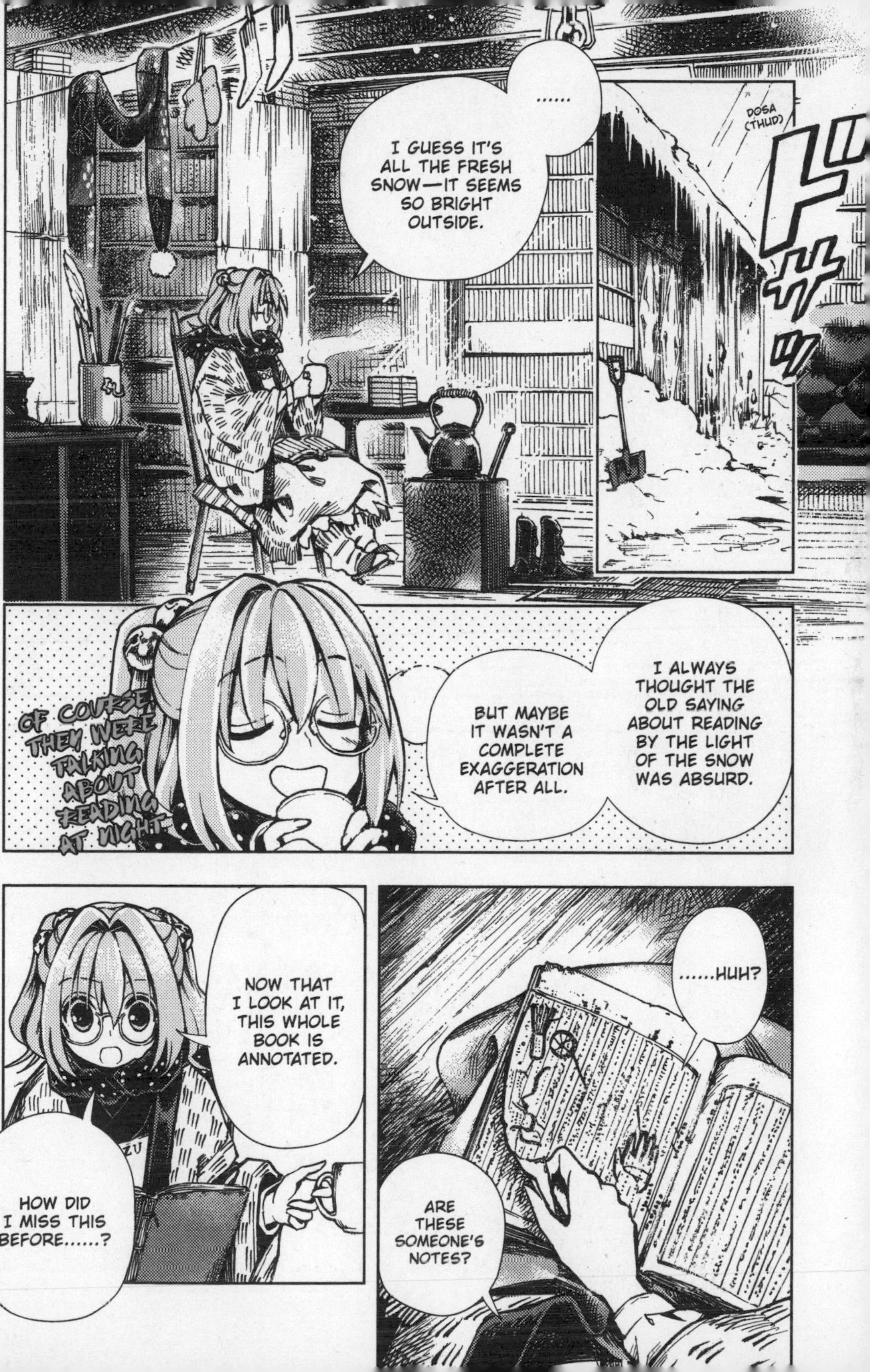
ドサッ
DOSA (THUD)
......
I GUESS IT'S ALL THE FRESH SNOW—IT SEEMS SO BRIGHT OUTSIDE.
I ALWAYS THOUGHT THE OLD SAYING ABOUT READING BY THE LIGHT OF THE SNOW WAS ABSURD.
BUT MAYBE IT WASN'T A COMPLETE EXAGGERATION AFTER ALL.
OF COURSE THEY WERE TALKING ABOUT READING AT NIGHT
......HUH?
ARE THESE SOMEONE'S NOTES?
NOW THAT I LOOK AT IT, THIS WHOLE BOOK IS ANNOTATED.
HOW DID I MISS THIS BEFORE......?

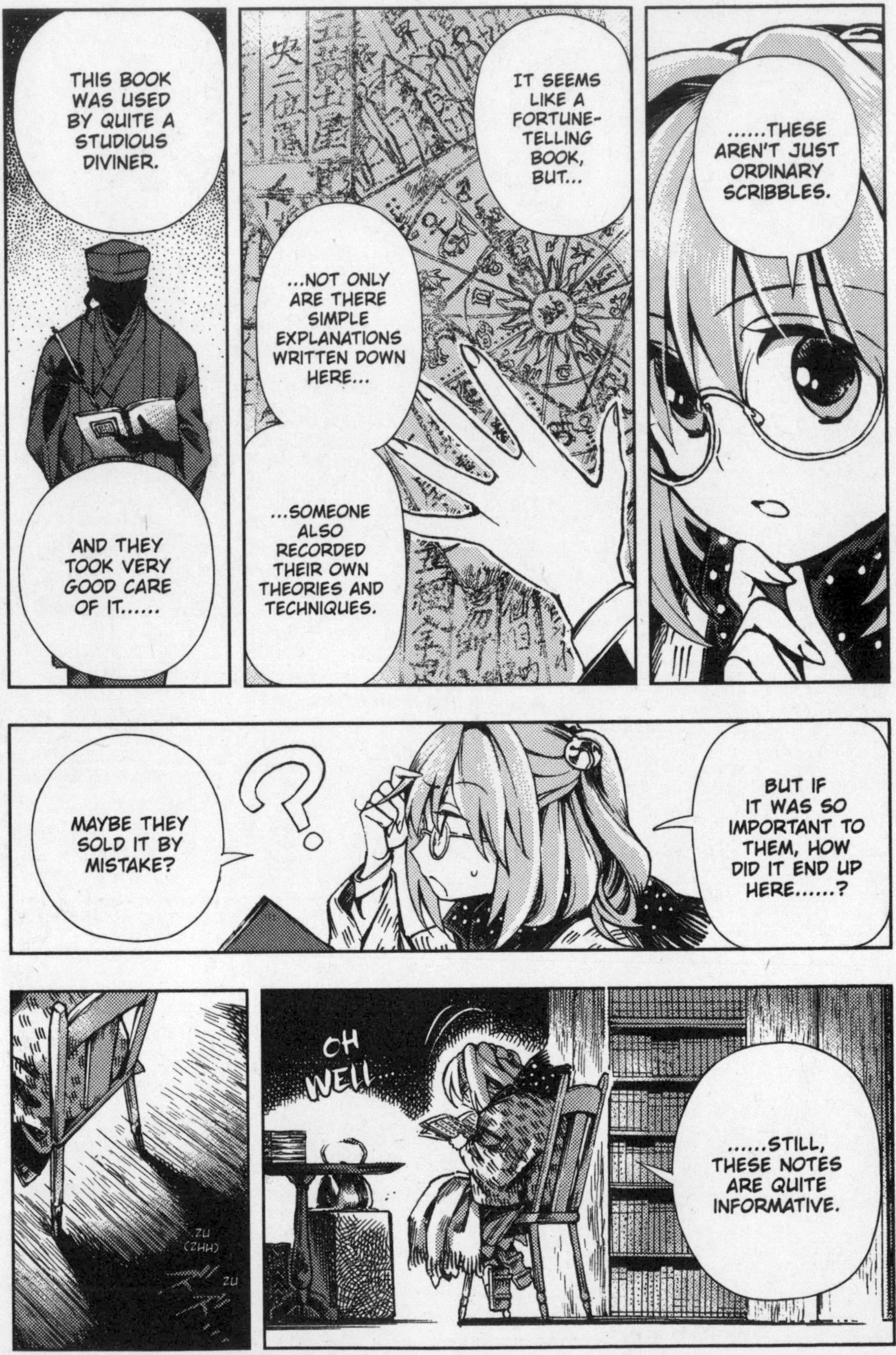
......THESE AREN'T JUST ORDINARY SCRIBBLES.
IT SEEMS LIKE A FORTUNE-TELLING BOOK, BUT...
...NOT ONLY ARE THERE SIMPLE EXPLANATIONS WRITTEN DOWN HERE...
...SOMEONE ALSO RECORDED THEIR OWN THEORIES AND TECHNIQUES.
THIS BOOK WAS USED BY QUITE A STUDIOUS DIVINER.
AND THEY TOOK VERY GOOD CARE OF IT......
BUT IF IT WAS SO IMPORTANT TO THEM, HOW DID IT END UP HERE......?
?
MAYBE THEY SOLD IT BY MISTAKE?
OH WELL...
......STILL, THESE NOTES ARE QUITE INFORMATIVE.
ZU (ZHH)
ZU

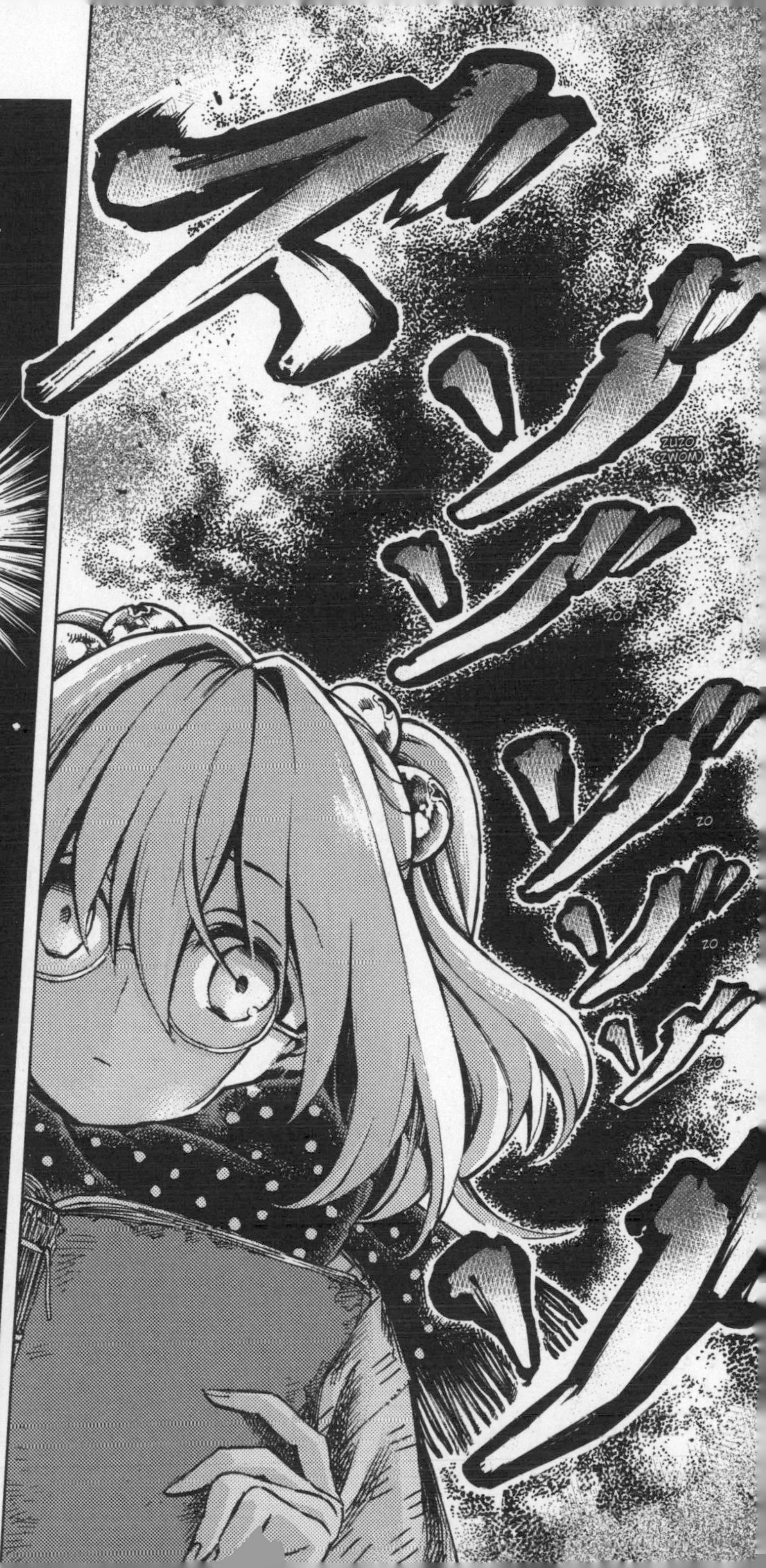
ZUZO
(ZWOM)
ZO
ZO
ZO
ZO
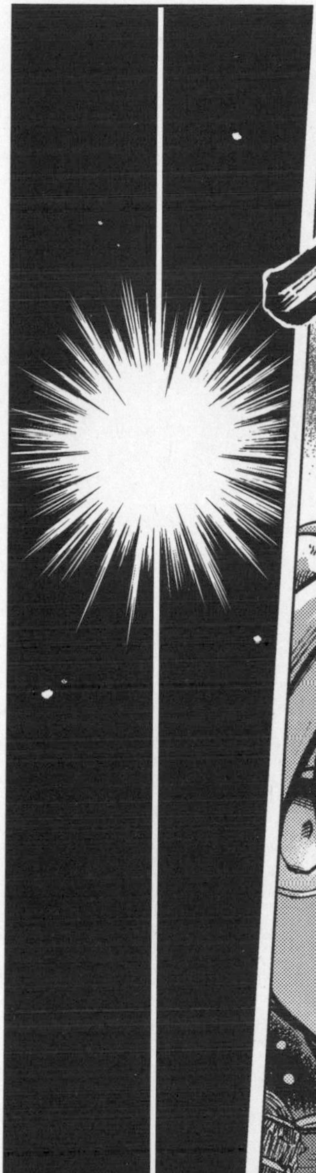

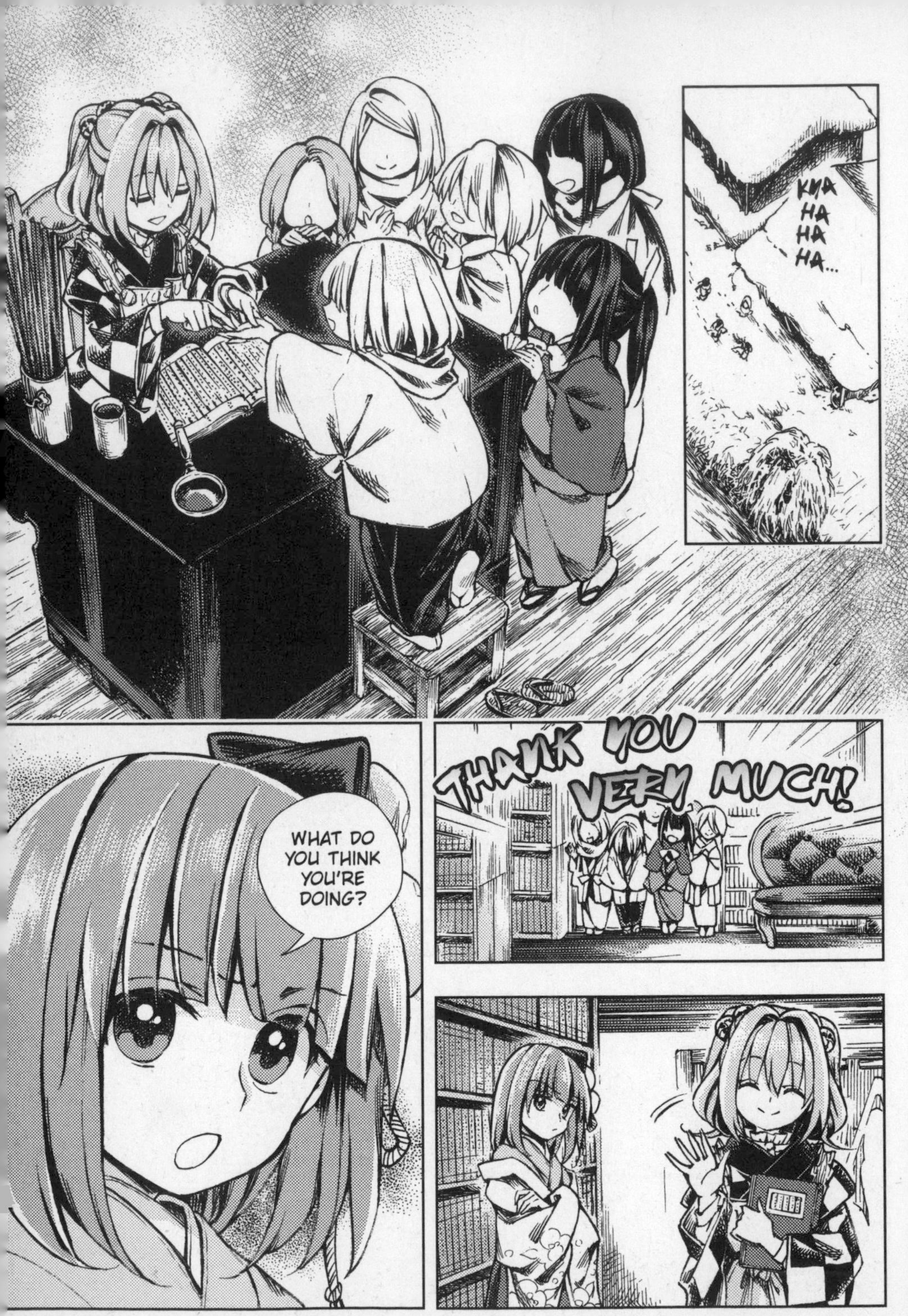
KYA HA HA HA...
THANK YOU VERY MUCH!
WHAT DO YOU THINK YOU'RE DOING?

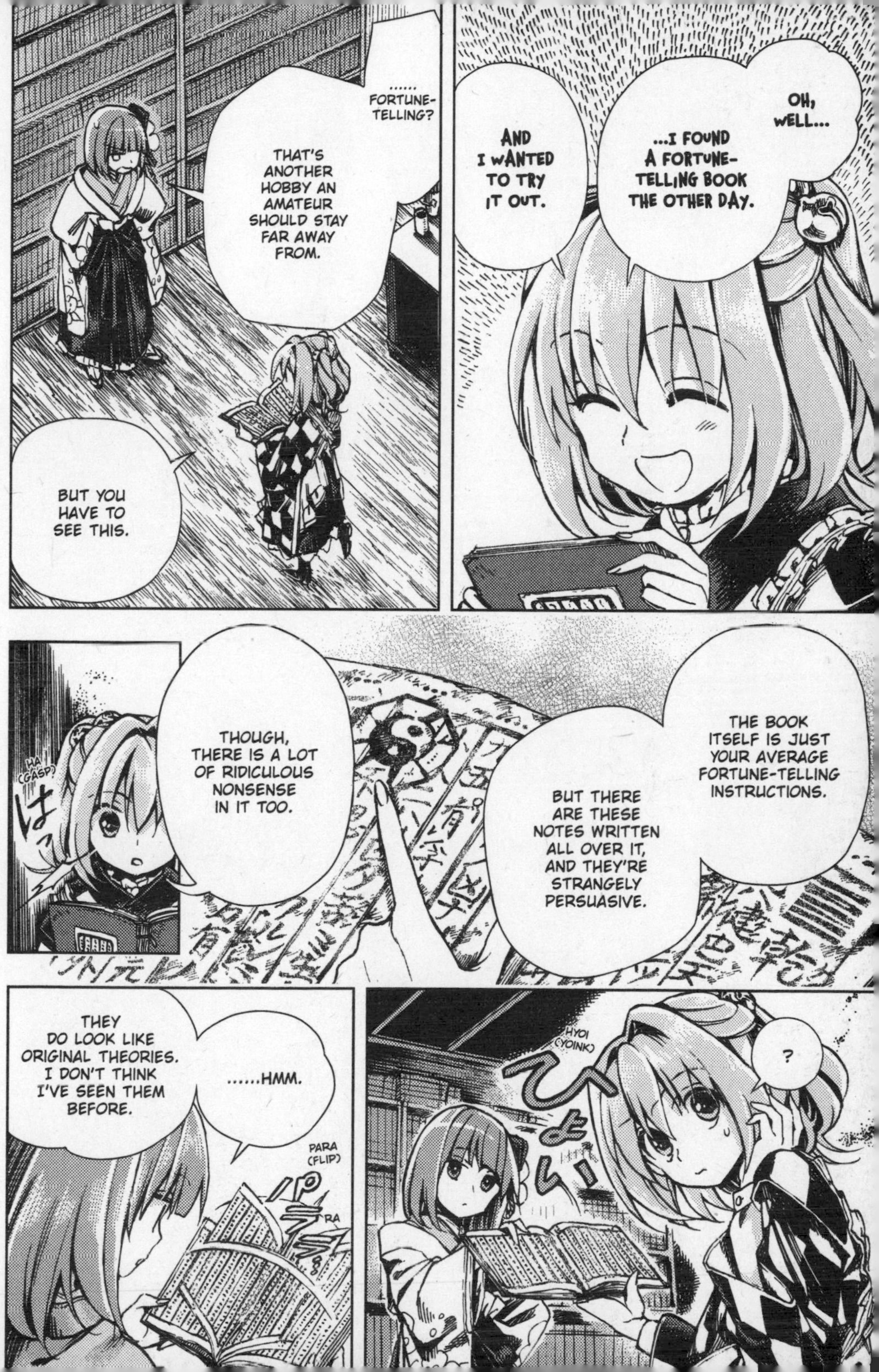
OH, WELL...
...I FOUND A FORTUNE-TELLING BOOK THE OTHER DAY.
AND I WANTED TO TRY IT OUT.
......FORTUNE-TELLING?
THAT'S ANOTHER HOBBY AN AMATEUR SHOULD STAY FAR AWAY FROM.
BUT YOU HAVE TO SEE THIS.
THE BOOK ITSELF IS JUST YOUR AVERAGE FORTUNE-TELLING INSTRUCTIONS.
BUT THERE ARE THESE NOTES WRITTEN ALL OVER IT, AND THEY'RE STRANGELY PERSUASIVE.
THOUGH, THERE IS A LOT OF RIDICULOUS NONSENSE IN IT TOO.
HA (GASP)
はっ
?
HYOI (YOINK)
ひょい
......HMM.
THEY DO LOOK LIKE ORIGINAL THEORIES. I DON'T THINK I'VE SEEN THEM BEFORE.
PARA (FLIP)
パラ
RA

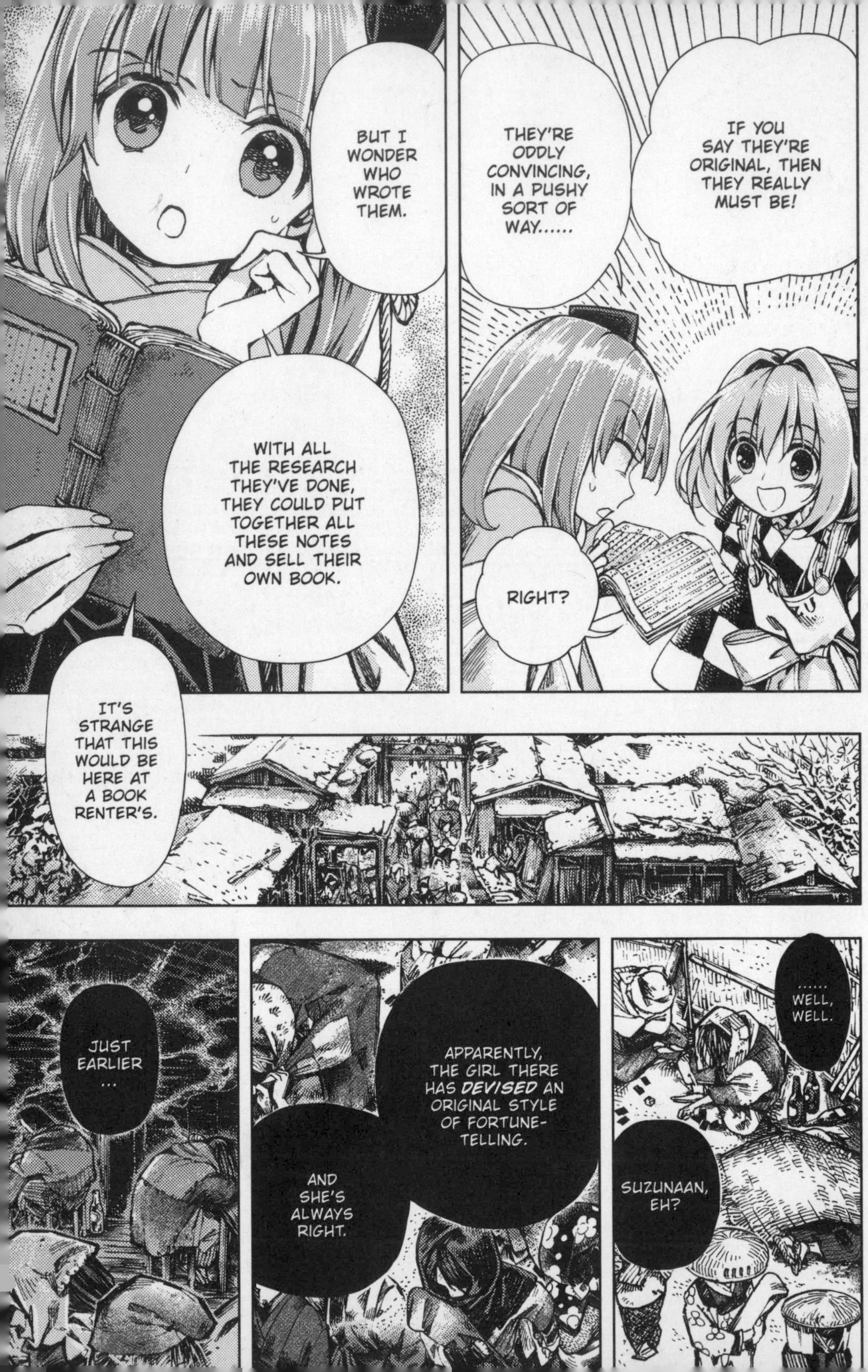
IF YOU SAY THEY'RE ORIGINAL, THEN THEY REALLY MUST BE!
THEY'RE ODDLY CONVINCING, IN A PUSHY SORT OF WAY......
RIGHT?
BUT I WONDER WHO WROTE THEM.
WITH ALL THE RESEARCH THEY'VE DONE, THEY COULD PUT TOGETHER ALL THESE NOTES AND SELL THEIR OWN BOOK.
IT'S STRANGE THAT THIS WOULD BE HERE AT A BOOK RENTER'S.
......WELL, WELL.
SUZUNAAN, EH?
APPARENTLY, THE GIRL THERE HAS *DEVISED* AN ORIGINAL STYLE OF FORTUNE-TELLING.
AND SHE'S ALWAYS RIGHT.
JUST EARLIER ...

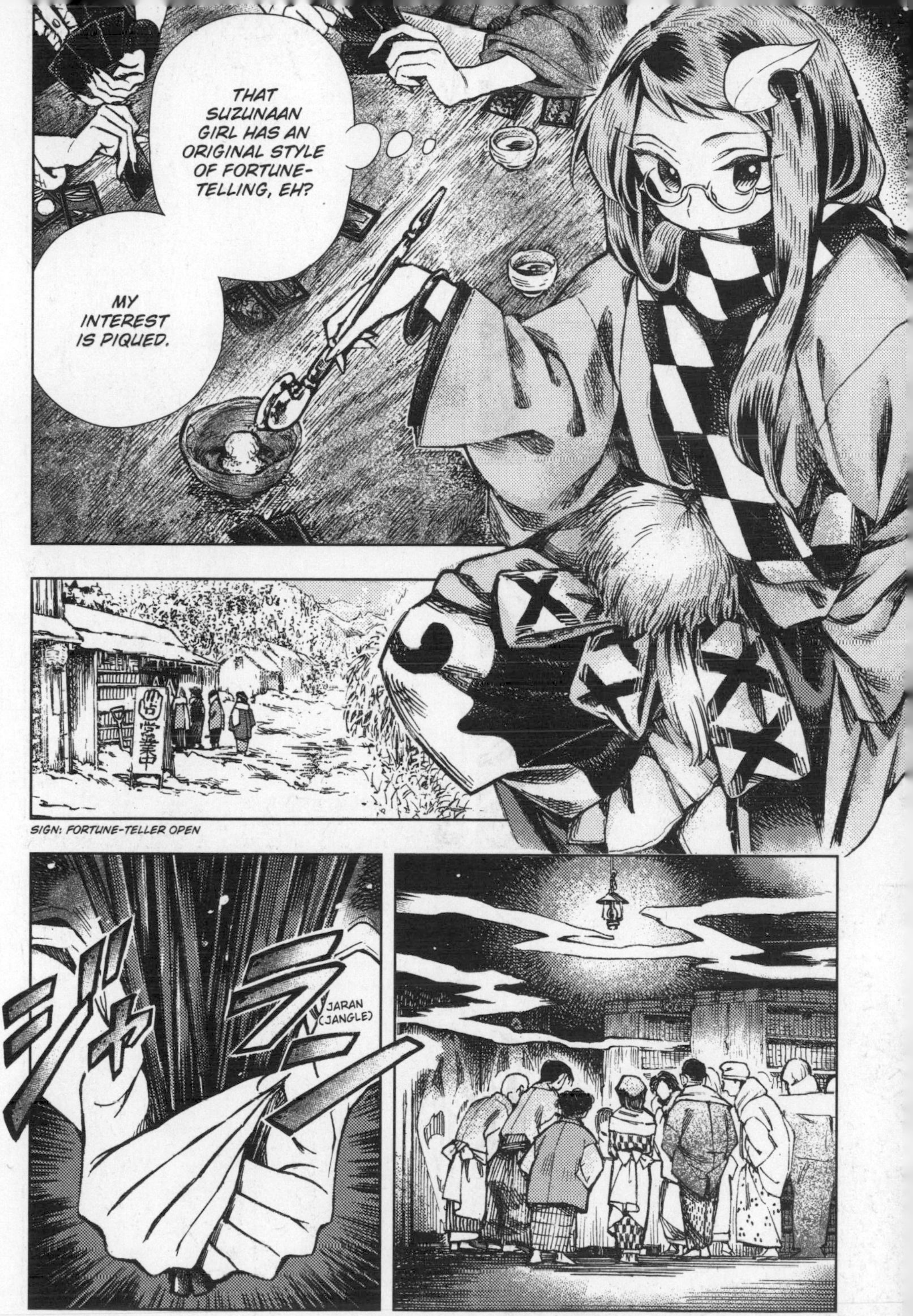
THAT SUZUNAAN GIRL HAS AN ORIGINAL STYLE OF FORTUNE-TELLING, EH?
MY INTEREST IS PIQUED.
SIGN: FORTUNE-TELLER OPEN
ジャラ
JARAN (JANGLE)

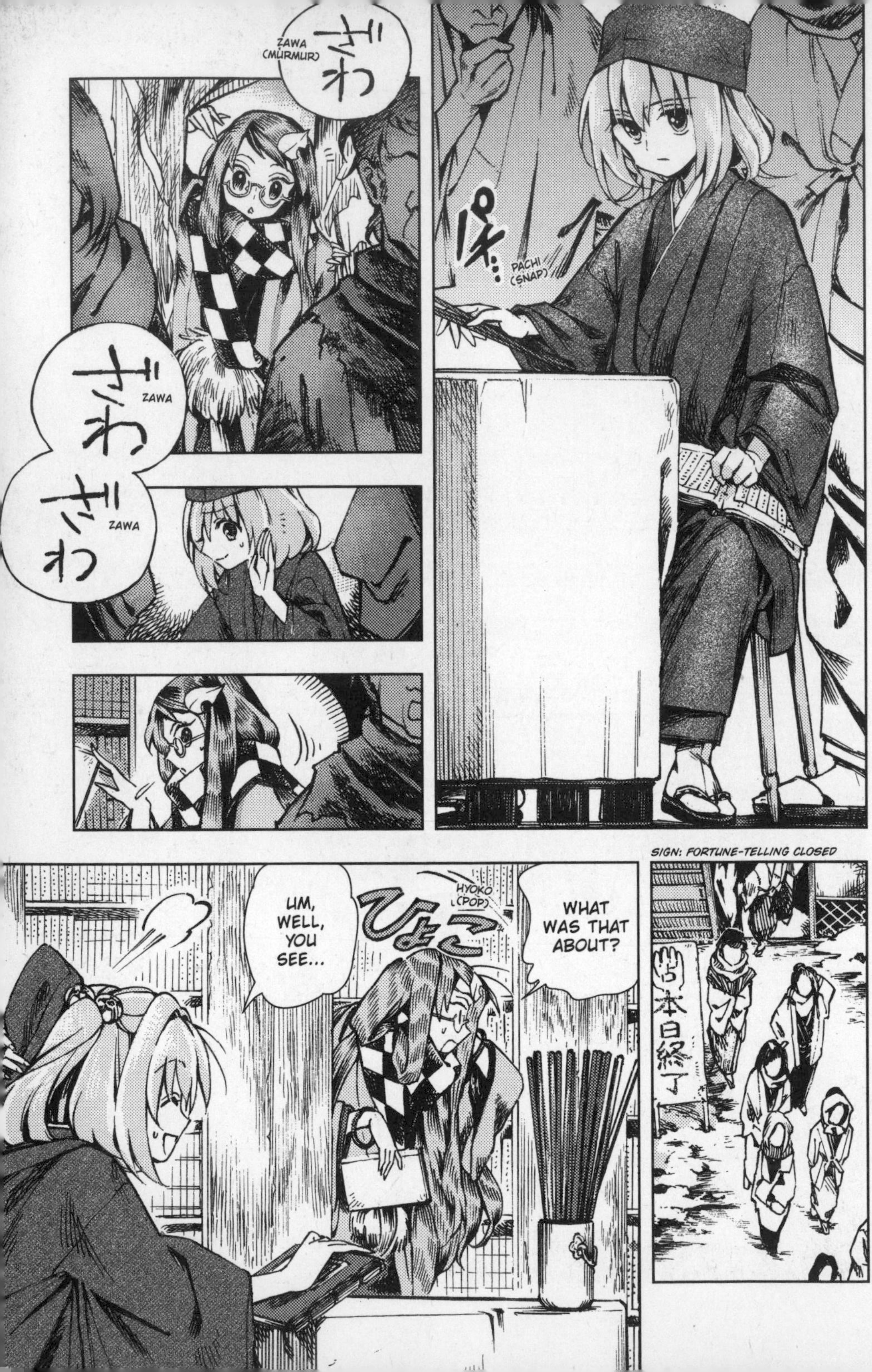
ぱち…
PACHI (SNAP)
ざわ
ZAWA (MURMUR)
ざわ
ZAWA
ざわ
ZAWA
SIGN: FORTUNE-TELLING CLOSED
占 本日終了
WHAT WAS THAT ABOUT?
ひょこ
HYOKO (POP)
UM, WELL, YOU SEE...

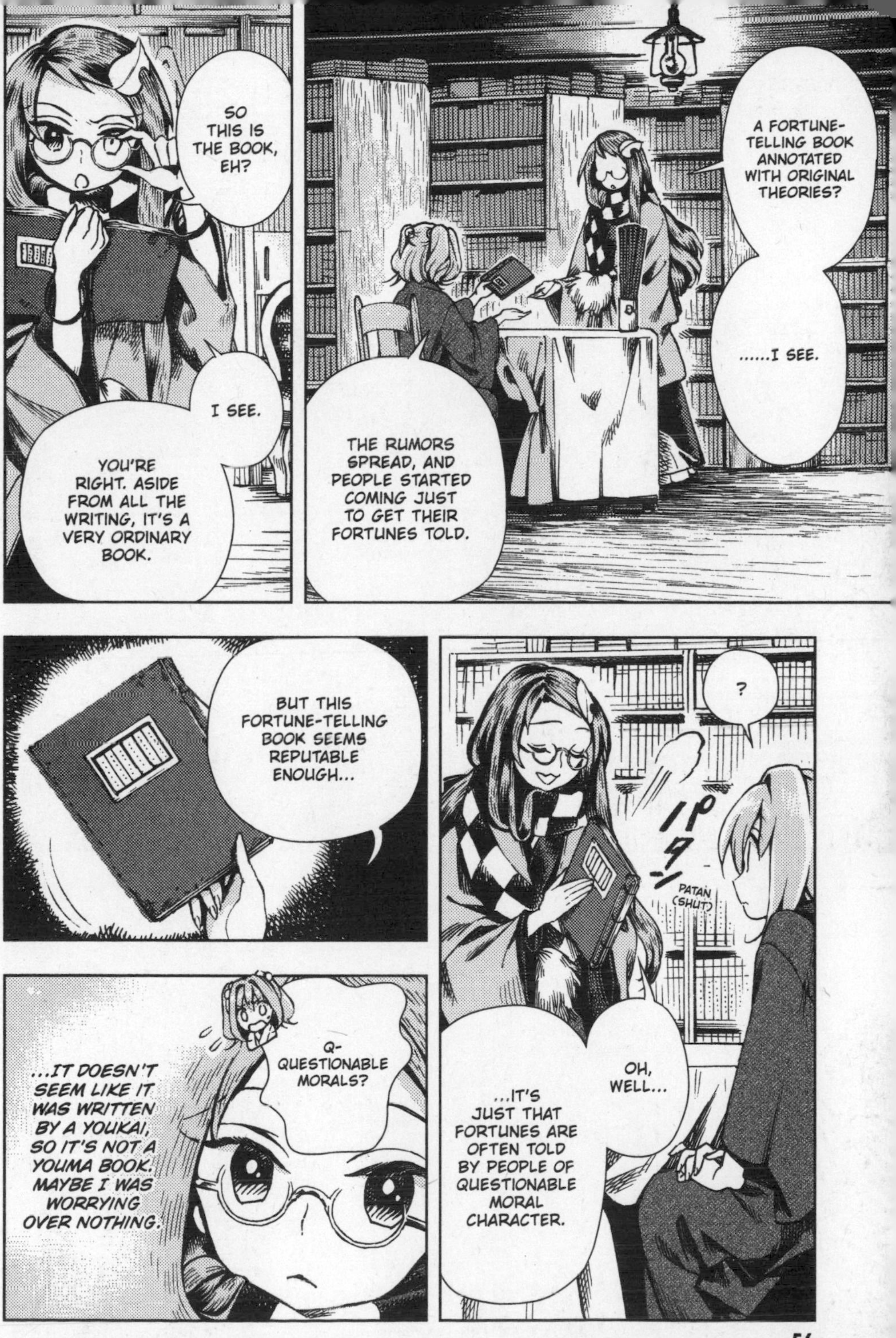
A FORTUNE-TELLING BOOK ANNOTATED WITH ORIGINAL THEORIES?
......I SEE.
THE RUMORS SPREAD, AND PEOPLE STARTED COMING JUST TO GET THEIR FORTUNES TOLD.
SO THIS IS THE BOOK, EH?
I SEE.
YOU'RE RIGHT. ASIDE FROM ALL THE WRITING, IT'S A VERY ORDINARY BOOK.
?
パタン
PATAN (SHUT)
OH, WELL...
...IT'S JUST THAT FORTUNES ARE OFTEN TOLD BY PEOPLE OF QUESTIONABLE MORAL CHARACTER.
BUT THIS FORTUNE-TELLING BOOK SEEMS REPUTABLE ENOUGH...
Q-QUESTIONABLE MORALS?
...IT DOESN'T SEEM LIKE IT WAS WRITTEN BY A YOUKAI, SO IT'S NOT A YOUMA BOOK. MAYBE I WAS WORRYING OVER NOTHING.

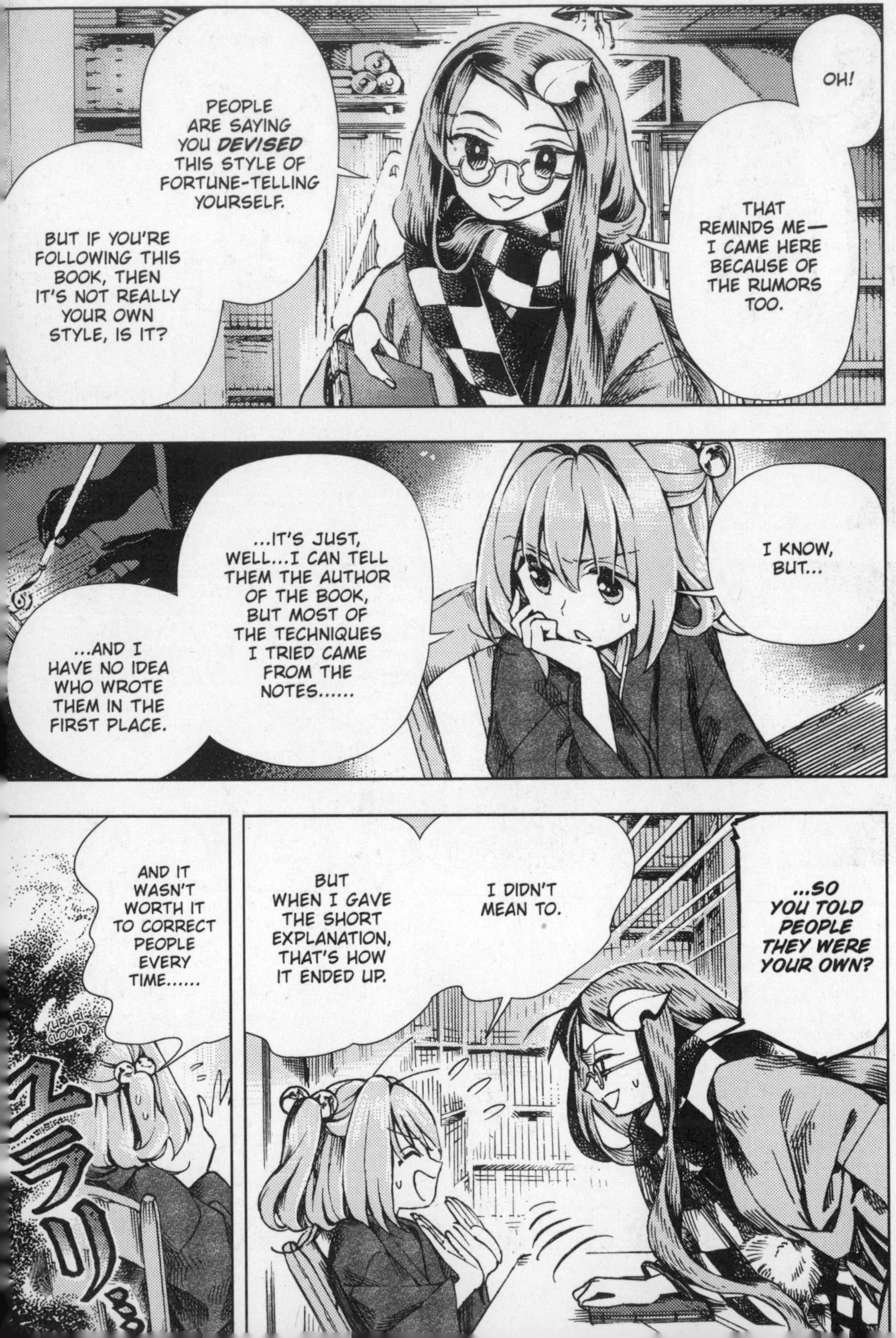
OH!
THAT REMINDS ME— I CAME HERE BECAUSE OF THE RUMORS TOO.
PEOPLE ARE SAYING YOU ***DEVISED*** THIS STYLE OF FORTUNE-TELLING YOURSELF.
BUT IF YOU'RE FOLLOWING THIS BOOK, THEN IT'S NOT REALLY YOUR OWN STYLE, IS IT?
I KNOW, BUT...
...IT'S JUST, WELL...I CAN TELL THEM THE AUTHOR OF THE BOOK, BUT MOST OF THE TECHNIQUES I TRIED CAME FROM THE NOTES......
...AND I HAVE NO IDEA WHO WROTE THEM IN THE FIRST PLACE.
...SO YOU TOLD PEOPLE THEY WERE YOUR OWN?
I DIDN'T MEAN TO.
BUT WHEN I GAVE THE SHORT EXPLANATION, THAT'S HOW IT ENDED UP.
AND IT WASN'T WORTH IT TO CORRECT PEOPLE EVERY TIME......
YURARI (LOOM)

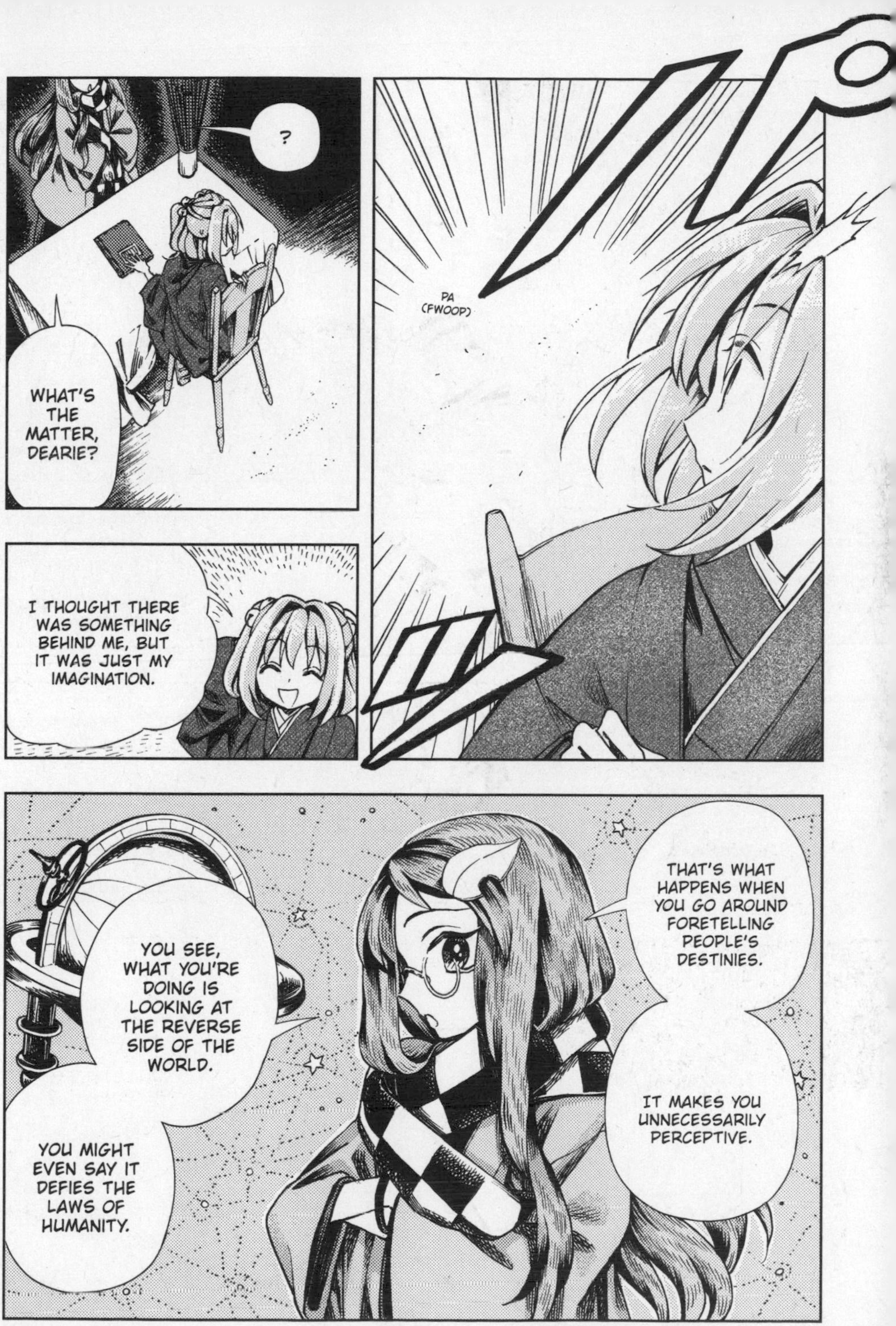
PA (FWOOP)
?
WHAT'S THE MATTER, DEARIE?
I THOUGHT THERE WAS SOMETHING BEHIND ME, BUT IT WAS JUST MY IMAGINATION.
THAT'S WHAT HAPPENS WHEN YOU GO AROUND FORETELLING PEOPLE'S DESTINIES.
IT MAKES YOU UNNECESSARILY PERCEPTIVE.
YOU SEE, WHAT YOU'RE DOING IS LOOKING AT THE REVERSE SIDE OF THE WORLD.
YOU MIGHT EVEN SAY IT DEFIES THE LAWS OF HUMANITY.

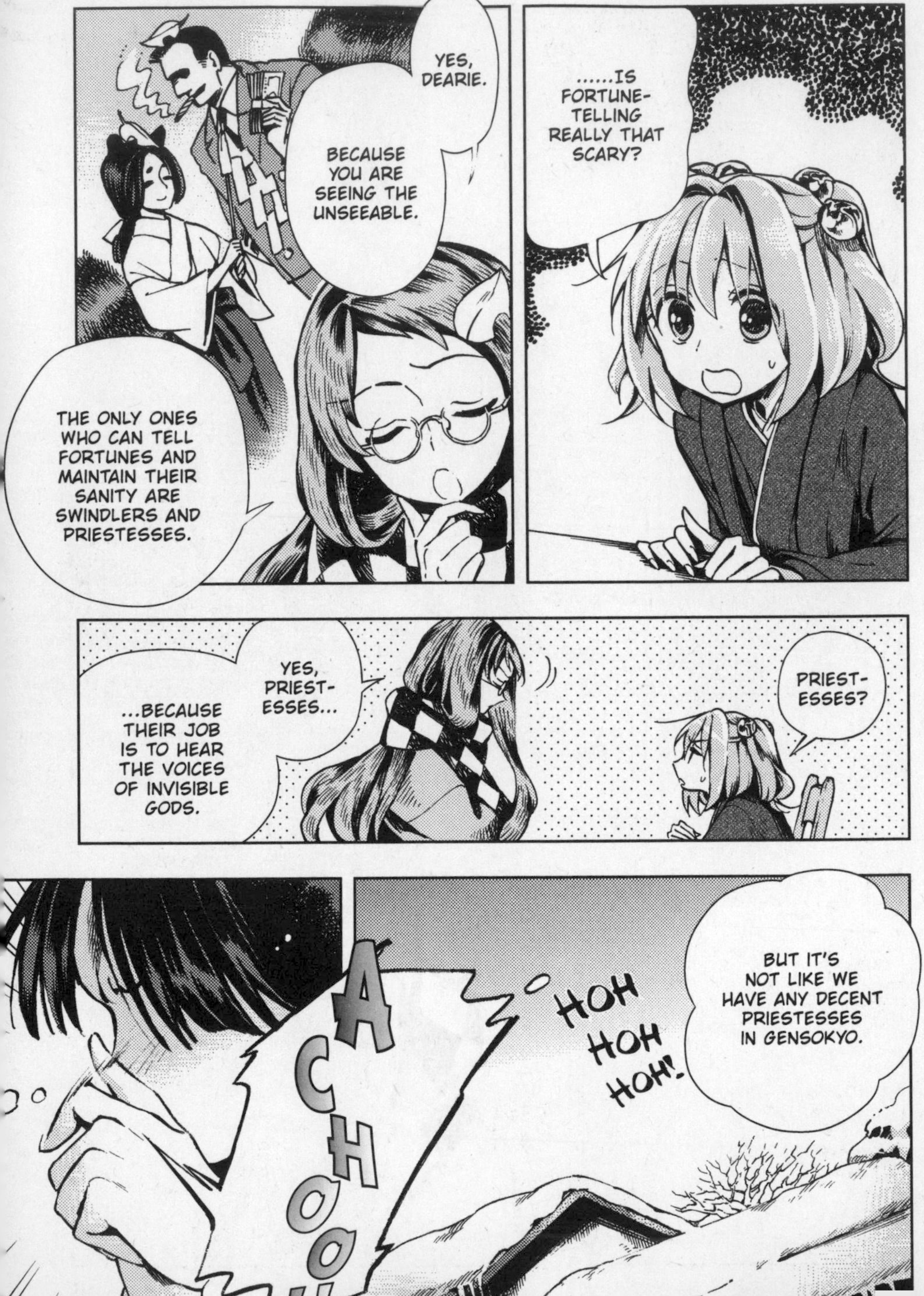
......IS FORTUNE-TELLING REALLY THAT SCARY?
YES, DEARIE.
BECAUSE YOU ARE SEEING THE UNSEEABLE.
THE ONLY ONES WHO CAN TELL FORTUNES AND MAINTAIN THEIR SANITY ARE SWINDLERS AND PRIESTESSES.
PRIEST-ESSES?
YES, PRIEST-ESSES...
...BECAUSE THEIR JOB IS TO HEAR THE VOICES OF INVISIBLE GODS.
BUT IT'S NOT LIKE WE HAVE ANY DECENT PRIESTESSES IN GENSOKYO.
HOH HOH HOH!
ACHOO!!

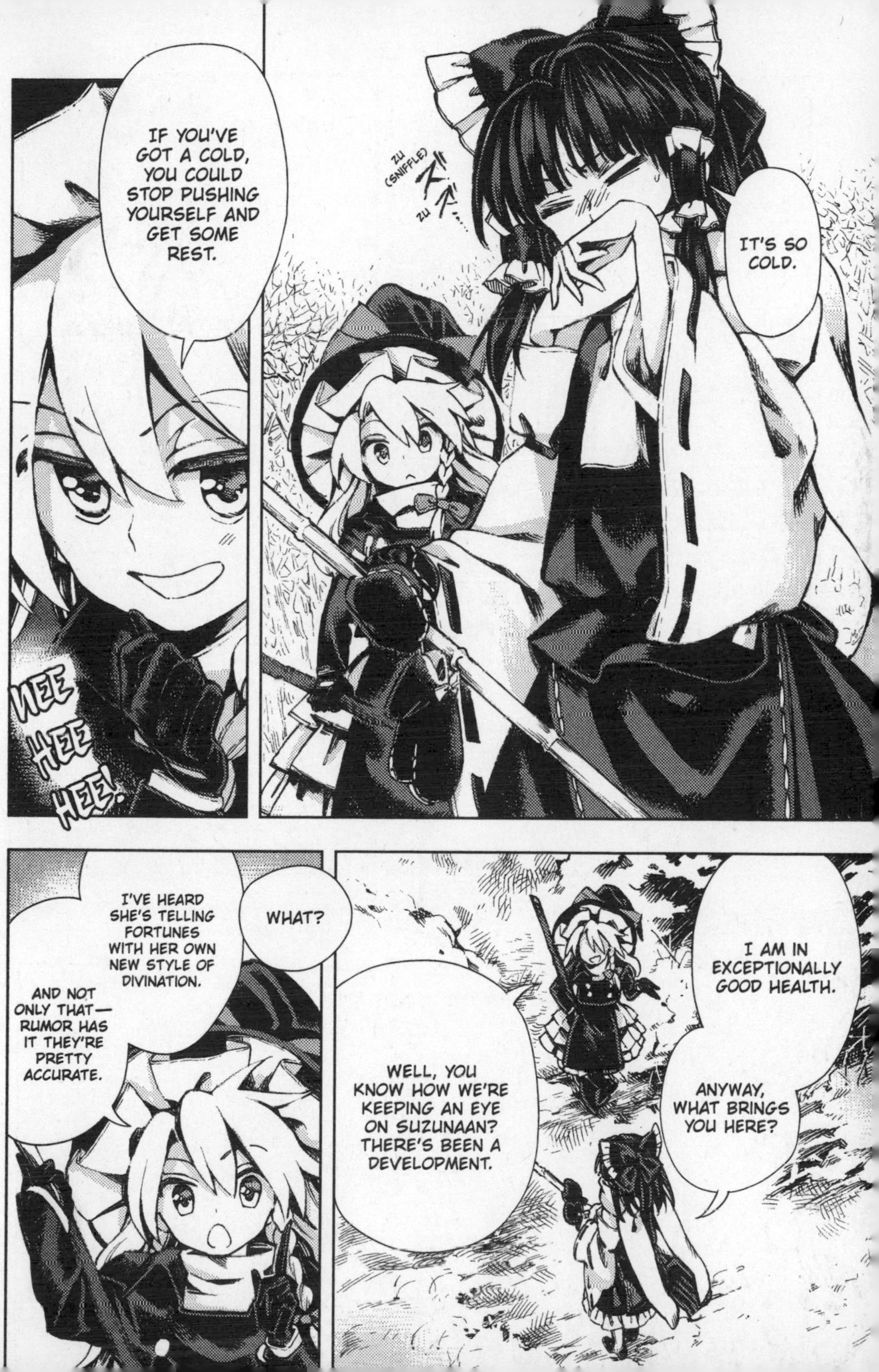
IT'S SO COLD.
ZU (SNIFFLE) ZU
IF YOU'VE GOT A COLD, YOU COULD STOP PUSHING YOURSELF AND GET SOME REST.
HEE HEE HEE!
I AM IN EXCEPTIONALLY GOOD HEALTH.
ANYWAY, WHAT BRINGS YOU HERE?
WELL, YOU KNOW HOW WE'RE KEEPING AN EYE ON SUZUNAAN? THERE'S BEEN A DEVELOPMENT.
WHAT?
I'VE HEARD SHE'S TELLING FORTUNES WITH HER OWN NEW STYLE OF DIVINATION.
AND NOT ONLY THAT— RUMOR HAS IT THEY'RE PRETTY ACCURATE.

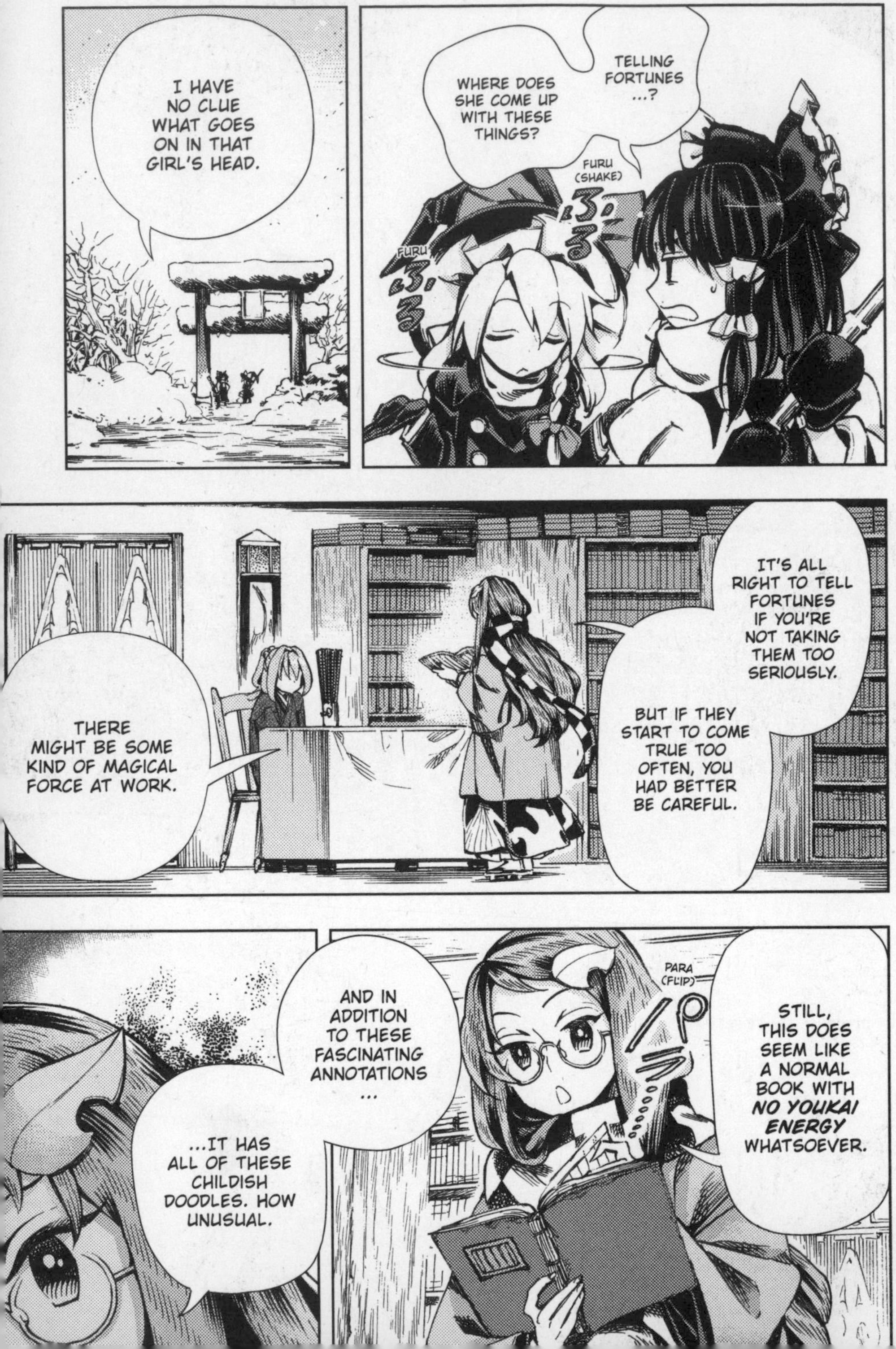
TELLING FORTUNES ...?
WHERE DOES SHE COME UP WITH THESE THINGS?
FURU (SHAKE)
FURU
I HAVE NO CLUE WHAT GOES ON IN THAT GIRL'S HEAD.
IT'S ALL RIGHT TO TELL FORTUNES IF YOU'RE NOT TAKING THEM TOO SERIOUSLY.
BUT IF THEY START TO COME TRUE TOO OFTEN, YOU HAD BETTER BE CAREFUL.
THERE MIGHT BE SOME KIND OF MAGICAL FORCE AT WORK.
PARA (FLIP)
STILL, THIS DOES SEEM LIKE A NORMAL BOOK WITH ***NO YOUKAI ENERGY*** WHATSOEVER.
AND IN ADDITION TO THESE FASCINATING ANNOTATIONS ...
...IT HAS ALL OF THESE CHILDISH DOODLES. HOW UNUSUAL.

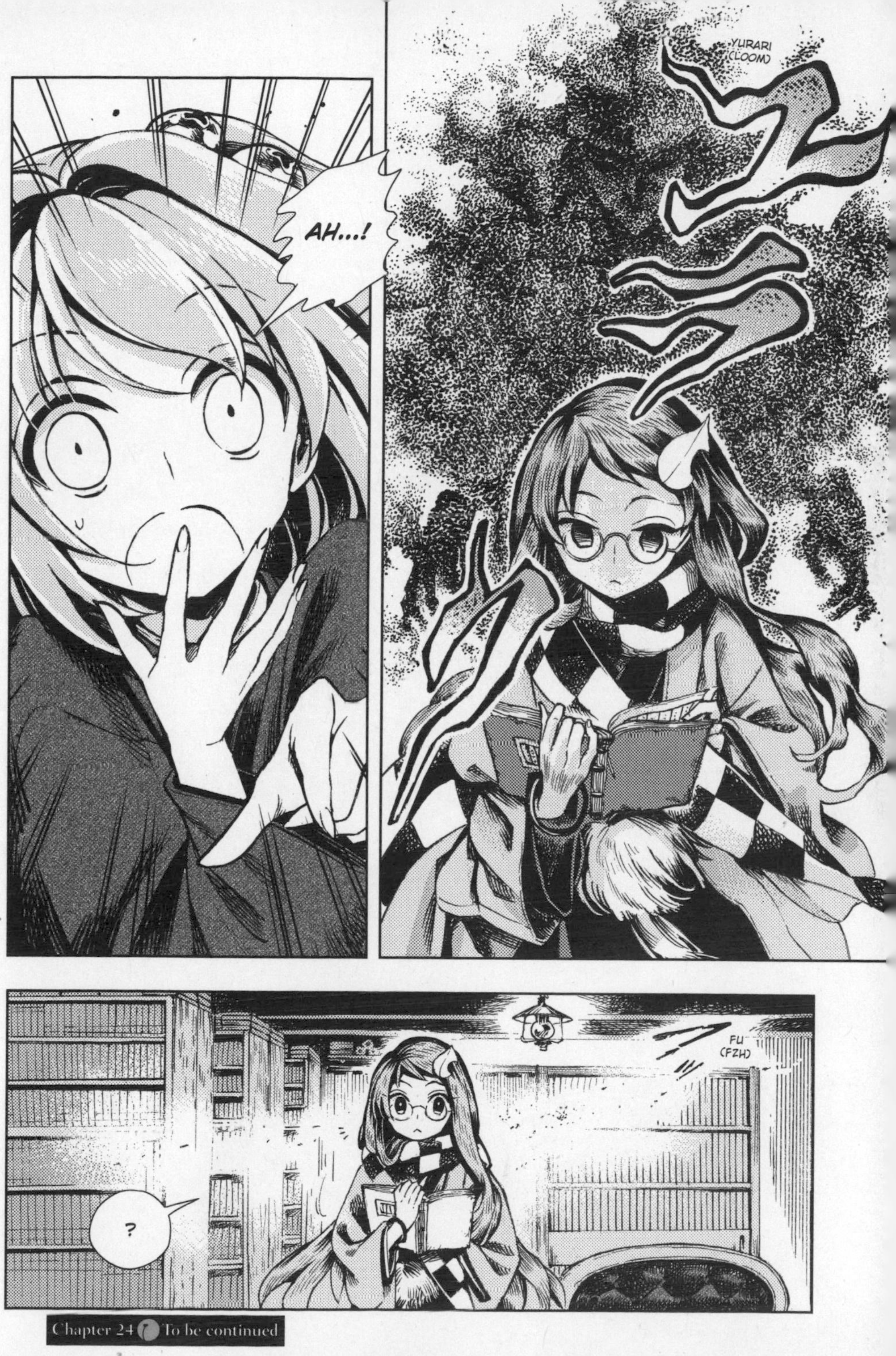
YURARI (CLOOM)
AH...!
FU (FZH)
?

Chapter 24 To be continued

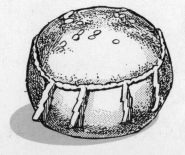

Forbidden Scrollery

Chapter 25 Anonymous Works Are Easily Plagiarized Part 2

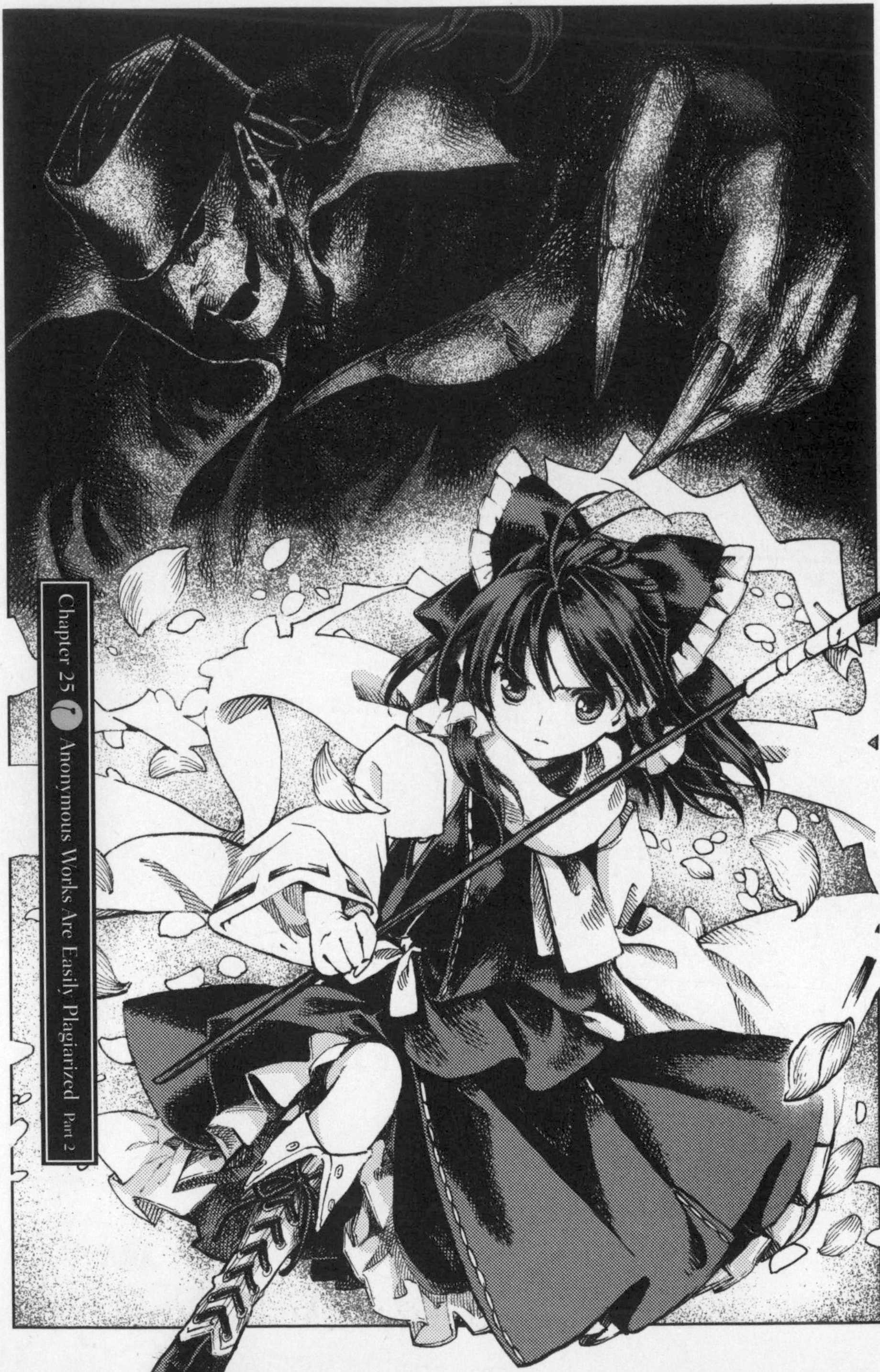

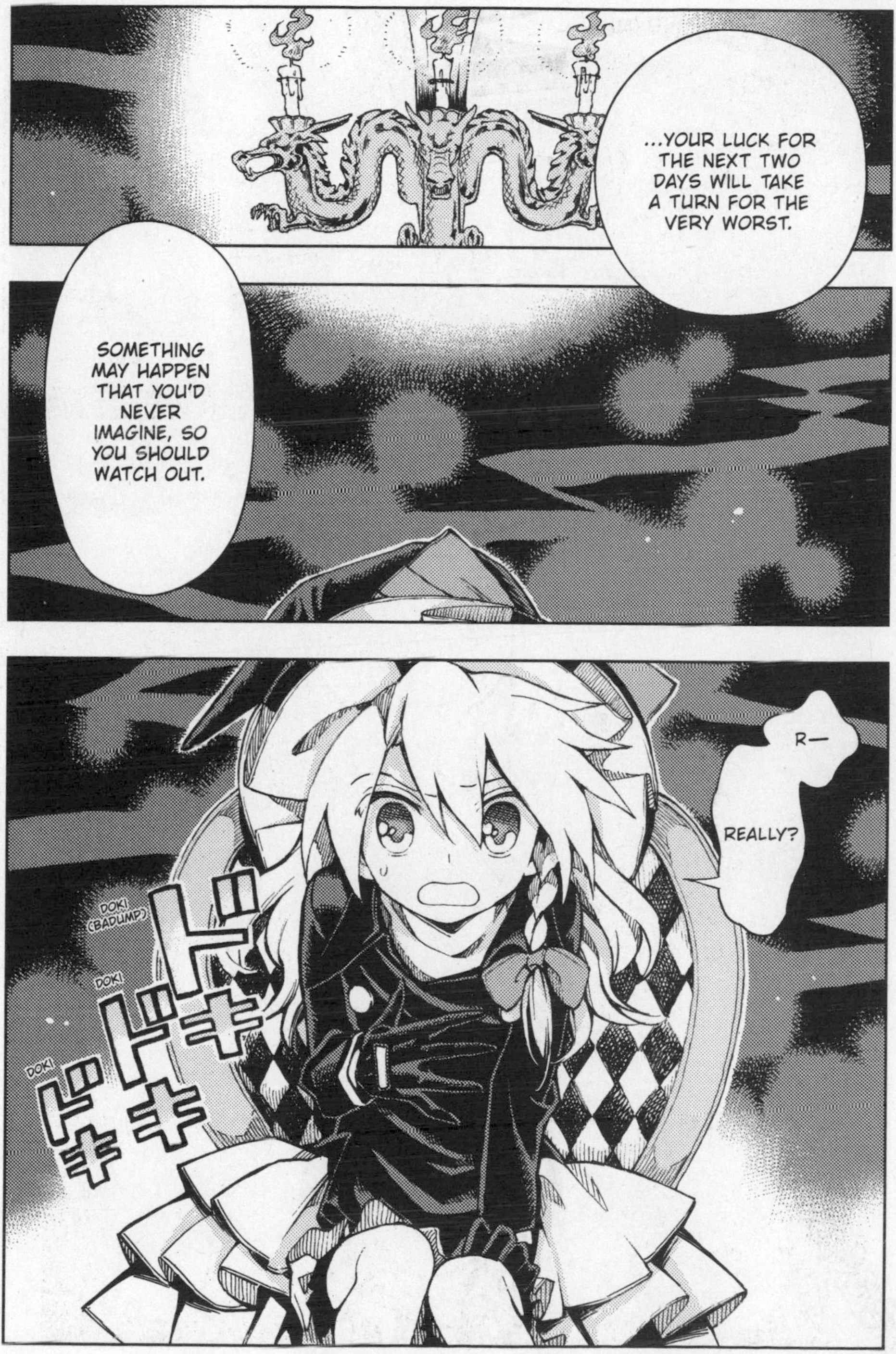
...YOUR LUCK FOR THE NEXT TWO DAYS WILL TAKE A TURN FOR THE VERY WORST.
SOMETHING MAY HAPPEN THAT YOU'D NEVER IMAGINE, SO YOU SHOULD WATCH OUT.
R—
REALLY?
ドキ
DOKI (BADUMP)
ドキ
DOKI
ドキ
DOKI

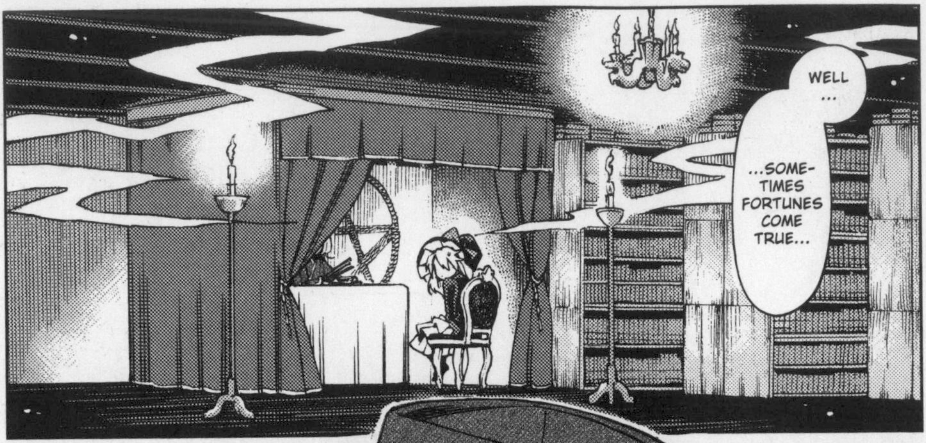
WELL ...
...SOME-TIMES FORTUNES COME TRUE...

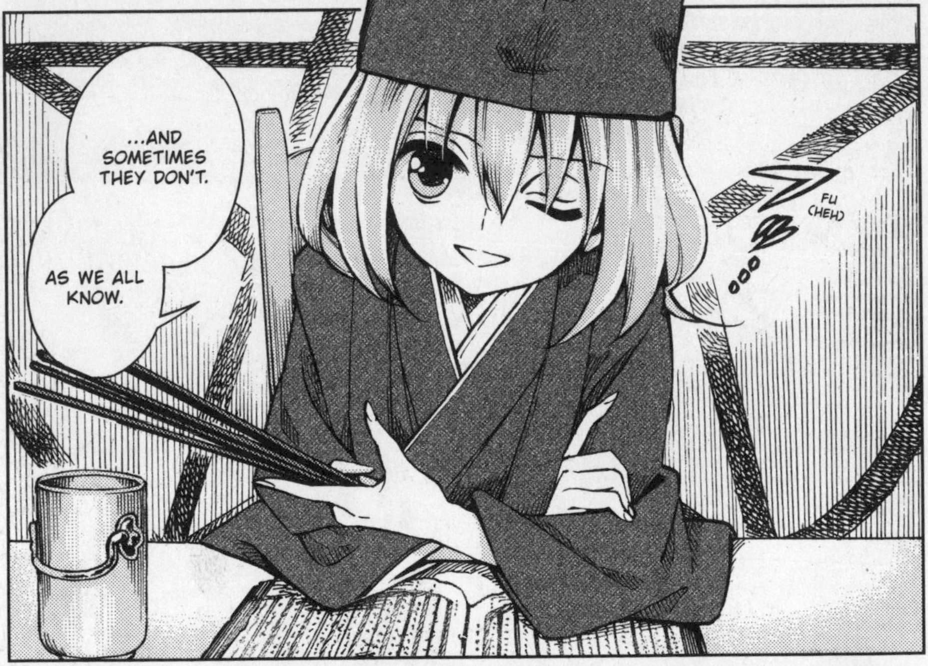
...AND SOMETIMES THEY DON'T.
AS WE ALL KNOW.
FU (HEH)

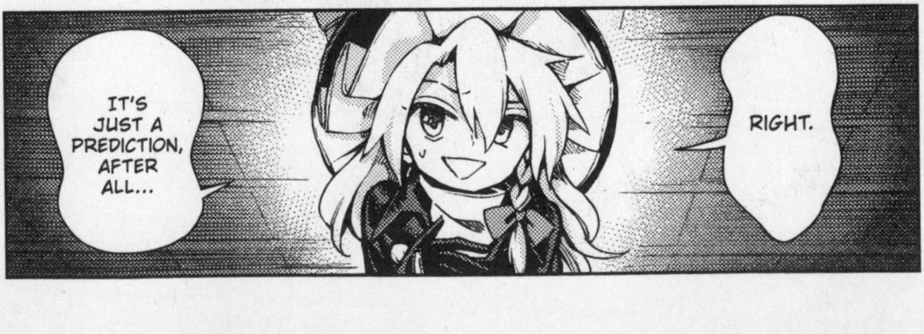
RIGHT.
IT'S JUST A PREDICTION, AFTER ALL...

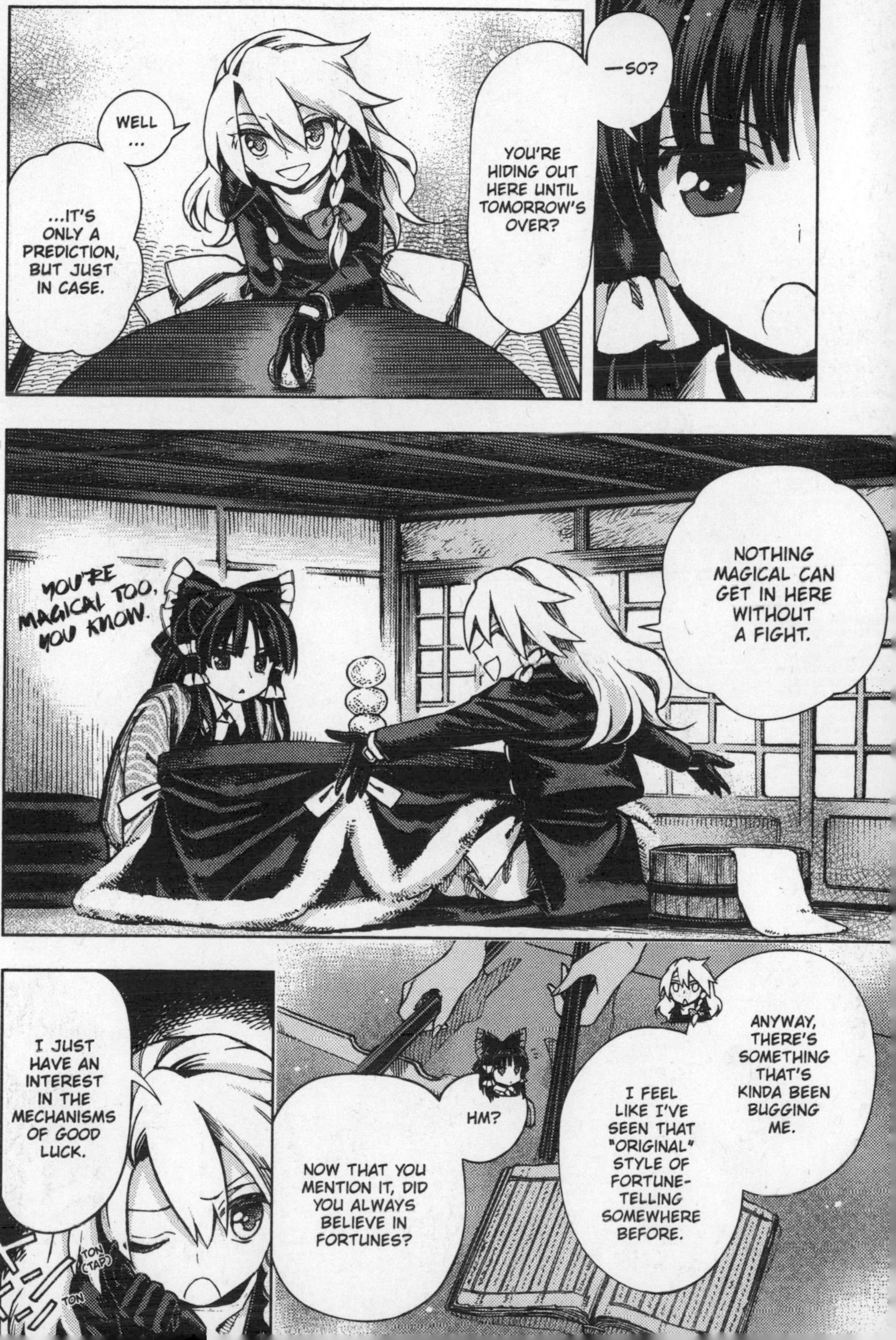
—SO?
YOU'RE HIDING OUT HERE UNTIL TOMORROW'S OVER?
WELL ...
...IT'S ONLY A PREDICTION, BUT JUST IN CASE.
NOTHING MAGICAL CAN GET IN HERE WITHOUT A FIGHT.
YOU'RE MAGICAL TOO, YOU KNOW.
ANYWAY, THERE'S SOMETHING THAT'S KINDA BEEN BUGGING ME.
I FEEL LIKE I'VE SEEN THAT "ORIGINAL" STYLE OF FORTUNE-TELLING SOMEWHERE BEFORE.
HM?
NOW THAT YOU MENTION IT, DID YOU ALWAYS BELIEVE IN FORTUNES?
I JUST HAVE AN INTEREST IN THE MECHANISMS OF GOOD LUCK.
TON (TAP)
TON

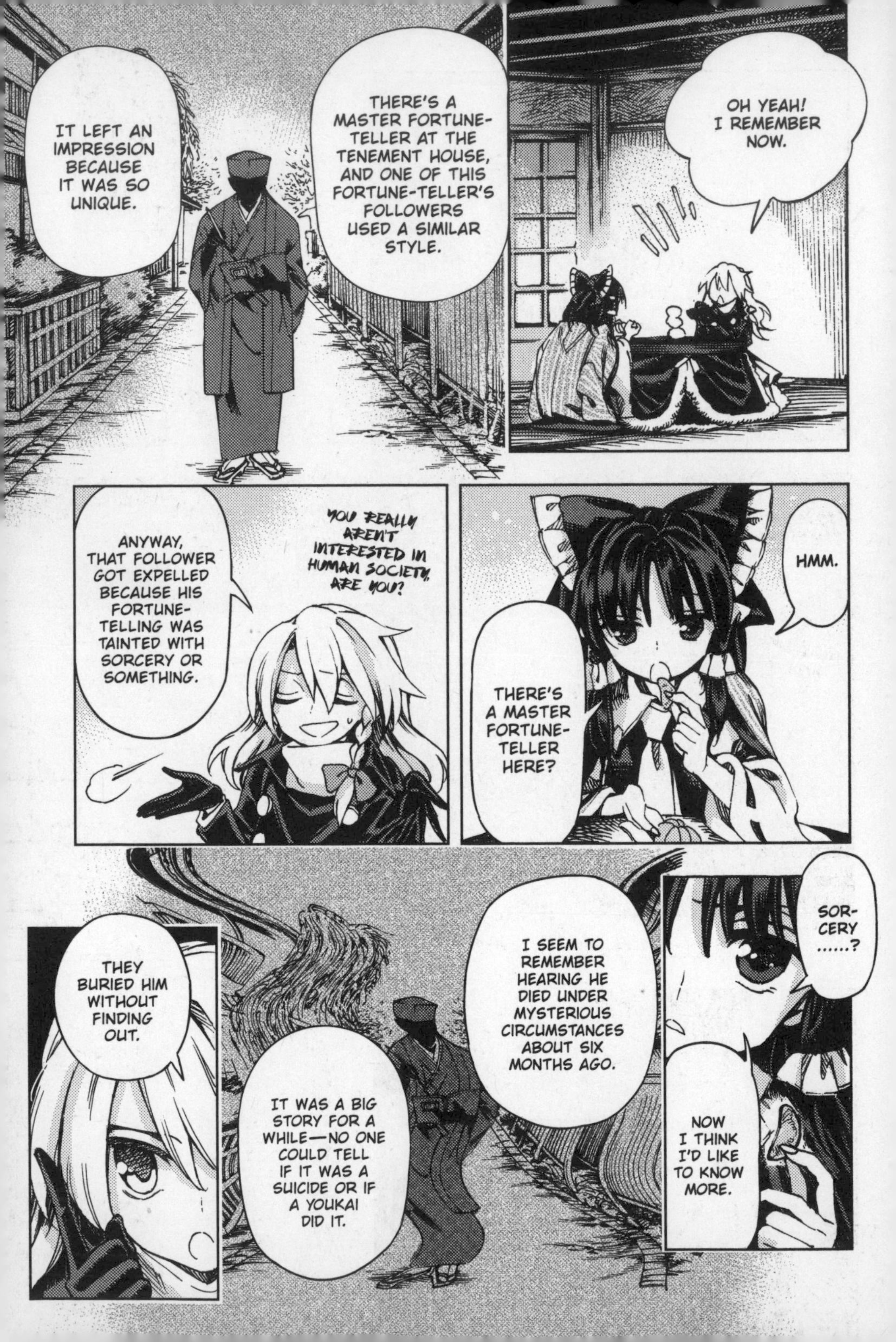
OH YEAH! I REMEMBER NOW.
THERE'S A MASTER FORTUNE-TELLER AT THE TENEMENT HOUSE, AND ONE OF THIS FORTUNE-TELLER'S FOLLOWERS USED A SIMILAR STYLE.
IT LEFT AN IMPRESSION BECAUSE IT WAS SO UNIQUE.
HMM.
THERE'S A MASTER FORTUNE-TELLER HERE?
YOU REALLY AREN'T INTERESTED IN HUMAN SOCIETY, ARE YOU?
ANYWAY, THAT FOLLOWER GOT EXPELLED BECAUSE HIS FORTUNE-TELLING WAS TAINTED WITH SORCERY OR SOMETHING.
SOR-CERY ......?
NOW I THINK I'D LIKE TO KNOW MORE.
I SEEM TO REMEMBER HEARING HE DIED UNDER MYSTERIOUS CIRCUMSTANCES ABOUT SIX MONTHS AGO.
IT WAS A BIG STORY FOR A WHILE—NO ONE COULD TELL IF IT WAS A SUICIDE OR IF A YOUKAI DID IT.
THEY BURIED HIM WITHOUT FINDING OUT.

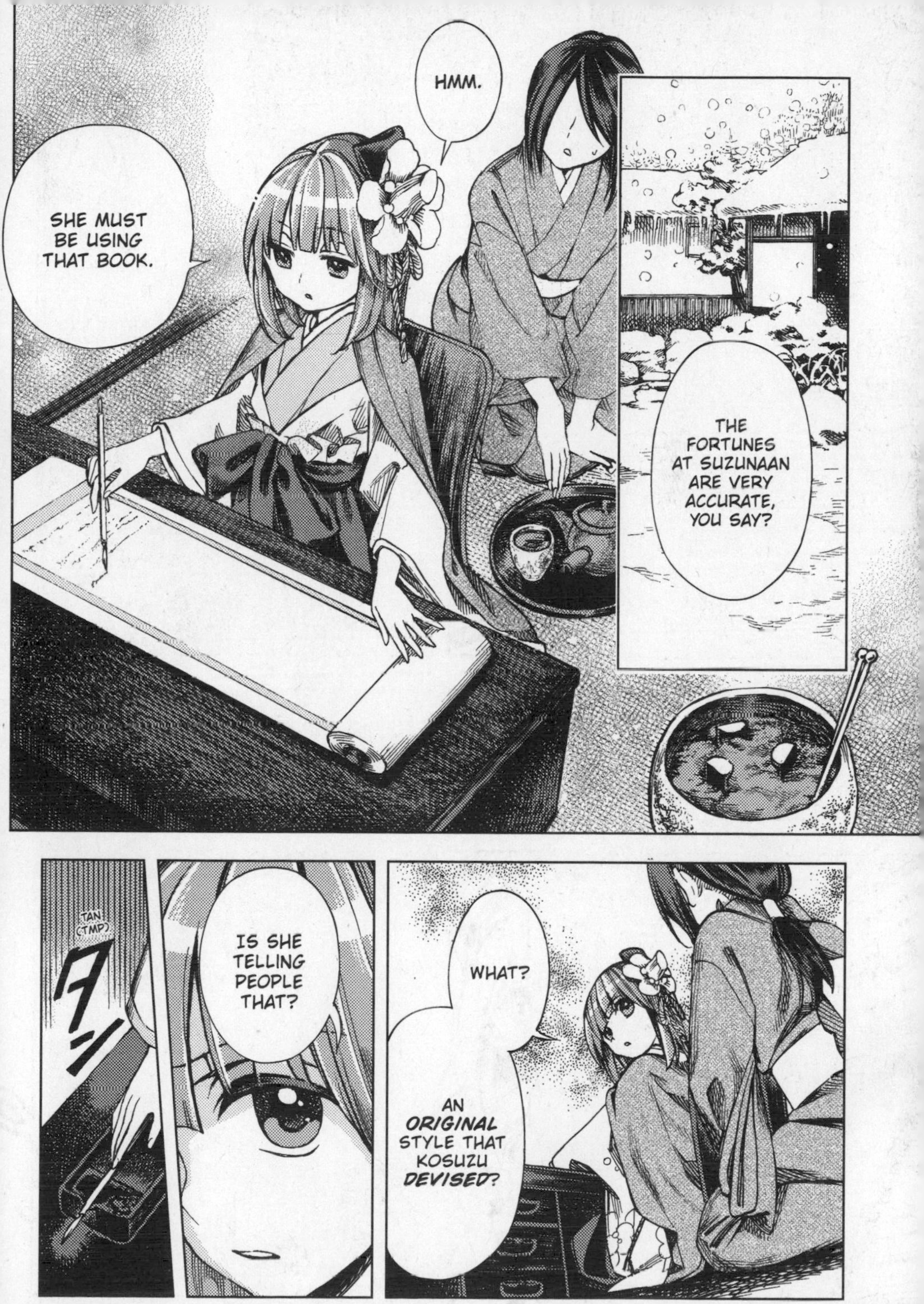
THE FORTUNES AT SUZUNAAN ARE VERY ACCURATE, YOU SAY?
HMM.
SHE MUST BE USING THAT BOOK.
WHAT?
AN *ORIGINAL* STYLE THAT KOSUZU *DEVISED*?
IS SHE TELLING PEOPLE THAT?
TAN (TMP)

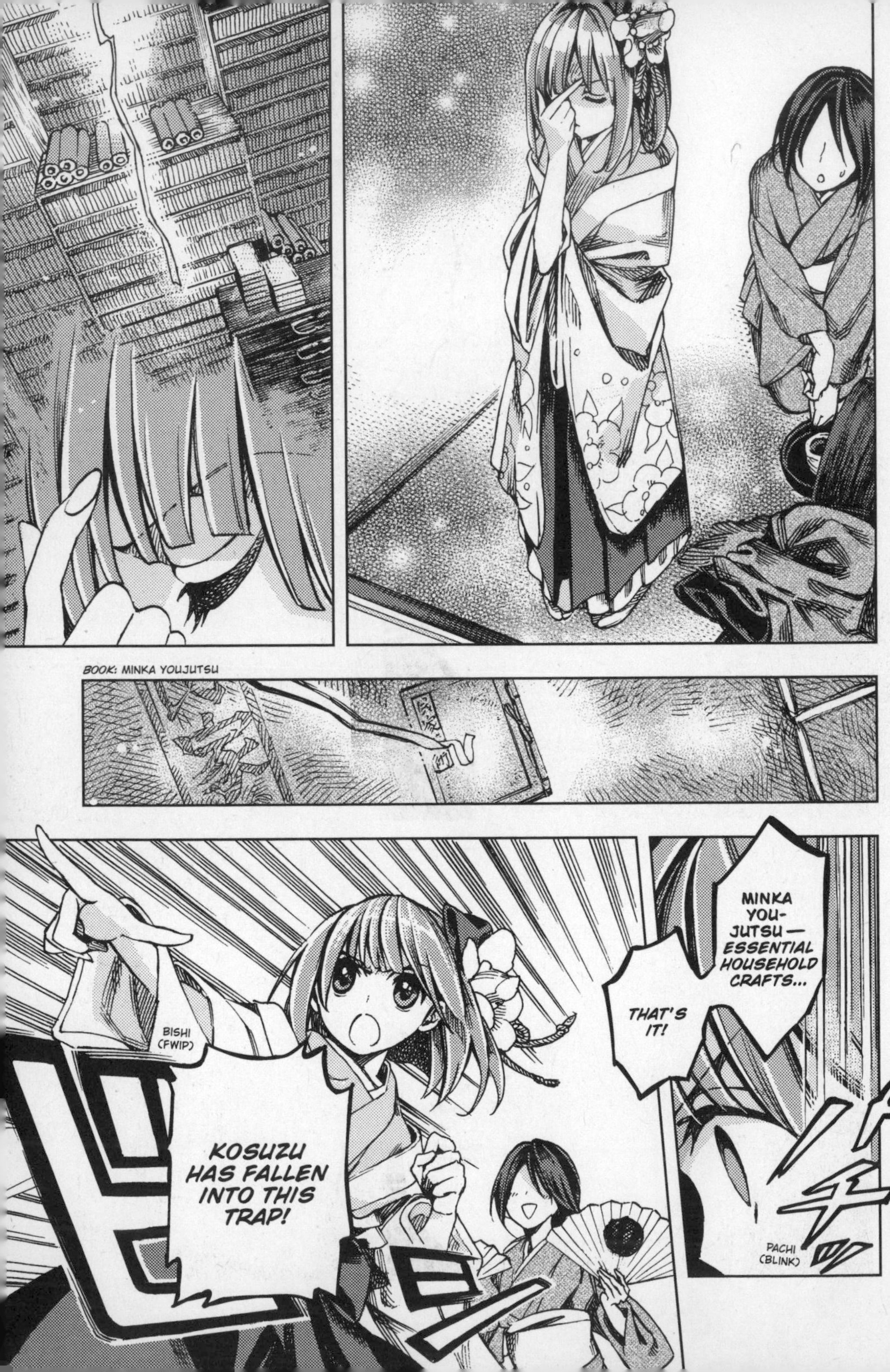
BOOK: MINKA YOUJUTSU
MINKA YOU-JUTSU—ESSENTIAL HOUSEHOLD CRAFTS...
THAT'S IT!
PACHI (BLINK)
BISHI (FWIP)
KOSUZU HAS FALLEN INTO THIS TRAP!

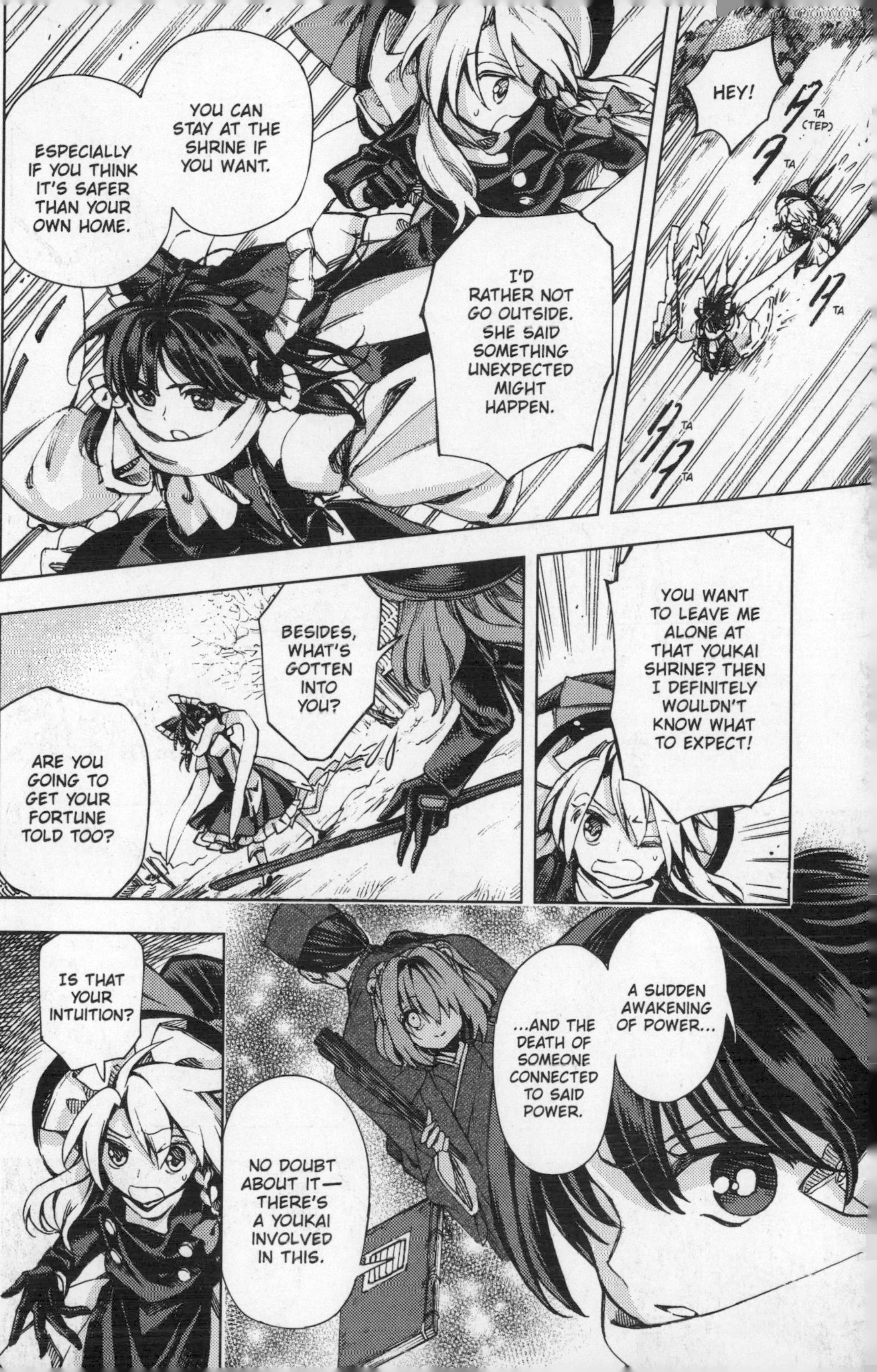
HEY!
TA (TEP)
TA
TA
TA
TA
I'D RATHER NOT GO OUTSIDE. SHE SAID SOMETHING UNEXPECTED MIGHT HAPPEN.
YOU CAN STAY AT THE SHRINE IF YOU WANT.
ESPECIALLY IF YOU THINK IT'S SAFER THAN YOUR OWN HOME.
YOU WANT TO LEAVE ME ALONE AT THAT YOUKAI SHRINE? THEN I DEFINITELY WOULDN'T KNOW WHAT TO EXPECT!
BESIDES, WHAT'S GOTTEN INTO YOU?
ARE YOU GOING TO GET YOUR FORTUNE TOLD TOO?
A SUDDEN AWAKENING OF POWER...
...AND THE DEATH OF SOMEONE CONNECTED TO SAID POWER.
NO DOUBT ABOUT IT—THERE'S A YOUKAI INVOLVED IN THIS.
IS THAT YOUR INTUITION?

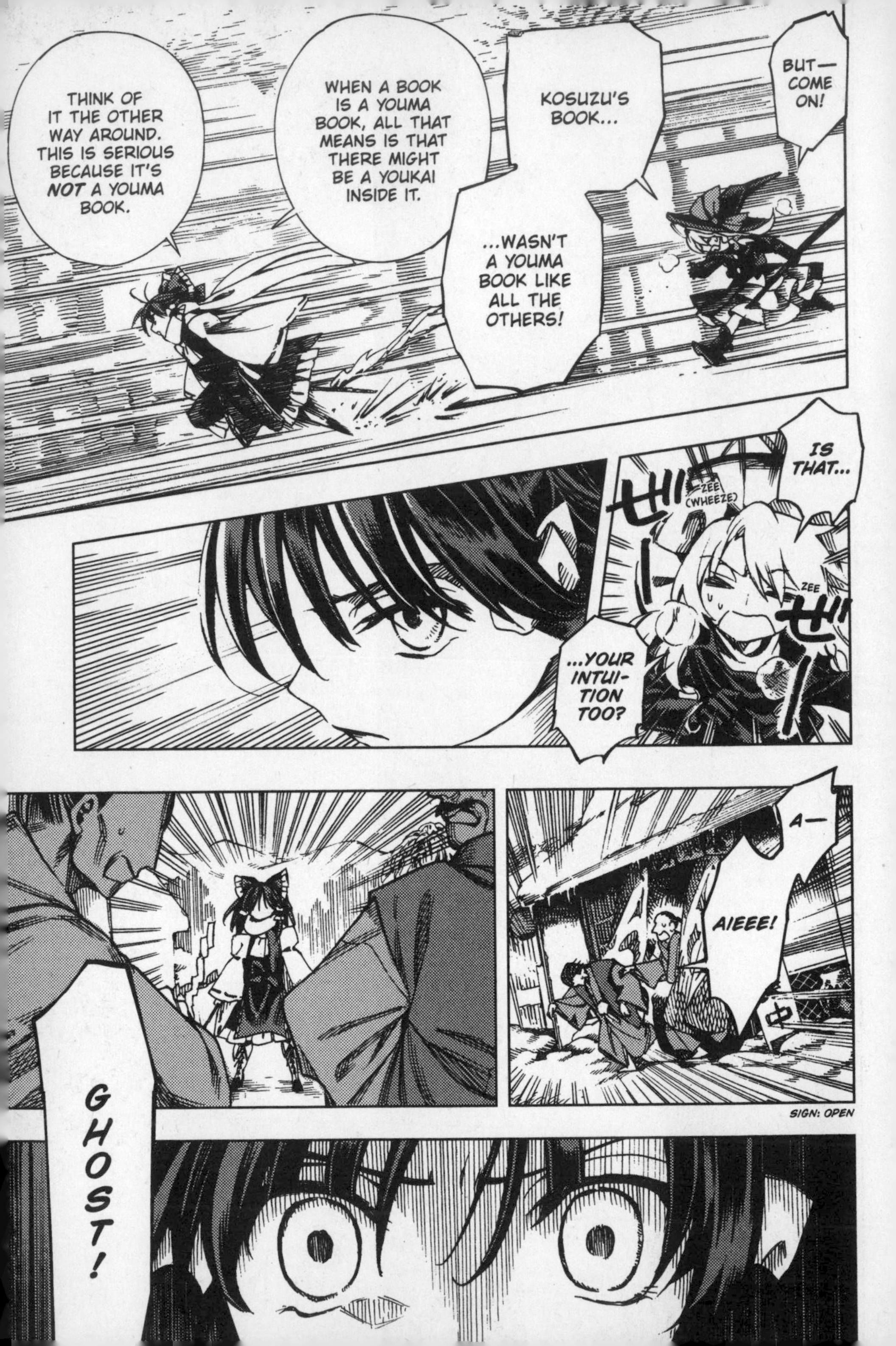
BUT— COME ON!
KOSUZU'S BOOK...
...WASN'T A YOUMA BOOK LIKE ALL THE OTHERS!
WHEN A BOOK IS A YOUMA BOOK, ALL THAT MEANS IS THAT THERE MIGHT BE A YOUKAI INSIDE IT.
THINK OF IT THE OTHER WAY AROUND. THIS IS SERIOUS BECAUSE IT'S *NOT* A YOUMA BOOK.
IS THAT...
ZEE (WHEEZE)
ZEE
...YOUR INTUITION TOO?
A—
AIEEE!
SIGN: OPEN
GHOST!

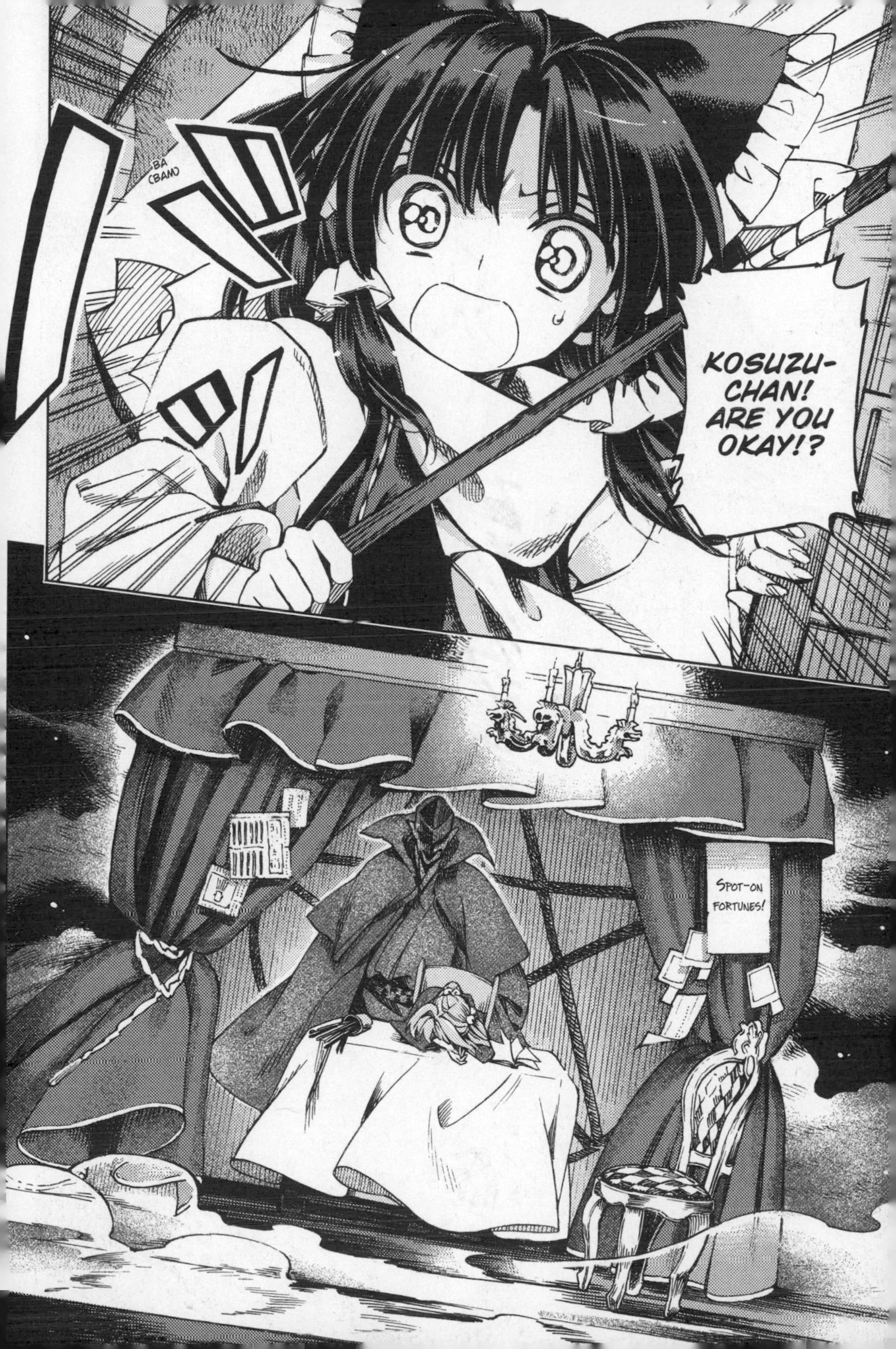
KOSUZU-CHAN! ARE YOU OKAY!?
BA (BAM)
Spot-on fortunes!

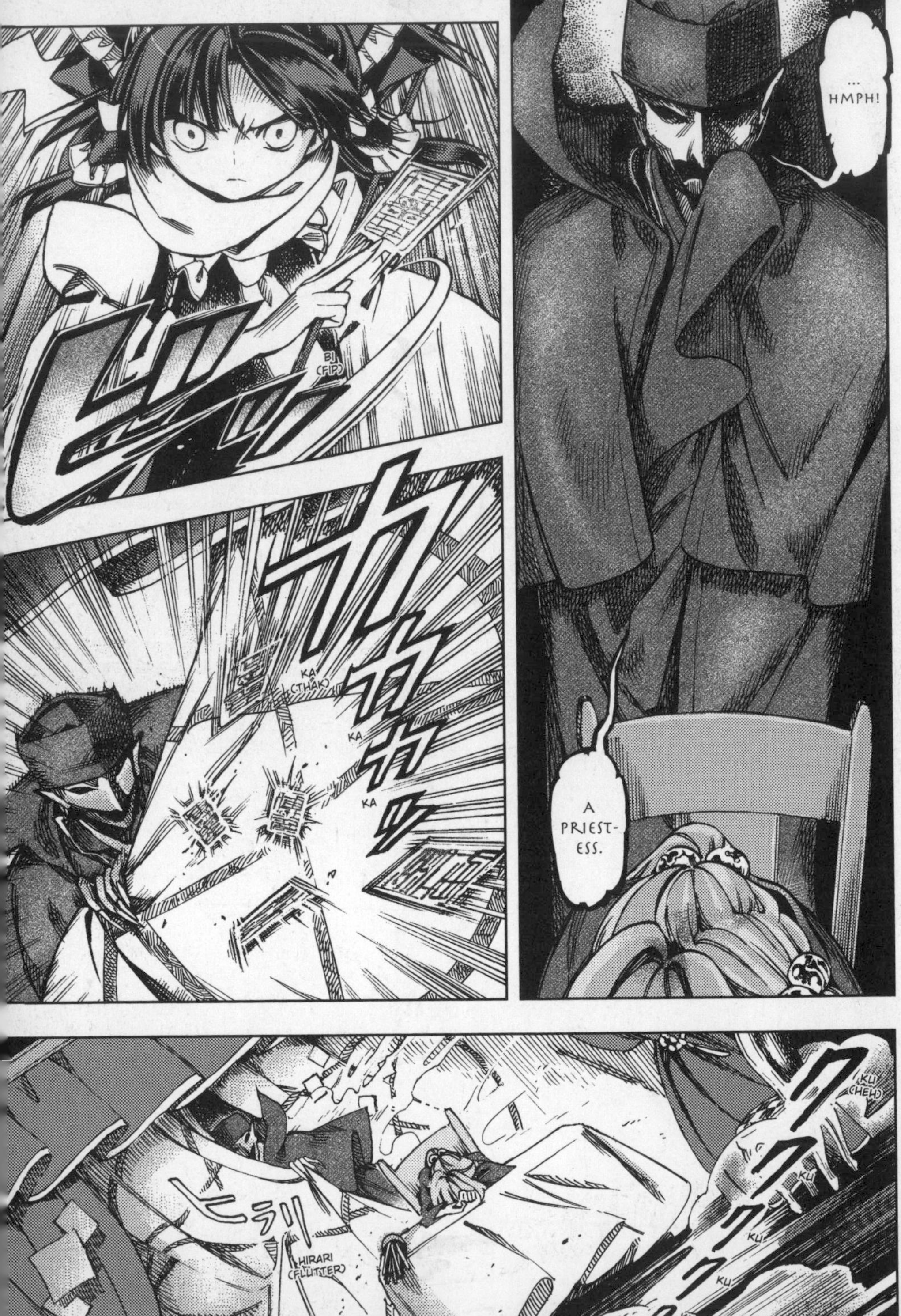

... HMPH!
A PRIEST-ESS.
BI (FIP)
KA (THAK)
KA
KA
KU (HEH)
KU
KU
KU
KU
HIRARI (FLUTTER)

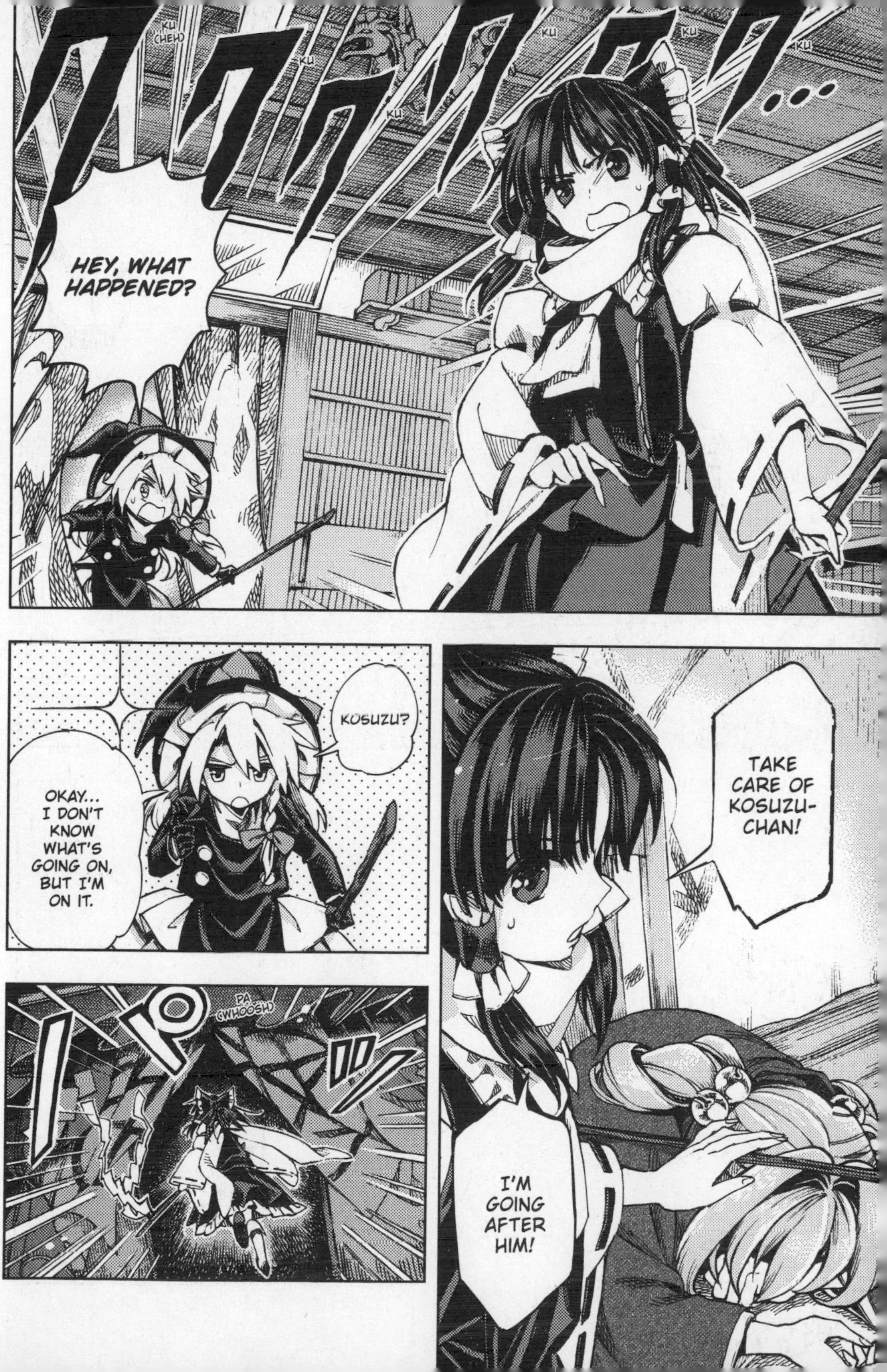
KU (CHEH)
KU
KU
KU
KU
KU
HEY, WHAT HAPPENED?
TAKE CARE OF KOSUZU-CHAN!
I'M GOING AFTER HIM!
KOSUZU?
OKAY... I DON'T KNOW WHAT'S GOING ON, BUT I'M ON IT.
PA (WHOOSH)

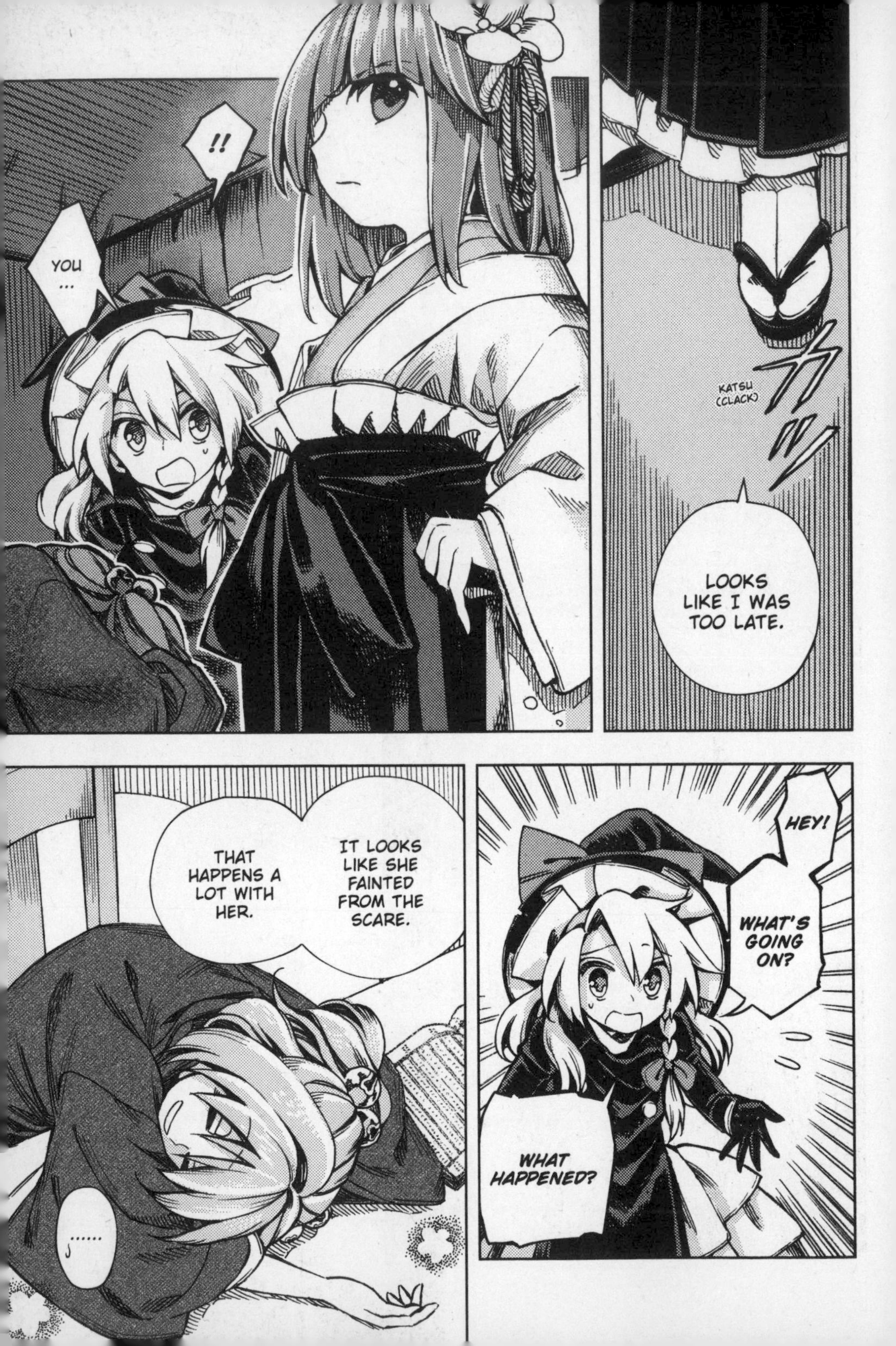
KATSU (CLACK)
LOOKS LIKE I WAS TOO LATE.
!!
YOU ...
HEY!
WHAT'S GOING ON?
WHAT HAPPENED?
IT LOOKS LIKE SHE FAINTED FROM THE SCARE.
THAT HAPPENS A LOT WITH HER.
......

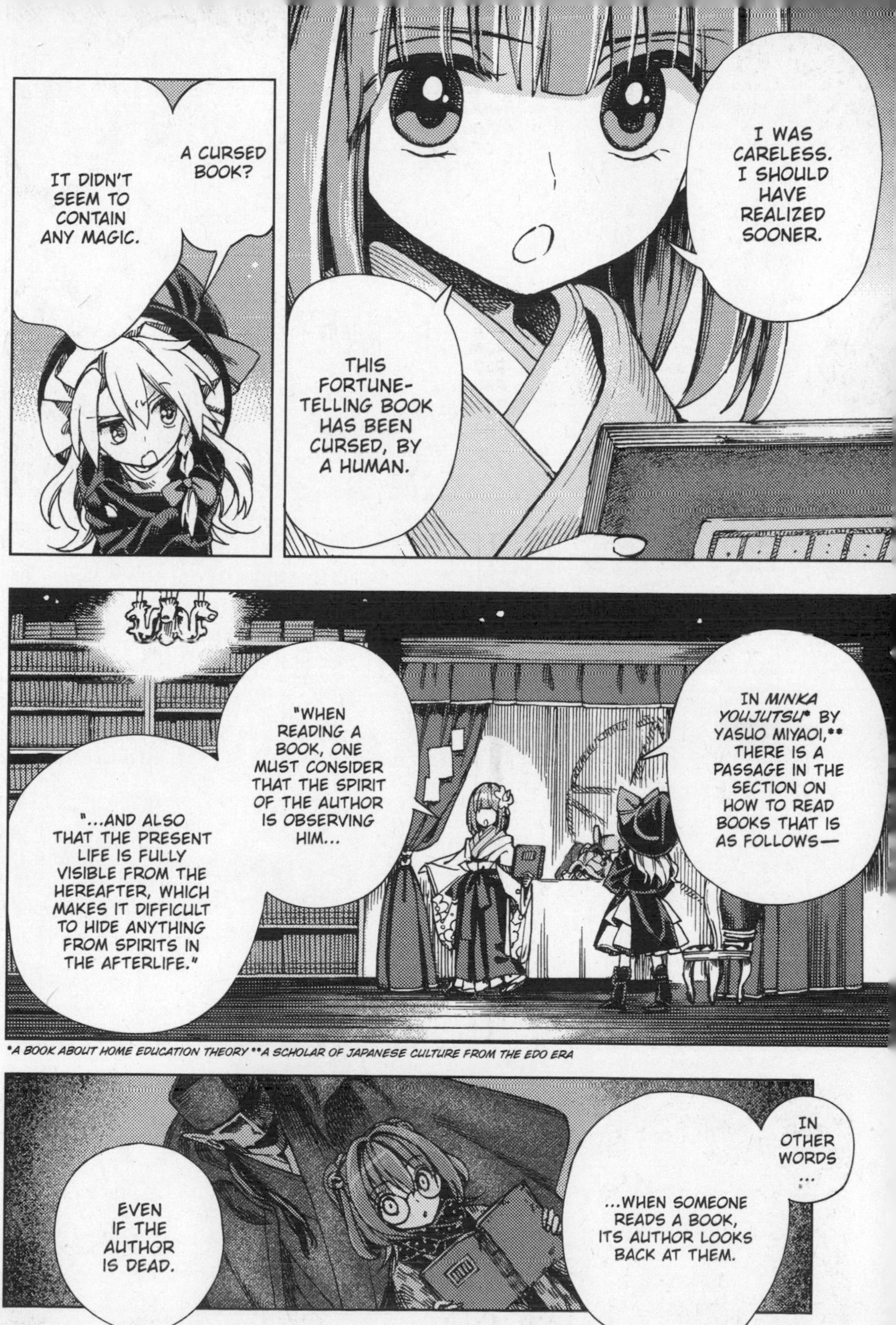
I WAS CARELESS. I SHOULD HAVE REALIZED SOONER.
THIS FORTUNE-TELLING BOOK HAS BEEN CURSED, BY A HUMAN.
A CURSED BOOK?
IT DIDN'T SEEM TO CONTAIN ANY MAGIC.
IN *MINKA YOUJUTSU** BY YASUO MIYAOI,** THERE IS A PASSAGE IN THE SECTION ON HOW TO READ BOOKS THAT IS AS FOLLOWS—
"WHEN READING A BOOK, ONE MUST CONSIDER THAT THE SPIRIT OF THE AUTHOR IS OBSERVING HIM...
"...AND ALSO THAT THE PRESENT LIFE IS FULLY VISIBLE FROM THE HEREAFTER, WHICH MAKES IT DIFFICULT TO HIDE ANYTHING FROM SPIRITS IN THE AFTERLIFE."
IN OTHER WORDS...
...WHEN SOMEONE READS A BOOK, ITS AUTHOR LOOKS BACK AT THEM.
EVEN IF THE AUTHOR IS DEAD.

*A BOOK ABOUT HOME EDUCATION THEORY **A SCHOLAR OF JAPANESE CULTURE FROM THE EDO ERA

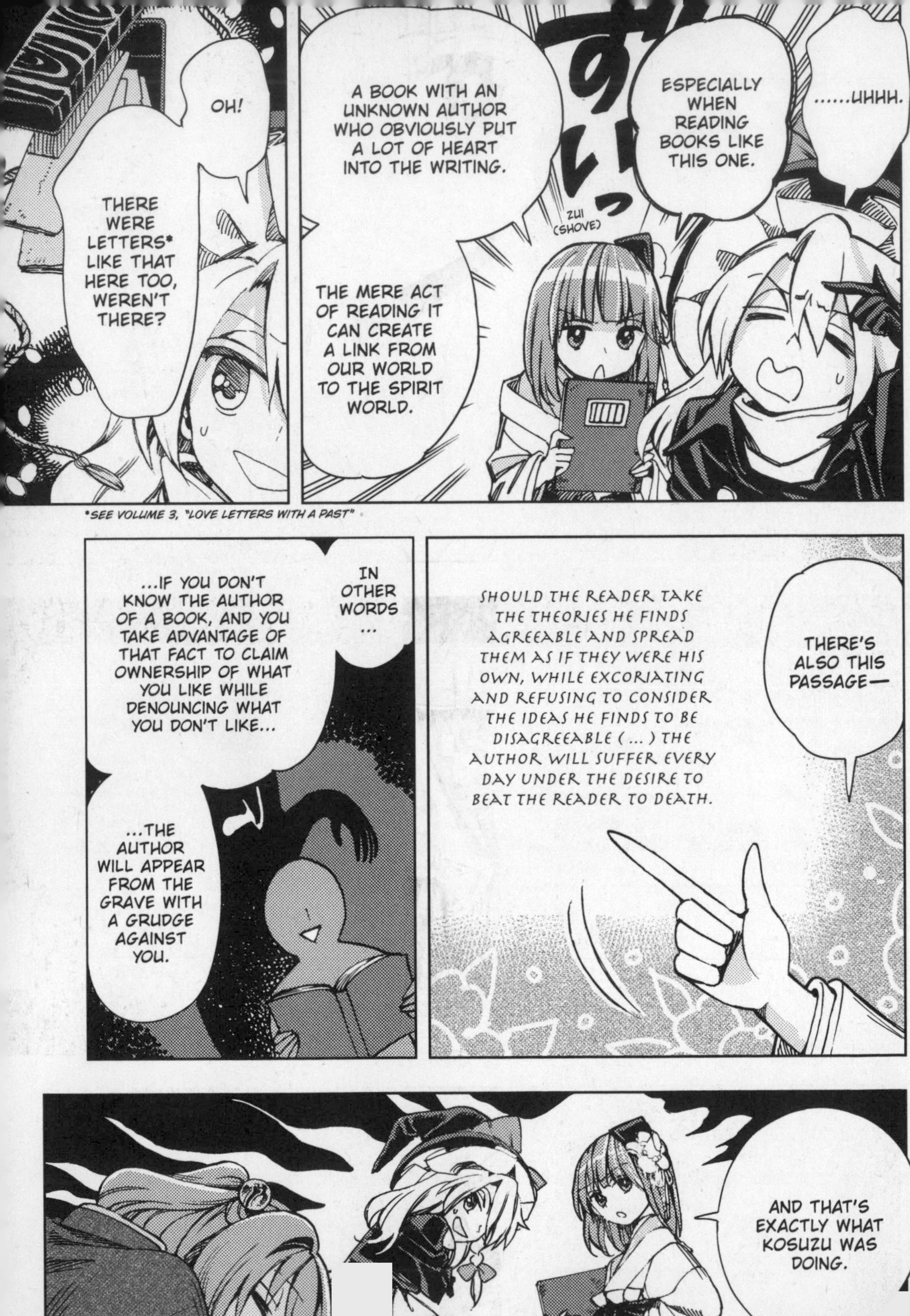
......UHHH.
ESPECIALLY WHEN READING BOOKS LIKE THIS ONE.
A BOOK WITH AN UNKNOWN AUTHOR WHO OBVIOUSLY PUT A LOT OF HEART INTO THE WRITING.
ZUI (SHOVE)
THE MERE ACT OF READING IT CAN CREATE A LINK FROM OUR WORLD TO THE SPIRIT WORLD.
OH!
THERE WERE LETTERS* LIKE THAT HERE TOO, WEREN'T THERE?
THERE'S ALSO THIS PASSAGE—
SHOULD THE READER TAKE THE THEORIES HE FINDS AGREEABLE AND SPREAD THEM AS IF THEY WERE HIS OWN, WHILE EXCORIATING AND REFUSING TO CONSIDER THE IDEAS HE FINDS TO BE DISAGREEABLE (...) THE AUTHOR WILL SUFFER EVERY DAY UNDER THE DESIRE TO BEAT THE READER TO DEATH.
IN OTHER WORDS ...
...IF YOU DON'T KNOW THE AUTHOR OF A BOOK, AND YOU TAKE ADVANTAGE OF THAT FACT TO CLAIM OWNERSHIP OF WHAT YOU LIKE WHILE DENOUNCING WHAT YOU DON'T LIKE...
...THE AUTHOR WILL APPEAR FROM THE GRAVE WITH A GRUDGE AGAINST YOU.
AND THAT'S EXACTLY WHAT KOSUZU WAS DOING.

*SEE VOLUME 3, "LOVE LETTERS WITH A PAST"

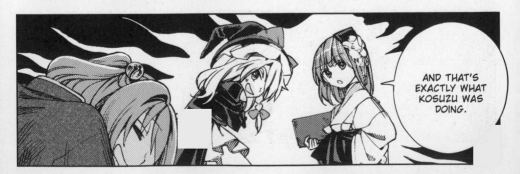

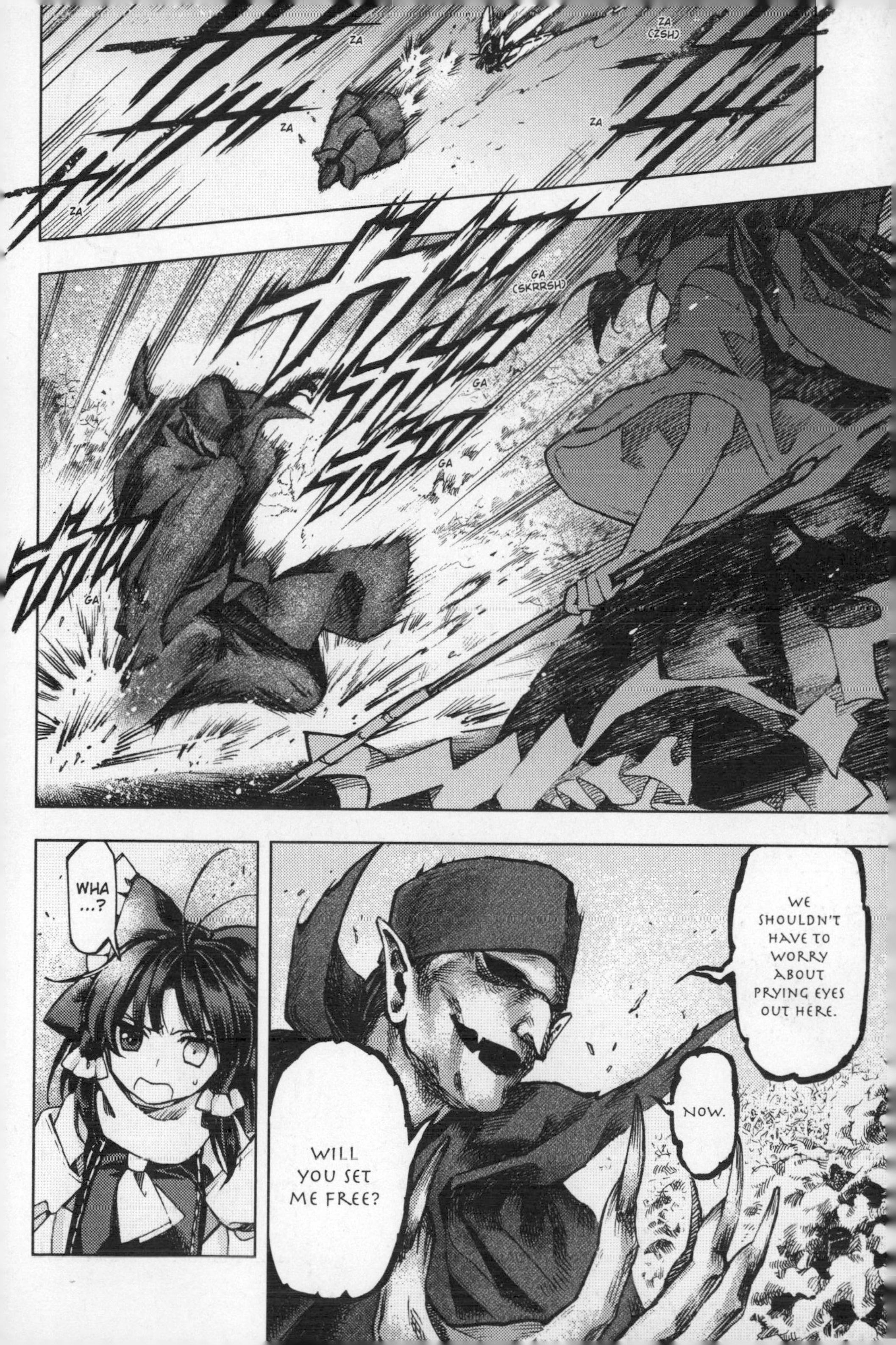
ZA (ZSH)
ZA
ZA
ZA
ZA
GA (SKRRSH)
GA
GA
GA
WE SHOULDN'T HAVE TO WORRY ABOUT PRYING EYES OUT HERE.
NOW.
WILL YOU SET ME FREE?
WHA ...?

Through my fortune-telling, I saw the reverse side of the world...
...and suddenly saw how wretched human existence is, and how much control youkai have.
I decided to take my leave of humanity.
When I learned I could return to this world through books, I devised a spell to turn myself into a youkai, and I took my own life.
The notes I scribbled down are made up of two parts—
The anonymous notes on fortune-telling and the art of elocution, simple enough for anyone to master...
...and the childish, ridiculous nonsense.
......
When someone rejected the nonsense part and flaunted the former as an **original style of fortune-telling**...
...my jealousy would enable me to return from the afterlife.

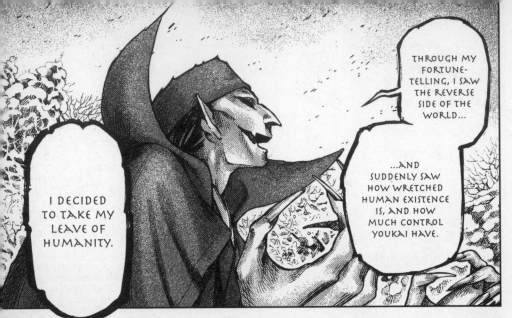

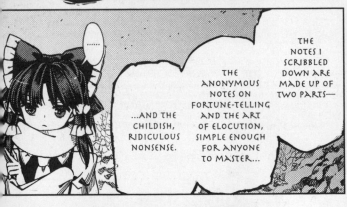

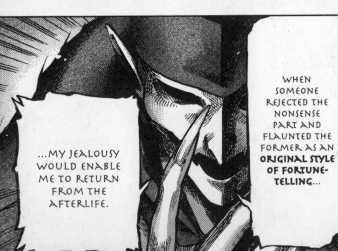

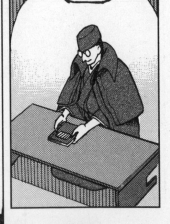

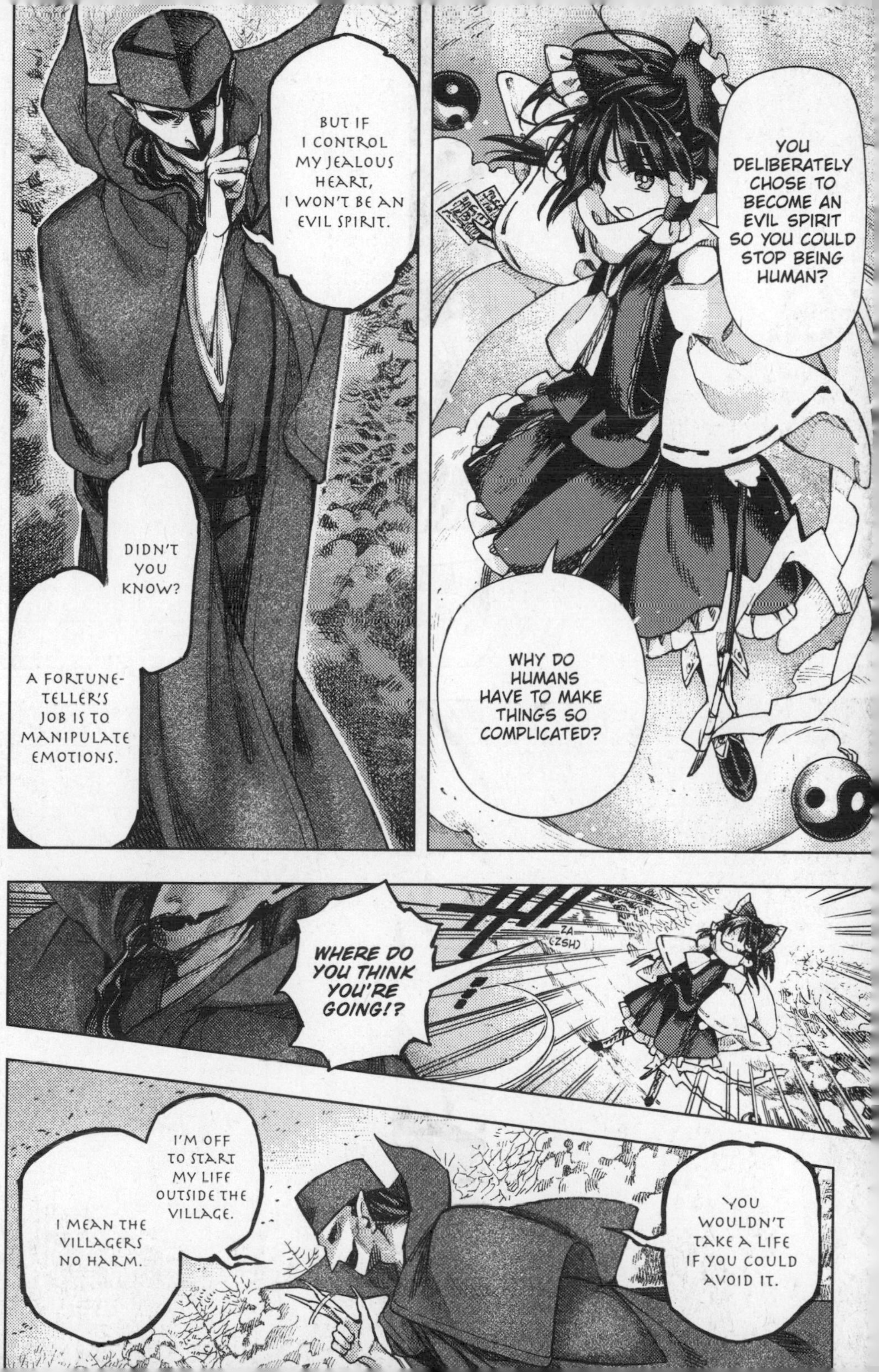
YOU DELIBERATELY CHOSE TO BECOME AN EVIL SPIRIT SO YOU COULD STOP BEING HUMAN?
WHY DO HUMANS HAVE TO MAKE THINGS SO COMPLICATED?
BUT IF I CONTROL MY JEALOUS HEART, I WON'T BE AN EVIL SPIRIT.
DIDN'T YOU KNOW?
A FORTUNE-TELLER'S JOB IS TO MANIPULATE EMOTIONS.
ZA (ZSH)
WHERE DO YOU THINK YOU'RE GOING!?
YOU WOULDN'T TAKE A LIFE IF YOU COULD AVOID IT.
I'M OFF TO START MY LIFE OUTSIDE THE VILLAGE.
I MEAN THE VILLAGERS NO HARM.

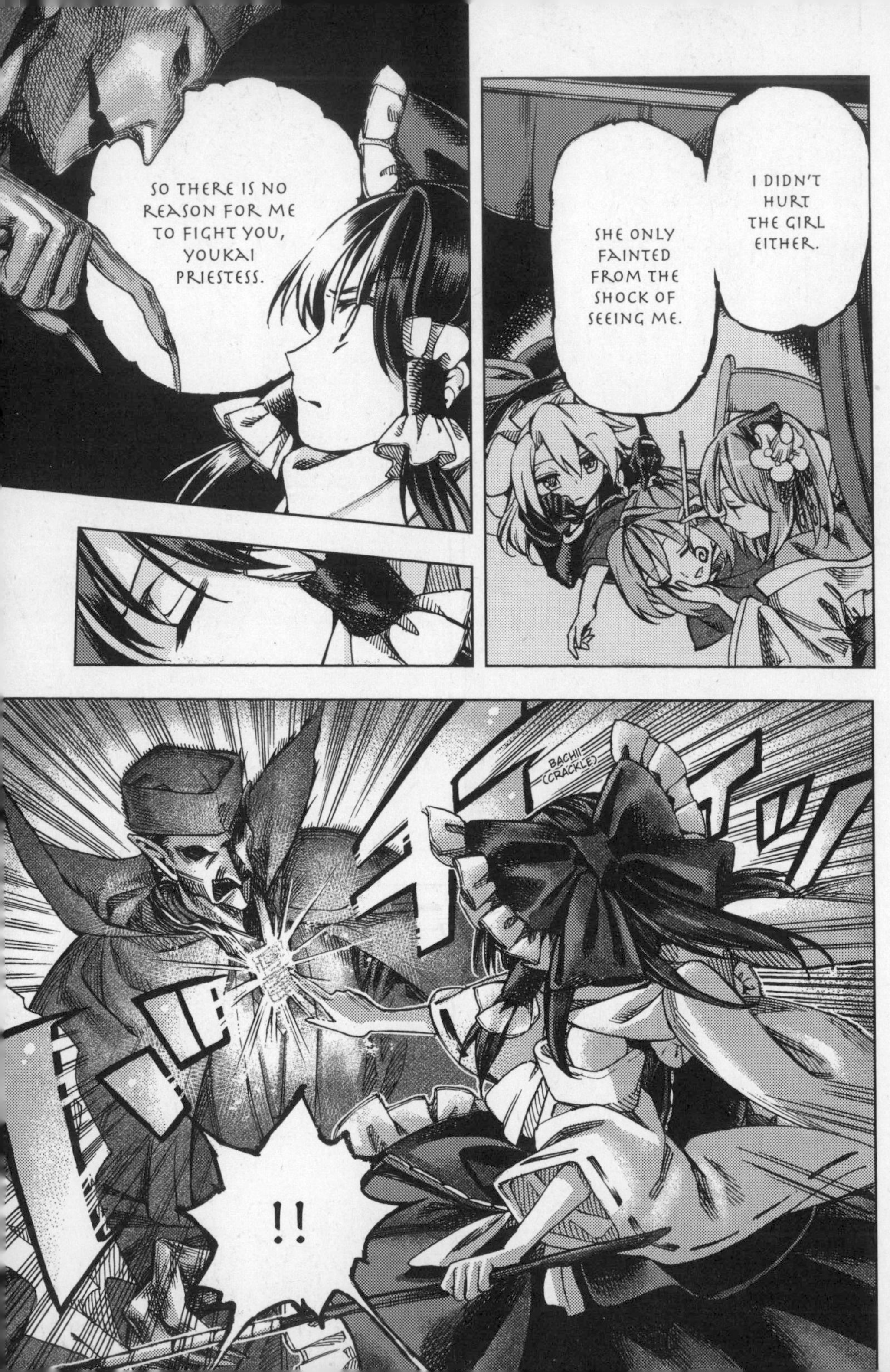
I DIDN'T HURT THE GIRL EITHER.
SHE ONLY FAINTED FROM THE SHOCK OF SEEING ME.
SO THERE IS NO REASON FOR ME TO FIGHT YOU, YOUKAI PRIESTESS.
BACHII (CRACKLE)
!!

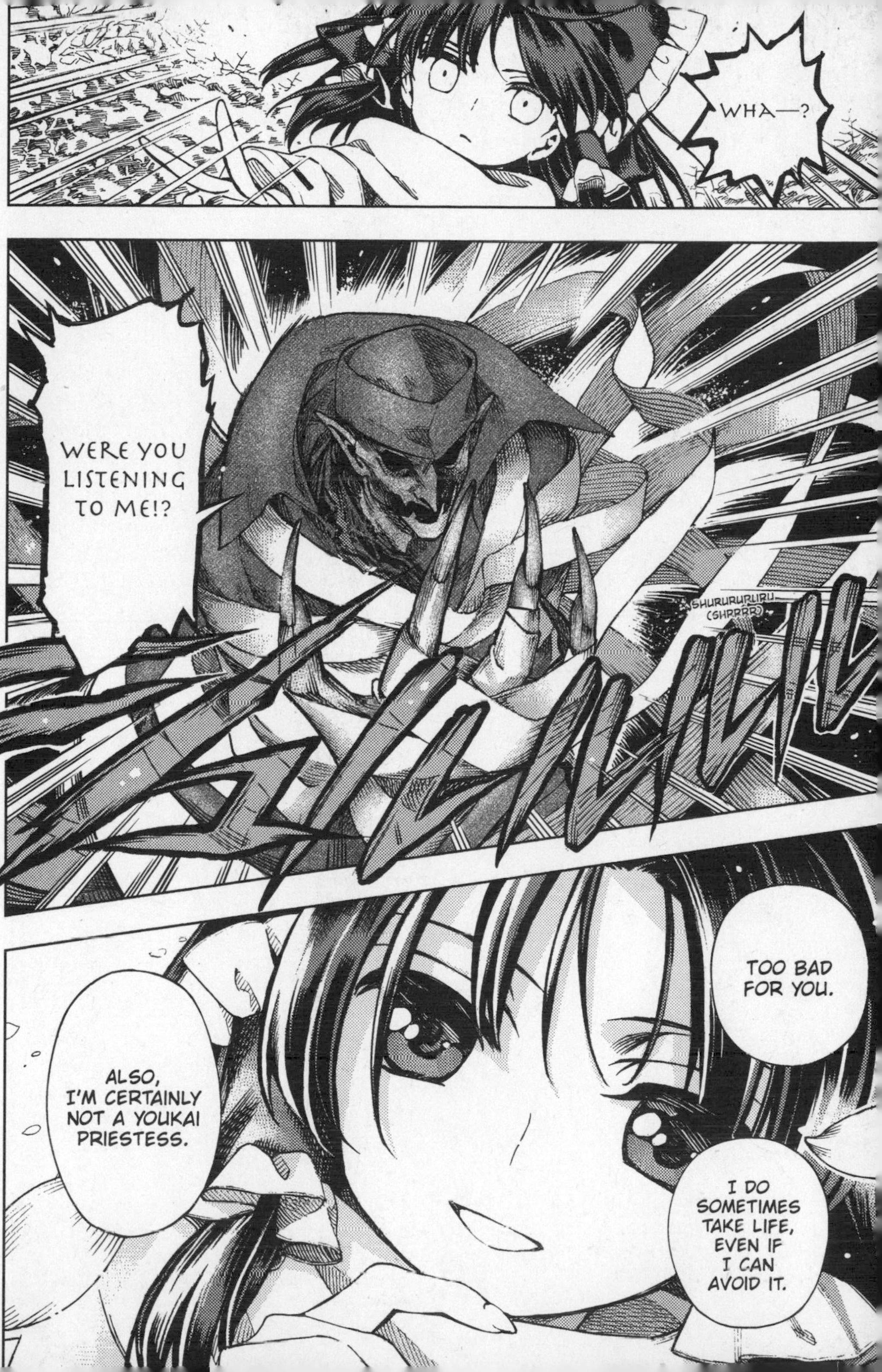
WHA—?
WERE YOU LISTENING TO ME!?
SHURURURURU (SHRRRR)
TOO BAD FOR YOU.
ALSO, I'M CERTAINLY NOT A YOUKAI PRIESTESS.
I DO SOMETIMES TAKE LIFE, EVEN IF I CAN AVOID IT.

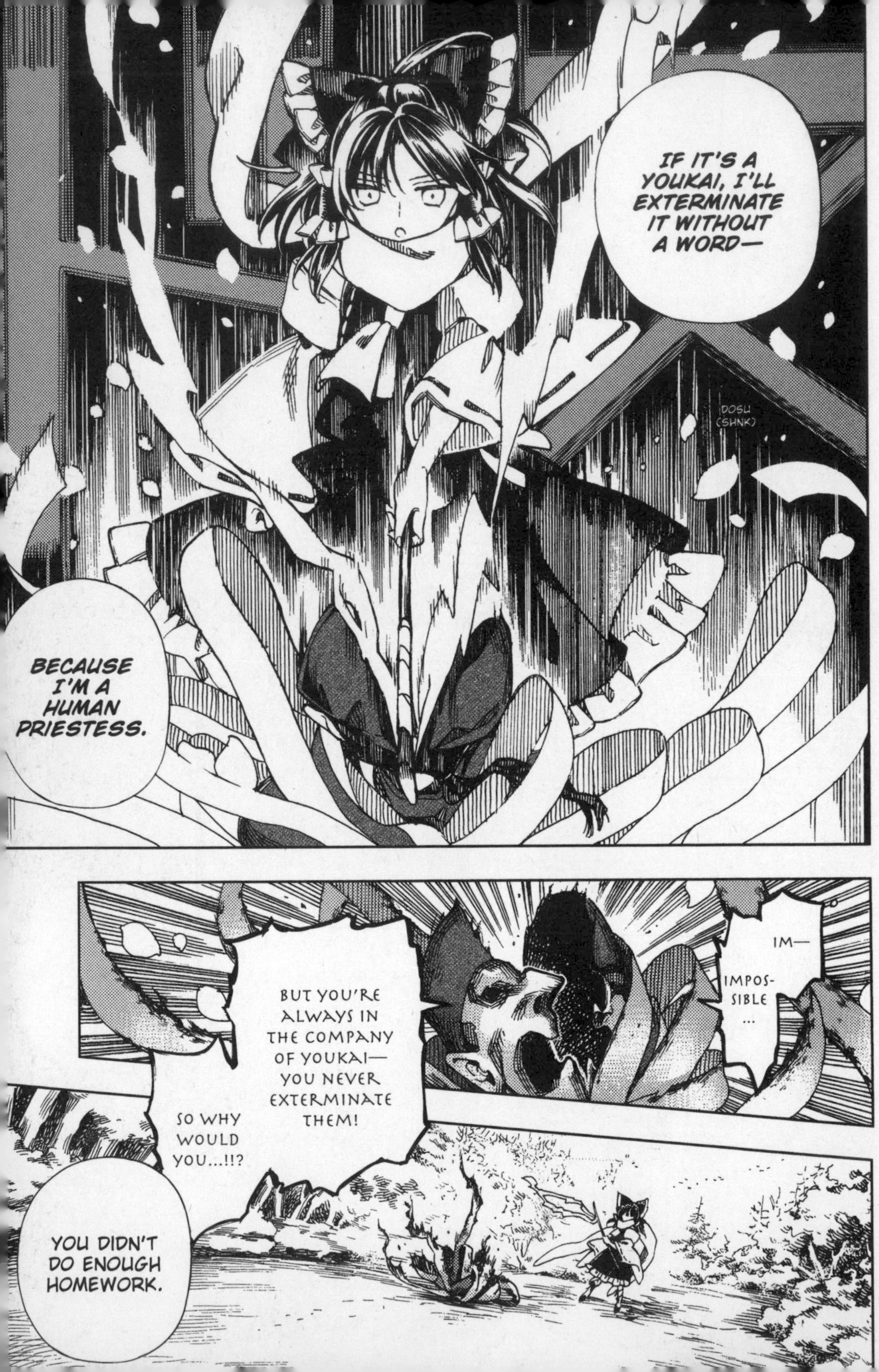
IF IT'S A YOUKAI, I'LL EXTERMINATE IT WITHOUT A WORD—
DOSU (SHNK)
BECAUSE I'M A HUMAN PRIESTESS.
IM—
IMPOS-SIBLE...
BUT YOU'RE ALWAYS IN THE COMPANY OF YOUKAI— YOU NEVER EXTERMINATE THEM!
SO WHY WOULD YOU...!!?
YOU DIDN'T DO ENOUGH HOMEWORK.

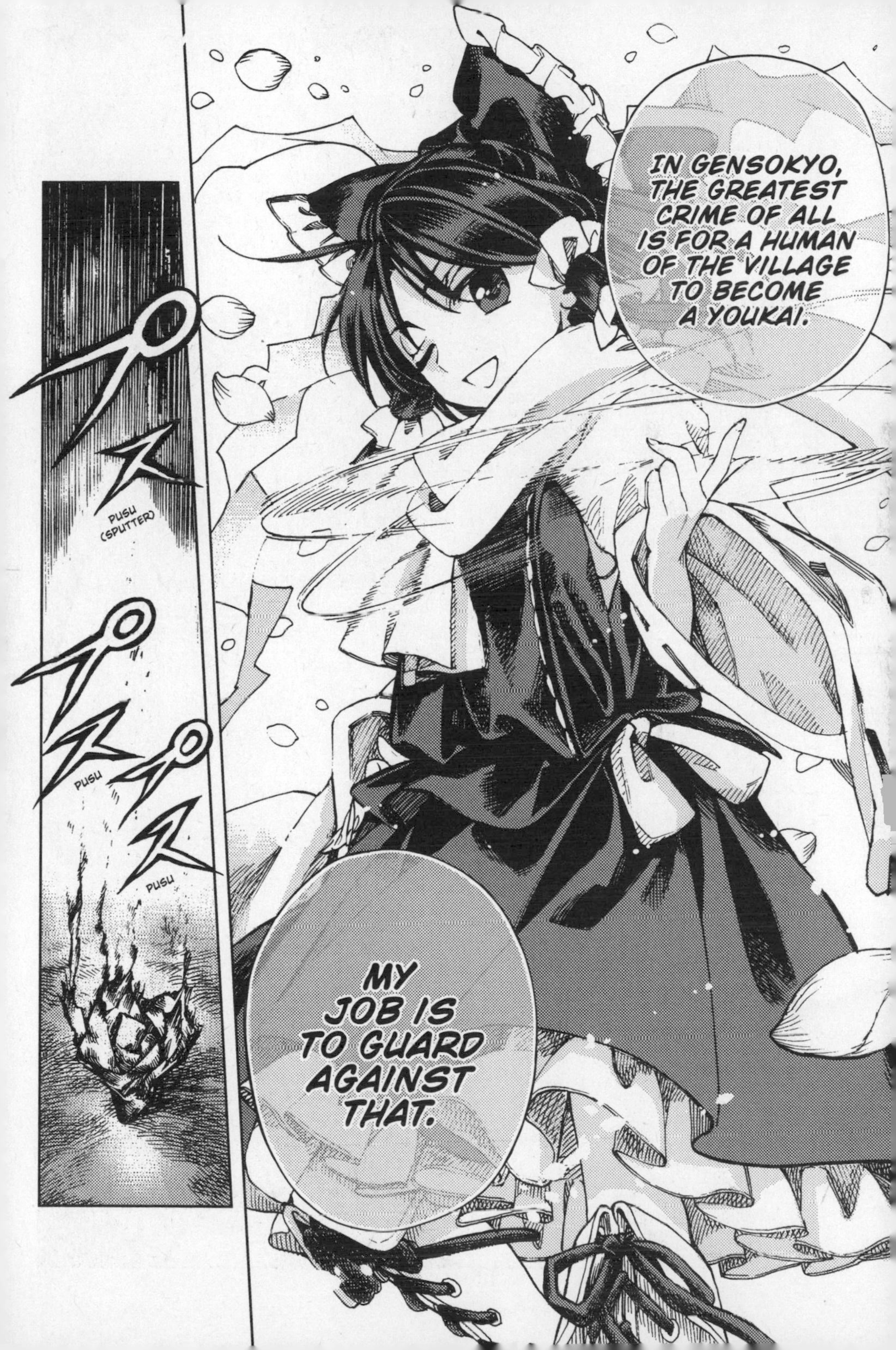
IN GENSOKYO, THE GREATEST CRIME OF ALL IS FOR A HUMAN OF THE VILLAGE TO BECOME A YOUKAI.
MY JOB IS TO GUARD AGAINST THAT.
PUSU (SPUTTER)
PUSU
PUSU

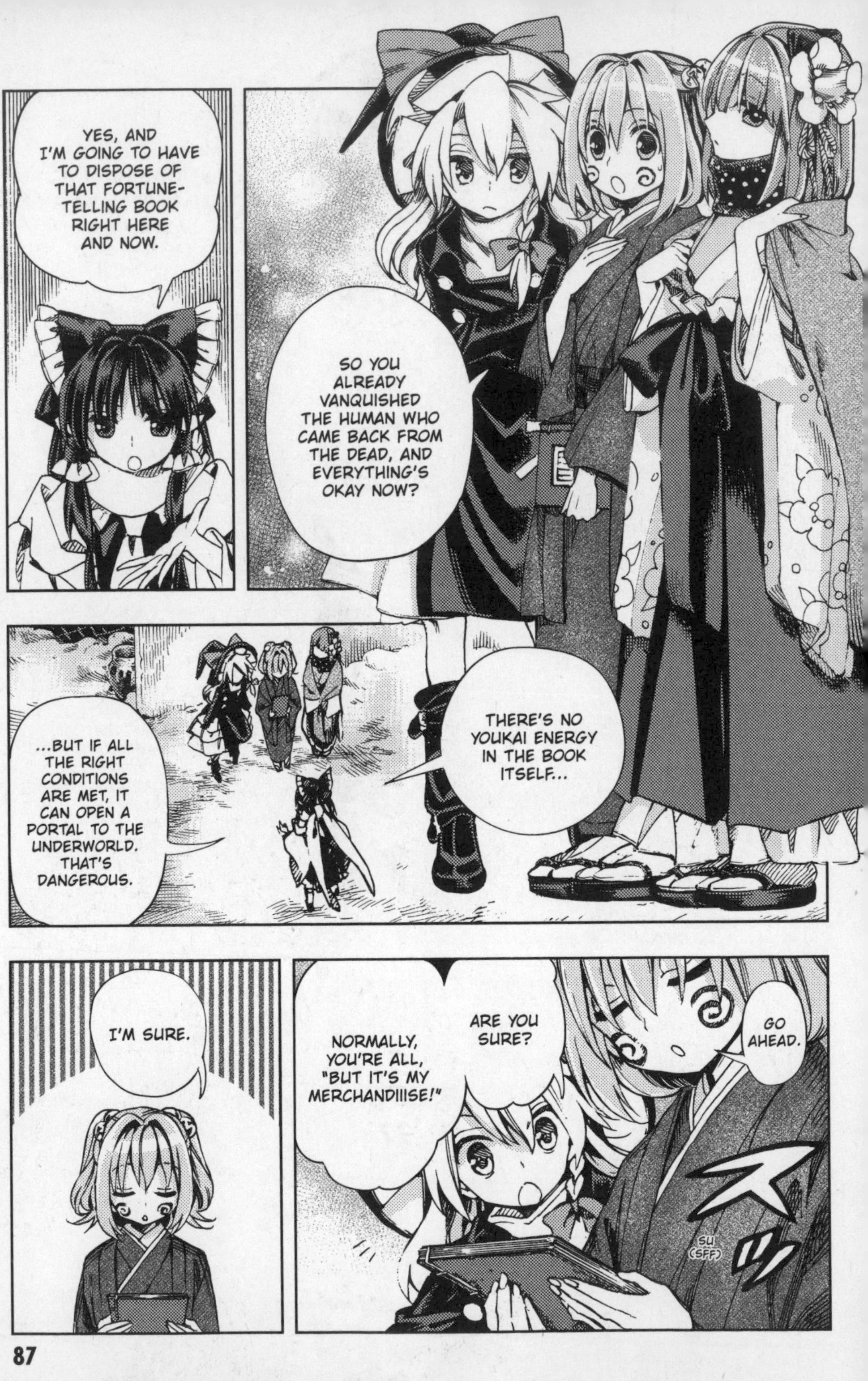
SO YOU ALREADY VANQUISHED THE HUMAN WHO CAME BACK FROM THE DEAD, AND EVERYTHING'S OKAY NOW?
YES, AND I'M GOING TO HAVE TO DISPOSE OF THAT FORTUNE-TELLING BOOK RIGHT HERE AND NOW.
THERE'S NO YOUKAI ENERGY IN THE BOOK ITSELF...
...BUT IF ALL THE RIGHT CONDITIONS ARE MET, IT CAN OPEN A PORTAL TO THE UNDERWORLD. THAT'S DANGEROUS.
GO AHEAD.
ARE YOU SURE?
NORMALLY, YOU'RE ALL, "BUT IT'S MY MERCHANDIIISE!"
SU (SFF)
I'M SURE.

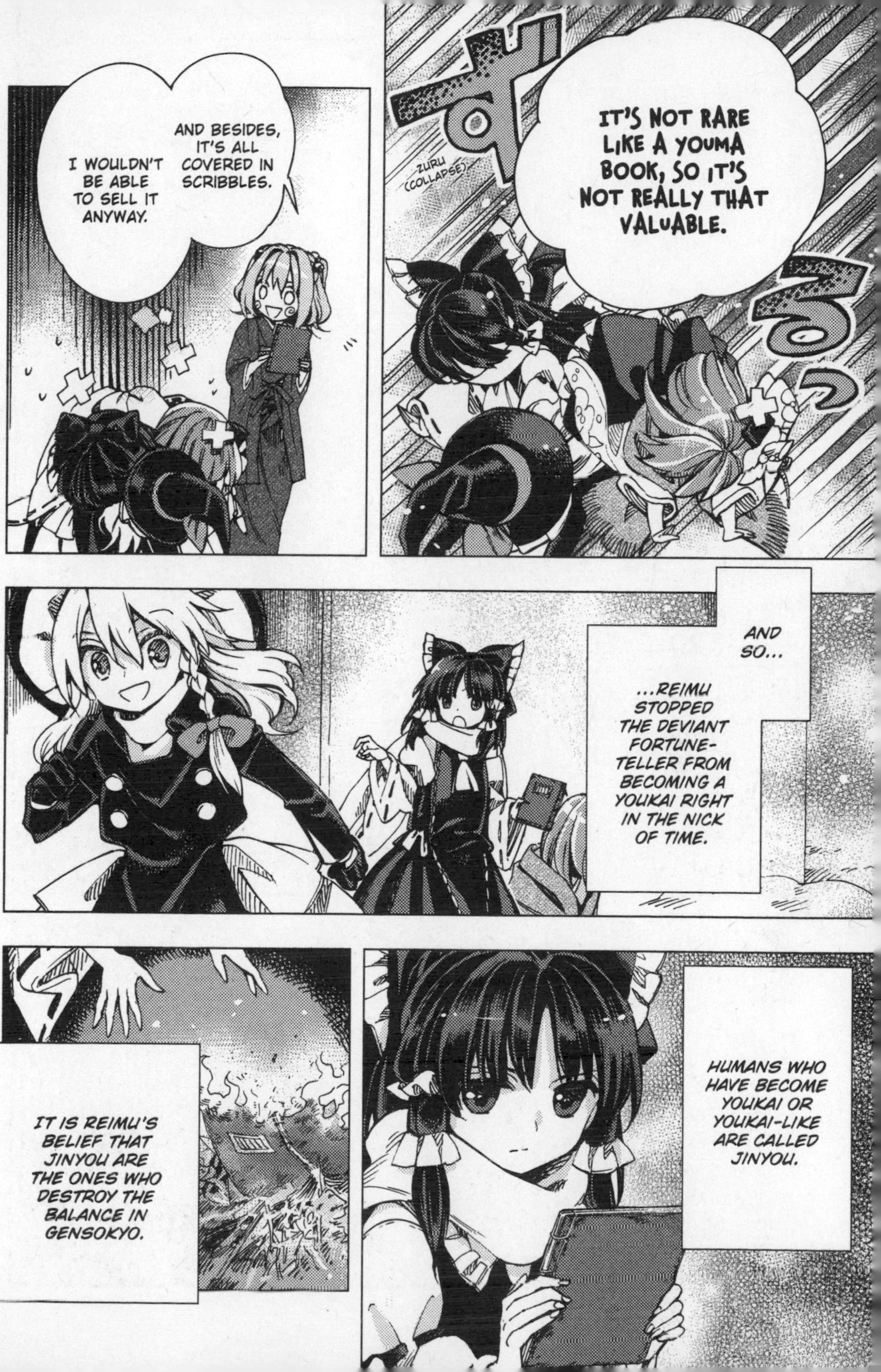
IT'S NOT RARE LIKE A YOUMA BOOK, SO IT'S NOT REALLY THAT VALUABLE.
ZURU (COLLAPSE)
AND BESIDES, IT'S ALL COVERED IN SCRIBBLES.
I WOULDN'T BE ABLE TO SELL IT ANYWAY.
AND SO...
...REIMU STOPPED THE DEVIANT FORTUNE-TELLER FROM BECOMING A YOUKAI RIGHT IN THE NICK OF TIME.
HUMANS WHO HAVE BECOME YOUKAI OR YOUKAI-LIKE ARE CALLED JINYOU.
IT IS REIMU'S BELIEF THAT JINYOU ARE THE ONES WHO DESTROY THE BALANCE IN GENSOKYO.

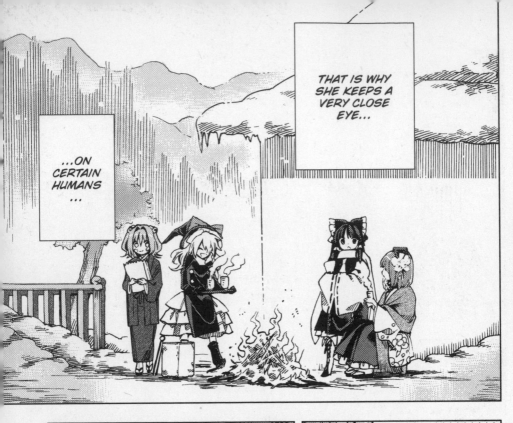

THAT IS WHY SHE KEEPS A VERY CLOSE EYE...
...ON CERTAIN HUMANS ...
す
SU (SFF)
ドサッ
KOSUZU
SPOT-ON FORTUNES!
NEW RELEASES
DOSSARI (THUD)
ふ
FUU (WHEW)
...AND ON SUZU-NAAN.

Chapter 25 End

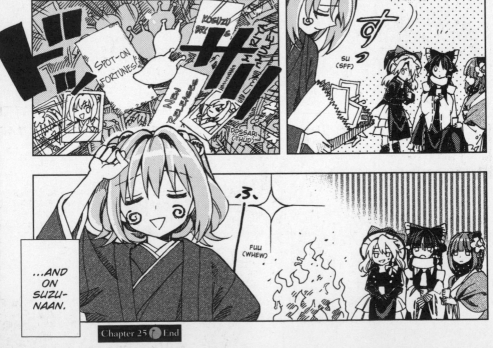

Forbidden Scrollery

Chapter 26 Kokkuri-san Scatters with the Cherry Blossoms Part 1

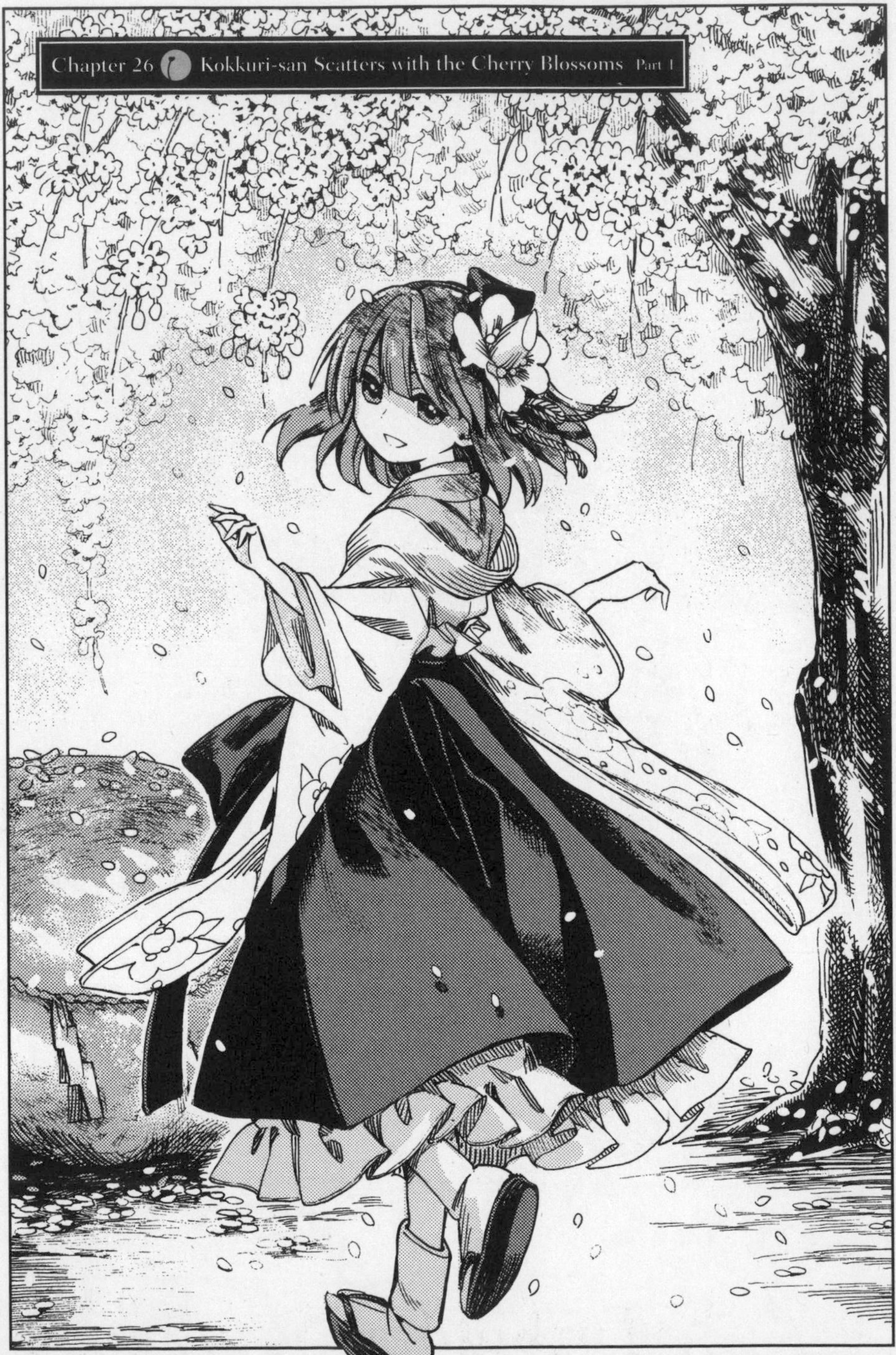

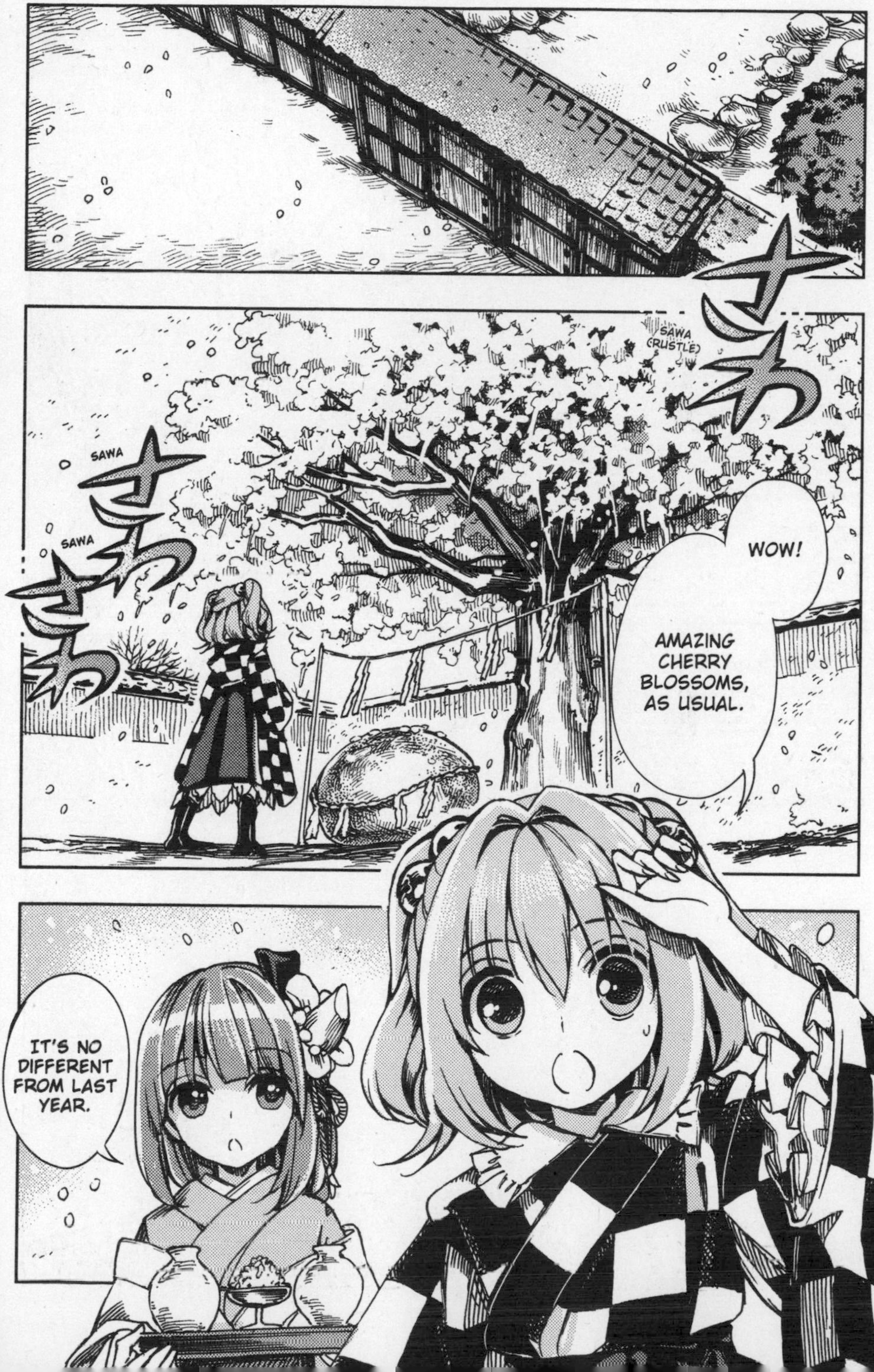
SAWA (RUSTLE)
WOW!
AMAZING CHERRY BLOSSOMS, AS USUAL.
SAWA
SAWA
IT'S NO DIFFERENT FROM LAST YEAR.

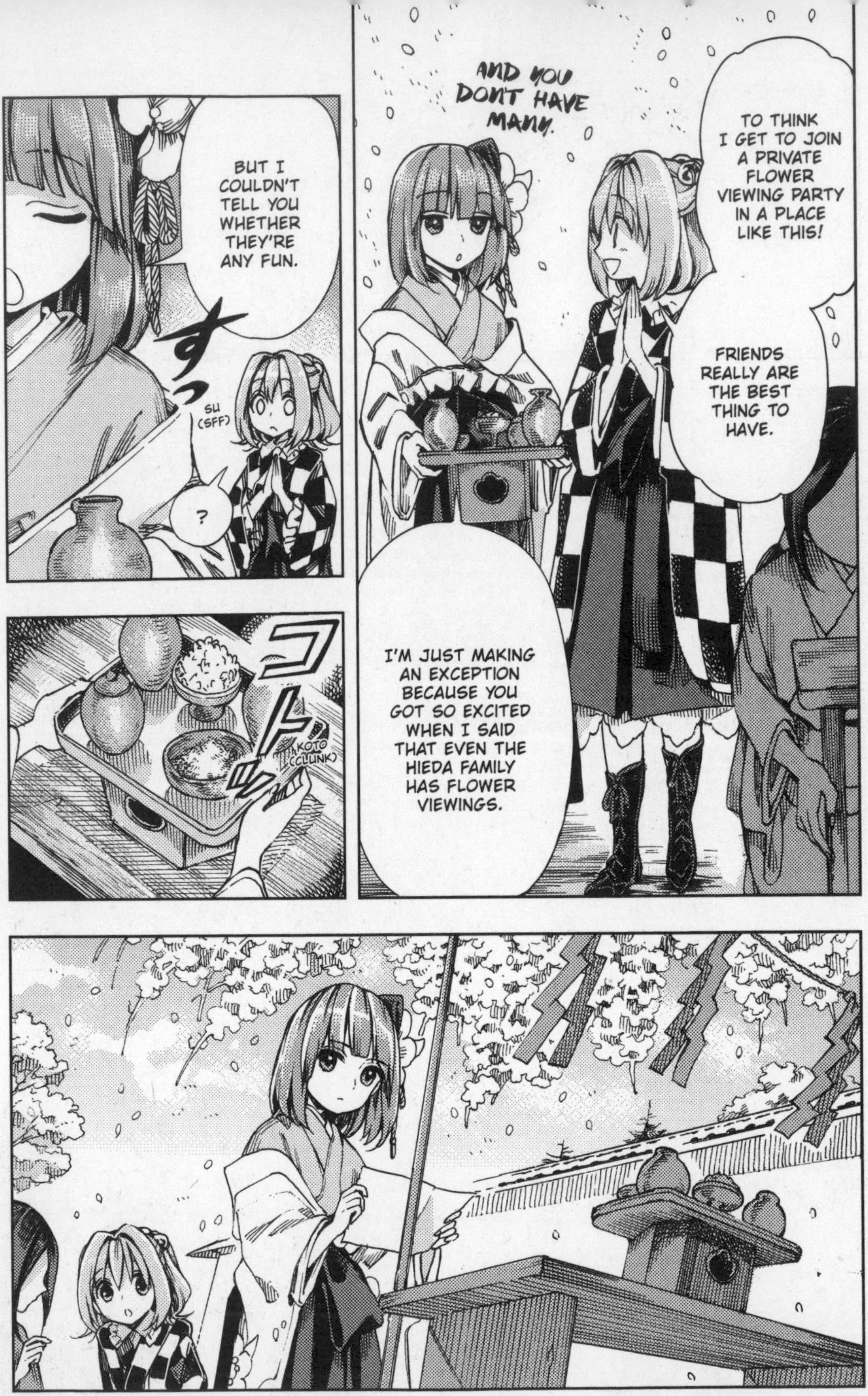
TO THINK I GET TO JOIN A PRIVATE FLOWER VIEWING PARTY IN A PLACE LIKE THIS!
FRIENDS REALLY ARE THE BEST THING TO HAVE.
AND YOU DON'T HAVE MANY.
I'M JUST MAKING AN EXCEPTION BECAUSE YOU GOT SO EXCITED WHEN I SAID THAT EVEN THE HIEDA FAMILY HAS FLOWER VIEWINGS.
BUT I COULDN'T TELL YOU WHETHER THEY'RE ANY FUN.
すっ
SU (SFF)
?
コトッ
KOTO (CLUNK)

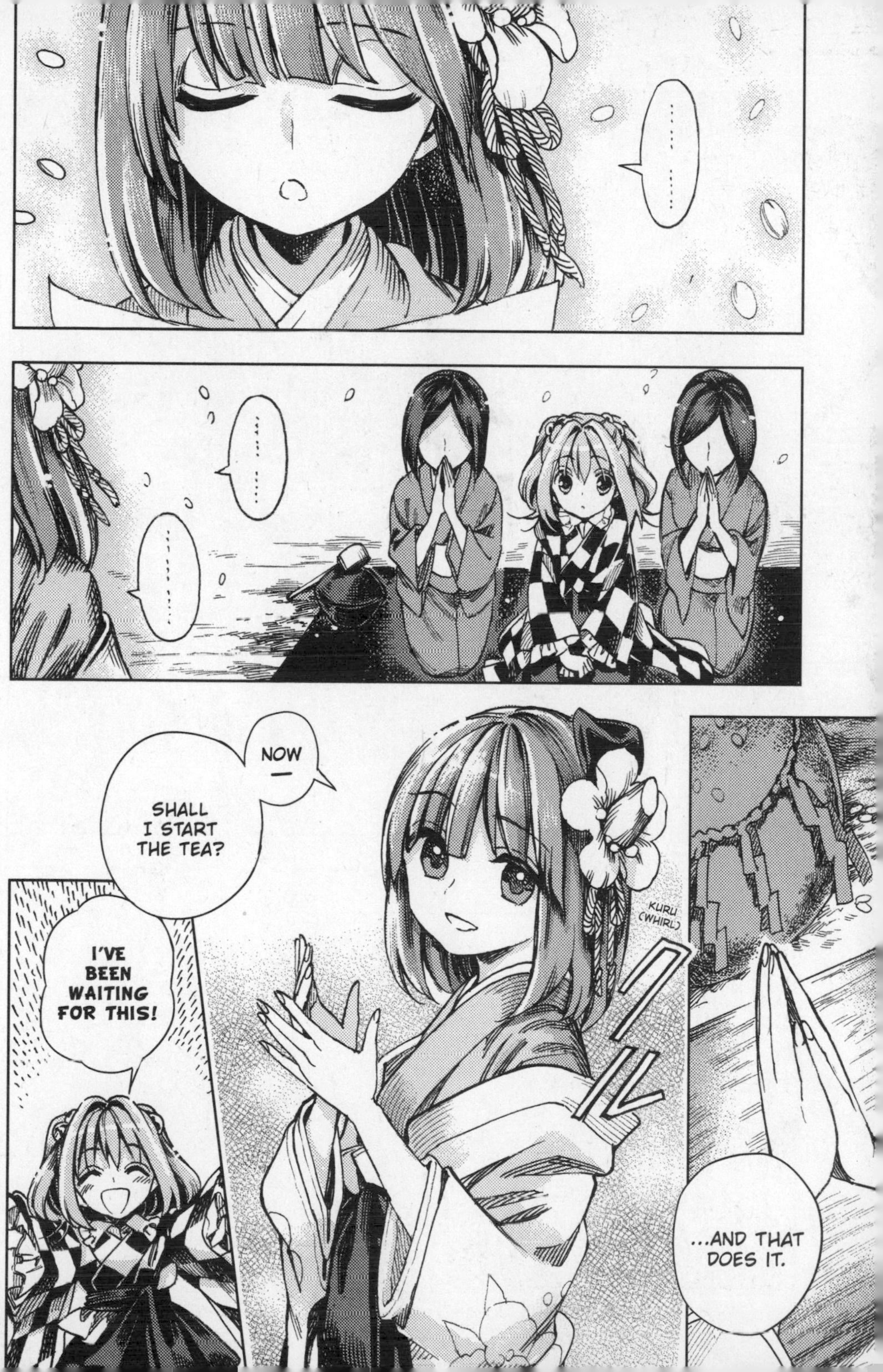
......
......
......
...AND THAT DOES IT.
NOW —
SHALL I START THE TEA?
KURU (WHIRL)
I'VE BEEN WAITING FOR THIS!

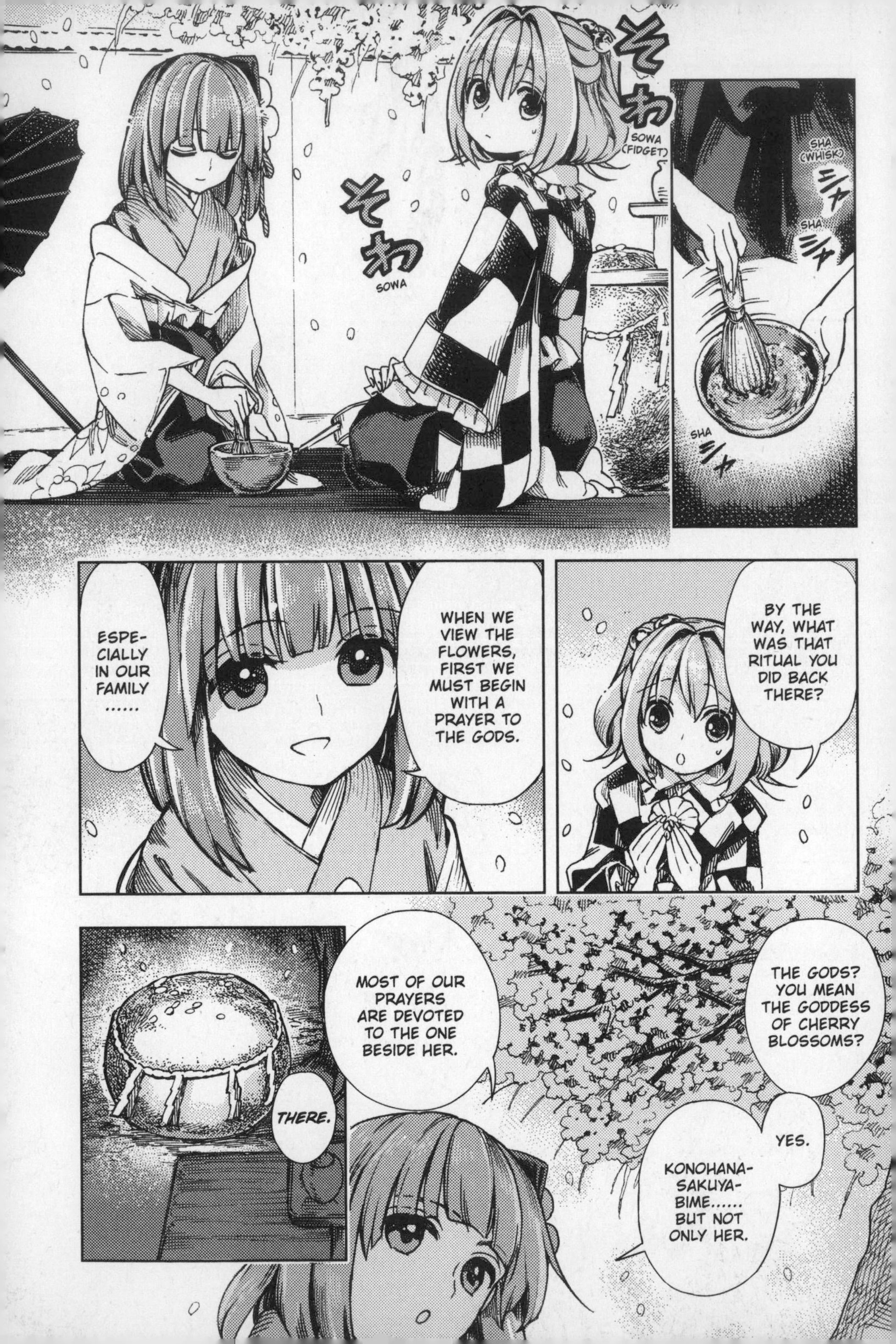
SHA (WHISK)
シャ
SHA
シャ
SHA
シャ
そわ
SOWA (FIDGET)
そわ
SOWA
BY THE WAY, WHAT WAS THAT RITUAL YOU DID BACK THERE?
WHEN WE VIEW THE FLOWERS, FIRST WE MUST BEGIN WITH A PRAYER TO THE GODS.
ESPE-CIALLY IN OUR FAMILY ......
THE GODS? YOU MEAN THE GODDESS OF CHERRY BLOSSOMS?
YES.
KONOHANA-SAKUYA-BIME...... BUT NOT ONLY HER.
MOST OF OUR PRAYERS ARE DEVOTED TO THE ONE BESIDE HER.
THERE.

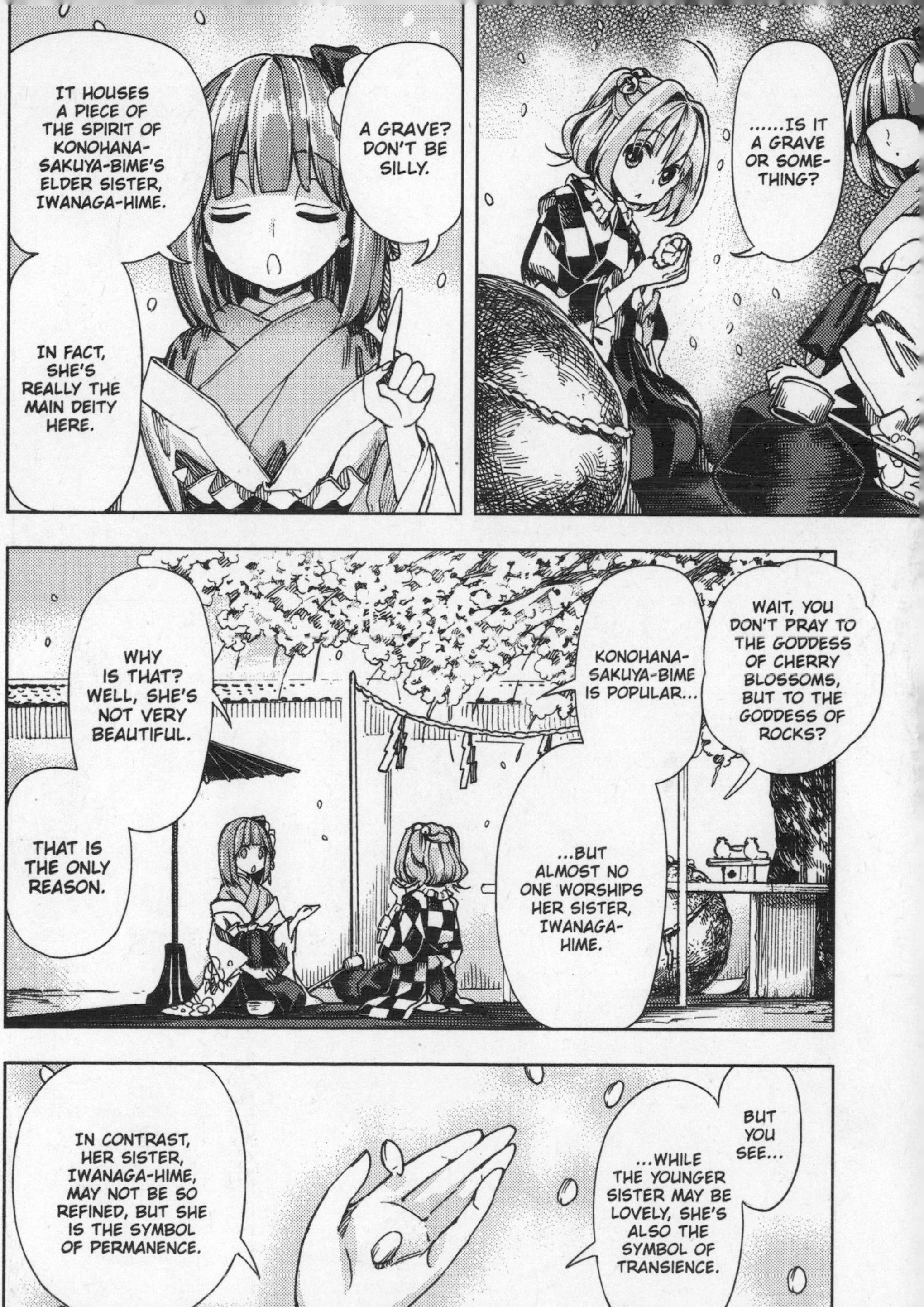
......IS IT A GRAVE OR SOME-THING?
A GRAVE? DON'T BE SILLY.
IT HOUSES A PIECE OF THE SPIRIT OF KONOHANA-SAKUYA-BIME'S ELDER SISTER, IWANAGA-HIME.
IN FACT, SHE'S REALLY THE MAIN DEITY HERE.
WAIT, YOU DON'T PRAY TO THE GODDESS OF CHERRY BLOSSOMS, BUT TO THE GODDESS OF ROCKS?
KONOHANA-SAKUYA-BIME IS POPULAR...
...BUT ALMOST NO ONE WORSHIPS HER SISTER, IWANAGA-HIME.
WHY IS THAT? WELL, SHE'S NOT VERY BEAUTIFUL.
THAT IS THE ONLY REASON.
BUT YOU SEE...
...WHILE THE YOUNGER SISTER MAY BE LOVELY, SHE'S ALSO THE SYMBOL OF TRANSIENCE.
IN CONTRAST, HER SISTER, IWANAGA-HIME, MAY NOT BE SO REFINED, BUT SHE IS THE SYMBOL OF PERMANENCE.

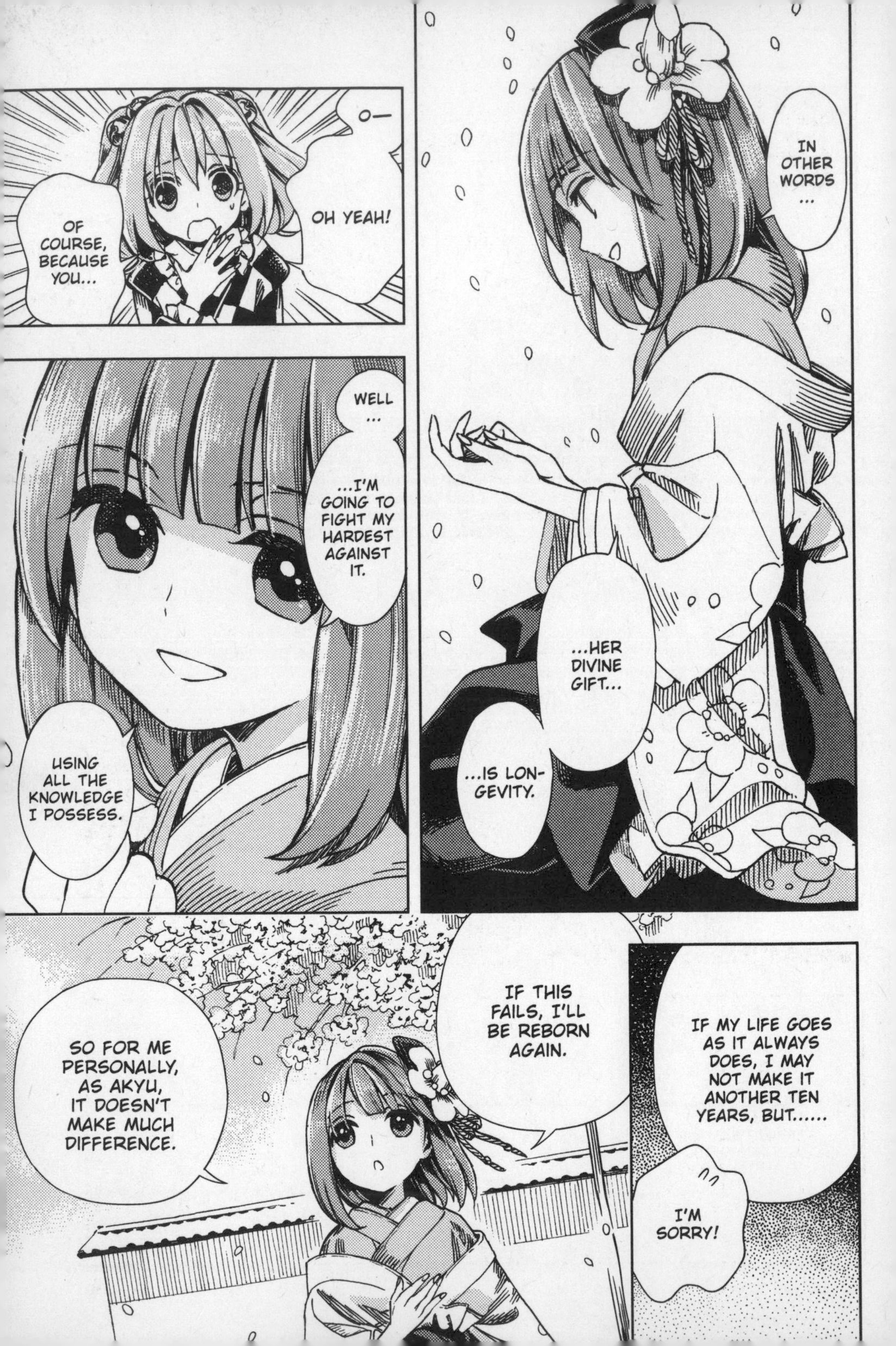
IN OTHER WORDS...
...HER DIVINE GIFT...
...IS LONGEVITY.
O—
OH YEAH!
OF COURSE, BECAUSE YOU...
WELL...
...I'M GOING TO FIGHT MY HARDEST AGAINST IT.
USING ALL THE KNOWLEDGE I POSSESS.
IF MY LIFE GOES AS IT ALWAYS DOES, I MAY NOT MAKE IT ANOTHER TEN YEARS, BUT......
I'M SORRY!
IF THIS FAILS, I'LL BE REBORN AGAIN.
SO FOR ME PERSONALLY, AS AKYU, IT DOESN'T MAKE MUCH DIFFERENCE.

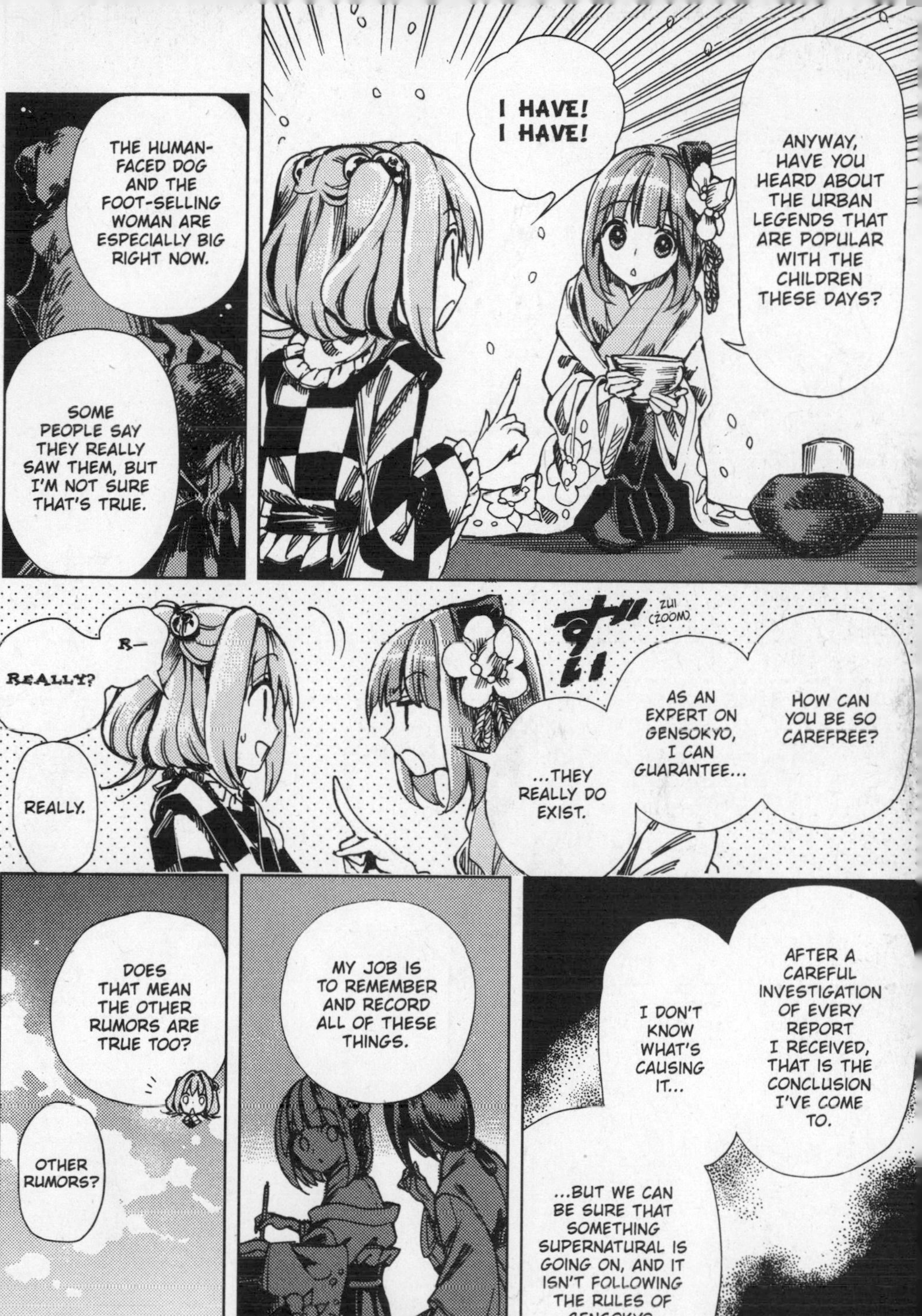
ANYWAY, HAVE YOU HEARD ABOUT THE URBAN LEGENDS THAT ARE POPULAR WITH THE CHILDREN THESE DAYS?
I HAVE! I HAVE!
THE HUMAN-FACED DOG AND THE FOOT-SELLING WOMAN ARE ESPECIALLY BIG RIGHT NOW.
SOME PEOPLE SAY THEY REALLY SAW THEM, BUT I'M NOT SURE THAT'S TRUE.
ZUI (ZOOM)
HOW CAN YOU BE SO CAREFREE?
AS AN EXPERT ON GENSOKYO, I CAN GUARANTEE...
...THEY REALLY DO EXIST.
R— REALLY?
REALLY.
AFTER A CAREFUL INVESTIGATION OF EVERY REPORT I RECEIVED, THAT IS THE CONCLUSION I'VE COME TO.
I DON'T KNOW WHAT'S CAUSING IT...
...BUT WE CAN BE SURE THAT SOMETHING SUPERNATURAL IS GOING ON, AND IT ISN'T FOLLOWING THE RULES OF GENSOKYO.
MY JOB IS TO REMEMBER AND RECORD ALL OF THESE THINGS.
DOES THAT MEAN THE OTHER RUMORS ARE TRUE TOO?
OTHER RUMORS?

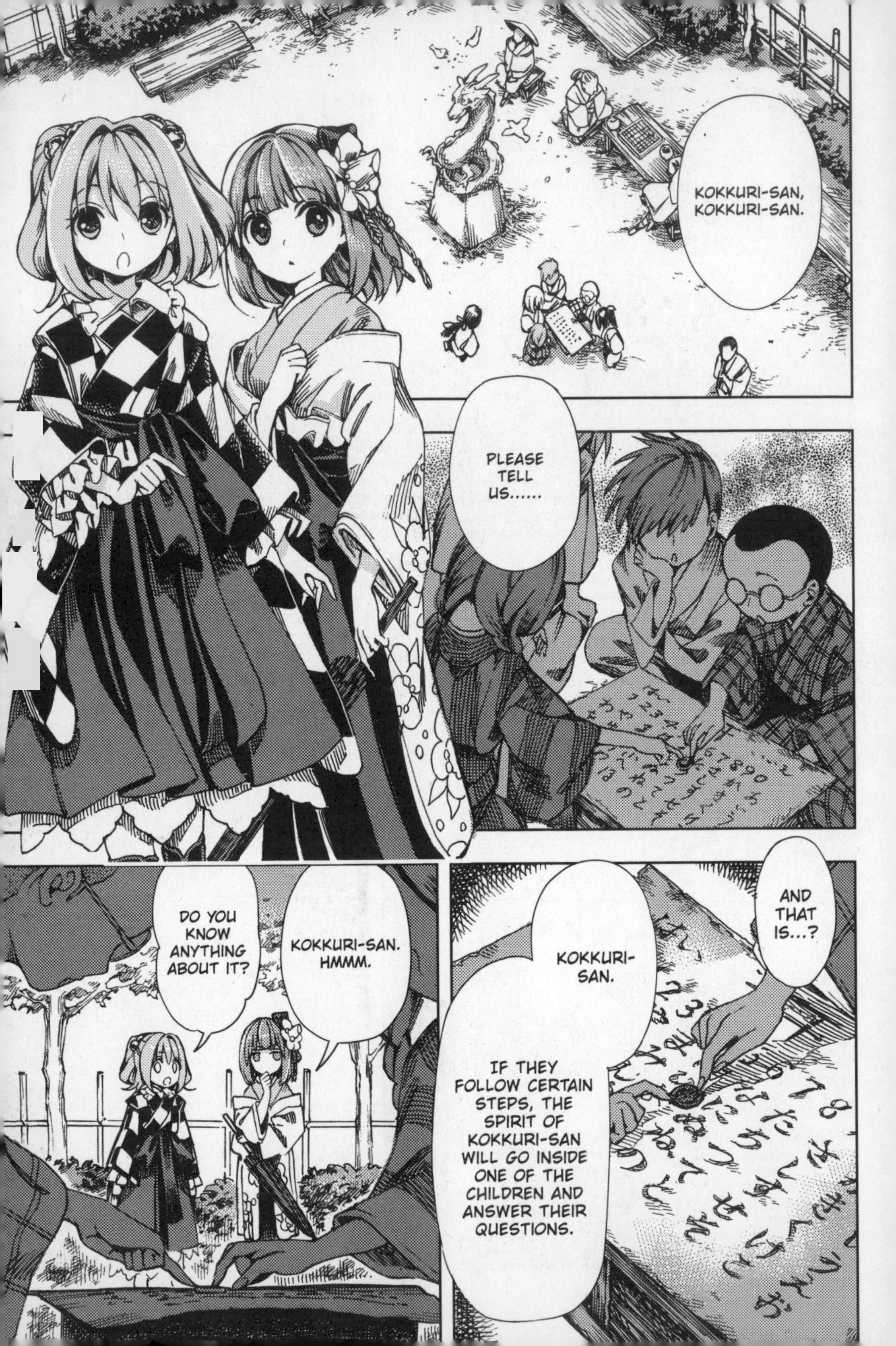
KOKKURI-SAN, KOKKURI-SAN.
PLEASE TELL US......
AND THAT IS...?
KOKKURI-SAN.
IF THEY FOLLOW CERTAIN STEPS, THE SPIRIT OF KOKKURI-SAN WILL GO INSIDE ONE OF THE CHILDREN AND ANSWER THEIR QUESTIONS.
KOKKURI-SAN. HMMM.
DO YOU KNOW ANYTHING ABOUT IT?

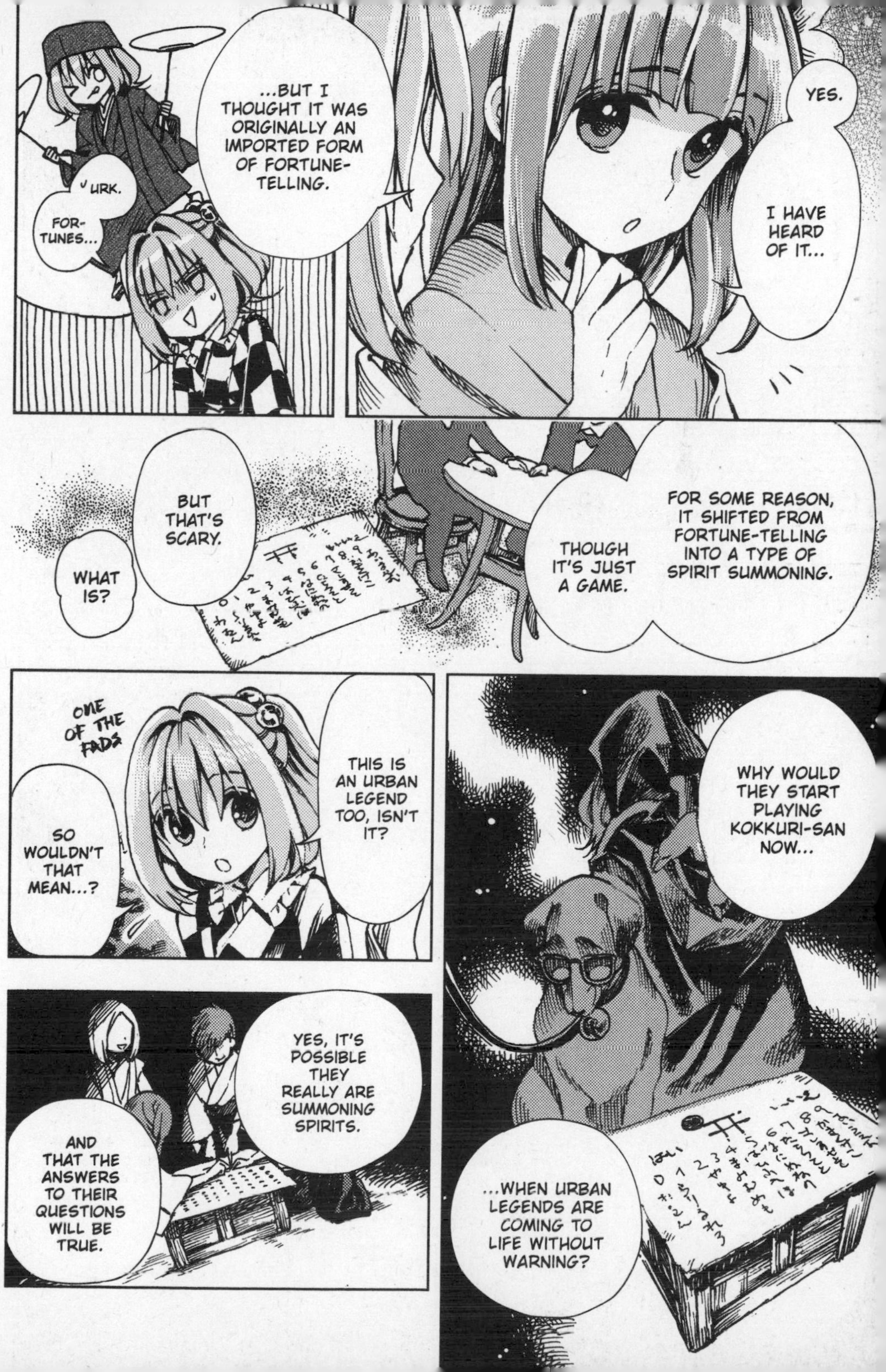
YES.
I HAVE HEARD OF IT...
...BUT I THOUGHT IT WAS ORIGINALLY AN IMPORTED FORM OF FORTUNE-TELLING.
URK.
FOR-TUNES...
FOR SOME REASON, IT SHIFTED FROM FORTUNE-TELLING INTO A TYPE OF SPIRIT SUMMONING.
THOUGH IT'S JUST A GAME.
BUT THAT'S SCARY.
WHAT IS?
WHY WOULD THEY START PLAYING KOKKURI-SAN NOW...
...WHEN URBAN LEGENDS ARE COMING TO LIFE WITHOUT WARNING?
THIS IS AN URBAN LEGEND TOO, ISN'T IT?
SO WOULDN'T THAT MEAN...?
ONE OF THE FADS
YES, IT'S POSSIBLE THEY REALLY ARE SUMMONING SPIRITS.
AND THAT THE ANSWERS TO THEIR QUESTIONS WILL BE TRUE.

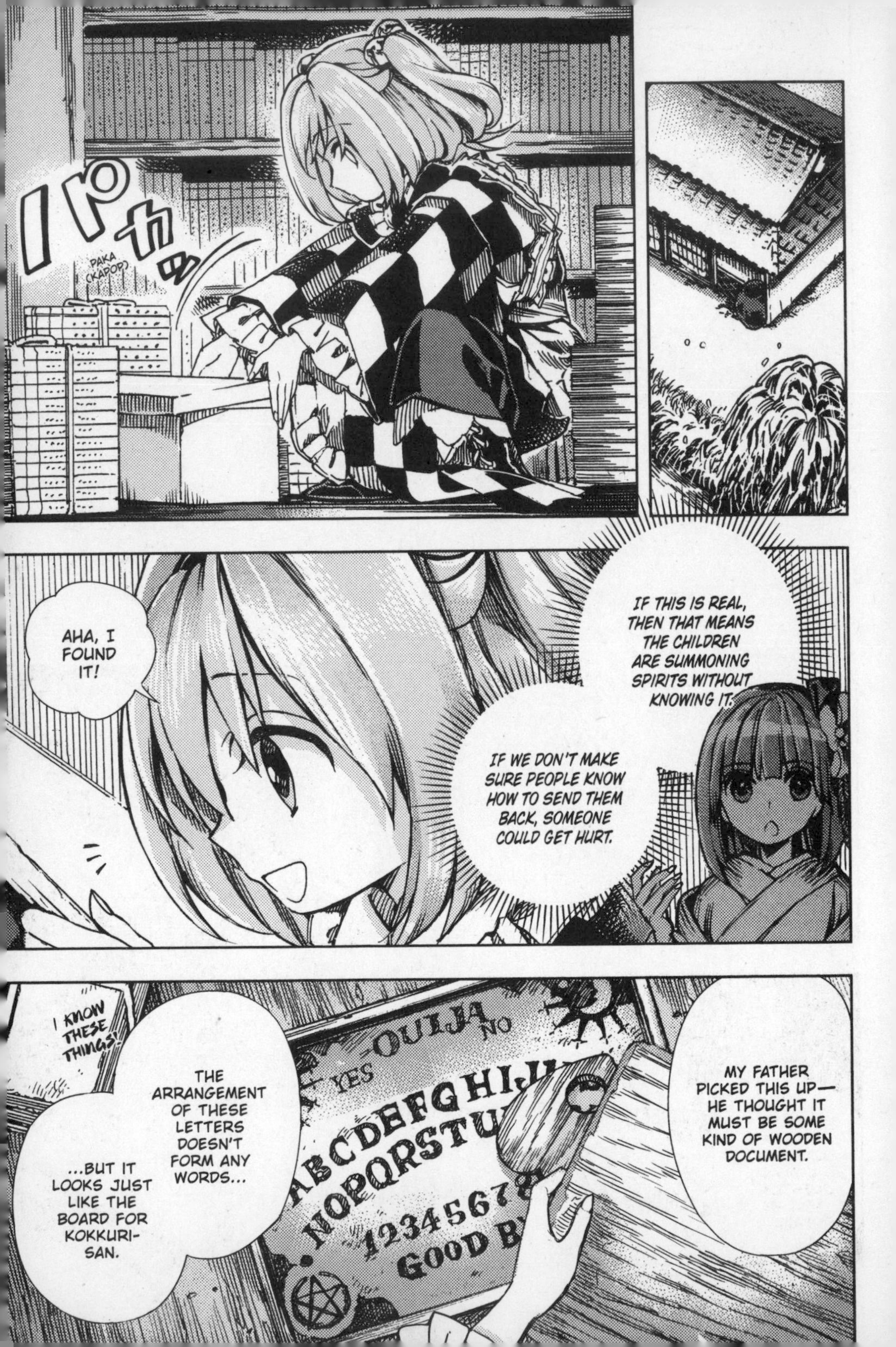
PAKA (KAPOP)
IF THIS IS REAL, THEN THAT MEANS THE CHILDREN ARE SUMMONING SPIRITS WITHOUT KNOWING IT.
IF WE DON'T MAKE SURE PEOPLE KNOW HOW TO SEND THEM BACK, SOMEONE COULD GET HURT.
AHA, I FOUND IT!
MY FATHER PICKED THIS UP— HE THOUGHT IT MUST BE SOME KIND OF WOODEN DOCUMENT.
THE ARRANGEMENT OF THESE LETTERS DOESN'T FORM ANY WORDS...
...BUT IT LOOKS JUST LIKE THE BOARD FOR KOKKURI-SAN.
I KNOW THESE THINGS!

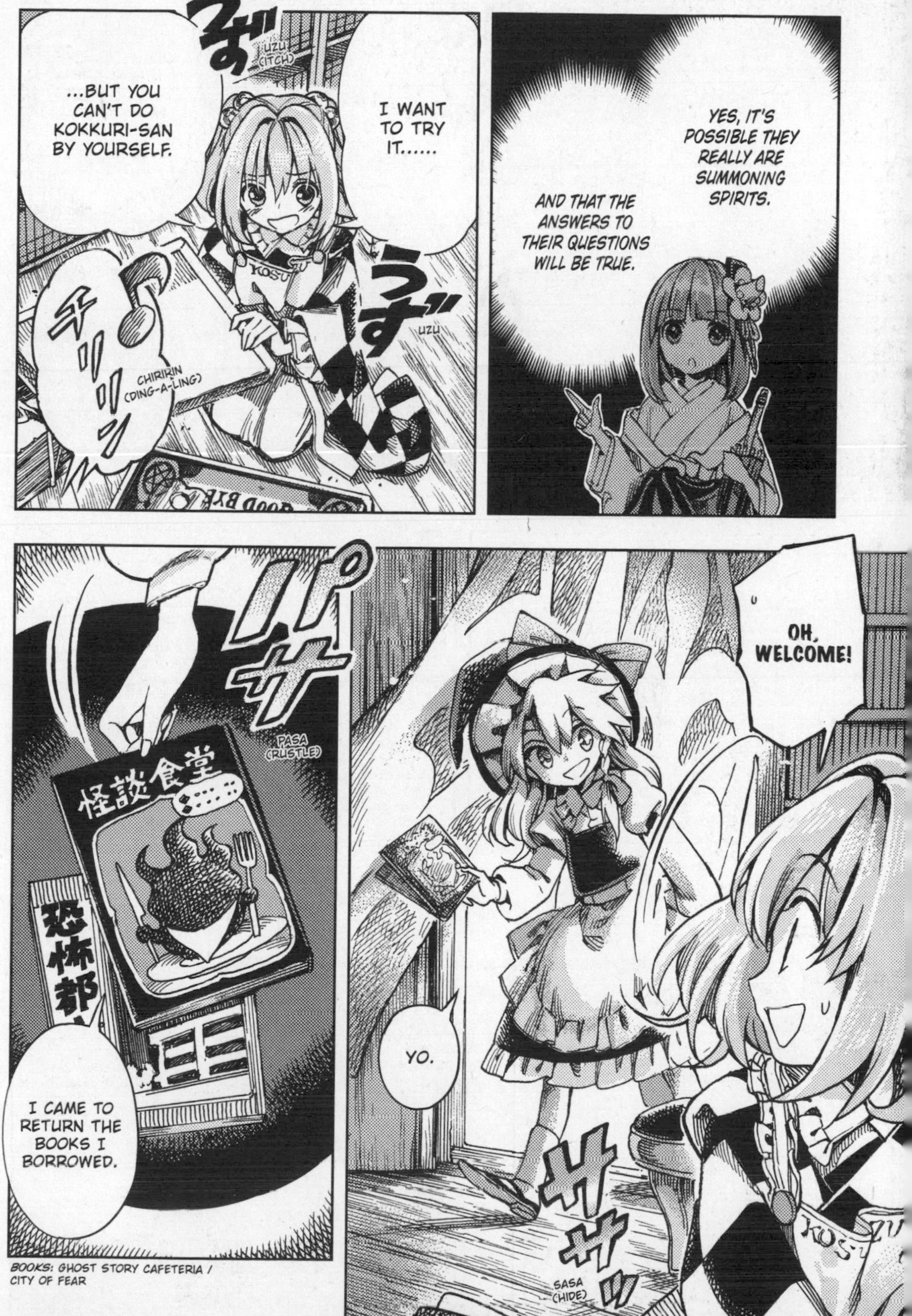
YES, IT'S POSSIBLE THEY REALLY ARE SUMMONING SPIRITS.
AND THAT THE ANSWERS TO THEIR QUESTIONS WILL BE TRUE.
うず
UZU (ITCH)
I WANT TO TRY IT......
...BUT YOU CAN'T DO KOKKURI-SAN BY YOURSELF.
うず
UZU
チリリン
CHIRIRIN (DING-A-LING)
GOOD BYE
OH, WELCOME!
YO.
ササッ
SASA (HIDE)
パサ
PASA (RUSTLE)
怪談食堂
恐怖都
I CAME TO RETURN THE BOOKS I BORROWED.

BOOKS: GHOST STORY CAFETERIA / CITY OF FEAR

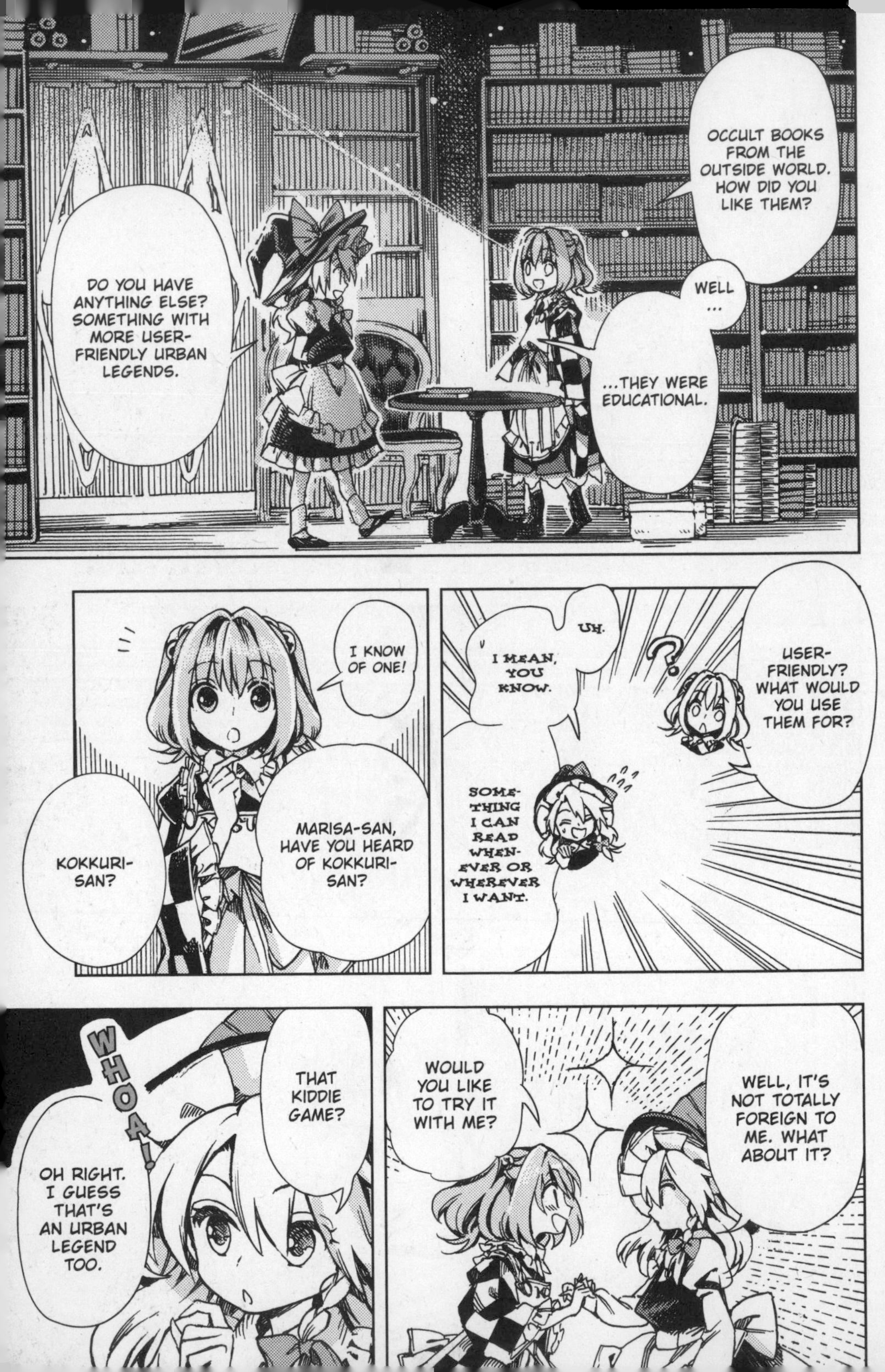
OCCULT BOOKS FROM THE OUTSIDE WORLD. HOW DID YOU LIKE THEM?
WELL ...
...THEY WERE EDUCATIONAL.
DO YOU HAVE ANYTHING ELSE? SOMETHING WITH MORE USER-FRIENDLY URBAN LEGENDS.
USER-FRIENDLY? WHAT WOULD YOU USE THEM FOR?
UH.
I MEAN, YOU KNOW.
SOMETHING I CAN READ WHENEVER OR WHEREVER I WANT.
I KNOW OF ONE!
MARISA-SAN, HAVE YOU HEARD OF KOKKURI-SAN?
KOKKURI-SAN?
WELL, IT'S NOT TOTALLY FOREIGN TO ME. WHAT ABOUT IT?
WOULD YOU LIKE TO TRY IT WITH ME?
WHOA!
THAT KIDDIE GAME?
OH RIGHT. I GUESS THAT'S AN URBAN LEGEND TOO.

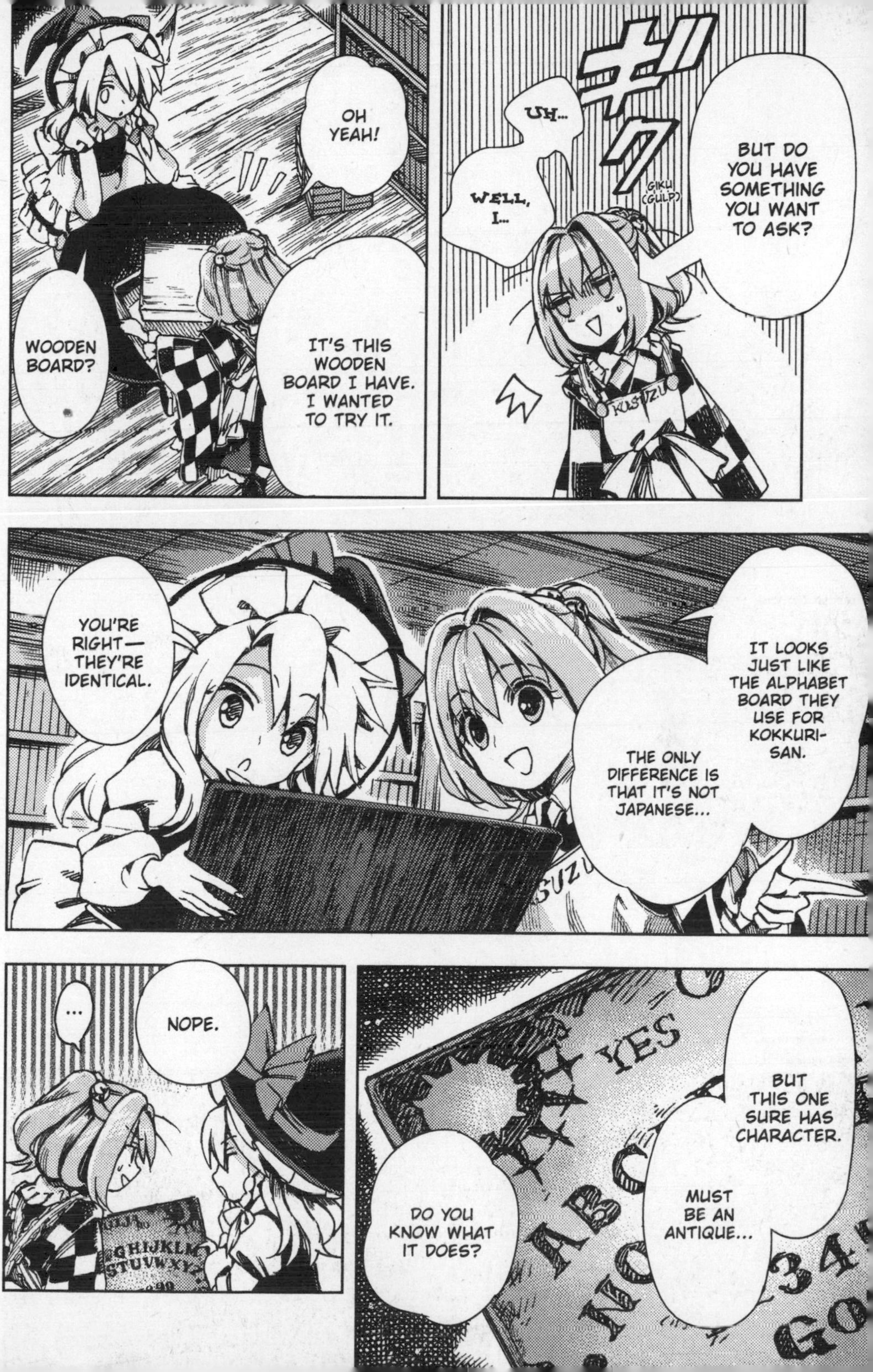
BUT DO YOU HAVE SOMETHING YOU WANT TO ASK?
GIKU (GULP)
UH...
WELL, I...
OH YEAH!
IT'S THIS WOODEN BOARD I HAVE. I WANTED TO TRY IT.
WOODEN BOARD?
IT LOOKS JUST LIKE THE ALPHABET BOARD THEY USE FOR KOKKURI-SAN.
THE ONLY DIFFERENCE IS THAT IT'S NOT JAPANESE...
YOU'RE RIGHT— THEY'RE IDENTICAL.
BUT THIS ONE SURE HAS CHARACTER.
MUST BE AN ANTIQUE...
DO YOU KNOW WHAT IT DOES?
YES
NOPE.
...

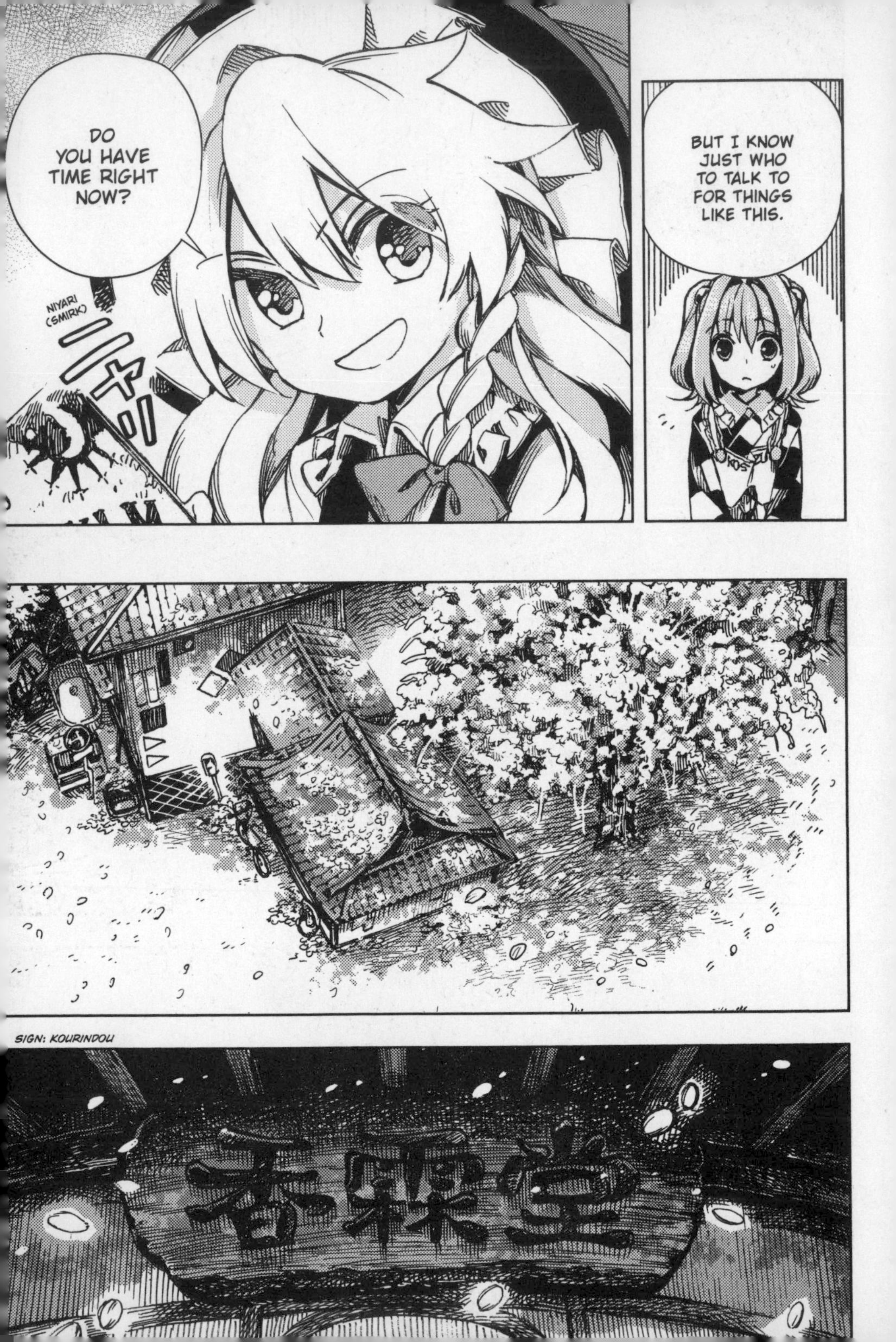
BUT I KNOW JUST WHO TO TALK TO FOR THINGS LIKE THIS.
DO YOU HAVE TIME RIGHT NOW?
NIYARI (SMIRK)
ニヤッ
SIGN: KOURINDOU

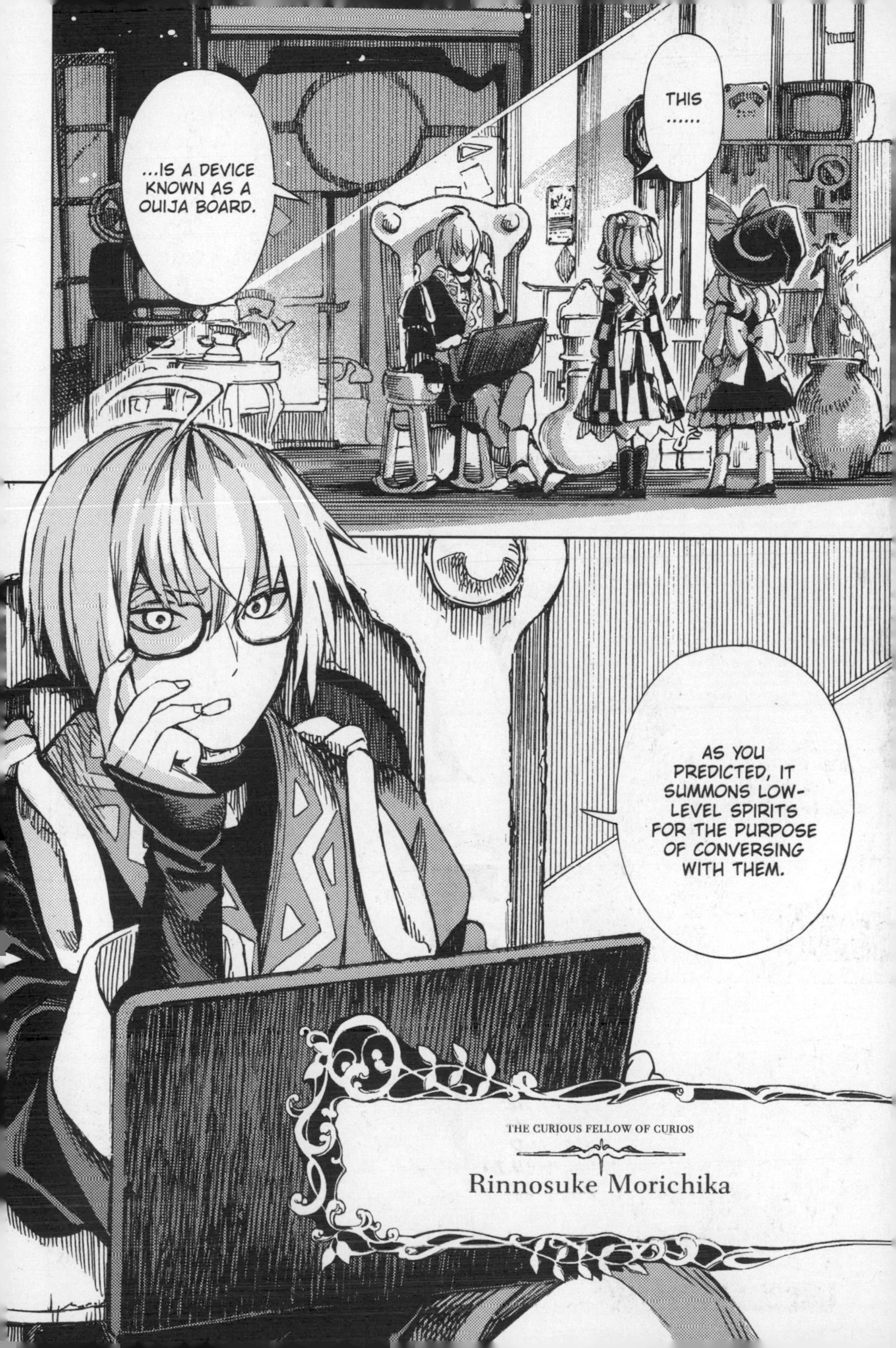
THIS ......
...IS A DEVICE KNOWN AS A OUIJA BOARD.
AS YOU PREDICTED, IT SUMMONS LOW-LEVEL SPIRITS FOR THE PURPOSE OF CONVERSING WITH THEM.
THE CURIOUS FELLOW OF CURIOS
Rinnosuke Morichika

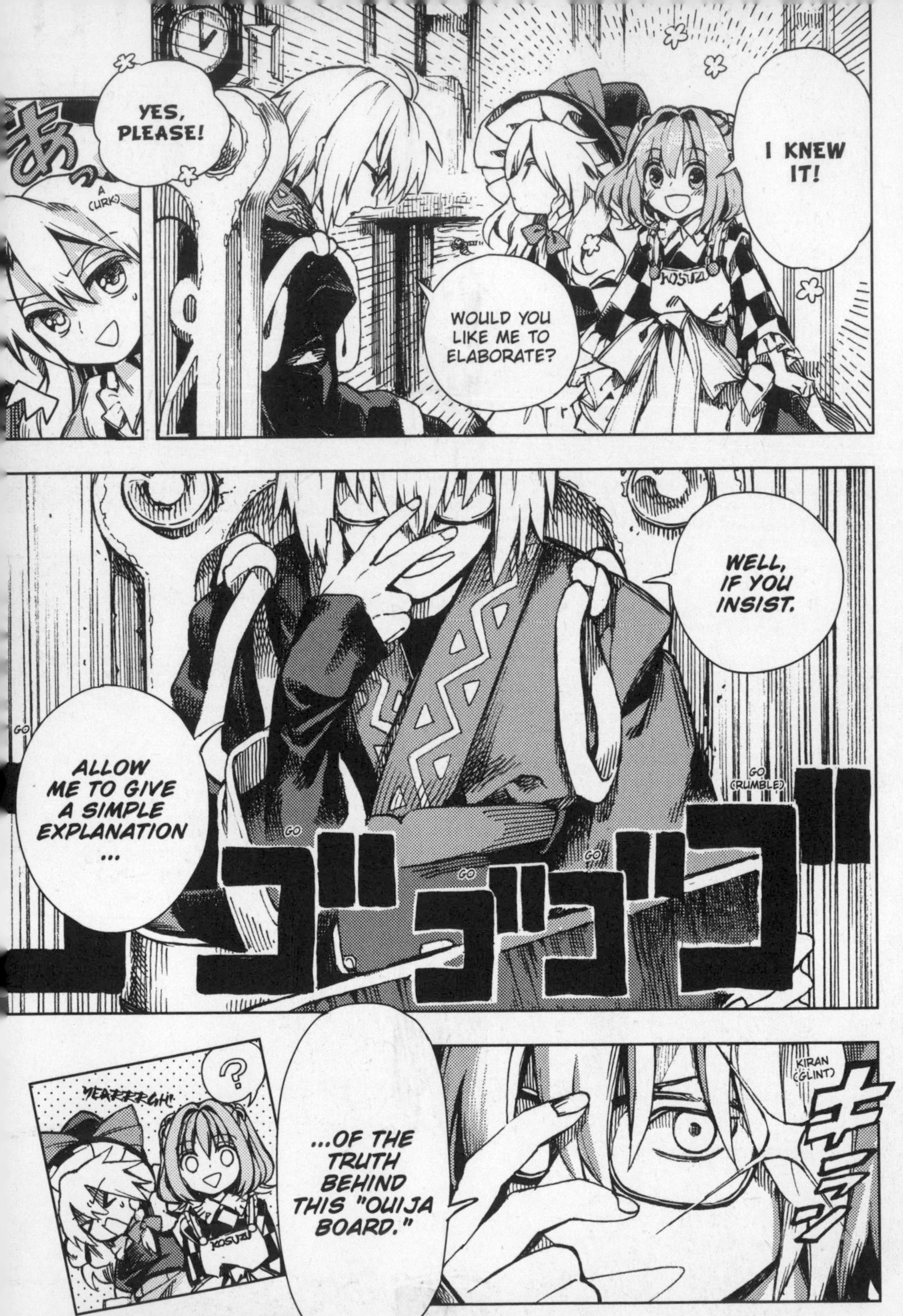
I KNEW IT!
WOULD YOU LIKE ME TO ELABORATE?
YES, PLEASE!
あっ
A (URK)
WELL, IF YOU INSIST.
GO (RUMBLE)
ゴゴゴゴ
GO
GO
GO
GO
ALLOW ME TO GIVE A SIMPLE EXPLANATION ...
KIRAN (GLINT)
キラン
...OF THE TRUTH BEHIND THIS "OUIJA BOARD."
?
YEARRRGH!
KOSUZU

Chapter 26 To be continued

Forbidden Scrollery

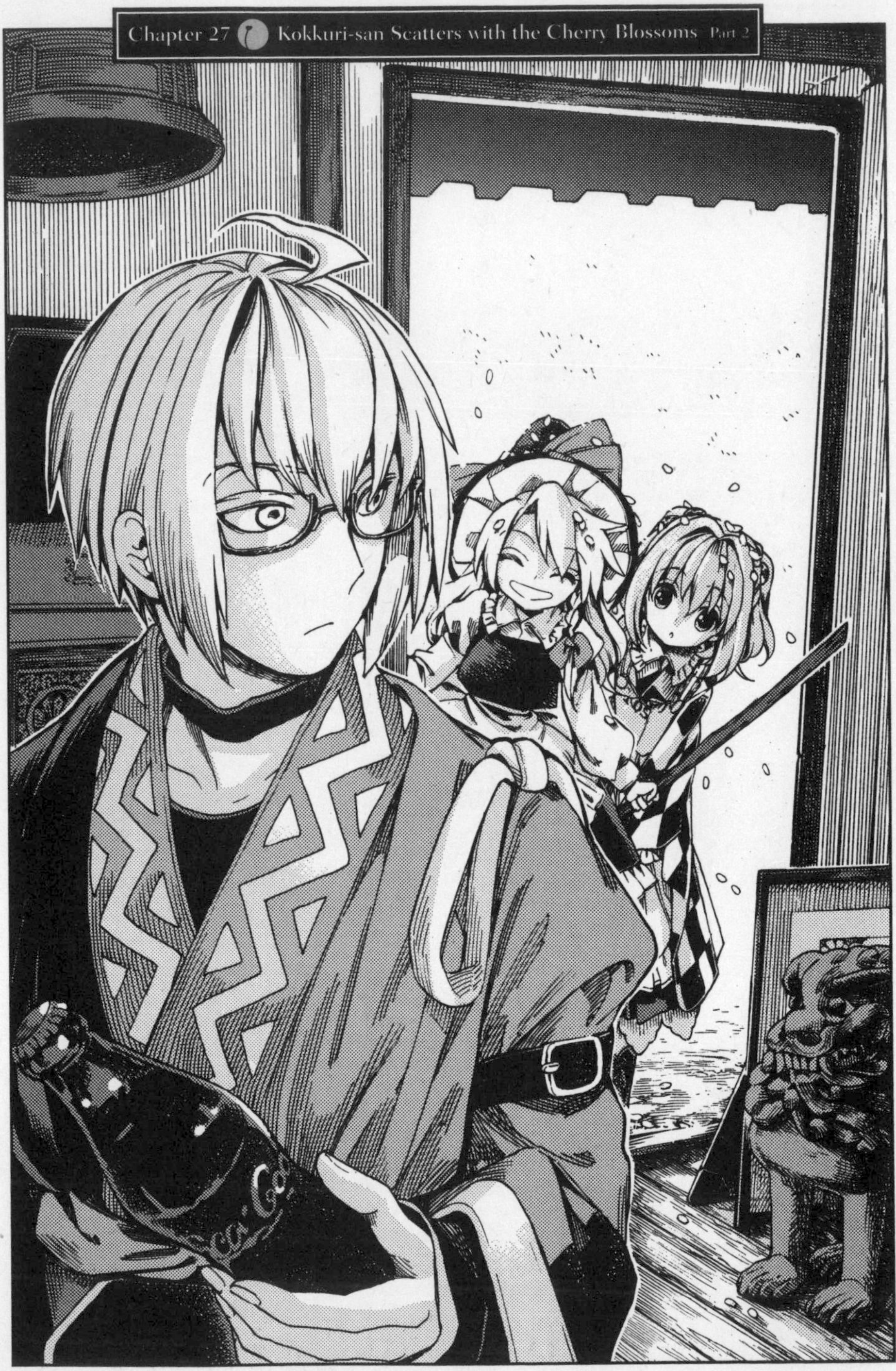
Chapter 27 Kokkuri-san Scatters with the Cherry Blossoms Part 2

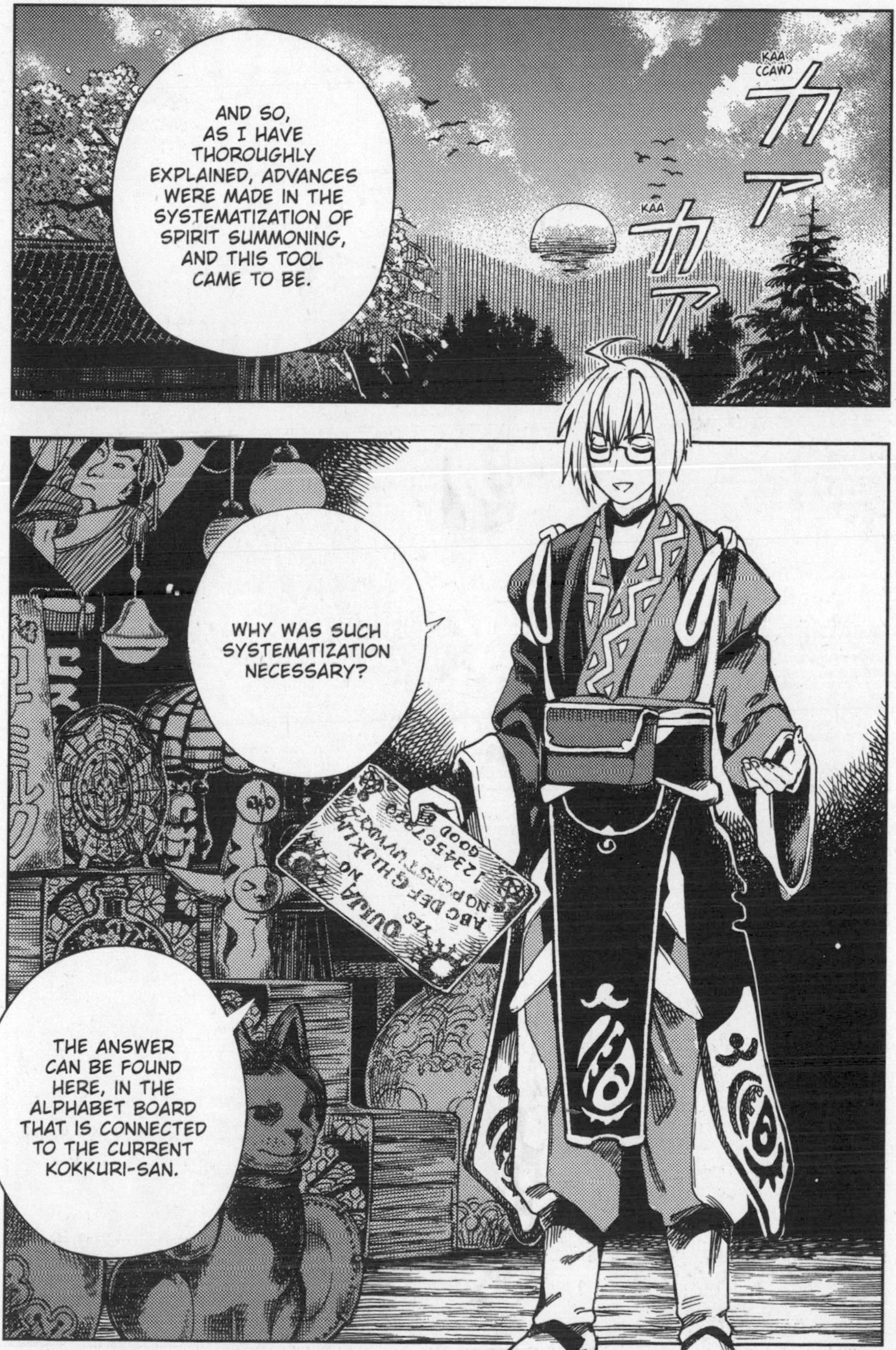
KAA (CAW)
カア
KAA
カア
AND SO, AS I HAVE THOROUGHLY EXPLAINED, ADVANCES WERE MADE IN THE SYSTEMATIZATION OF SPIRIT SUMMONING, AND THIS TOOL CAME TO BE.
WHY WAS SUCH SYSTEMATIZATION NECESSARY?
THE ANSWER CAN BE FOUND HERE, IN THE ALPHABET BOARD THAT IS CONNECTED TO THE CURRENT KOKKURI-SAN.

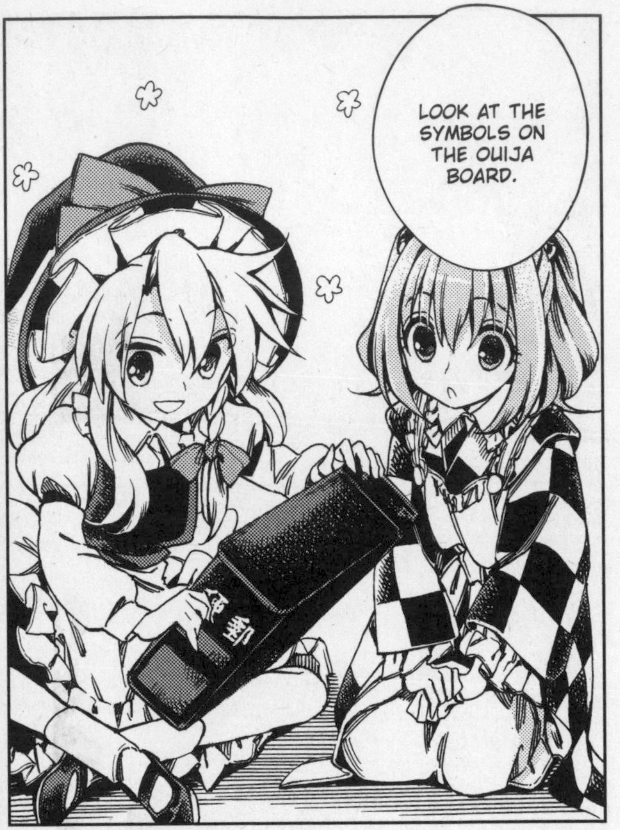
LOOK AT THE SYMBOLS ON THE OUIJA BOARD.
BOX: POST

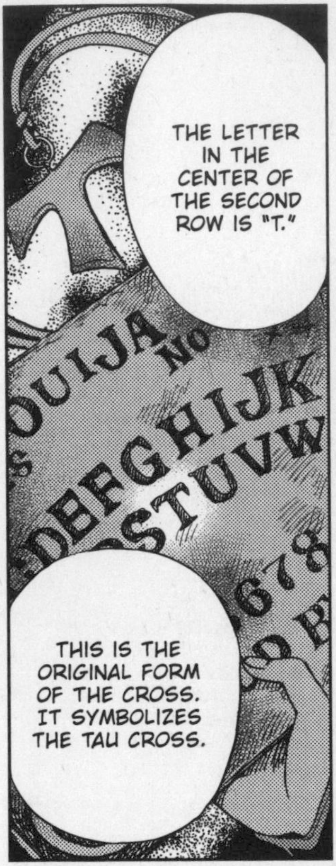
THE LETTER IN THE CENTER OF THE SECOND ROW IS "T."
OUIJA
NO
THIS IS THE ORIGINAL FORM OF THE CROSS. IT SYMBOLIZES THE TAU CROSS.

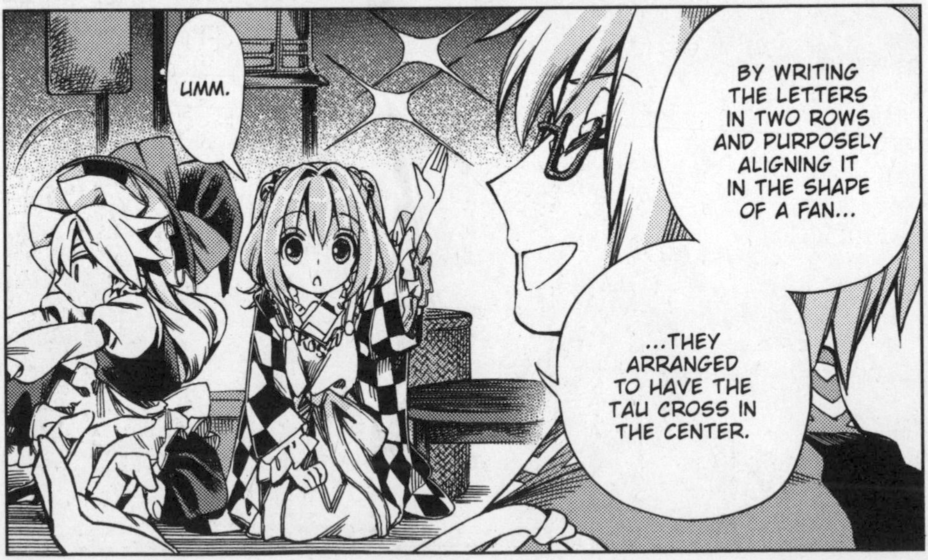
BY WRITING THE LETTERS IN TWO ROWS AND PURPOSELY ALIGNING IT IN THE SHAPE OF A FAN...
UMM.
...THEY ARRANGED TO HAVE THE TAU CROSS IN THE CENTER.

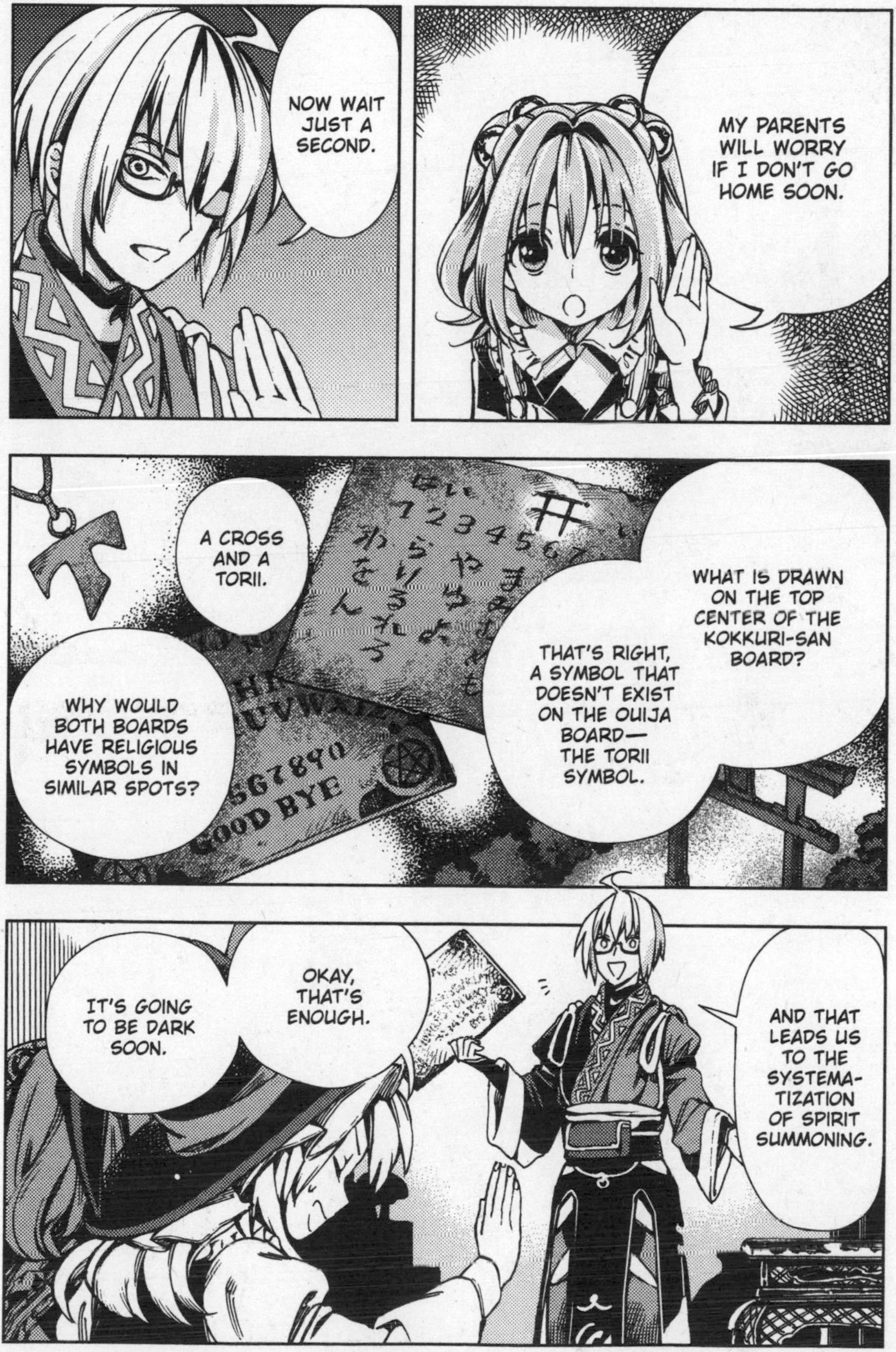
MY PARENTS WILL WORRY IF I DON'T GO HOME SOON.
NOW WAIT JUST A SECOND.
WHAT IS DRAWN ON THE TOP CENTER OF THE KOKKURI-SAN BOARD?
THAT'S RIGHT, A SYMBOL THAT DOESN'T EXIST ON THE OUIJA BOARD— THE TORII SYMBOL.
A CROSS AND A TORII.
WHY WOULD BOTH BOARDS HAVE RELIGIOUS SYMBOLS IN SIMILAR SPOTS?
GOOD BYE
AND THAT LEADS US TO THE SYSTEMA-TIZATION OF SPIRIT SUMMONING.
OKAY, THAT'S ENOUGH.
IT'S GOING TO BE DARK SOON.

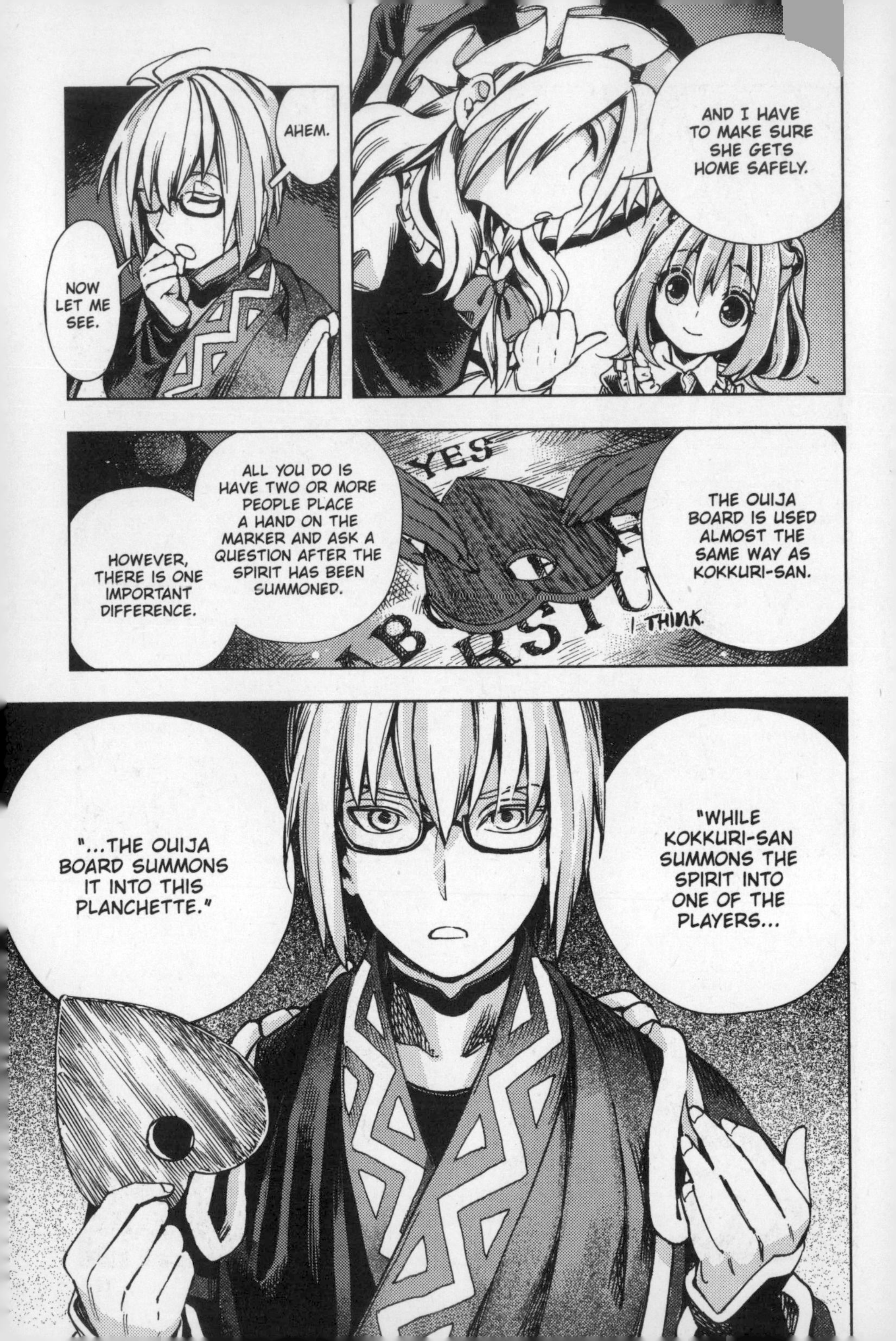
AND I HAVE TO MAKE SURE SHE GETS HOME SAFELY.
AHEM.
NOW LET ME SEE.
THE OUIJA BOARD IS USED ALMOST THE SAME WAY AS KOKKURI-SAN.
I THINK.
YES
ALL YOU DO IS HAVE TWO OR MORE PEOPLE PLACE A HAND ON THE MARKER AND ASK A QUESTION AFTER THE SPIRIT HAS BEEN SUMMONED.
HOWEVER, THERE IS ONE IMPORTANT DIFFERENCE.
"WHILE KOKKURI-SAN SUMMONS THE SPIRIT INTO ONE OF THE PLAYERS...
"...THE OUIJA BOARD SUMMONS IT INTO THIS PLANCHETTE."

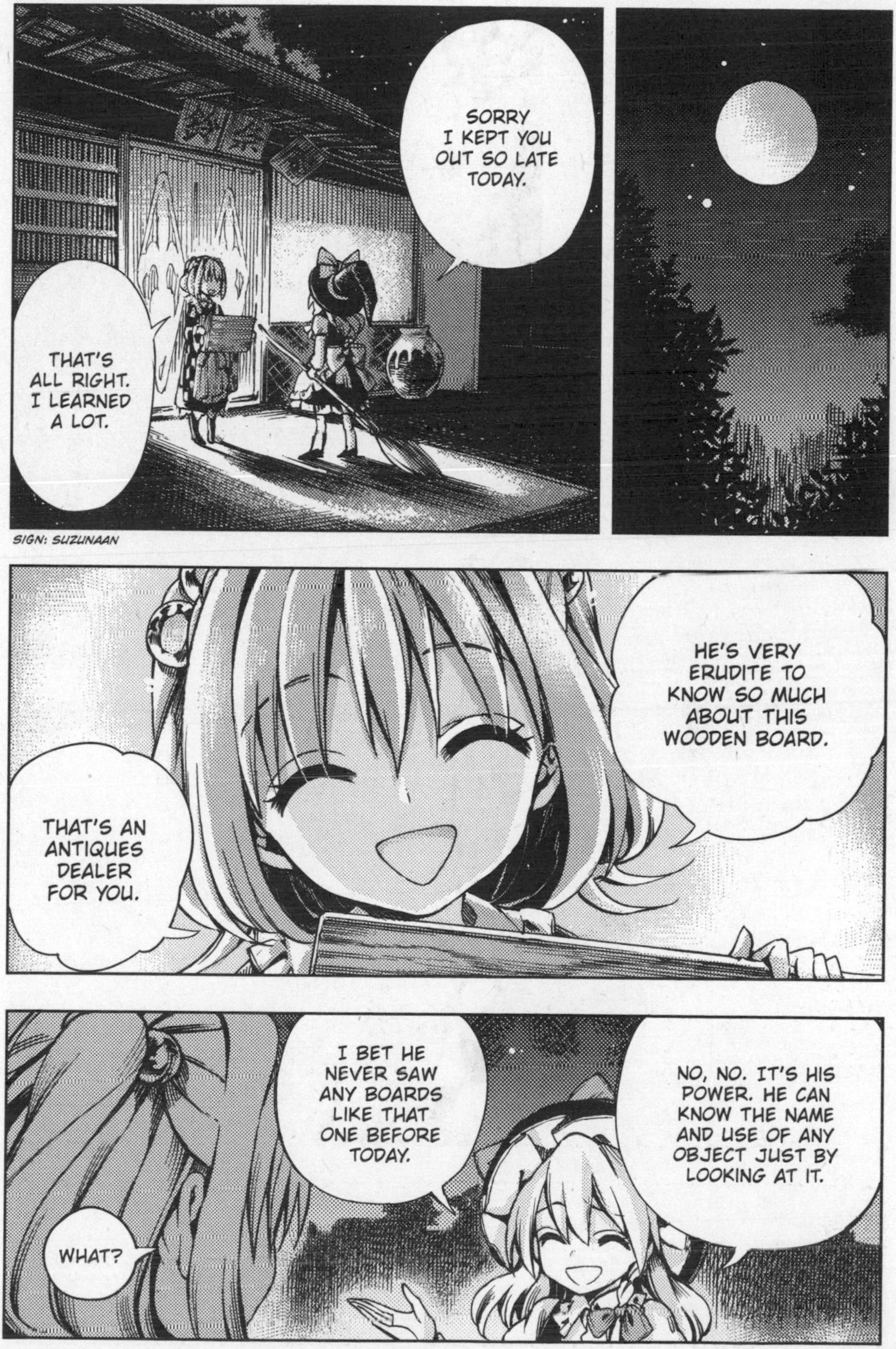
SORRY I KEPT YOU OUT SO LATE TODAY.
THAT'S ALL RIGHT. I LEARNED A LOT.
SIGN: SUZUNAAN
HE'S VERY ERUDITE TO KNOW SO MUCH ABOUT THIS WOODEN BOARD.
THAT'S AN ANTIQUES DEALER FOR YOU.
NO, NO. IT'S HIS POWER. HE CAN KNOW THE NAME AND USE OF ANY OBJECT JUST BY LOOKING AT IT.
I BET HE NEVER SAW ANY BOARDS LIKE THAT ONE BEFORE TODAY.
WHAT?

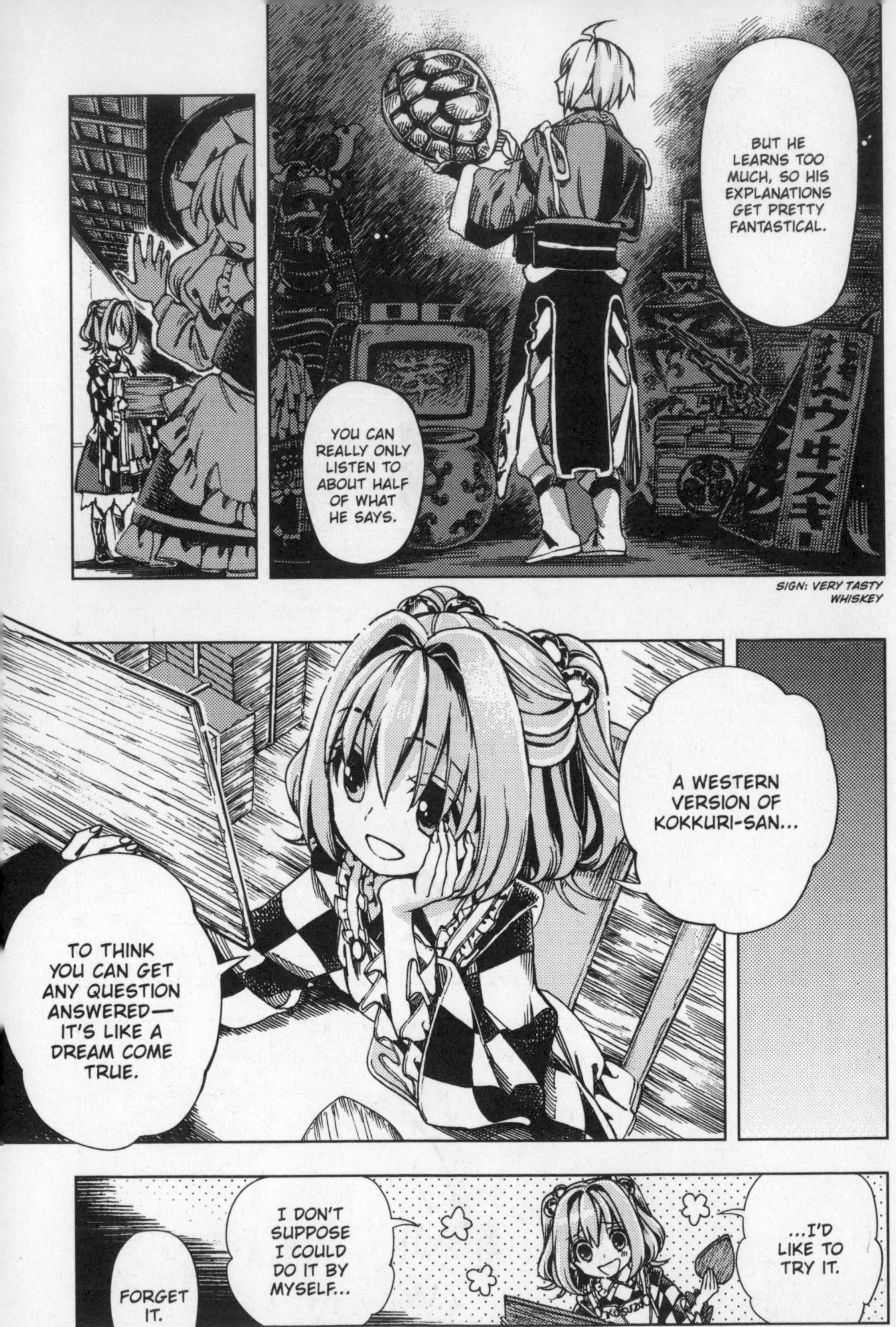
BUT HE LEARNS TOO MUCH, SO HIS EXPLANATIONS GET PRETTY FANTASTICAL.
YOU CAN REALLY ONLY LISTEN TO ABOUT HALF OF WHAT HE SAYS.
SIGN: VERY TASTY WHISKEY
A WESTERN VERSION OF KOKKURI-SAN...
TO THINK YOU CAN GET ANY QUESTION ANSWERED— IT'S LIKE A DREAM COME TRUE.
...I'D LIKE TO TRY IT.
I DON'T SUPPOSE I COULD DO IT BY MYSELF...
FORGET IT.

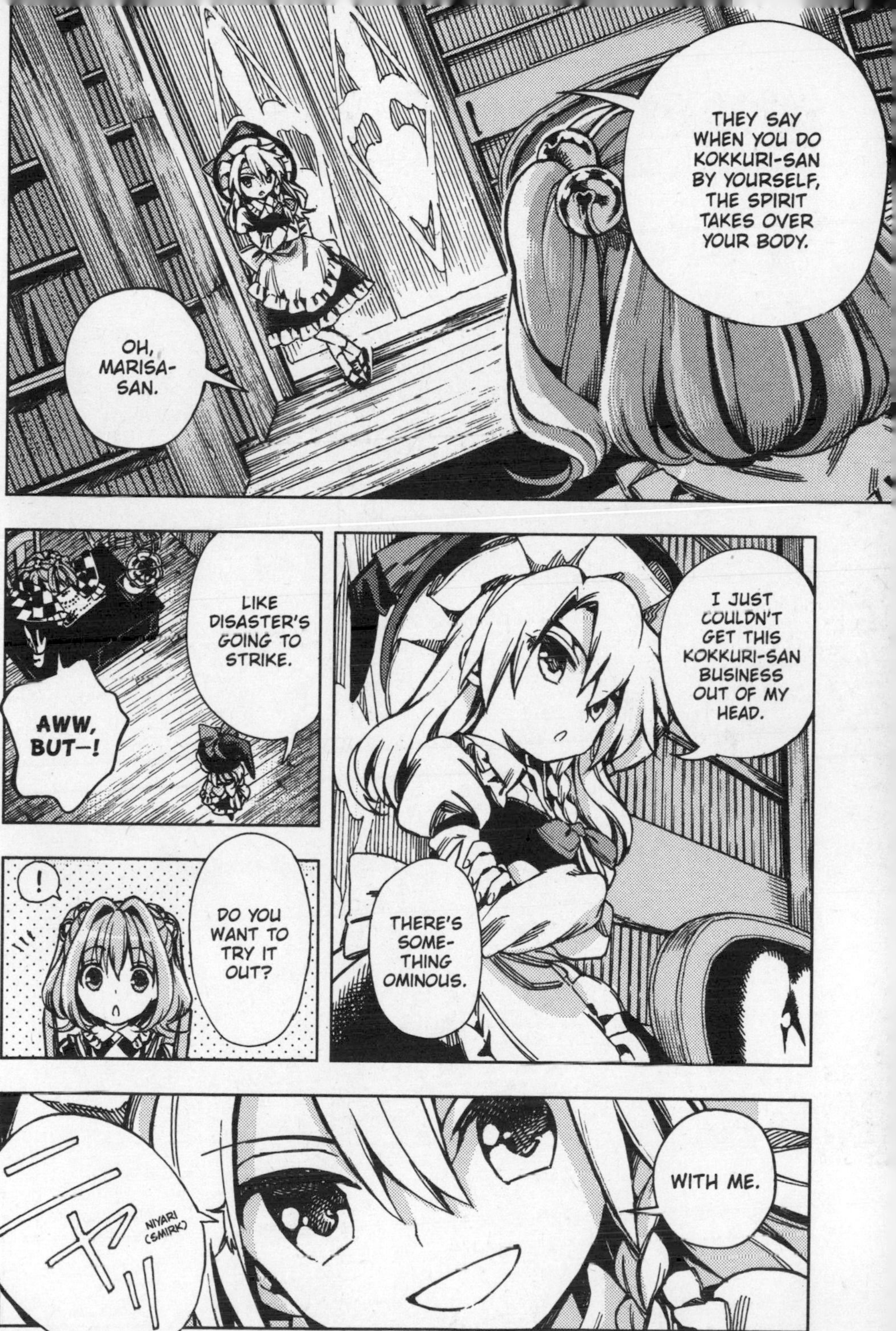
THEY SAY WHEN YOU DO KOKKURI-SAN BY YOURSELF, THE SPIRIT TAKES OVER YOUR BODY.
OH, MARISA-SAN.
I JUST COULDN'T GET THIS KOKKURI-SAN BUSINESS OUT OF MY HEAD.
THERE'S SOME-THING OMINOUS.
LIKE DISASTER'S GOING TO STRIKE.
AWW, BUT—!
!
DO YOU WANT TO TRY IT OUT?
WITH ME.
ニヤッ
NIYARI (SMIRK)

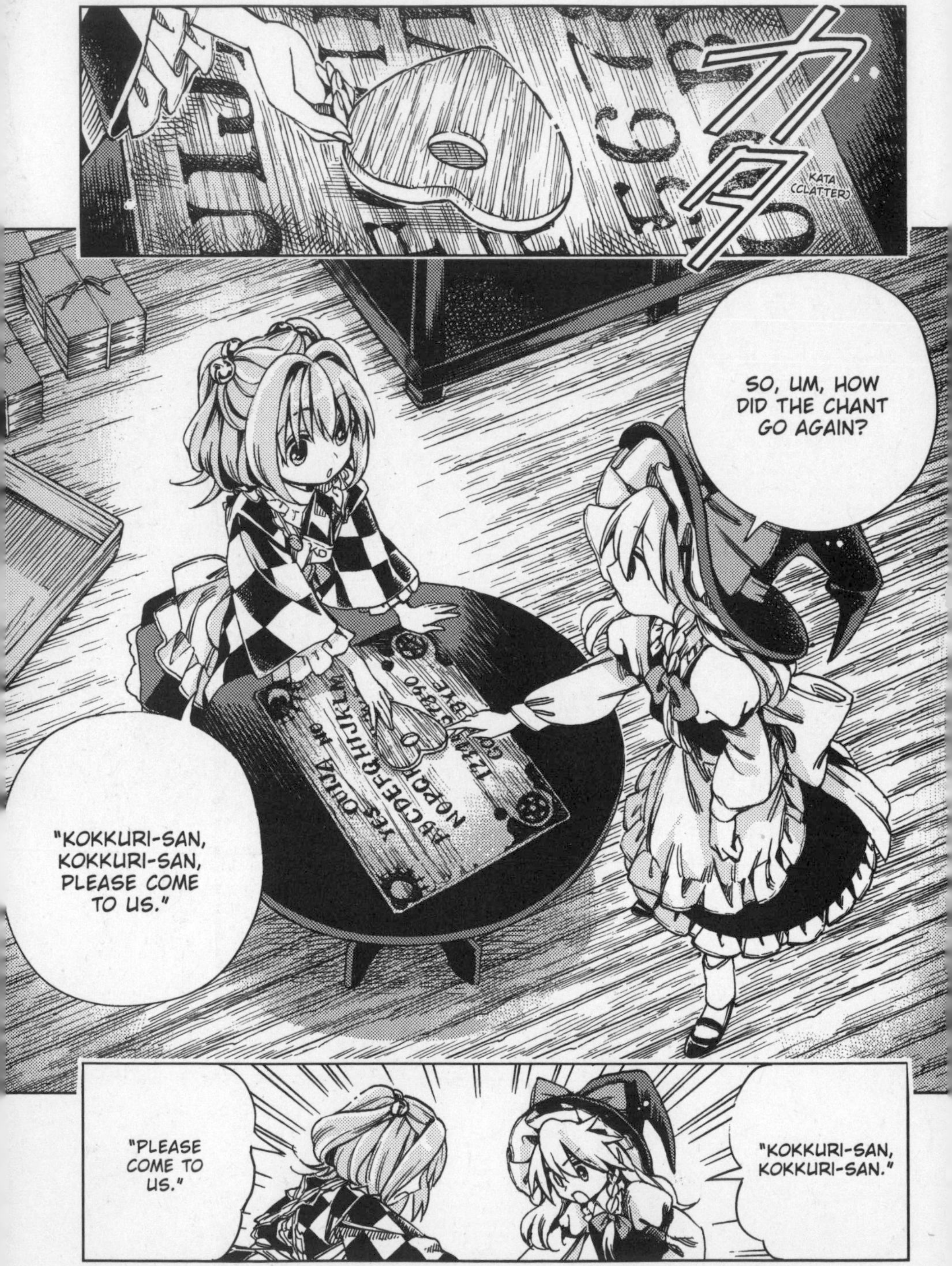
KATA
(CLATTER)
SO, UM, HOW DID THE CHANT GO AGAIN?
"KOKKURI-SAN, KOKKURI-SAN, PLEASE COME TO US."
"KOKKURI-SAN, KOKKURI-SAN."
"PLEASE COME TO US."

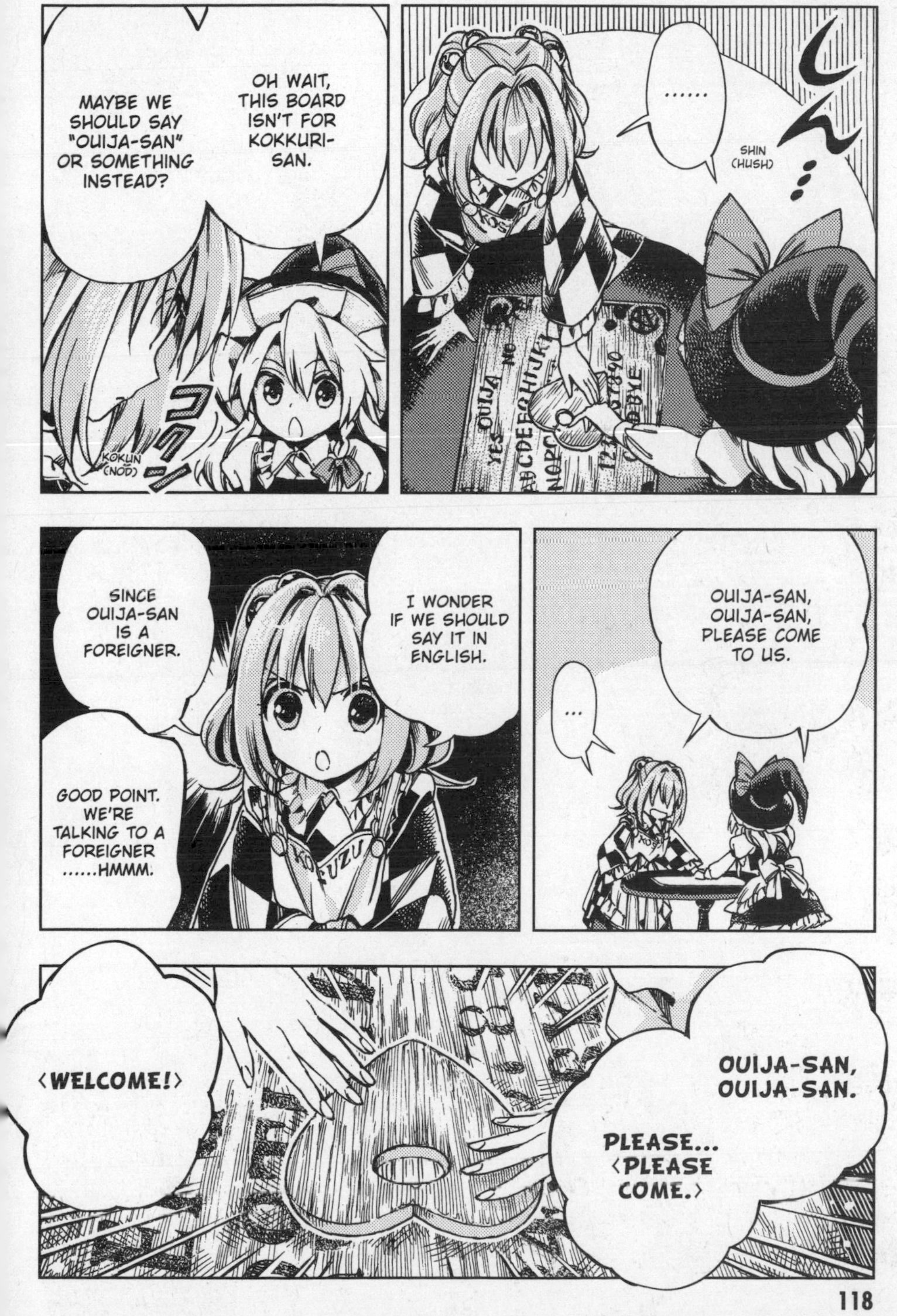
......
SHIN (HUSH)
OH WAIT, THIS BOARD ISN'T FOR KOKKURI-SAN.
MAYBE WE SHOULD SAY "OUIJA-SAN" OR SOMETHING INSTEAD?
KOKUN (NOD)
OUIJA-SAN, OUIJA-SAN, PLEASE COME TO US.
...
I WONDER IF WE SHOULD SAY IT IN ENGLISH.
SINCE OUIJA-SAN IS A FOREIGNER.
GOOD POINT. WE'RE TALKING TO A FOREIGNER ......HMMM.
OUIJA-SAN, OUIJA-SAN.
PLEASE... ‹PLEASE COME.›
‹WELCOME!›

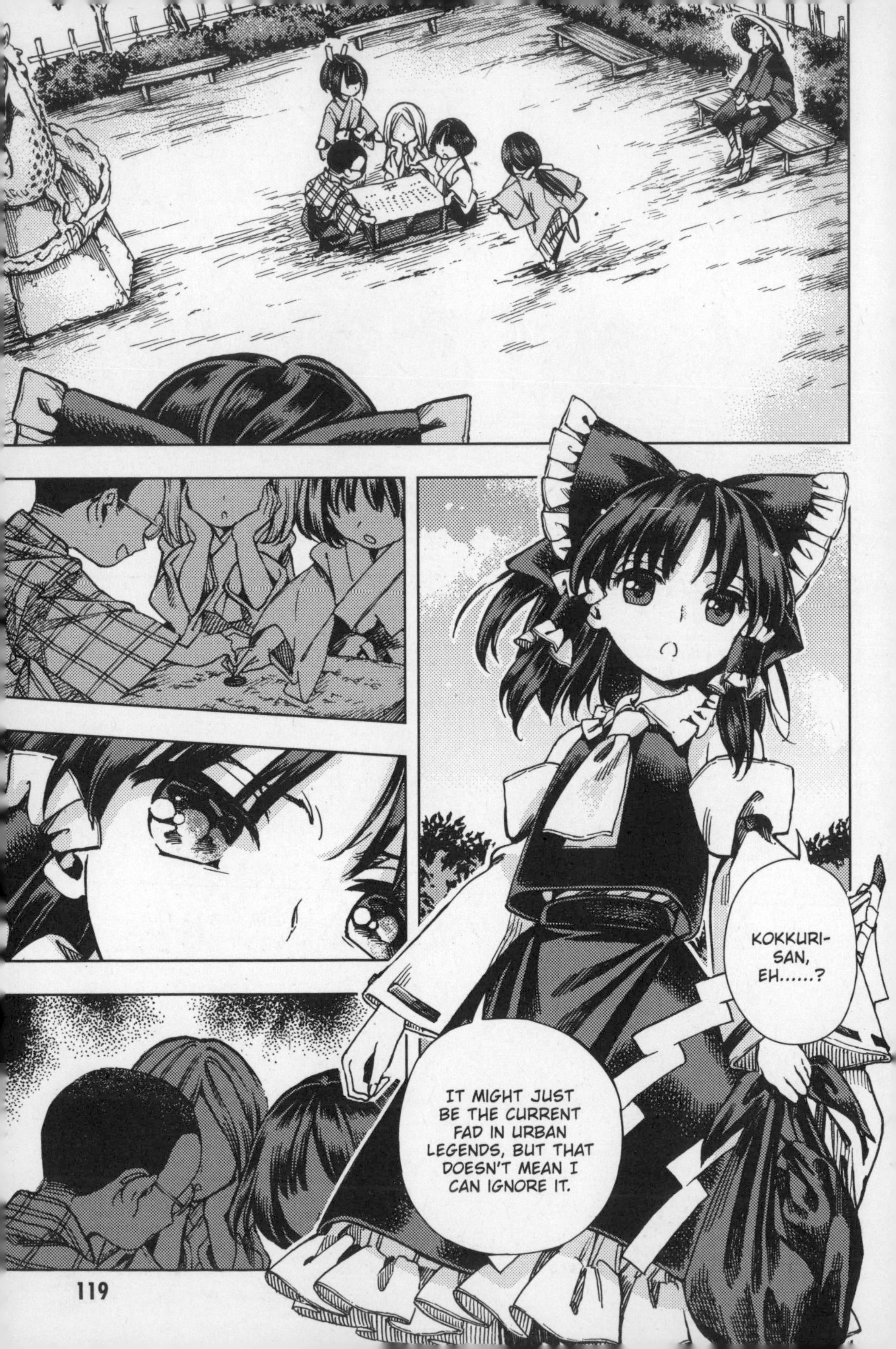
KOKKURI-SAN, EH......?
IT MIGHT JUST BE THE CURRENT FAD IN URBAN LEGENDS, BUT THAT DOESN'T MEAN I CAN IGNORE IT.

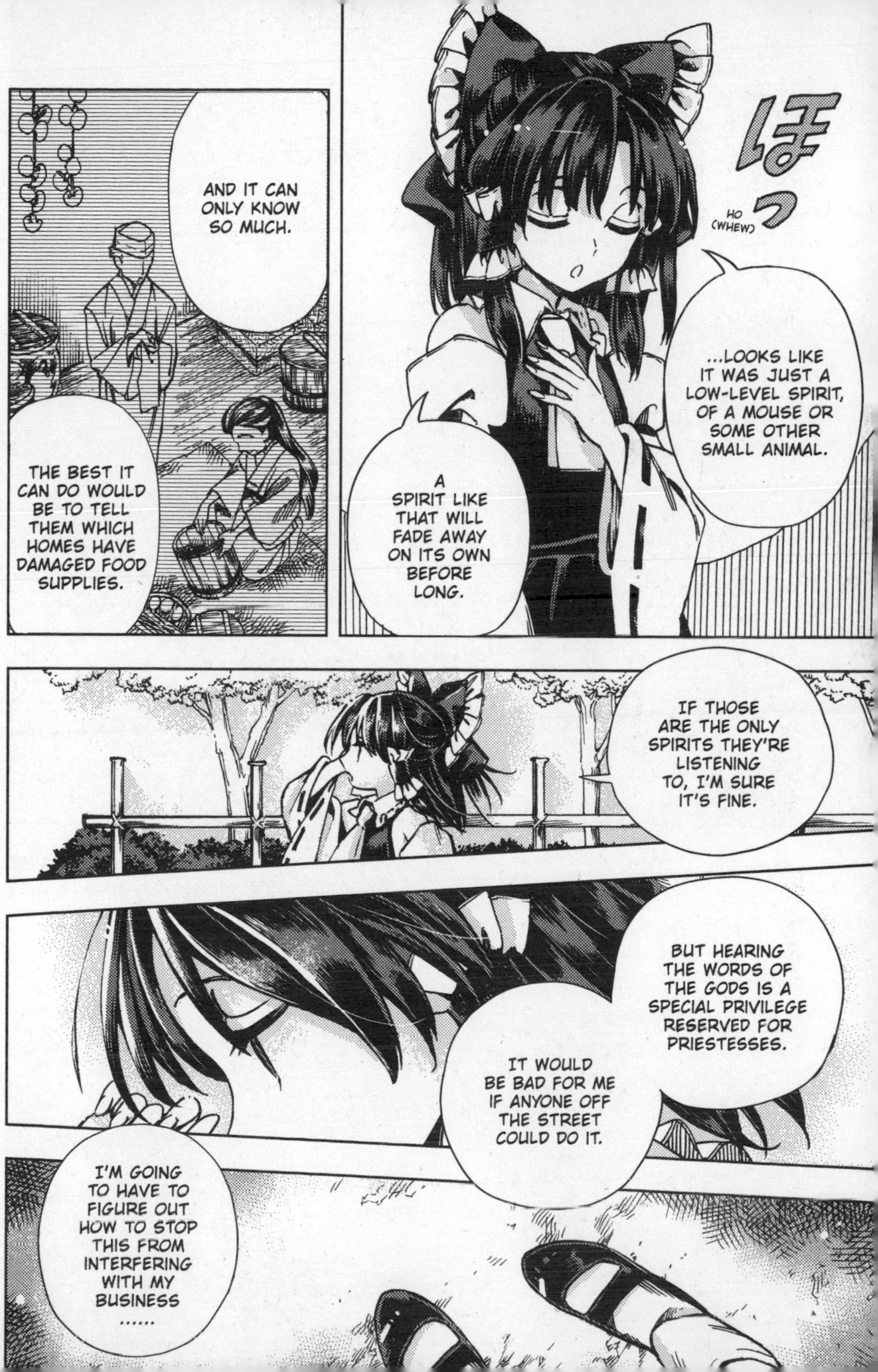
ほっ
HO (WHEW)
...LOOKS LIKE IT WAS JUST A LOW-LEVEL SPIRIT, OF A MOUSE OR SOME OTHER SMALL ANIMAL.
A SPIRIT LIKE THAT WILL FADE AWAY ON ITS OWN BEFORE LONG.
AND IT CAN ONLY KNOW SO MUCH.
THE BEST IT CAN DO WOULD BE TO TELL THEM WHICH HOMES HAVE DAMAGED FOOD SUPPLIES.
IF THOSE ARE THE ONLY SPIRITS THEY'RE LISTENING TO, I'M SURE IT'S FINE.
BUT HEARING THE WORDS OF THE GODS IS A SPECIAL PRIVILEGE RESERVED FOR PRIESTESSES.
IT WOULD BE BAD FOR ME IF ANYONE OFF THE STREET COULD DO IT.
I'M GOING TO HAVE TO FIGURE OUT HOW TO STOP THIS FROM INTERFERING WITH MY BUSINESS ......

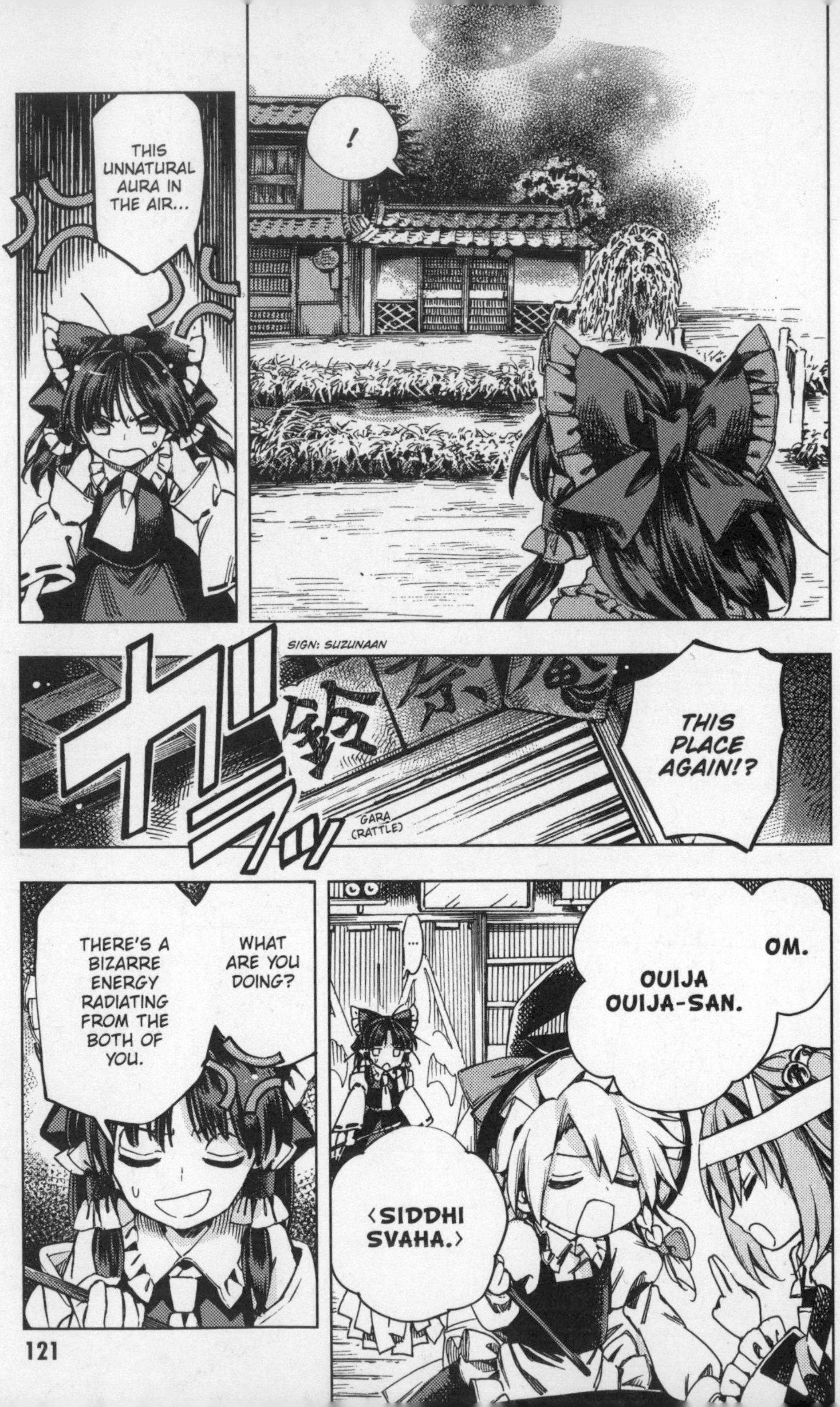
!
THIS UNNATURAL AURA IN THE AIR...
SIGN: SUZUNAAN
GARA (RATTLE)
THIS PLACE AGAIN!?
OM.
OUIJA OUIJA-SAN.
...
‹SIDDHI SVAHA.›
WHAT ARE YOU DOING?
THERE'S A BIZARRE ENERGY RADIATING FROM THE BOTH OF YOU.

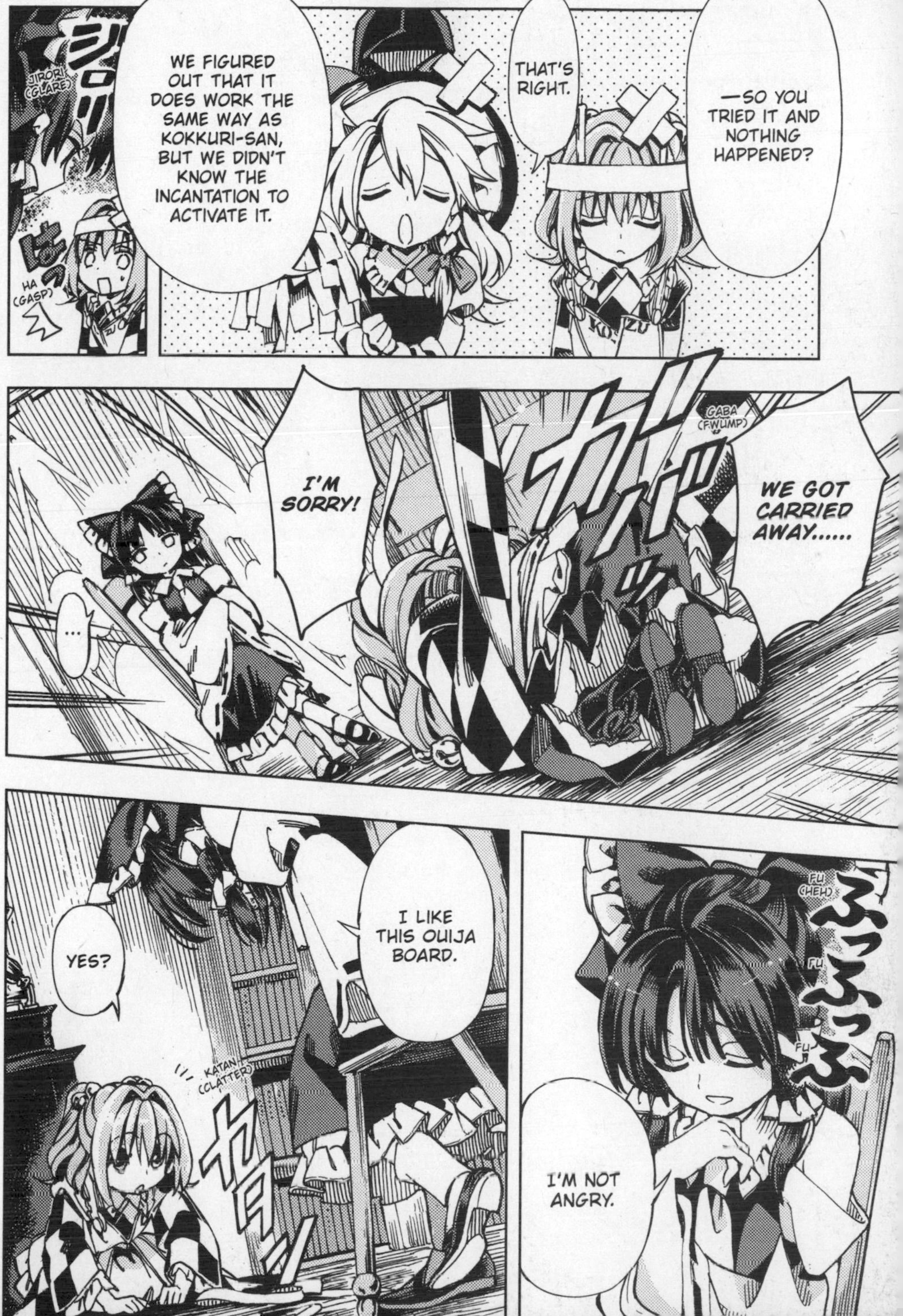
—SO YOU TRIED IT AND NOTHING HAPPENED?
THAT'S RIGHT.
WE FIGURED OUT THAT IT DOES WORK THE SAME WAY AS KOKKURI-SAN, BUT WE DIDN'T KNOW THE INCANTATION TO ACTIVATE IT.
JIRORI (GLARE)
HA (GASP)
WE GOT CARRIED AWAY......
GABA (FWUMP)
I'M SORRY!
...
FU (HEH)
FU
FU
I'M NOT ANGRY.
I LIKE THIS OUIJA BOARD.
YES?
KATAN (CLATTER)

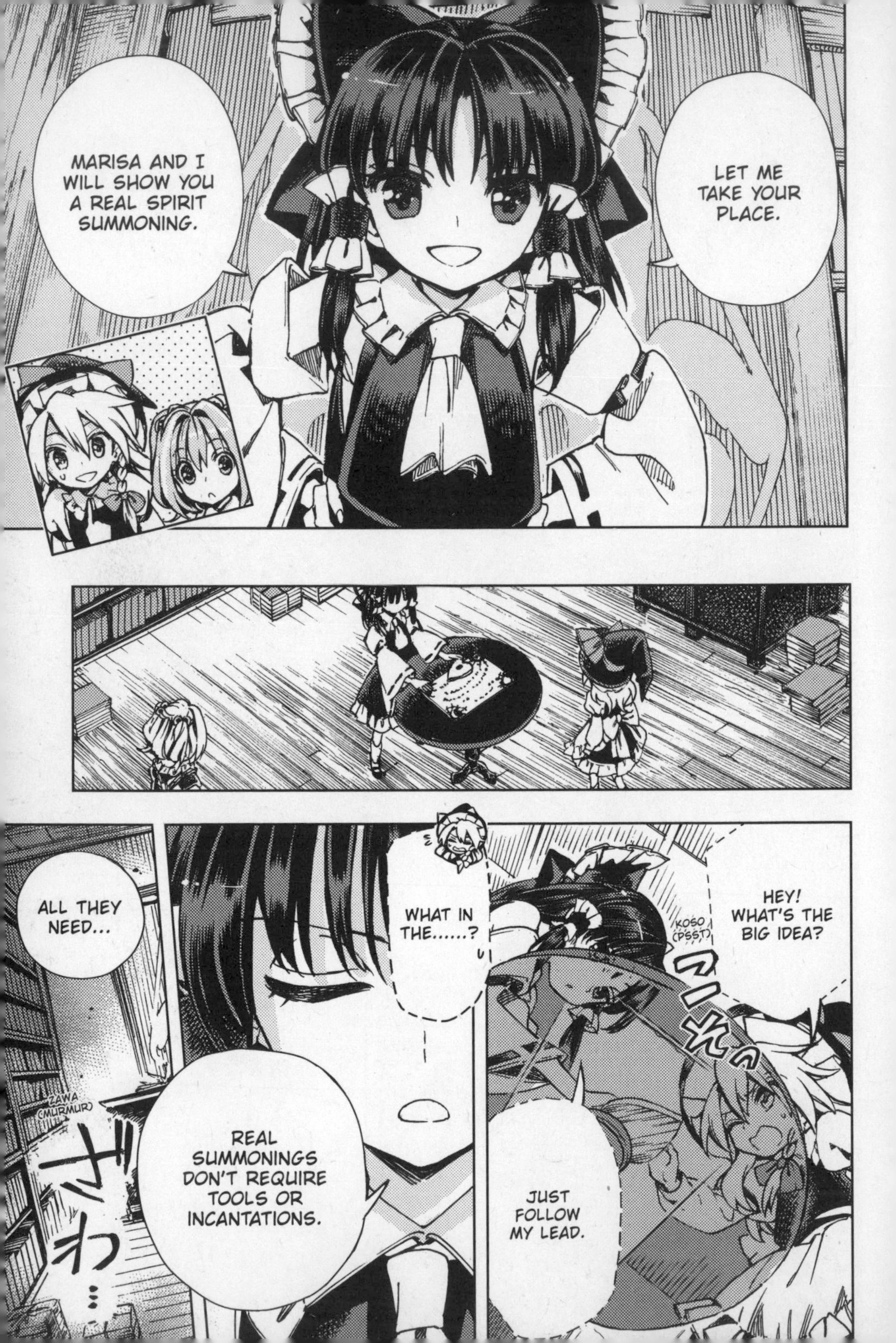
LET ME TAKE YOUR PLACE.
MARISA AND I WILL SHOW YOU A REAL SPIRIT SUMMONING.
HEY! WHAT'S THE BIG IDEA?
KOSO (PSST)
WHAT IN THE......?
JUST FOLLOW MY LEAD.
REAL SUMMONINGS DON'T REQUIRE TOOLS OR INCANTATIONS.
ALL THEY NEED...
ZAWA (MURMUR)

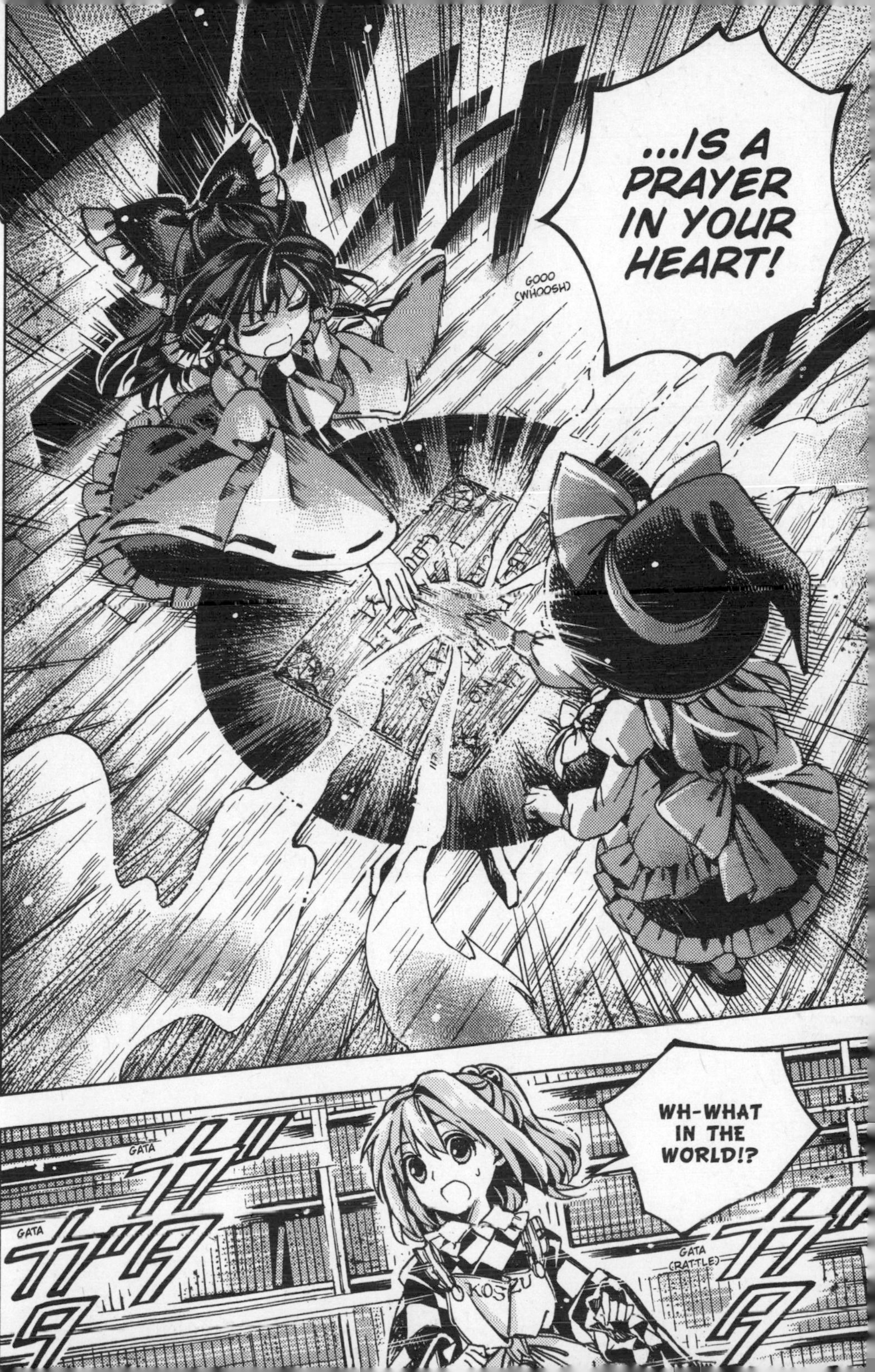
...IS A PRAYER IN YOUR HEART!
GOOO (WHOOSH)
WH-WHAT IN THE WORLD!?
GATA (RATTLE)
GATA
GATA

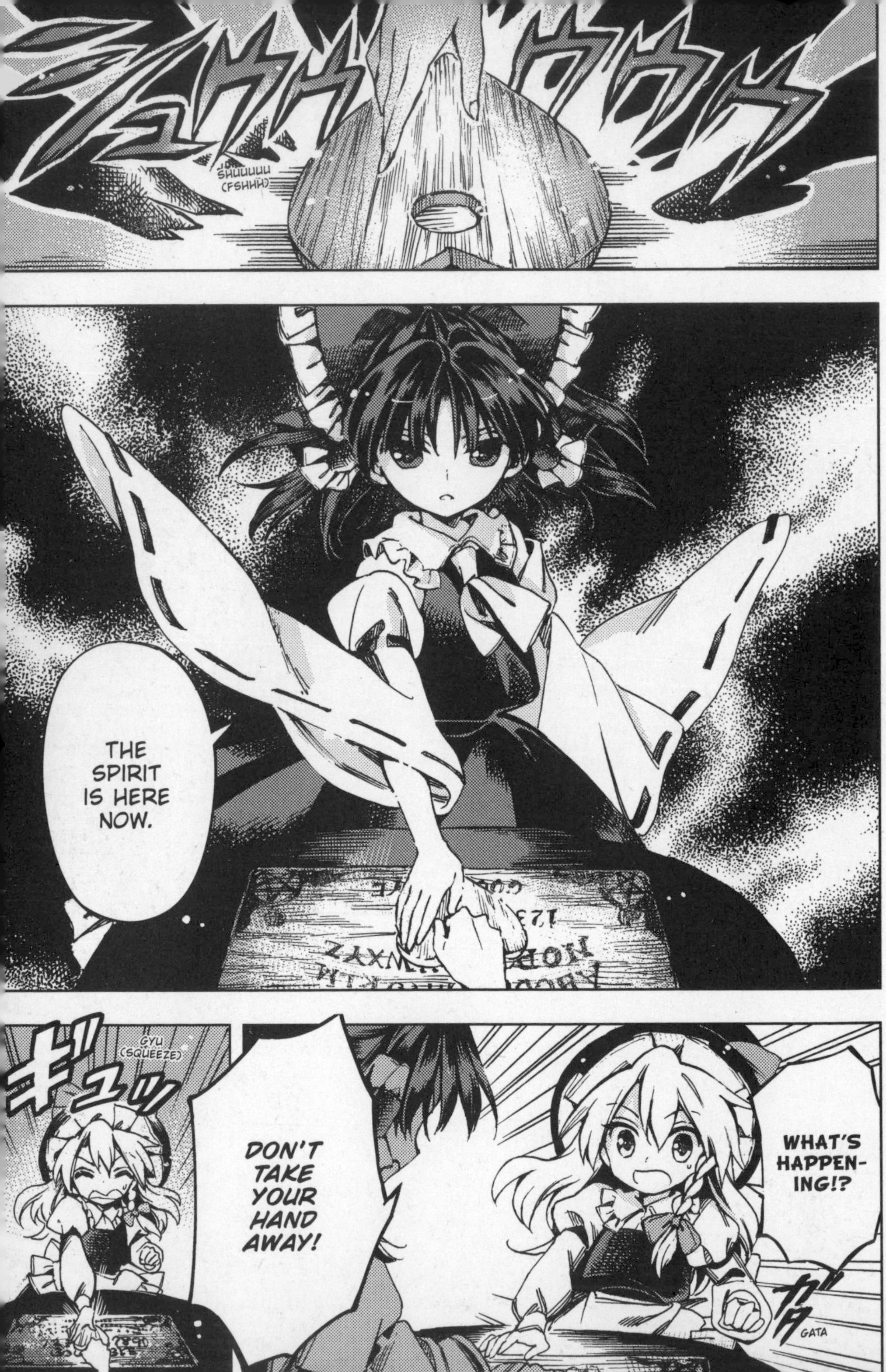

SHUUUUU (FSHHH)
THE SPIRIT IS HERE NOW.
WHAT'S HAPPEN-ING!?
DON'T TAKE YOUR HAND AWAY!
GATA
GYU (SQUEEZE)

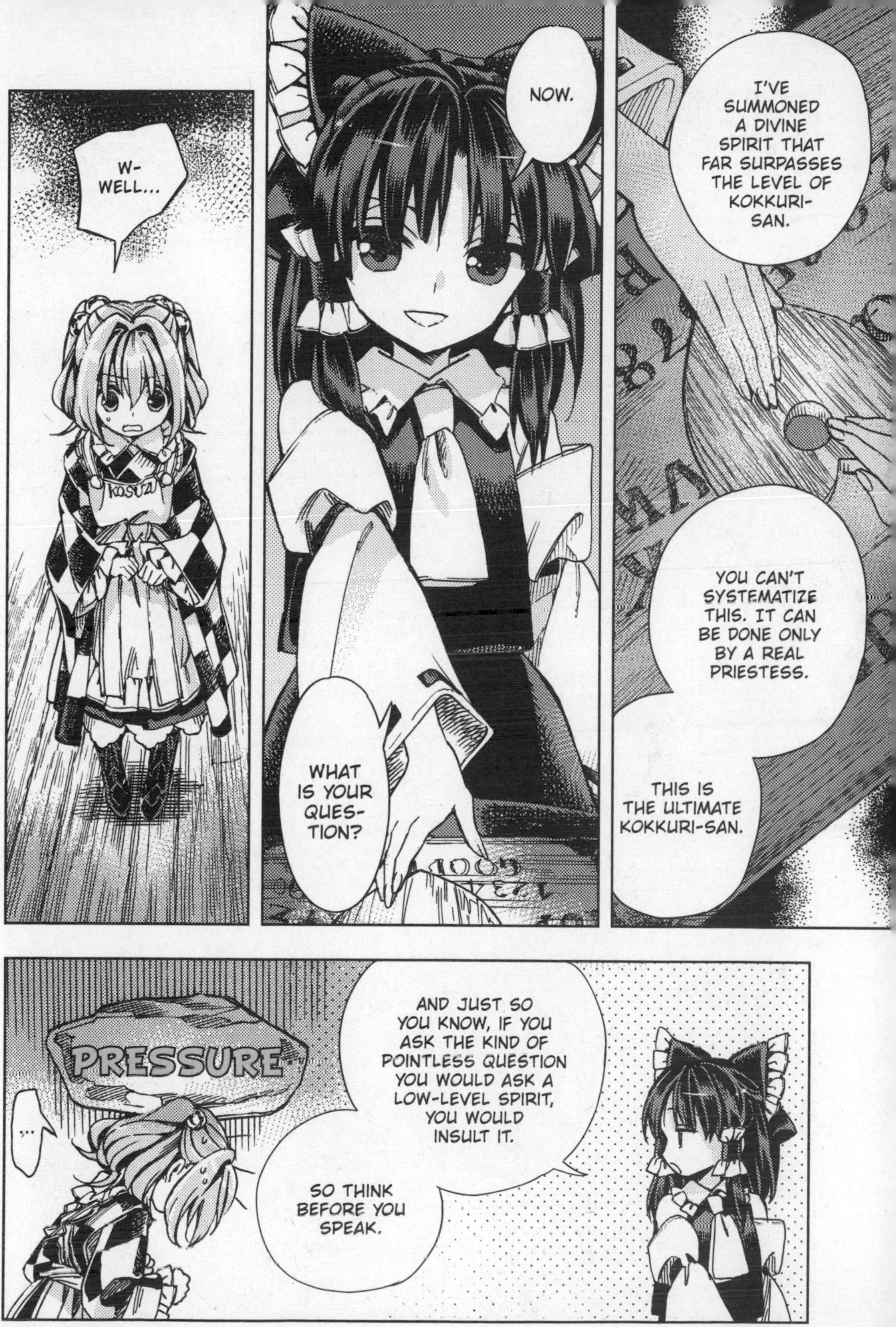
I'VE SUMMONED A DIVINE SPIRIT THAT FAR SURPASSES THE LEVEL OF KOKKURI-SAN.
YOU CAN'T SYSTEMATIZE THIS. IT CAN BE DONE ONLY BY A REAL PRIESTESS.
THIS IS THE ULTIMATE KOKKURI-SAN.
NOW.
WHAT IS YOUR QUES-TION?
W-WELL...
AND JUST SO YOU KNOW, IF YOU ASK THE KIND OF POINTLESS QUESTION YOU WOULD ASK A LOW-LEVEL SPIRIT, YOU WOULD INSULT IT.
SO THINK BEFORE YOU SPEAK.
PRESSURE
...

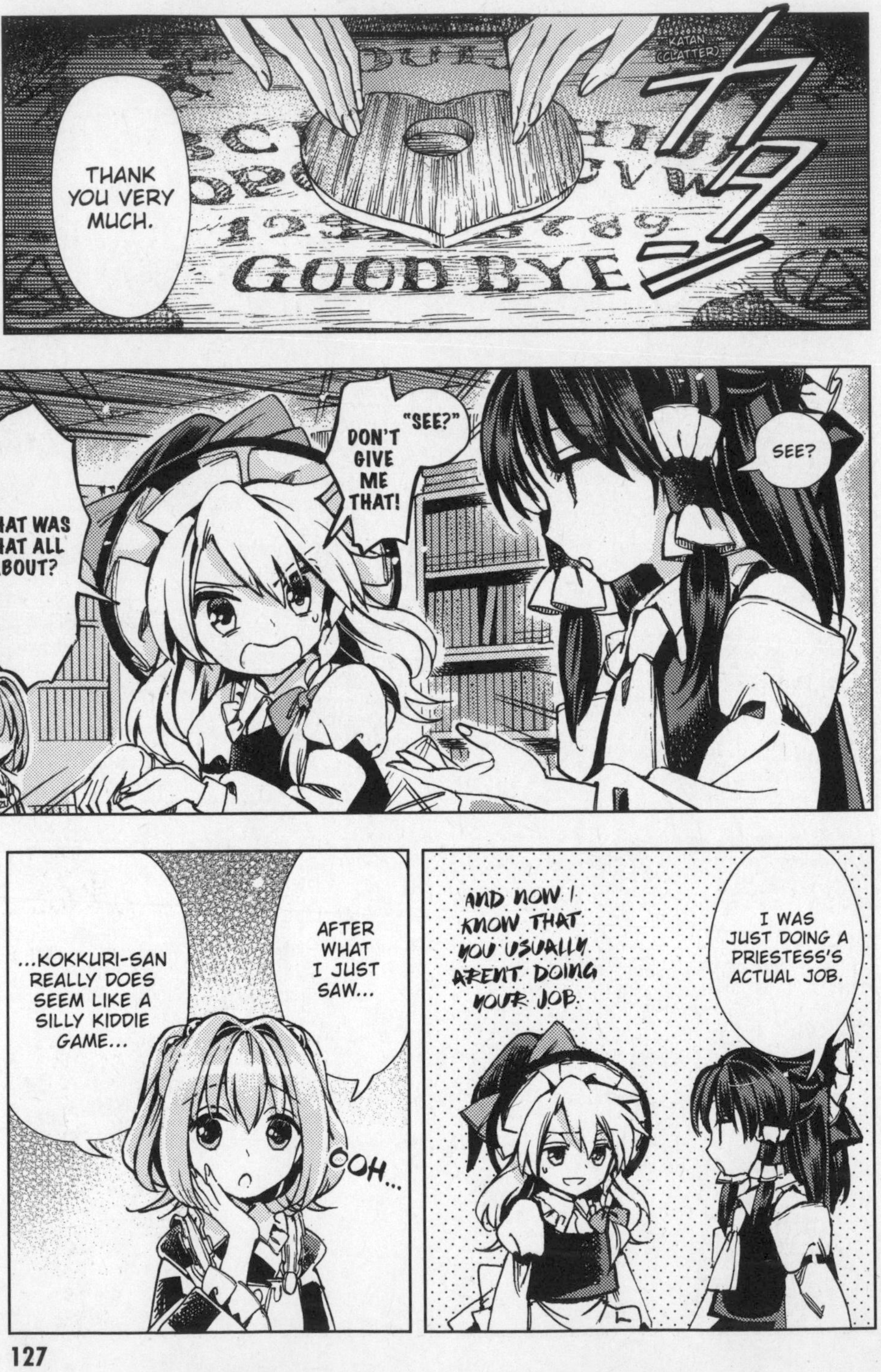

KATAN (CLATTER)
THANK YOU VERY MUCH.
SEE?
"SEE?" DON'T GIVE ME THAT!
WHAT WAS THAT ALL ABOUT?
I WAS JUST DOING A PRIESTESS'S ACTUAL JOB.
AND NOW I KNOW THAT YOU USUALLY ARENT DOING YOUR JOB.
AFTER WHAT I JUST SAW...
...KOKKURI-SAN REALLY DOES SEEM LIKE A SILLY KIDDIE GAME...
OOH...

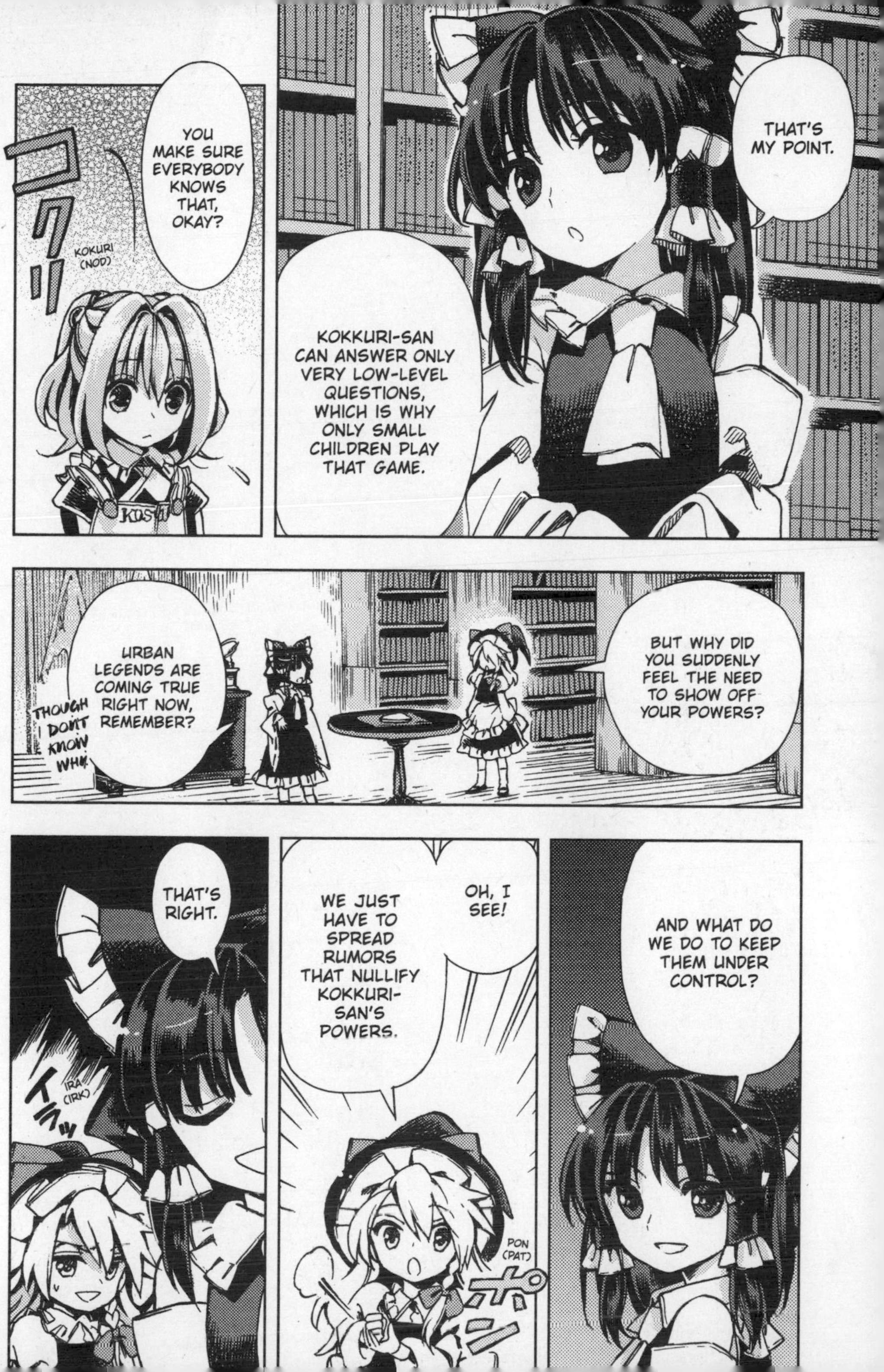
THAT'S MY POINT.
KOKKURI-SAN CAN ANSWER ONLY VERY LOW-LEVEL QUESTIONS, WHICH IS WHY ONLY SMALL CHILDREN PLAY THAT GAME.
YOU MAKE SURE EVERYBODY KNOWS THAT, OKAY?
KOKURI (NOD)
BUT WHY DID YOU SUDDENLY FEEL THE NEED TO SHOW OFF YOUR POWERS?
URBAN LEGENDS ARE COMING TRUE RIGHT NOW, REMEMBER?
THOUGH I DON'T KNOW WHY
AND WHAT DO WE DO TO KEEP THEM UNDER CONTROL?
OH, I SEE!
WE JUST HAVE TO SPREAD RUMORS THAT NULLIFY KOKKURI-SAN'S POWERS.
PON (PAT)
THAT'S RIGHT.
IRA (IRK)

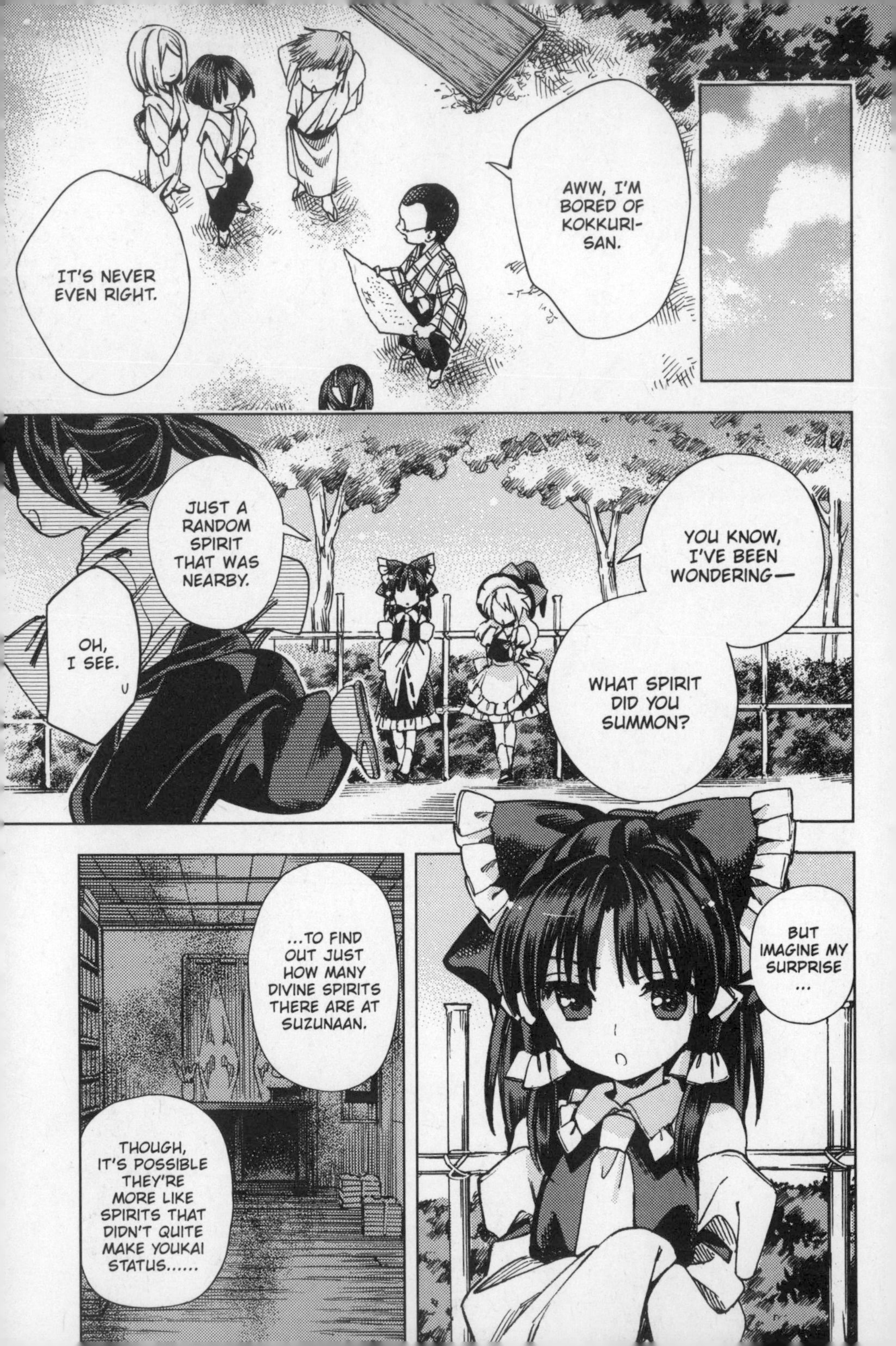
AWW, I'M BORED OF KOKKURI-SAN.
IT'S NEVER EVEN RIGHT.
YOU KNOW, I'VE BEEN WONDERING—
WHAT SPIRIT DID YOU SUMMON?
JUST A RANDOM SPIRIT THAT WAS NEARBY.
OH, I SEE.
BUT IMAGINE MY SURPRISE ...
...TO FIND OUT JUST HOW MANY DIVINE SPIRITS THERE ARE AT SUZUNAAN.
THOUGH, IT'S POSSIBLE THEY'RE MORE LIKE SPIRITS THAT DIDN'T QUITE MAKE YOUKAI STATUS......

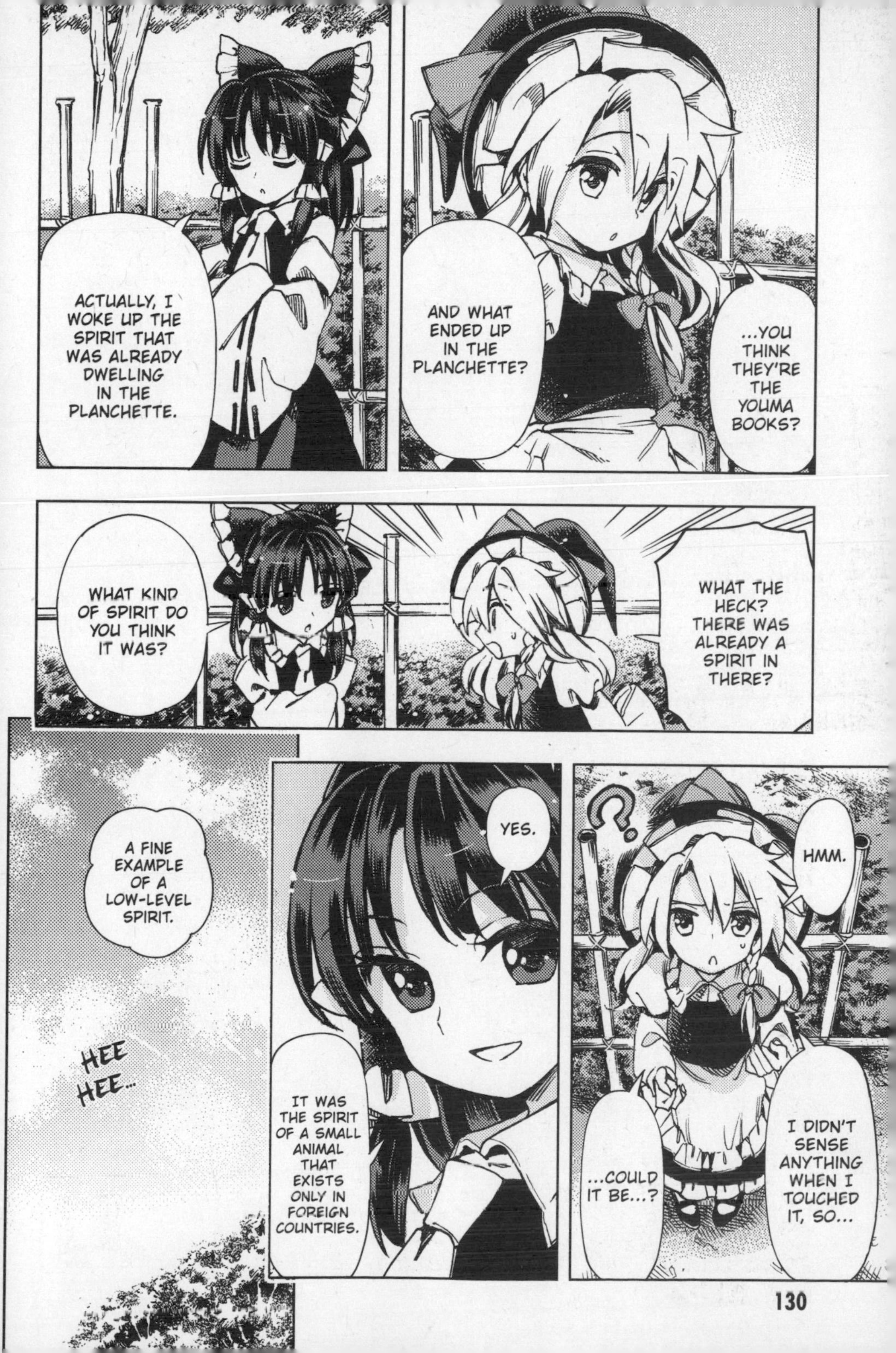
...YOU THINK THEY'RE THE YOUMA BOOKS?
AND WHAT ENDED UP IN THE PLANCHETTE?
ACTUALLY, I WOKE UP THE SPIRIT THAT WAS ALREADY DWELLING IN THE PLANCHETTE.
WHAT THE HECK? THERE WAS ALREADY A SPIRIT IN THERE?
WHAT KIND OF SPIRIT DO YOU THINK IT WAS?
HMM.
I DIDN'T SENSE ANYTHING WHEN I TOUCHED IT, SO...
...COULD IT BE...?
YES.
IT WAS THE SPIRIT OF A SMALL ANIMAL THAT EXISTS ONLY IN FOREIGN COUNTRIES.
A FINE EXAMPLE OF A LOW-LEVEL SPIRIT.
HEE HEE...

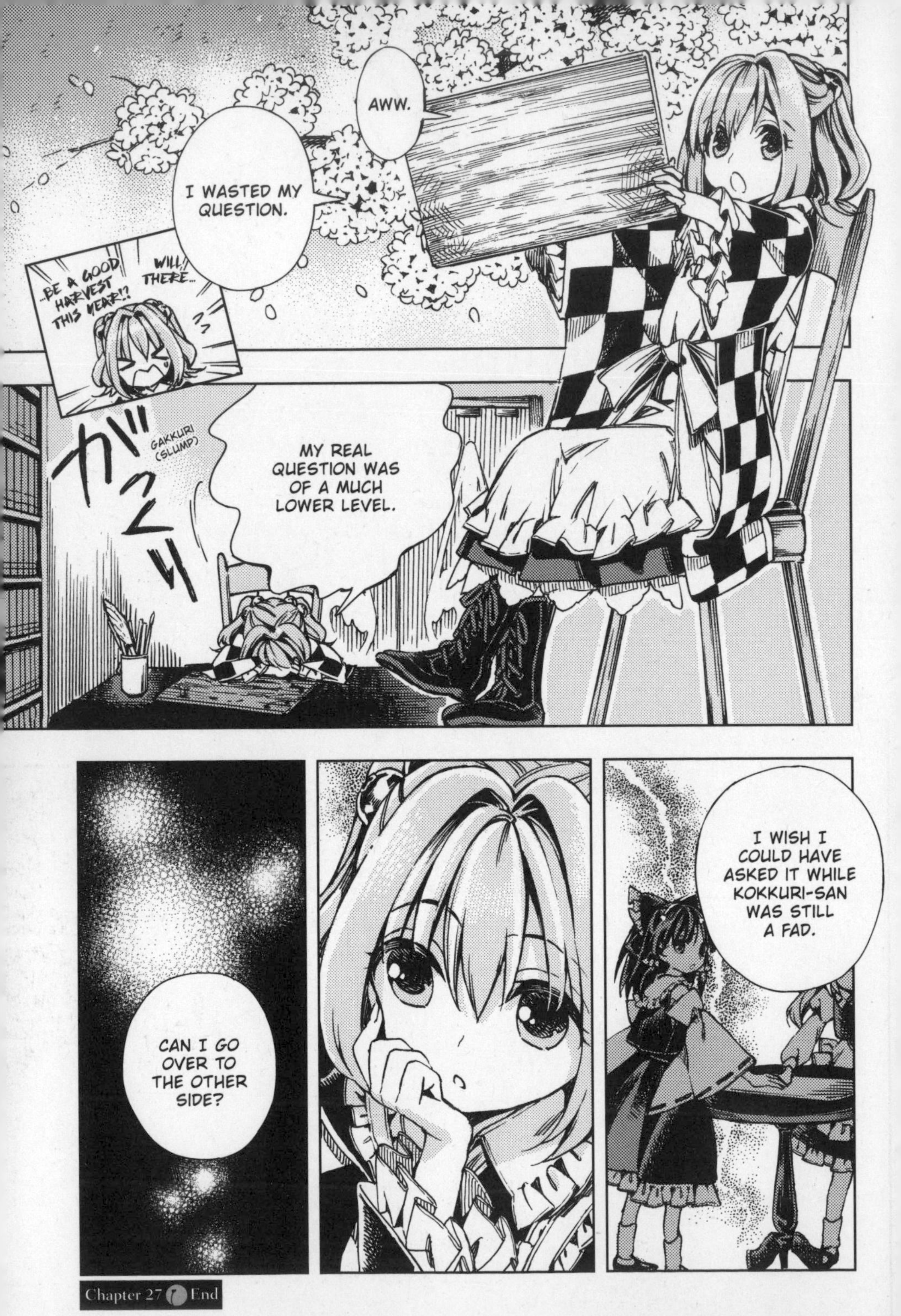
AWW.
I WASTED MY QUESTION.
WILL THERE...
...BE A GOOD HARVEST THIS YEAR!?
MY REAL QUESTION WAS OF A MUCH LOWER LEVEL.
GAKKURI (SLUMP)
I WISH I COULD HAVE ASKED IT WHILE KOKKURI-SAN WAS STILL A FAD.
CAN I GO OVER TO THE OTHER SIDE?

Chapter 27 End

Forbidden Scrollery

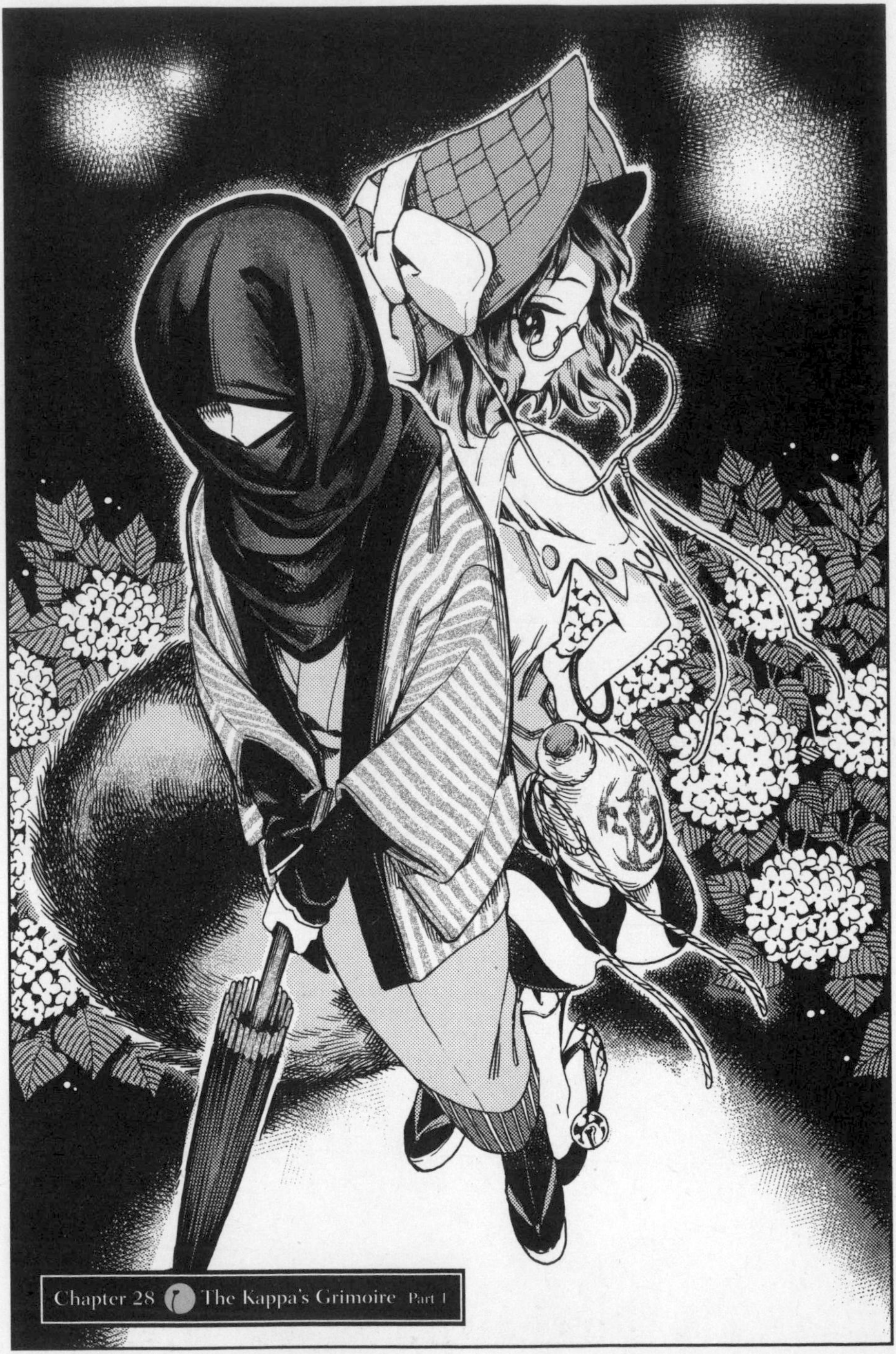
Chapter 28 The Kappa's Grimoire Part 1

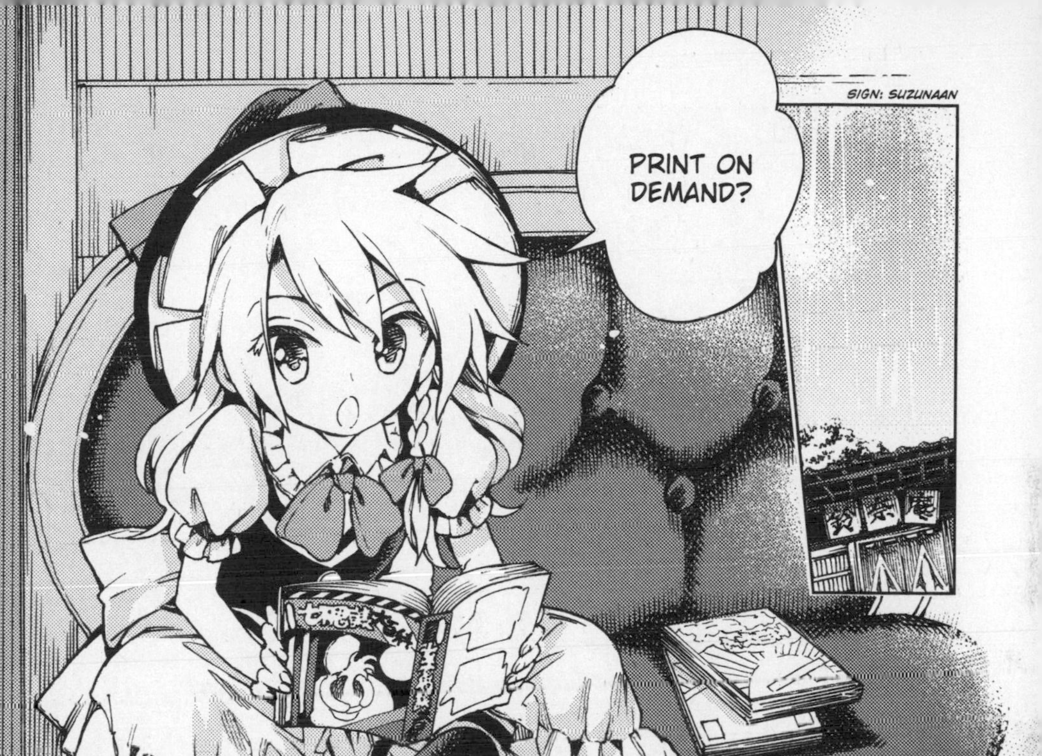
SIGN: SUZUNAAN
PRINT ON DEMAND?
BOOK: BIG ENCYCLOPEDIA OF SEVEN WONDERS

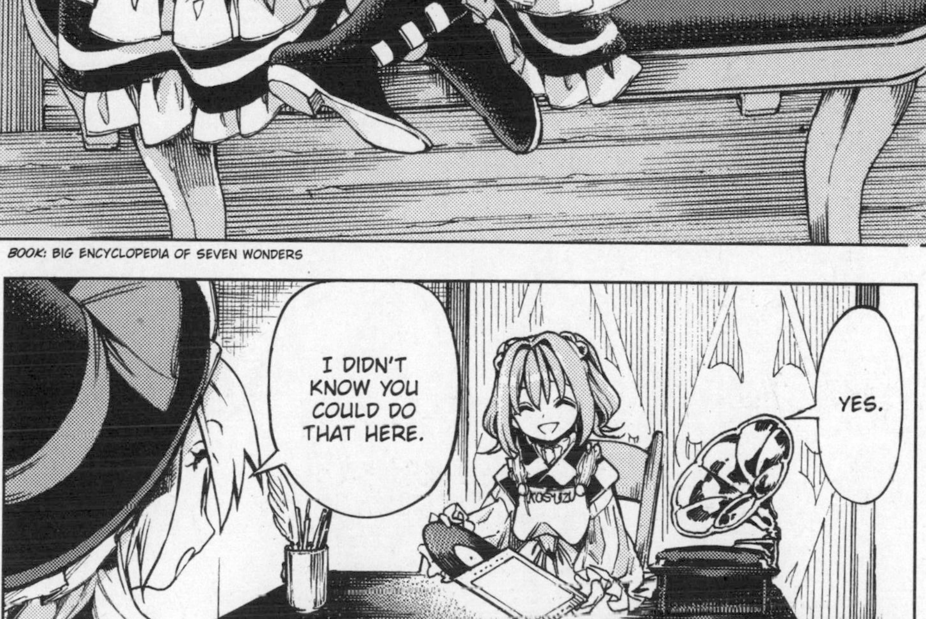
YES.
I DIDN'T KNOW YOU COULD DO THAT HERE.
KOSUZU

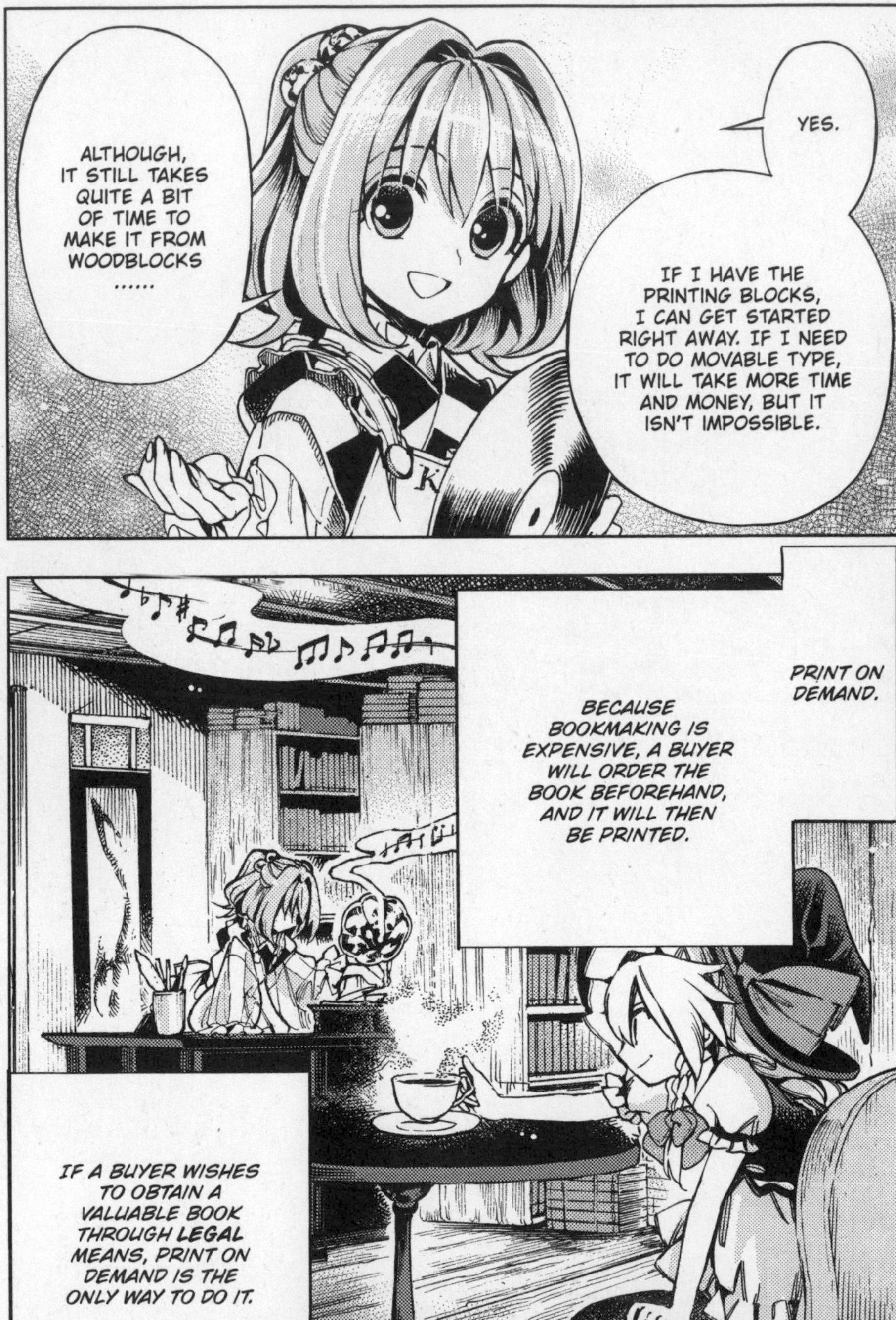
YES.
IF I HAVE THE PRINTING BLOCKS, I CAN GET STARTED RIGHT AWAY. IF I NEED TO DO MOVABLE TYPE, IT WILL TAKE MORE TIME AND MONEY, BUT IT ISN'T IMPOSSIBLE.
ALTHOUGH, IT STILL TAKES QUITE A BIT OF TIME TO MAKE IT FROM WOODBLOCKS ......
PRINT ON DEMAND.
BECAUSE BOOKMAKING IS EXPENSIVE, A BUYER WILL ORDER THE BOOK BEFOREHAND, AND IT WILL THEN BE PRINTED.
IF A BUYER WISHES TO OBTAIN A VALUABLE BOOK THROUGH LEGAL MEANS, PRINT ON DEMAND IS THE ONLY WAY TO DO IT.

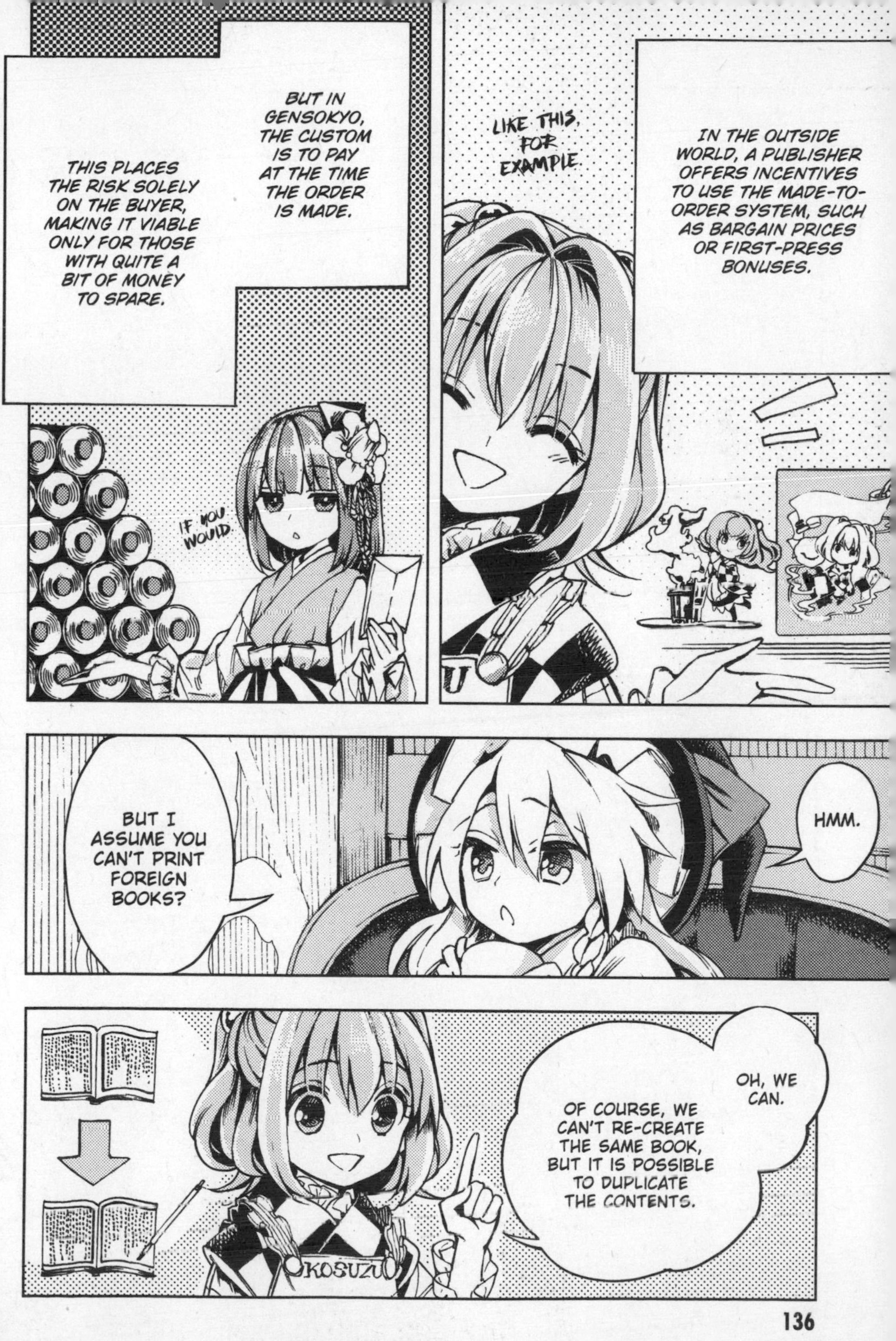
IN THE OUTSIDE WORLD, A PUBLISHER OFFERS INCENTIVES TO USE THE MADE-TO-ORDER SYSTEM, SUCH AS BARGAIN PRICES OR FIRST-PRESS BONUSES.
LIKE THIS, FOR EXAMPLE.
BUT IN GENSOKYO, THE CUSTOM IS TO PAY AT THE TIME THE ORDER IS MADE.
THIS PLACES THE RISK SOLELY ON THE BUYER, MAKING IT VIABLE ONLY FOR THOSE WITH QUITE A BIT OF MONEY TO SPARE.
IF YOU WOULD.
HMM.
BUT I ASSUME YOU CAN'T PRINT FOREIGN BOOKS?
OH, WE CAN.
OF COURSE, WE CAN'T RE-CREATE THE SAME BOOK, BUT IT IS POSSIBLE TO DUPLICATE THE CONTENTS.
KOSUZU

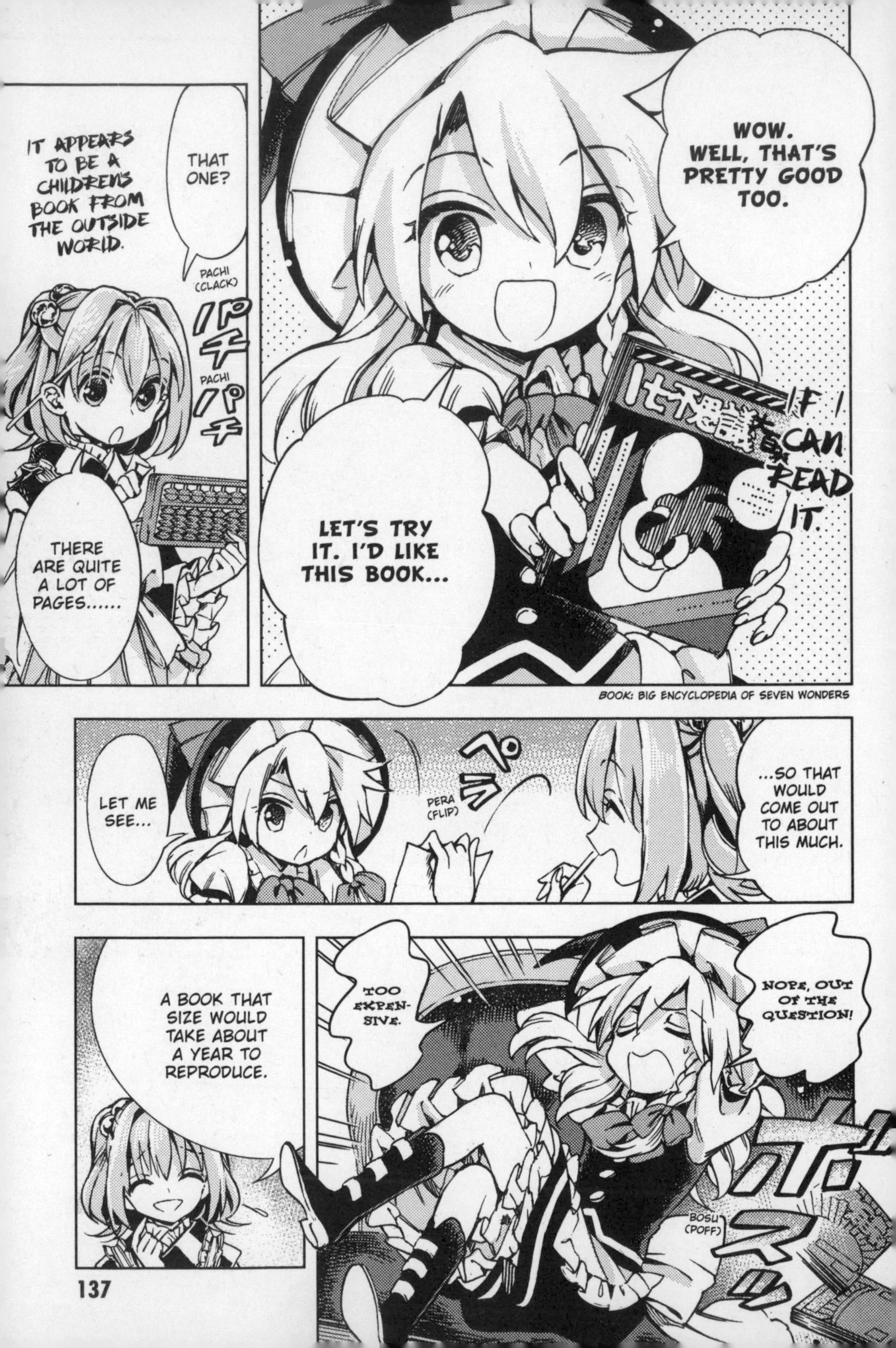
WOW. WELL, THAT'S PRETTY GOOD TOO.
IF I CAN READ IT.
LET'S TRY IT. I'D LIKE THIS BOOK...
BOOK: BIG ENCYCLOPEDIA OF SEVEN WONDERS
THAT ONE?
IT APPEARS TO BE A CHILDREN'S BOOK FROM THE OUTSIDE WORLD.
PACHI (CLACK)
パチ
PACHI
パチ
THERE ARE QUITE A LOT OF PAGES......
...SO THAT WOULD COME OUT TO ABOUT THIS MUCH.
PERA (FLIP)
ペラ
LET ME SEE...
NOPE, OUT OF THE QUESTION!
TOO EXPENSIVE.
BOSU (POFF)
A BOOK THAT SIZE WOULD TAKE ABOUT A YEAR TO REPRODUCE.

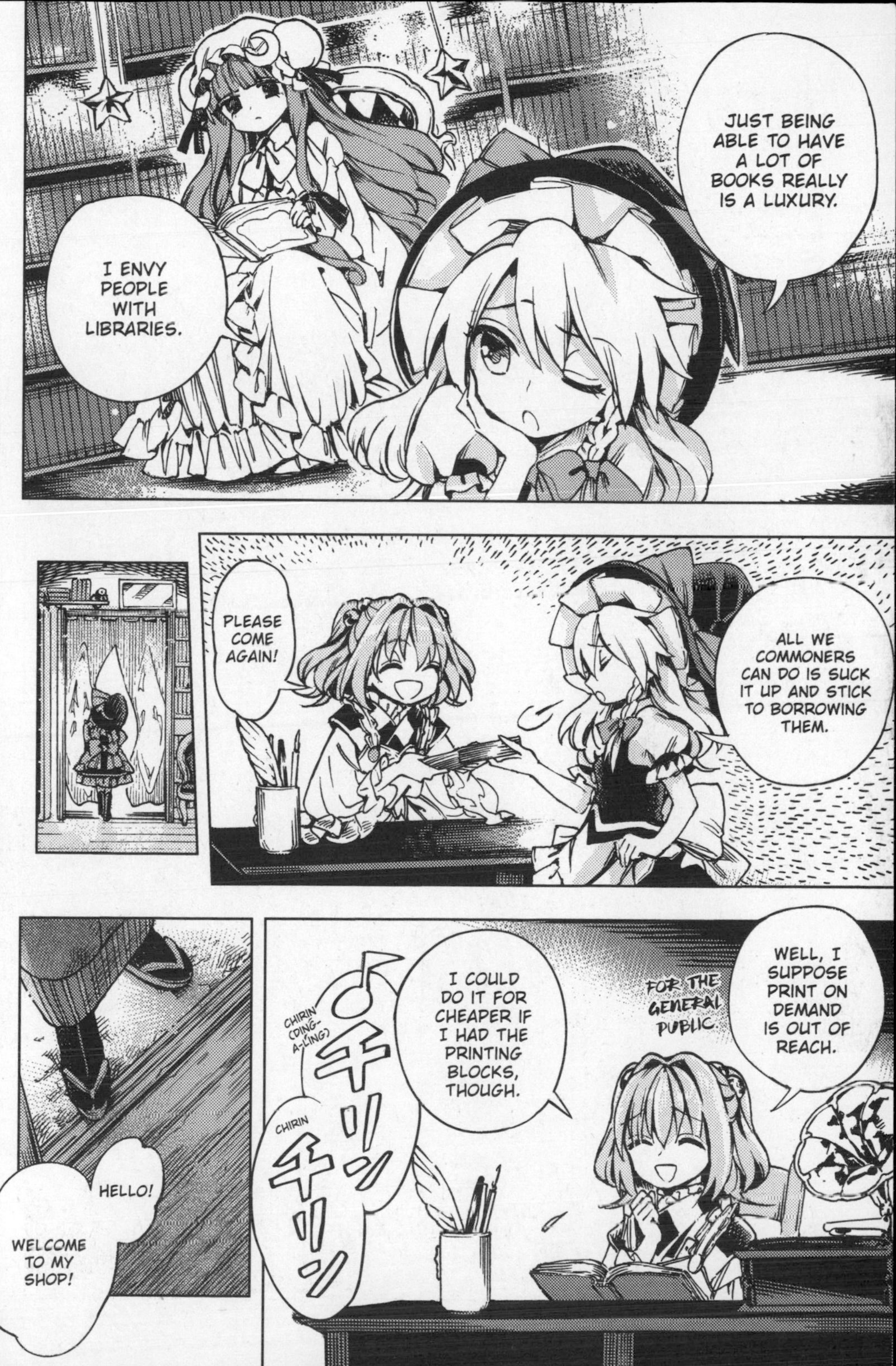
JUST BEING ABLE TO HAVE A LOT OF BOOKS REALLY IS A LUXURY.
I ENVY PEOPLE WITH LIBRARIES.
ALL WE COMMONERS CAN DO IS SUCK IT UP AND STICK TO BORROWING THEM.
PLEASE COME AGAIN!
WELL, I SUPPOSE PRINT ON DEMAND IS OUT OF REACH.
FOR THE GENERAL PUBLIC.
I COULD DO IT FOR CHEAPER IF I HAD THE PRINTING BLOCKS, THOUGH.
チリン
CHIRIN (DING-A-LING)
チリン
CHIRIN
HELLO!
WELCOME TO MY SHOP!

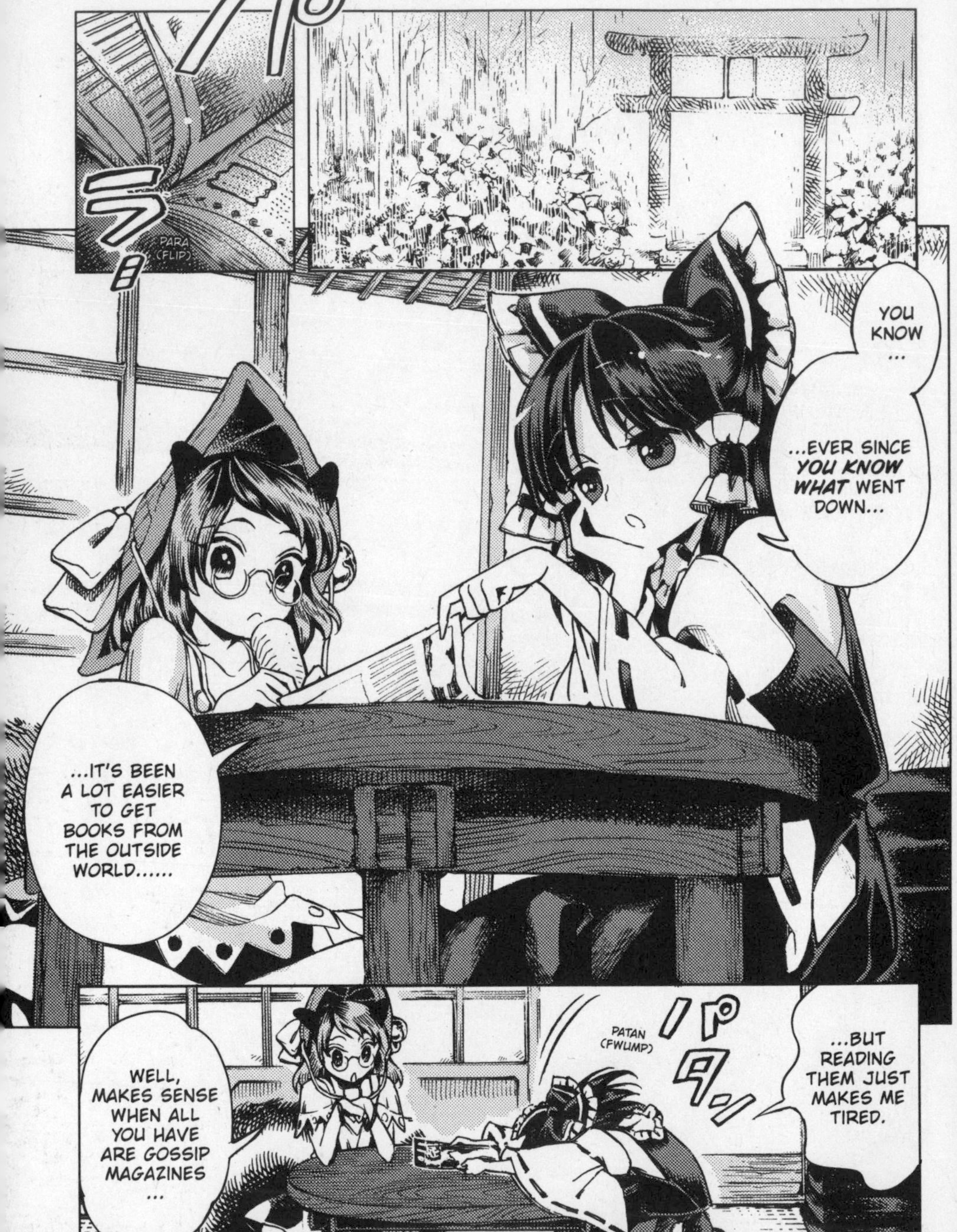

パラ
PARA (FLIP)
YOU KNOW ...
...EVER SINCE *YOU KNOW WHAT* WENT DOWN...
...IT'S BEEN A LOT EASIER TO GET BOOKS FROM THE OUTSIDE WORLD......
...BUT READING THEM JUST MAKES ME TIRED.
パタン
PATAN (FWUMP)
WELL, MAKES SENSE WHEN ALL YOU HAVE ARE GOSSIP MAGAZINES ...

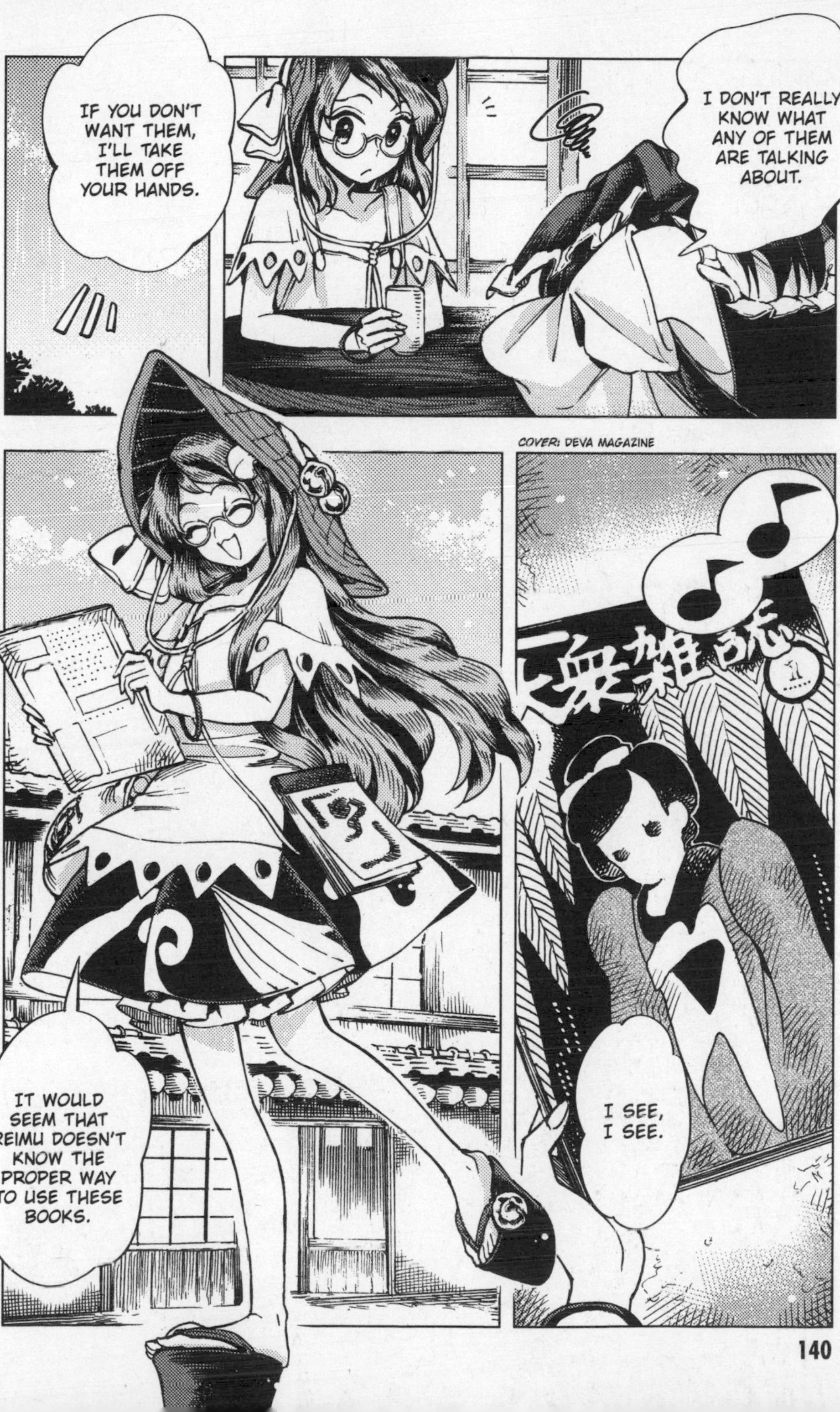
I DON'T REALLY KNOW WHAT ANY OF THEM ARE TALKING ABOUT.
IF YOU DON'T WANT THEM, I'LL TAKE THEM OFF YOUR HANDS.
COVER: DEVA MAGAZINE
I SEE, I SEE.
IT WOULD SEEM THAT REIMU DOESN'T KNOW THE PROPER WAY TO USE THESE BOOKS.

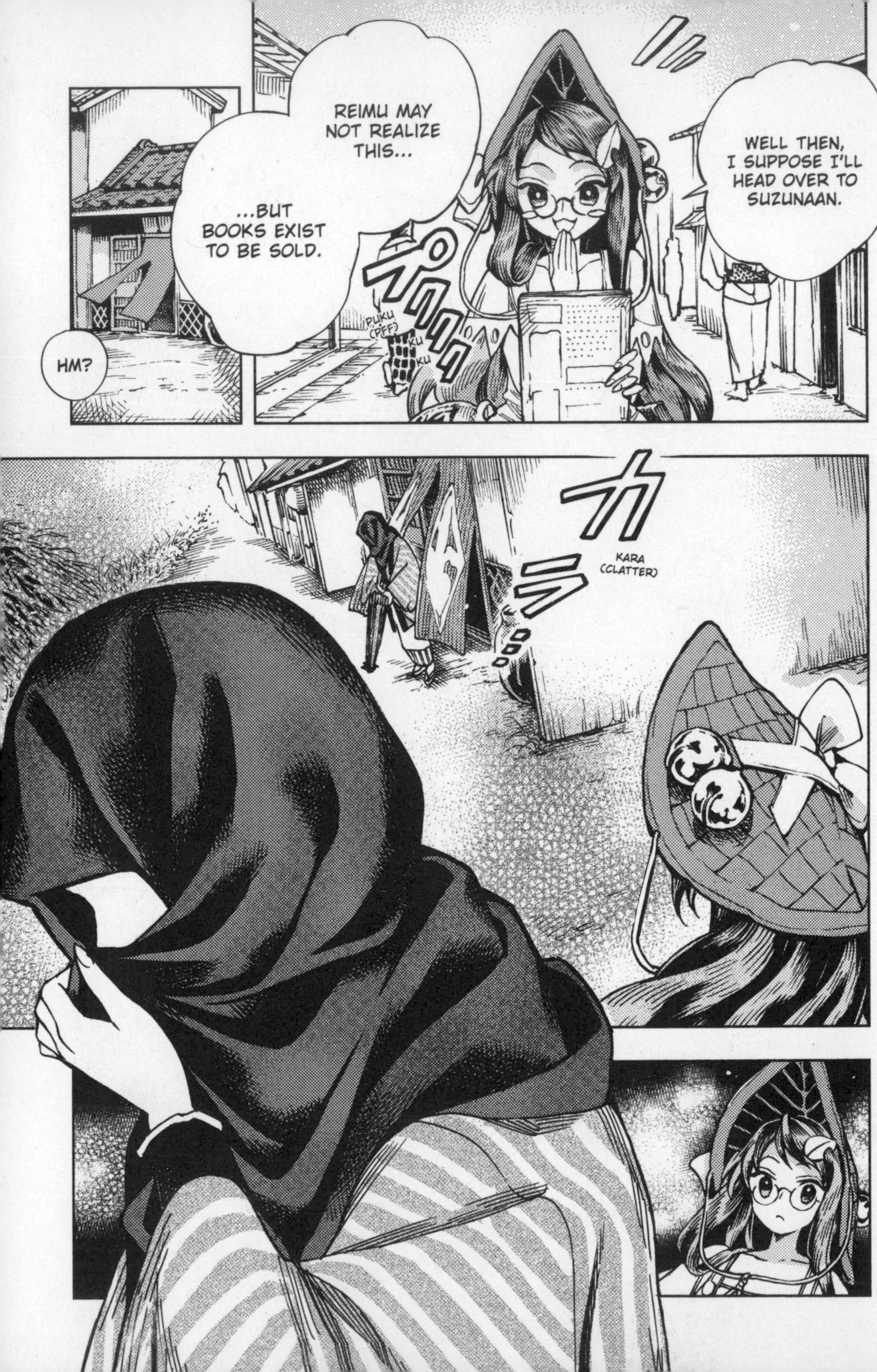
REIMU MAY NOT REALIZE THIS...
...BUT BOOKS EXIST TO BE SOLD.
PUKU (PFF)
KU
KU
WELL THEN, I SUPPOSE I'LL HEAD OVER TO SUZUNAAN.
HM?
KARA (CLATTER)

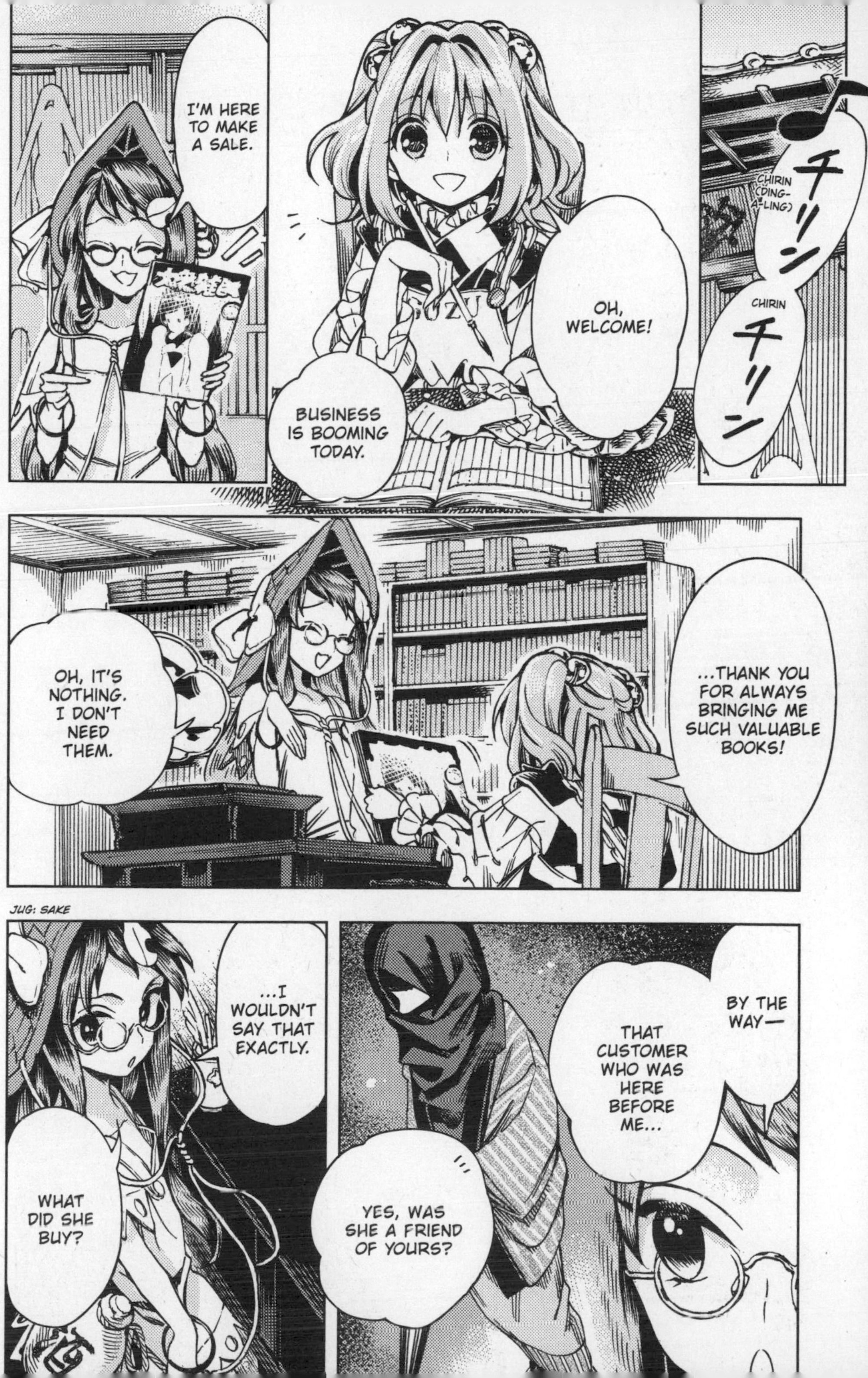

チリン
CHIRIN (DING-A-LING)
チリン
CHIRIN
OH, WELCOME!
BUSINESS IS BOOMING TODAY.
I'M HERE TO MAKE A SALE.
...THANK YOU FOR ALWAYS BRINGING ME SUCH VALUABLE BOOKS!
OH, IT'S NOTHING. I DON'T NEED THEM.
JUG: SAKE
BY THE WAY—
THAT CUSTOMER WHO WAS HERE BEFORE ME...
YES, WAS SHE A FRIEND OF YOURS?
...I WOULDN'T SAY THAT EXACTLY.
WHAT DID SHE BUY?

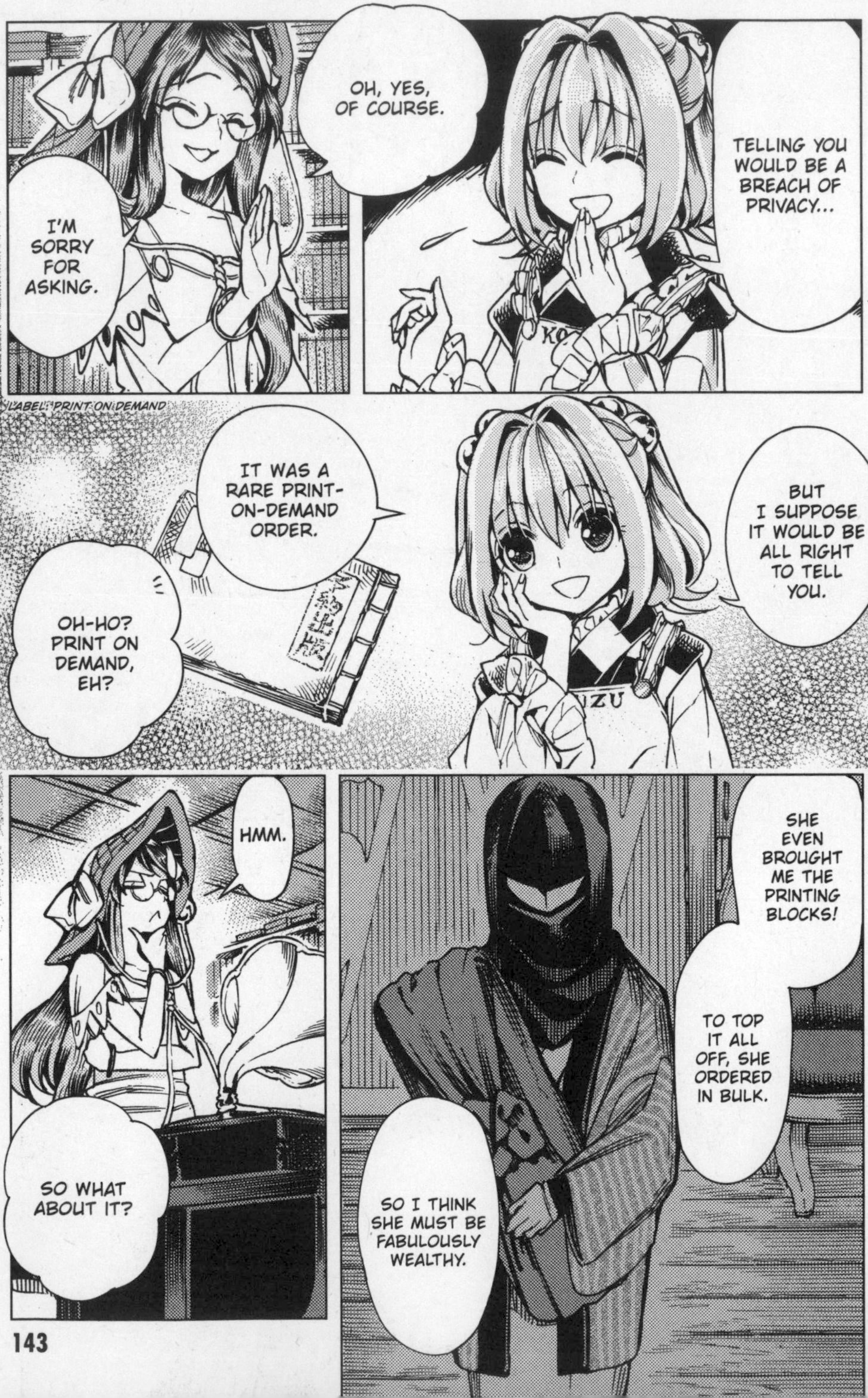
TELLING YOU WOULD BE A BREACH OF PRIVACY...
OH, YES, OF COURSE.
I'M SORRY FOR ASKING.
BUT I SUPPOSE IT WOULD BE ALL RIGHT TO TELL YOU.
IT WAS A RARE PRINT-ON-DEMAND ORDER.
LABEL: PRINT ON DEMAND
OH-HO? PRINT ON DEMAND, EH?
SHE EVEN BROUGHT ME THE PRINTING BLOCKS!
TO TOP IT ALL OFF, SHE ORDERED IN BULK.
SO I THINK SHE MUST BE FABULOUSLY WEALTHY.
HMM.
SO WHAT ABOUT IT?

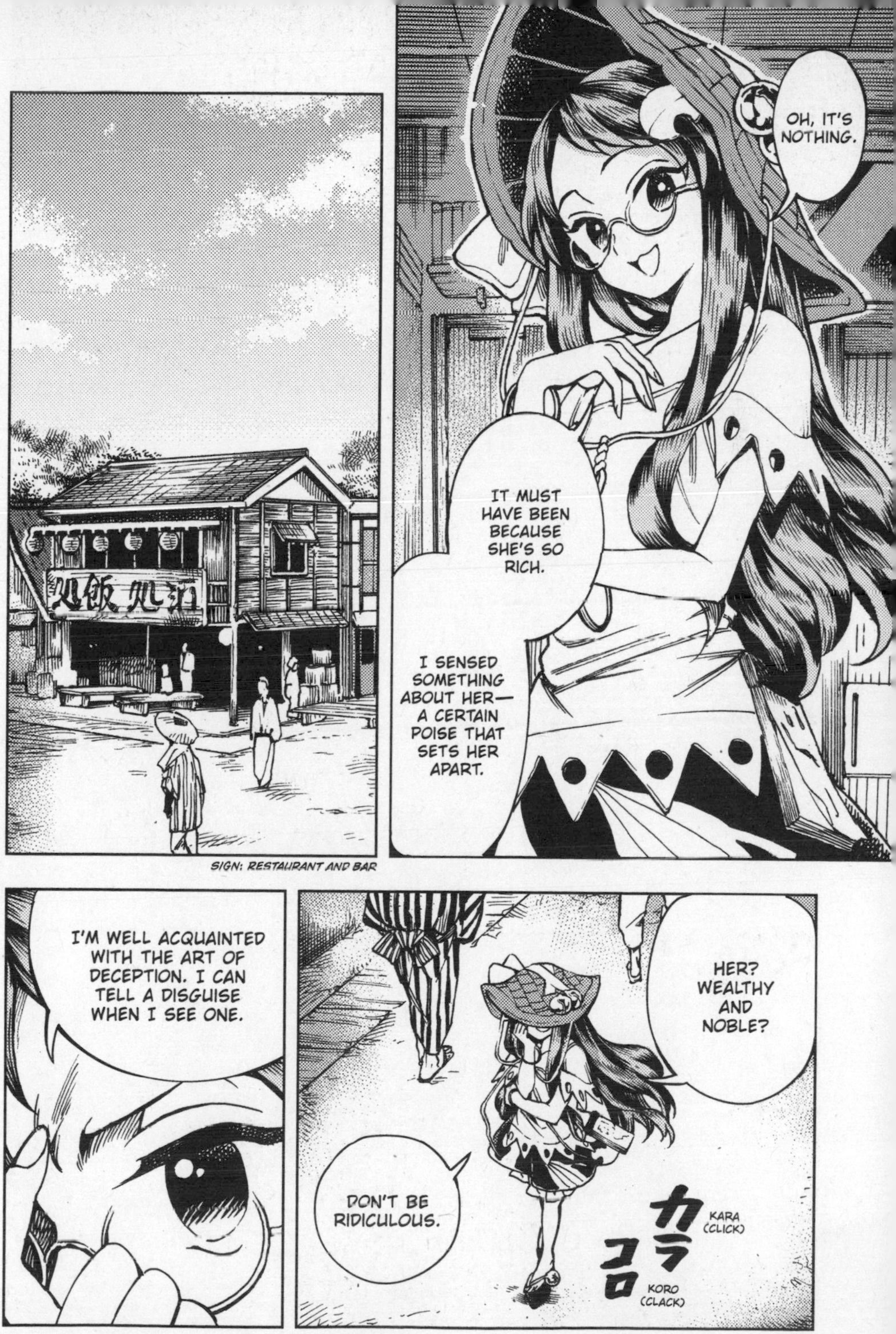
OH, IT'S NOTHING.
IT MUST HAVE BEEN BECAUSE SHE'S SO RICH.
I SENSED SOMETHING ABOUT HER— A CERTAIN POISE THAT SETS HER APART.
処飯処酒
SIGN: RESTAURANT AND BAR
HER? WEALTHY AND NOBLE?
DON'T BE RIDICULOUS.
カラ
KARA (CLICK)
コロ
KORO (CLACK)
I'M WELL ACQUAINTED WITH THE ART OF DECEPTION. I CAN TELL A DISGUISE WHEN I SEE ONE.

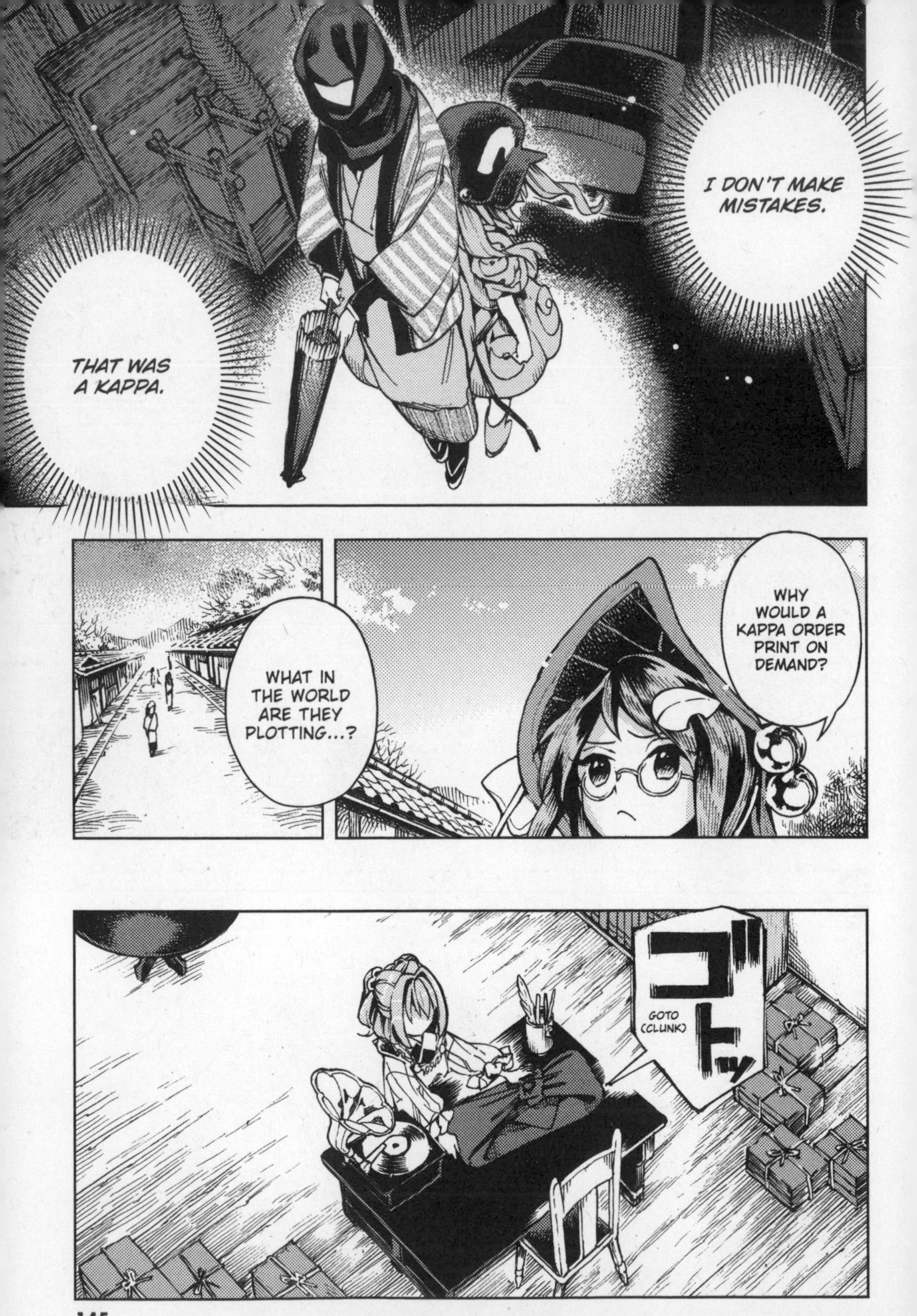
I DON'T MAKE MISTAKES.
THAT WAS A KAPPA.
WHY WOULD A KAPPA ORDER PRINT ON DEMAND?
WHAT IN THE WORLD ARE THEY PLOTTING...?
ゴトッ
GOTO (CLUNK)

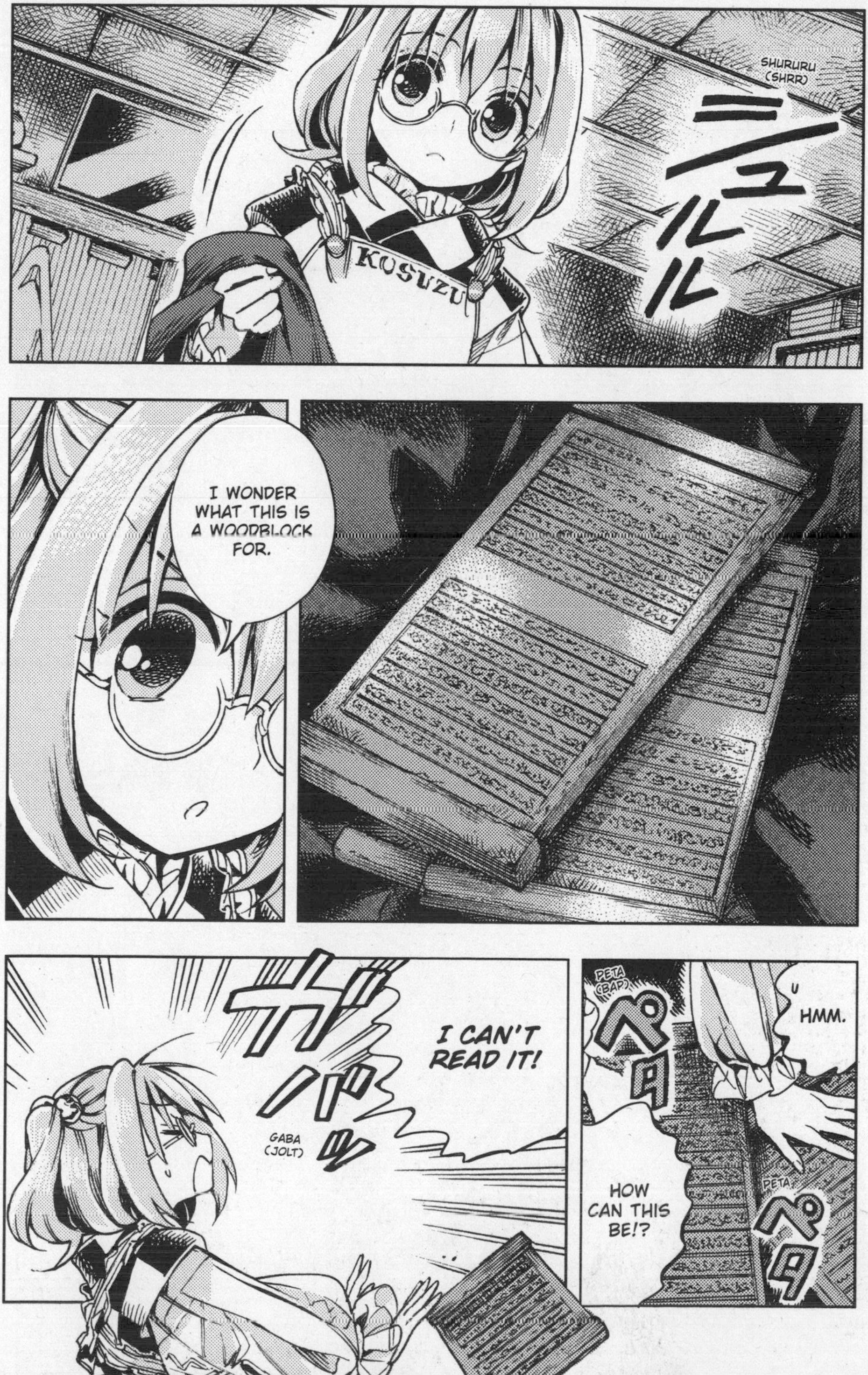
SHURURU (SHRR)
I WONDER WHAT THIS IS A WOODBLOCK FOR.
PETA (BAP)
U HMM.
HOW CAN THIS BE!?
PETA
I CAN'T READ IT!
GABA (JOLT)

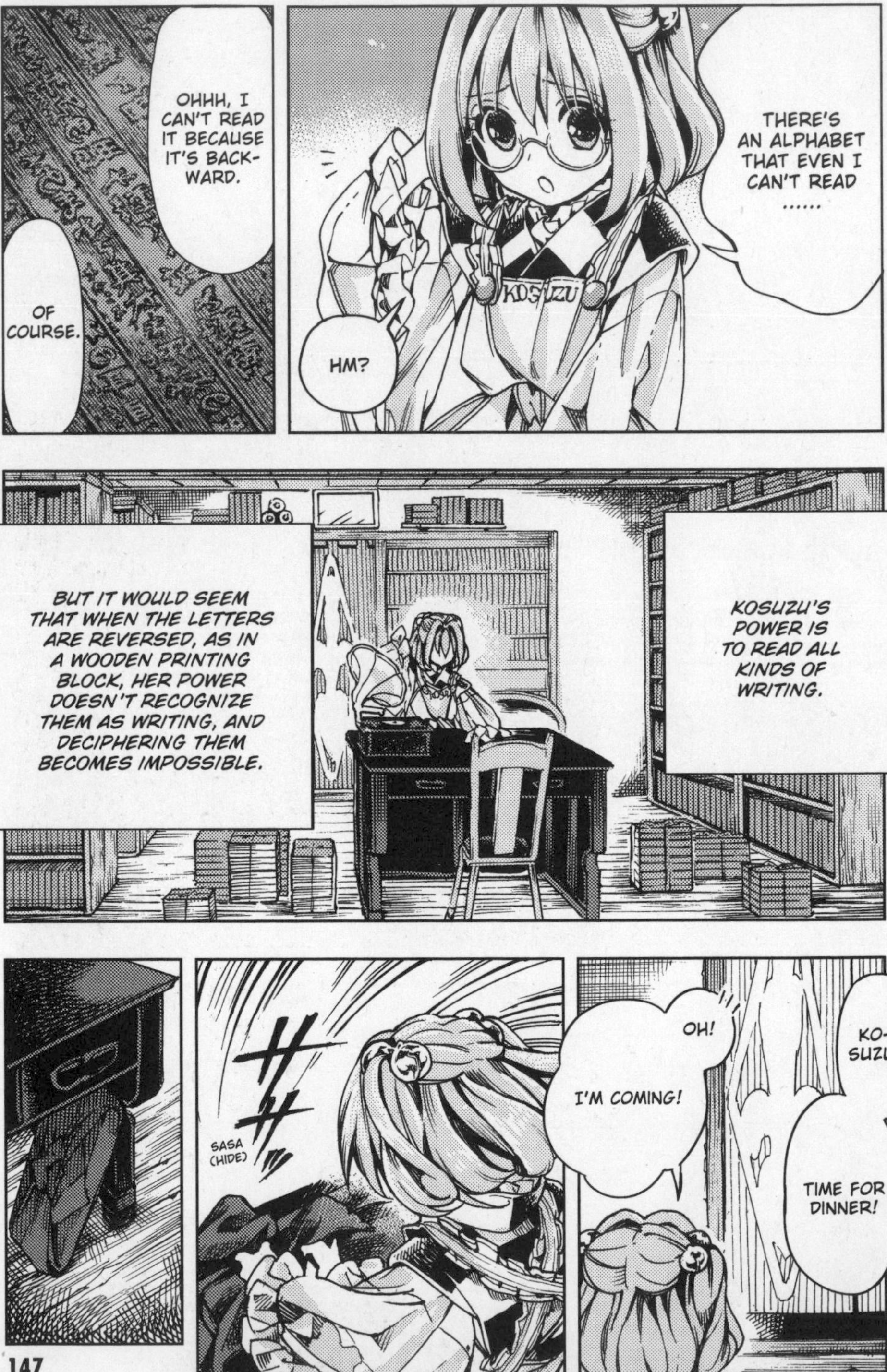
THERE'S AN ALPHABET THAT EVEN I CAN'T READ ......
HM?
OHHH, I CAN'T READ IT BECAUSE IT'S BACK-WARD.
OF COURSE.
KOSUZU'S POWER IS TO READ ALL KINDS OF WRITING.
BUT IT WOULD SEEM THAT WHEN THE LETTERS ARE REVERSED, AS IN A WOODEN PRINTING BLOCK, HER POWER DOESN'T RECOGNIZE THEM AS WRITING, AND DECIPHERING THEM BECOMES IMPOSSIBLE.
KO-SUZU!
TIME FOR DINNER!
OH!
I'M COMING!
SASA (HIDE)

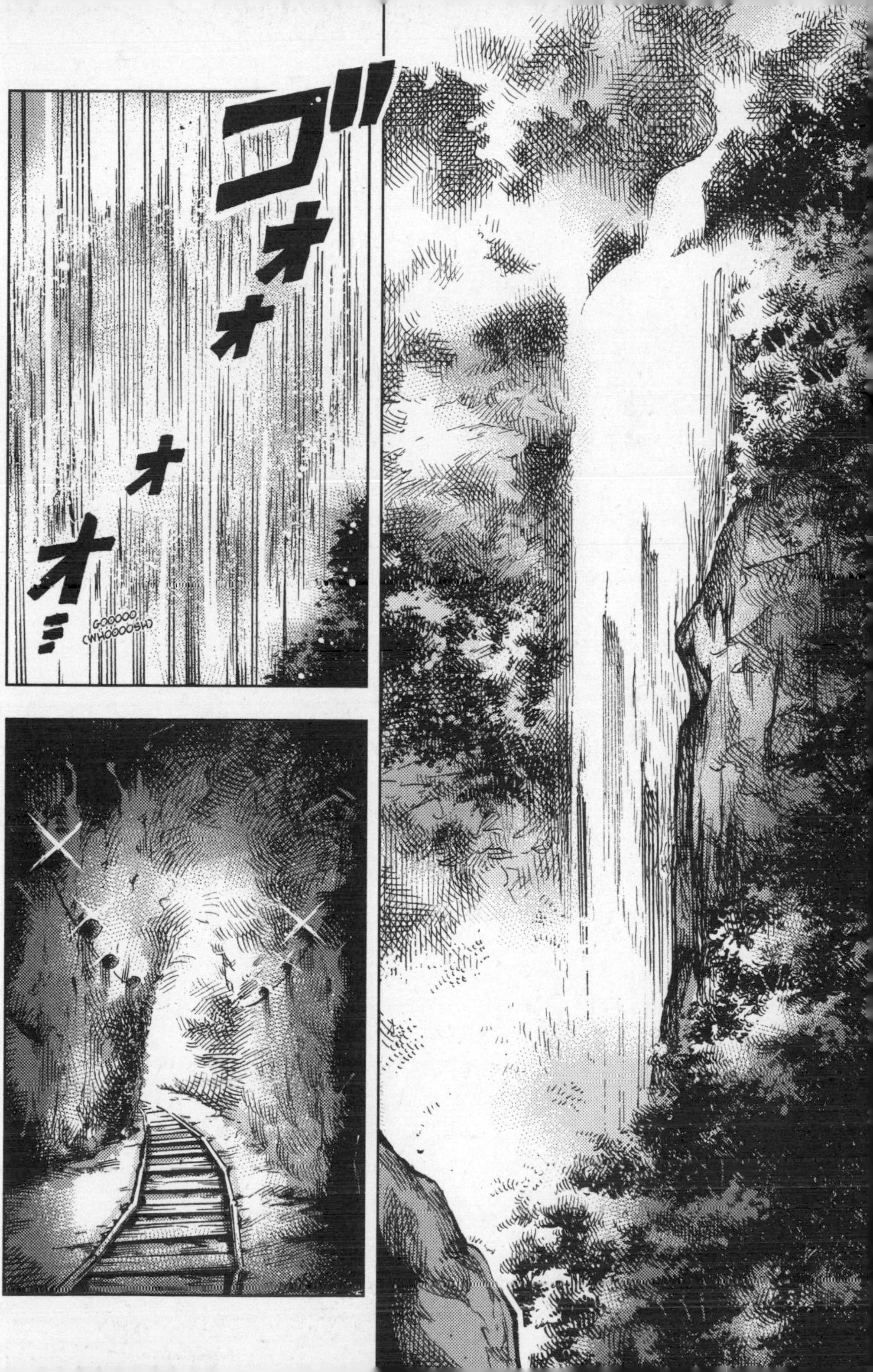
ゴオオオオ
GOOOOO (WHOOOOSH)

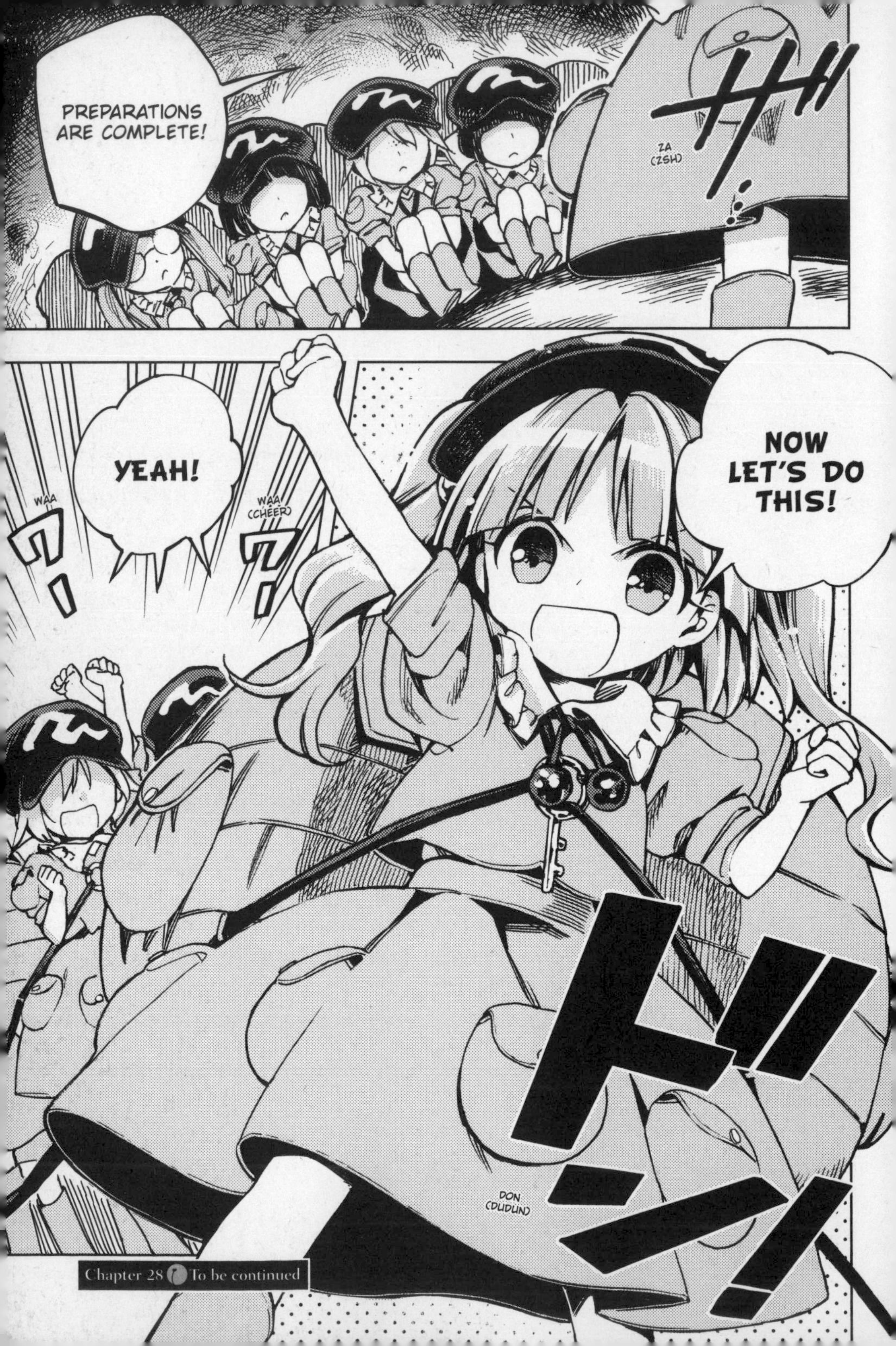
ZA
(ZSH)
PREPARATIONS ARE COMPLETE!
NOW LET'S DO THIS!
WAA
(CHEER)
YEAH!
WAA
DON
(DUDUN)
Chapter 28 To be continued

Forbidden Scrollery

Chapter 29 The Kappa's Grimoire Part 2

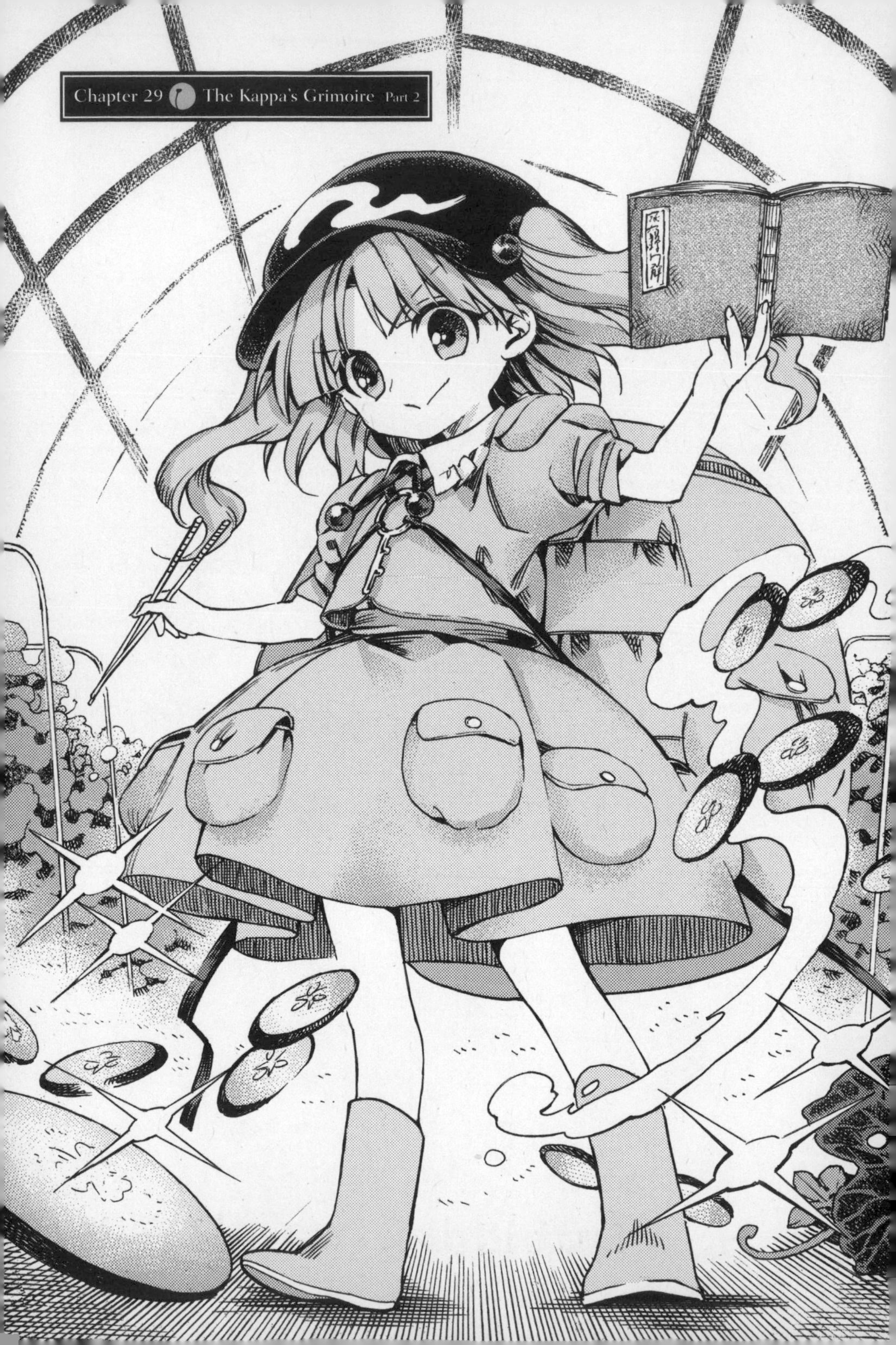

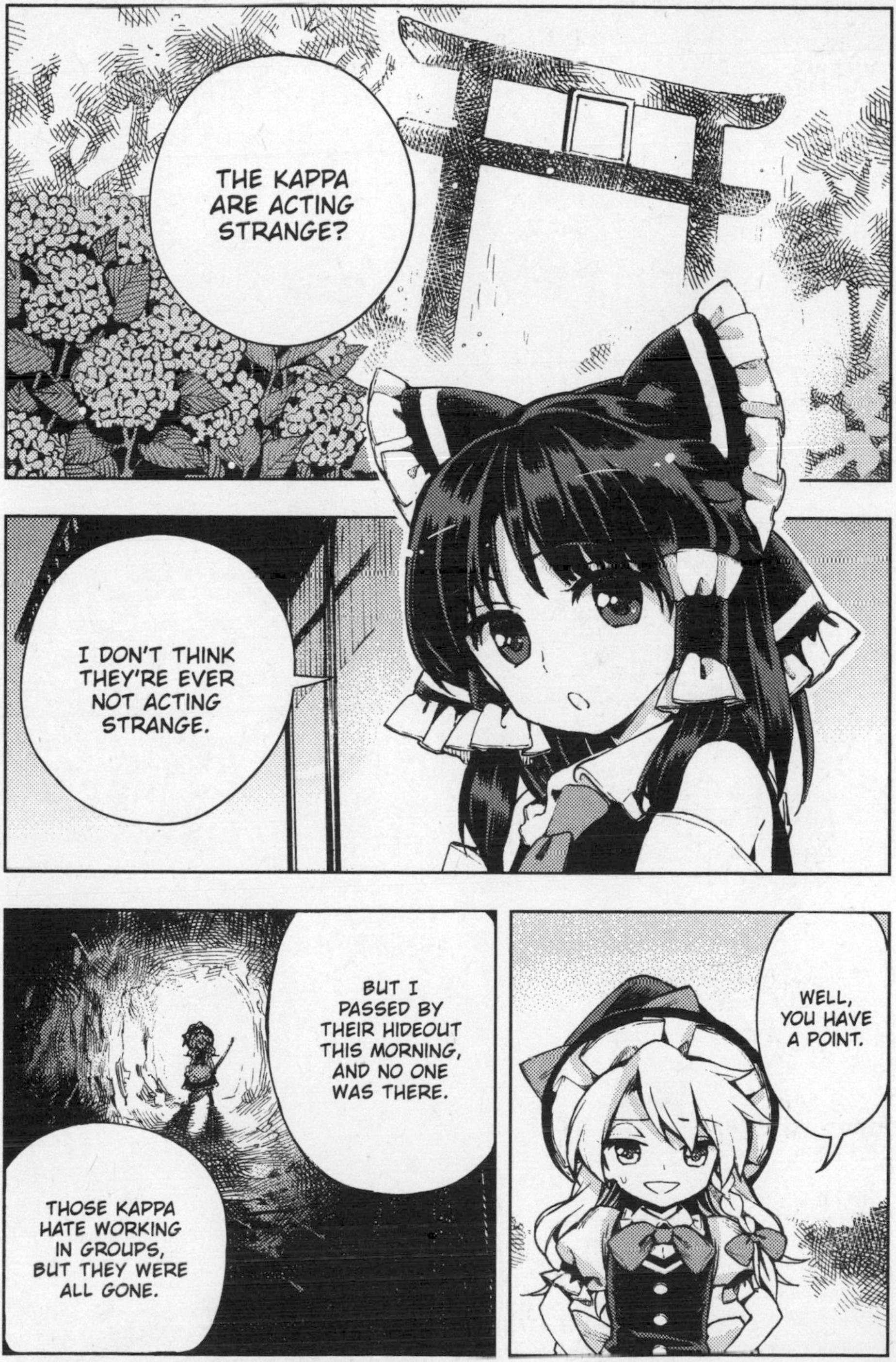
THE KAPPA ARE ACTING STRANGE?
I DON'T THINK THEY'RE EVER NOT ACTING STRANGE.
WELL, YOU HAVE A POINT.
BUT I PASSED BY THEIR HIDEOUT THIS MORNING, AND NO ONE WAS THERE.
THOSE KAPPA HATE WORKING IN GROUPS, BUT THEY WERE ALL GONE.

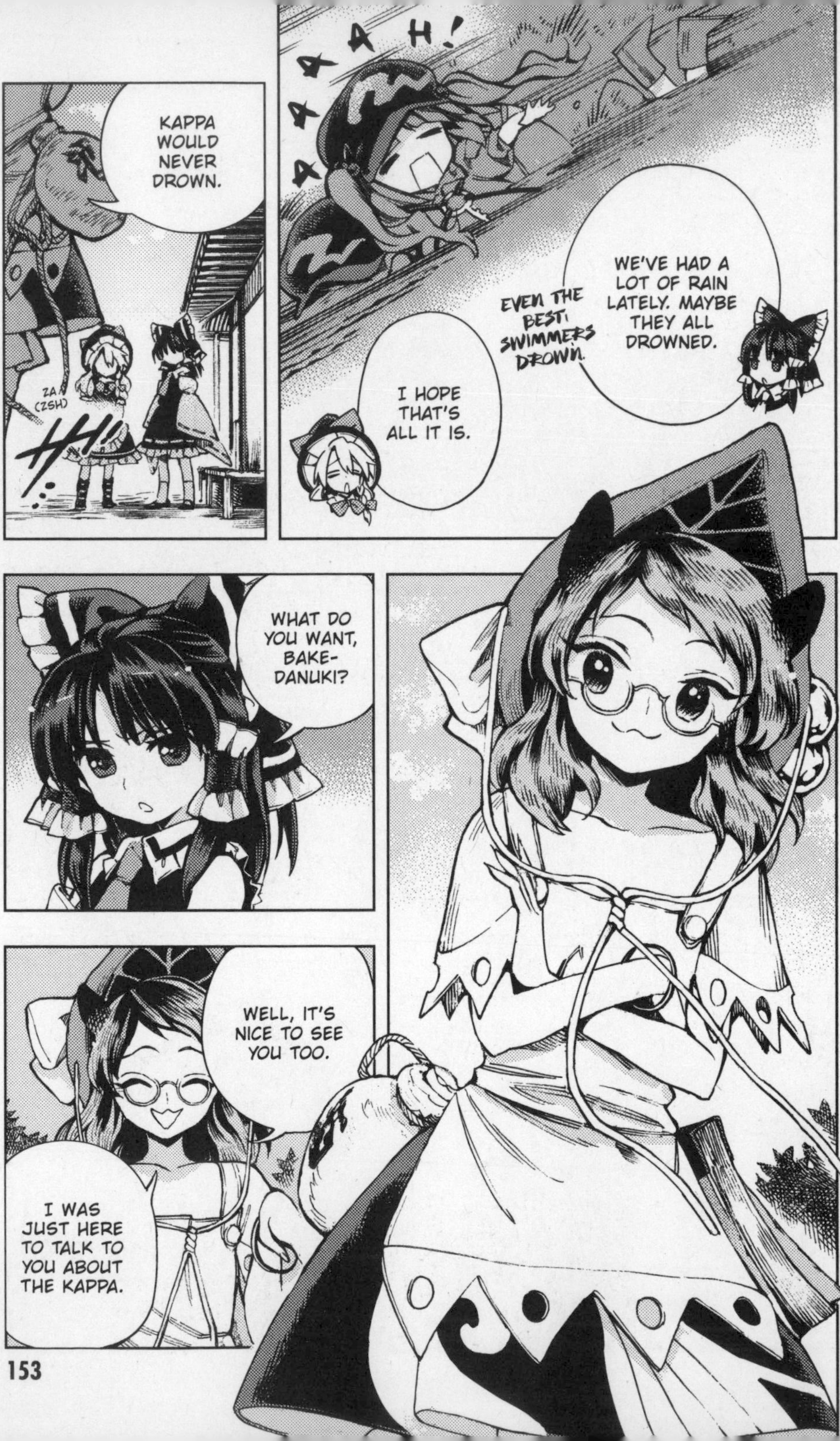
AAAAAH!
WE'VE HAD A LOT OF RAIN LATELY. MAYBE THEY ALL DROWNED.
EVEN THE BEST SWIMMERS DROWN.
I HOPE THAT'S ALL IT IS.
KAPPA WOULD NEVER DROWN.
ZA (ZSH)
WHAT DO YOU WANT, BAKE-DANUKI?
WELL, IT'S NICE TO SEE YOU TOO.
I WAS JUST HERE TO TALK TO YOU ABOUT THE KAPPA.

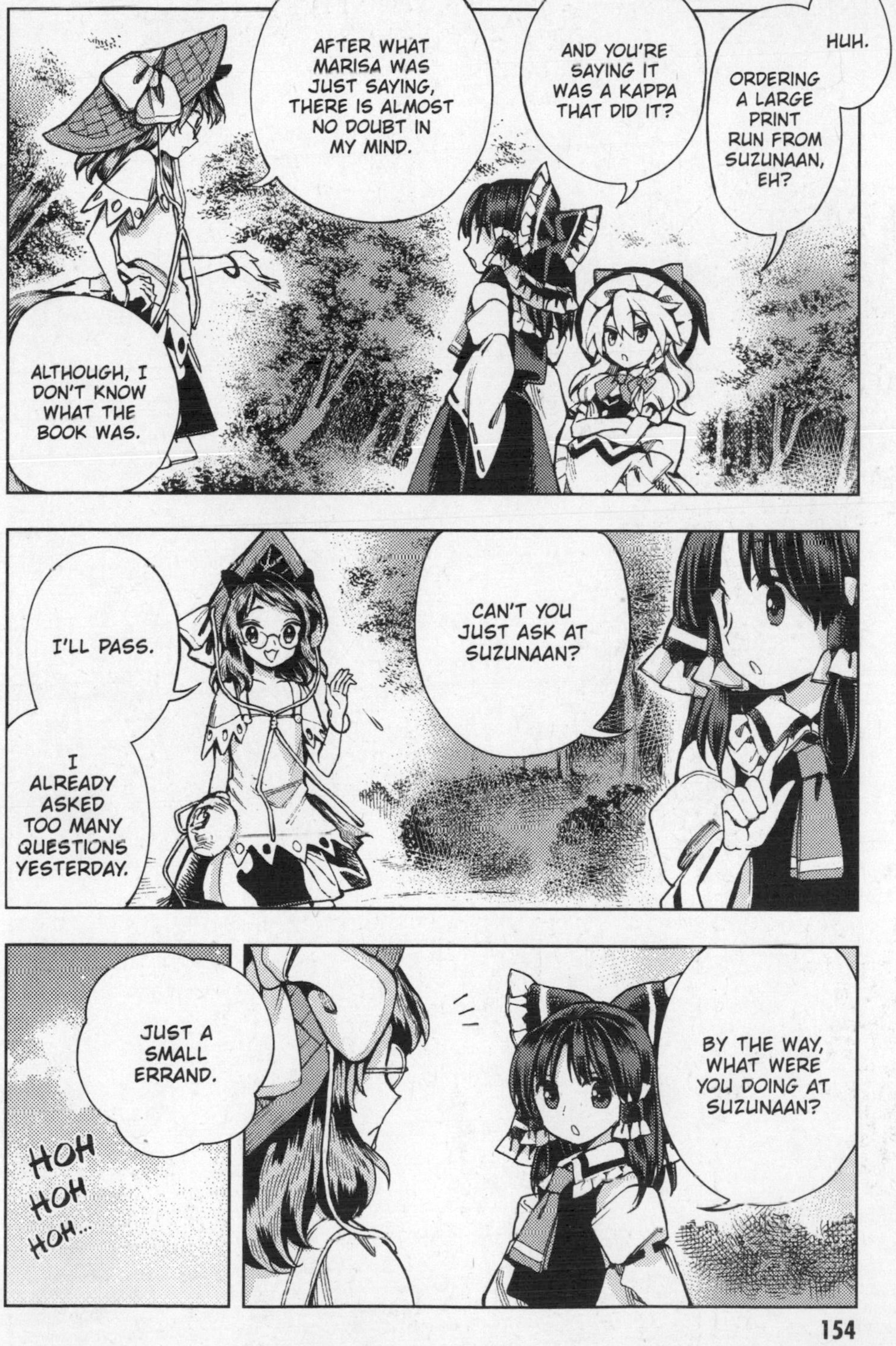
HUH.
ORDERING A LARGE PRINT RUN FROM SUZUNAAN, EH?
AND YOU'RE SAYING IT WAS A KAPPA THAT DID IT?
AFTER WHAT MARISA WAS JUST SAYING, THERE IS ALMOST NO DOUBT IN MY MIND.
ALTHOUGH, I DON'T KNOW WHAT THE BOOK WAS.
CAN'T YOU JUST ASK AT SUZUNAAN?
I'LL PASS.
I ALREADY ASKED TOO MANY QUESTIONS YESTERDAY.
BY THE WAY, WHAT WERE YOU DOING AT SUZUNAAN?
JUST A SMALL ERRAND.
HOH HOH HOH...

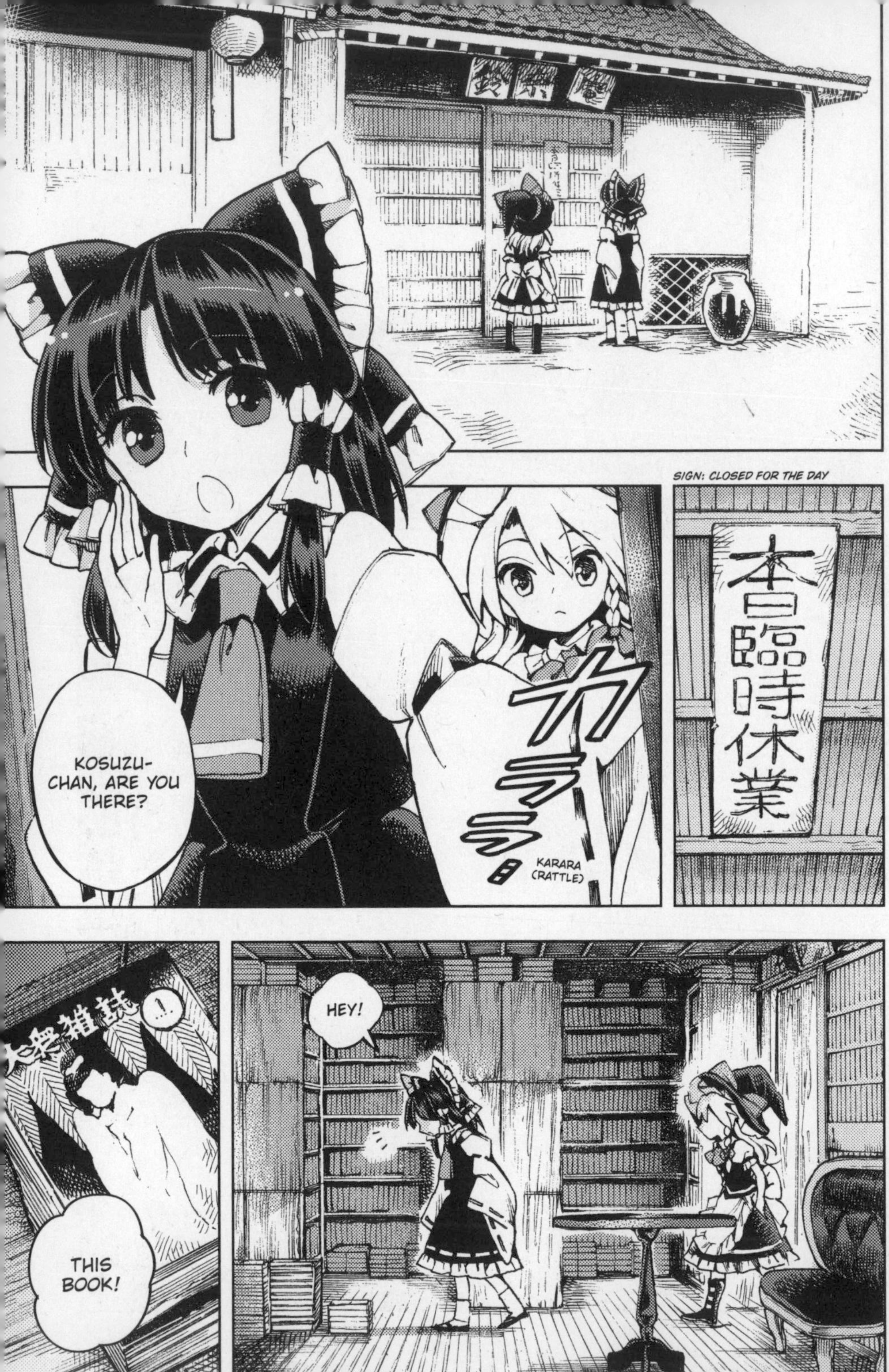
鈴奈庵
SIGN: CLOSED FOR THE DAY
本日臨時休業
カラララ
KARARA (RATTLE)
KOSUZU-CHAN, ARE YOU THERE?
HEY!
!
THIS BOOK!

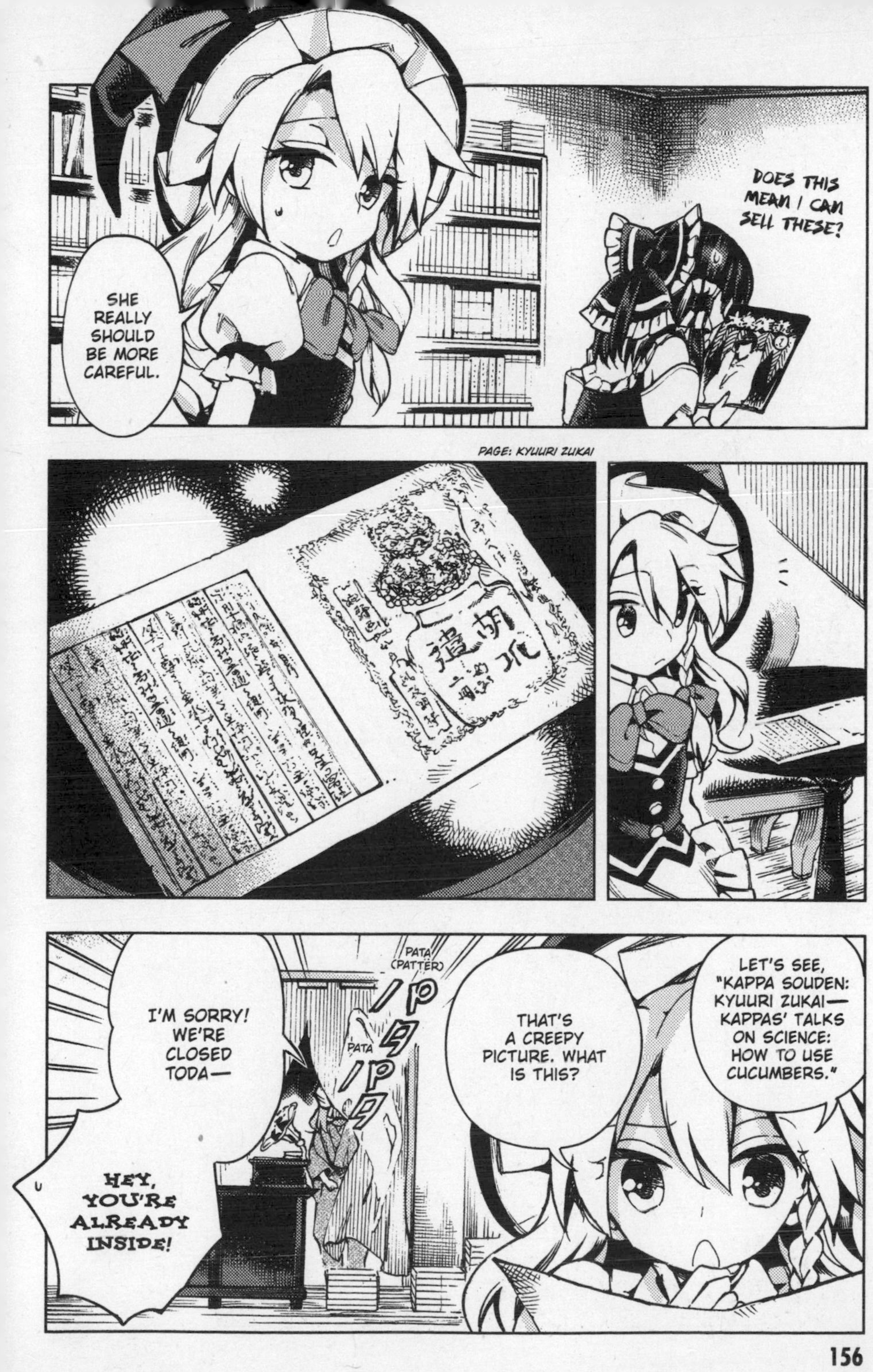

DOES THIS MEAN I CAN SELL THESE?
SHE REALLY SHOULD BE MORE CAREFUL.
PAGE: KYUURI ZUKAI
LET'S SEE, "KAPPA SOUDEN: KYUURI ZUKAI— KAPPAS' TALKS ON SCIENCE: HOW TO USE CUCUMBERS."
THAT'S A CREEPY PICTURE. WHAT IS THIS?
PATA (PATTER)
PATA
I'M SORRY! WE'RE CLOSED TODA—
HEY, YOU'RE ALREADY INSIDE!

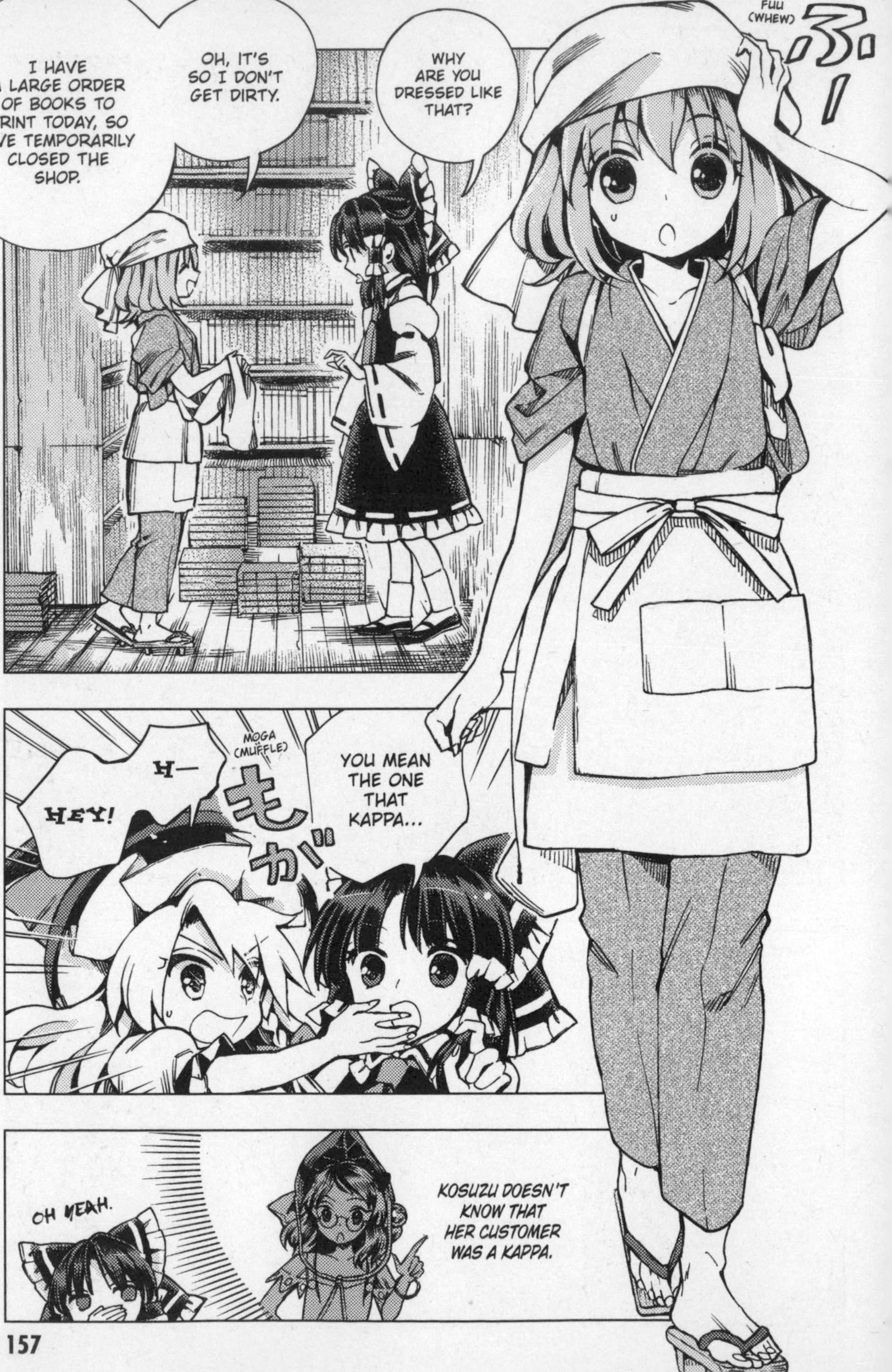
FUU (WHEW)
ふっ
WHY ARE YOU DRESSED LIKE THAT?
OH, IT'S SO I DON'T GET DIRTY.
I HAVE A LARGE ORDER OF BOOKS TO PRINT TODAY, SO I'VE TEMPORARILY CLOSED THE SHOP.
YOU MEAN THE ONE THAT KAPPA...
MOGA (MUFFLE)
もが
H—
HEY!
KOSUZU DOESN'T KNOW THAT HER CUSTOMER WAS A KAPPA.
OH YEAH.

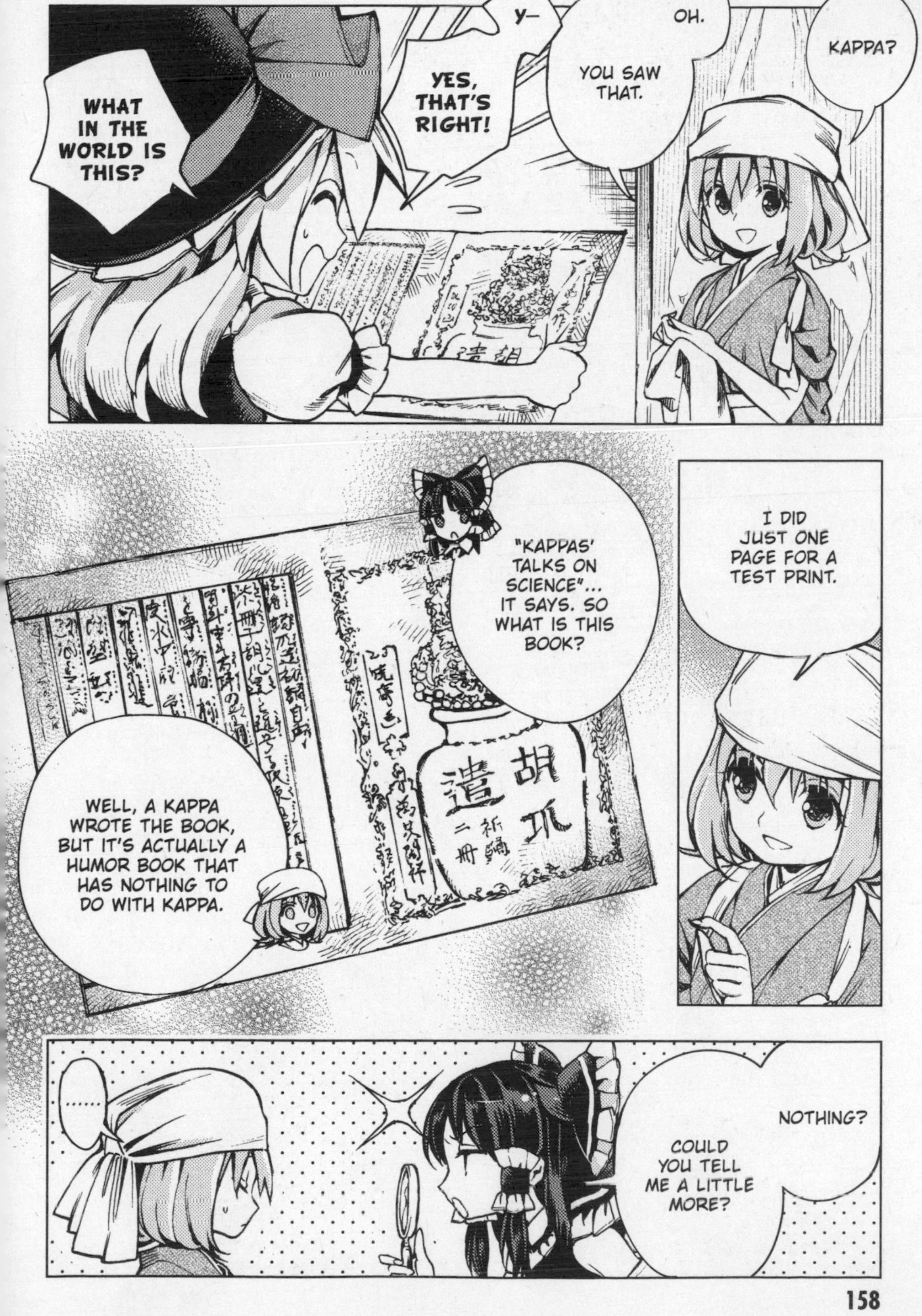
KAPPA?
OH.
YOU SAW THAT.
Y—
YES, THAT'S RIGHT!
WHAT IN THE WORLD IS THIS?
I DID JUST ONE PAGE FOR A TEST PRINT.
"KAPPAS' TALKS ON SCIENCE"... IT SAYS. SO WHAT IS THIS BOOK?
WELL, A KAPPA WROTE THE BOOK, BUT IT'S ACTUALLY A HUMOR BOOK THAT HAS NOTHING TO DO WITH KAPPA.
NOTHING?
COULD YOU TELL ME A LITTLE MORE?
......

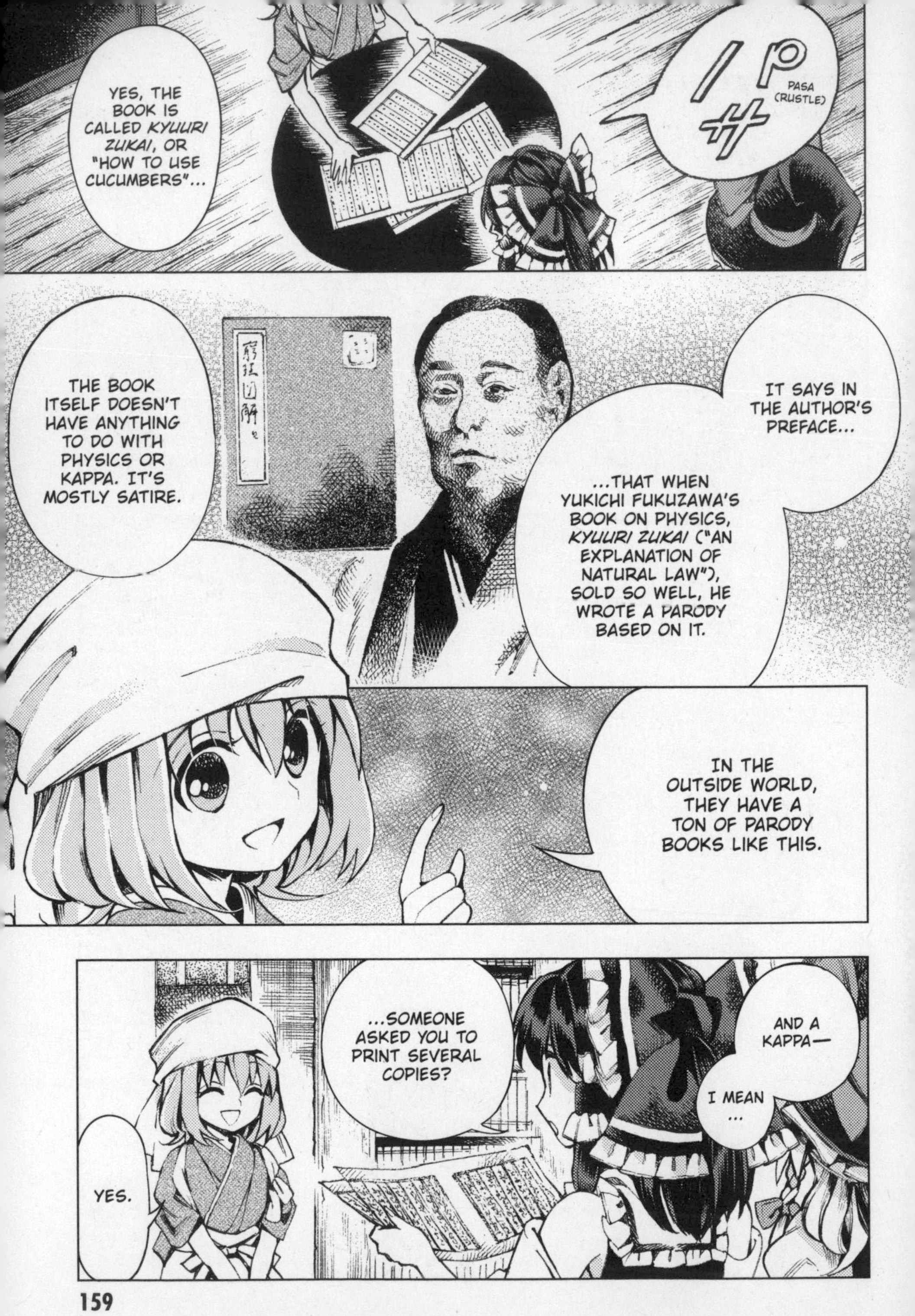
PASA (RUSTLE)
YES, THE BOOK IS CALLED *KYUURI ZUKAI*, OR "HOW TO USE CUCUMBERS"...
IT SAYS IN THE AUTHOR'S PREFACE...
...THAT WHEN YUKICHI FUKUZAWA'S BOOK ON PHYSICS, *KYUURI ZUKAI* ("AN EXPLANATION OF NATURAL LAW"), SOLD SO WELL, HE WROTE A PARODY BASED ON IT.
THE BOOK ITSELF DOESN'T HAVE ANYTHING TO DO WITH PHYSICS OR KAPPA. IT'S MOSTLY SATIRE.
IN THE OUTSIDE WORLD, THEY HAVE A TON OF PARODY BOOKS LIKE THIS.
AND A KAPPA—
I MEAN ...
...SOMEONE ASKED YOU TO PRINT SEVERAL COPIES?
YES.

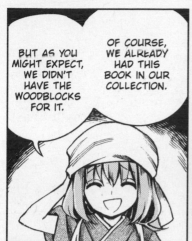

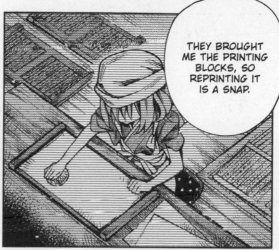

THEY BROUGHT ME THE PRINTING BLOCKS, SO REPRINTING IT IS A SNAP.
OF COURSE, WE ALREADY HAD THIS BOOK IN OUR COLLECTION.
BUT AS YOU MIGHT EXPECT, WE DIDN'T HAVE THE WOODBLOCKS FOR IT.
UH.
RIGHT.
ARE YOU SERIOUS...?
FROM THE LOOK OF IT, IT'S JUST A NORMAL BOOK PRINTED ON NORMAL PAPER.
?
YES, AND...?
IS THERE SOMETHING WRONG WITH THE BOOK?
OH, IT'S NOTHING.
WE'RE SORRY FOR INTERRUPTING YOUR WORK.
PASA (RUSTLE)

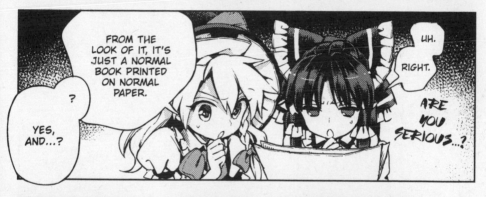

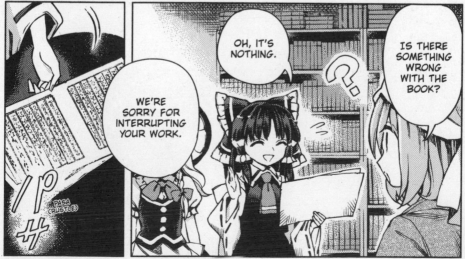

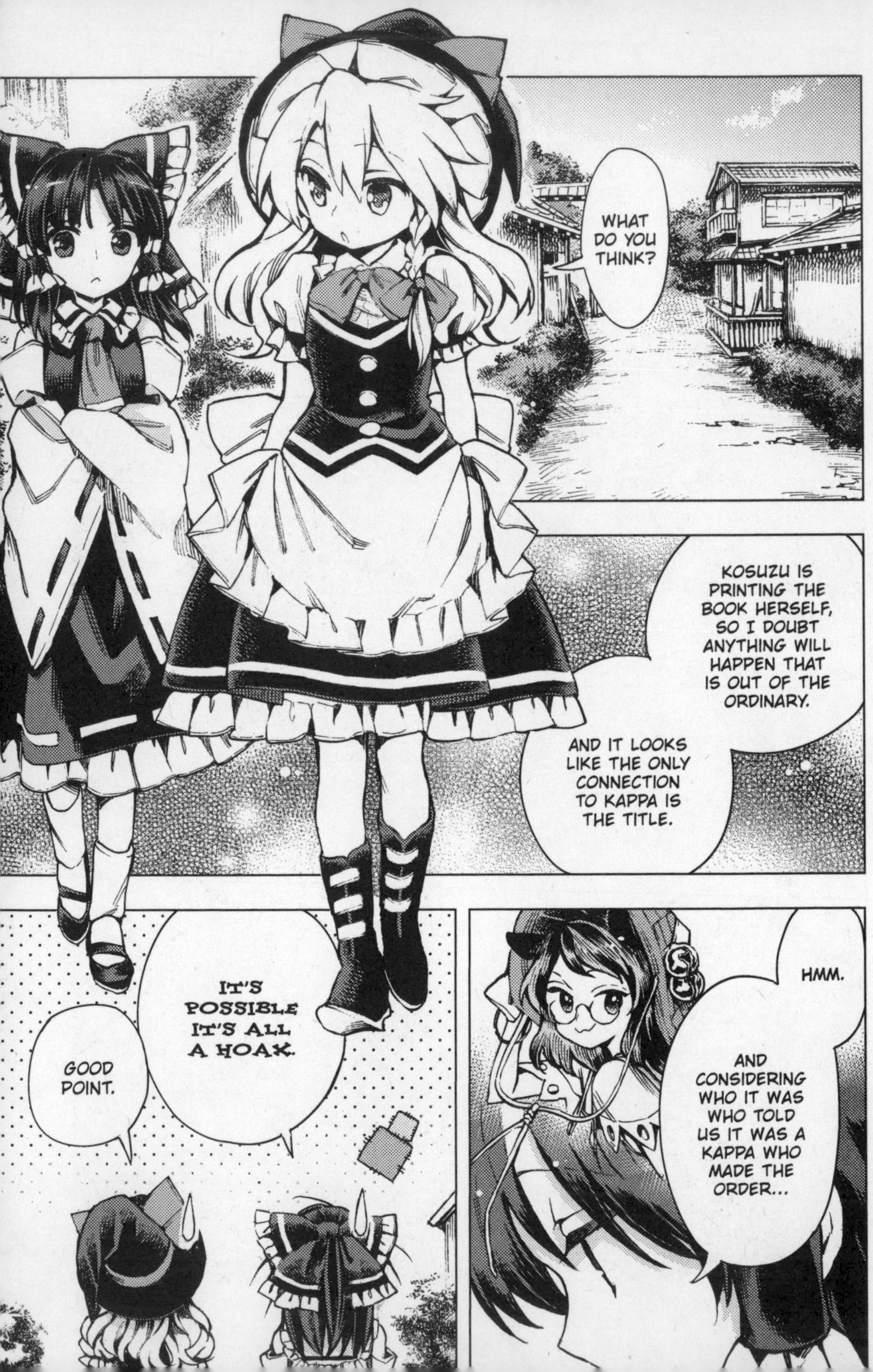
WHAT DO YOU THINK?
KOSUZU IS PRINTING THE BOOK HERSELF, SO I DOUBT ANYTHING WILL HAPPEN THAT IS OUT OF THE ORDINARY.
AND IT LOOKS LIKE THE ONLY CONNECTION TO KAPPA IS THE TITLE.
HMM.
AND CONSIDERING WHO IT WAS WHO TOLD US IT WAS A KAPPA WHO MADE THE ORDER...
IT'S POSSIBLE IT'S ALL A HOAX.
GOOD POINT.

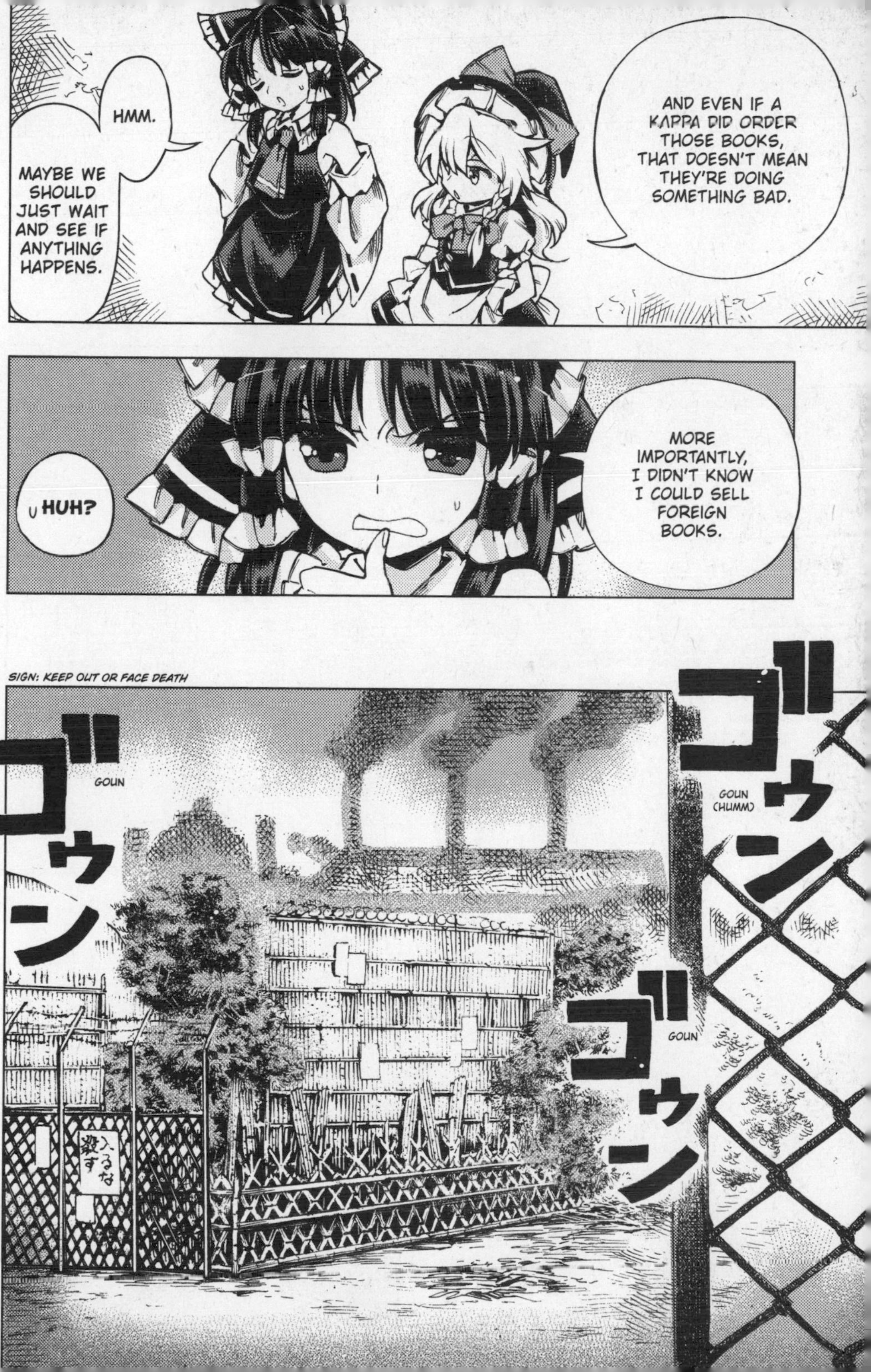
AND EVEN IF A KAPPA DID ORDER THOSE BOOKS, THAT DOESN'T MEAN THEY'RE DOING SOMETHING BAD.
HMM.
MAYBE WE SHOULD JUST WAIT AND SEE IF ANYTHING HAPPENS.
MORE IMPORTANTLY, I DIDN'T KNOW I COULD SELL FOREIGN BOOKS.
HUH?
SIGN: KEEP OUT OR FACE DEATH
ゴウン
GOUN (HUMM)
ゴウン
GOUN
ゴウン
GOUN
入るな
殺す

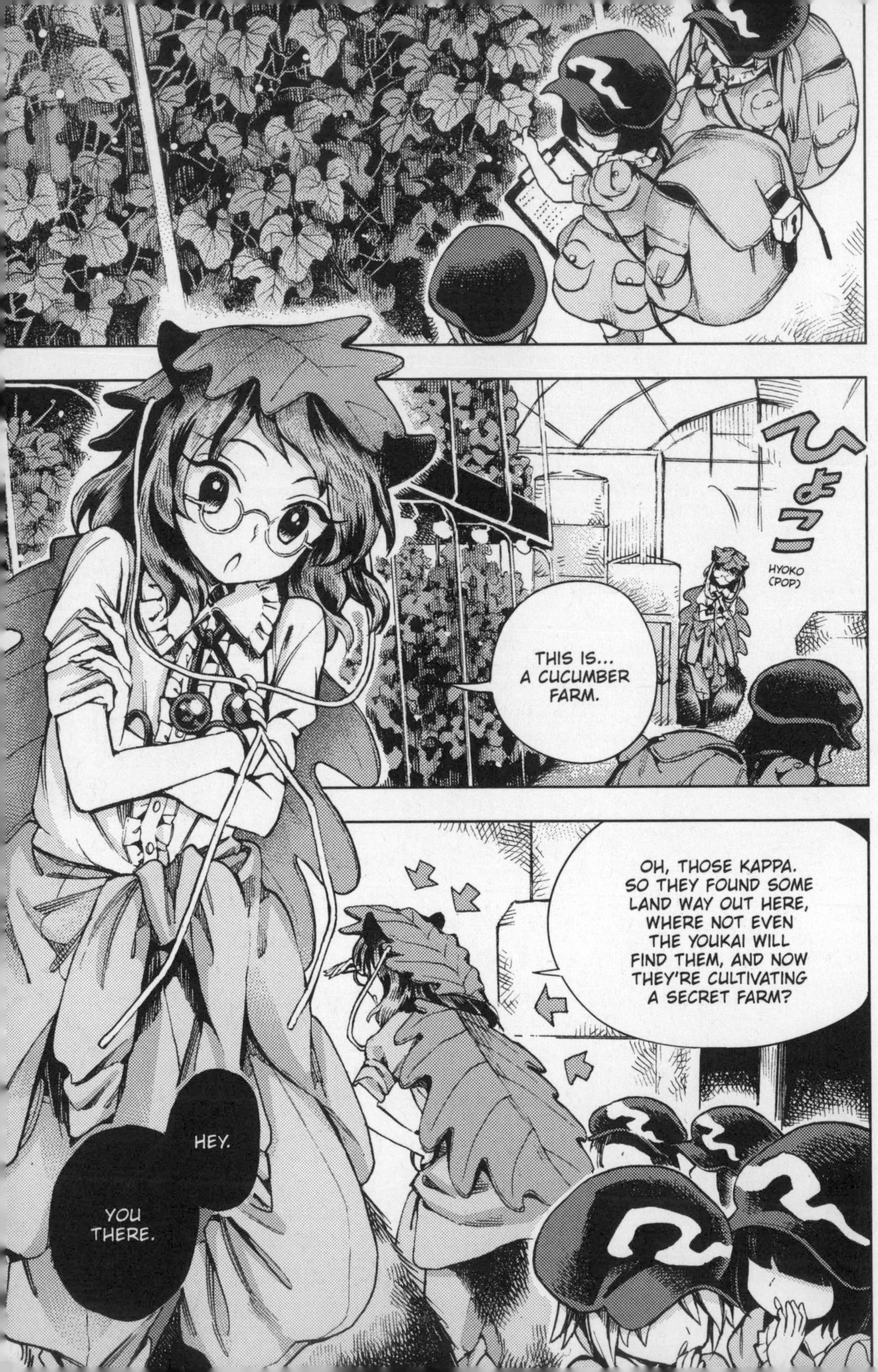
ひょっこ
HYOKO (POP)
THIS IS... A CUCUMBER FARM.
OH, THOSE KAPPA. SO THEY FOUND SOME LAND WAY OUT HERE, WHERE NOT EVEN THE YOUKAI WILL FIND THEM, AND NOW THEY'RE CULTIVATING A SECRET FARM?
HEY.
YOU THERE.

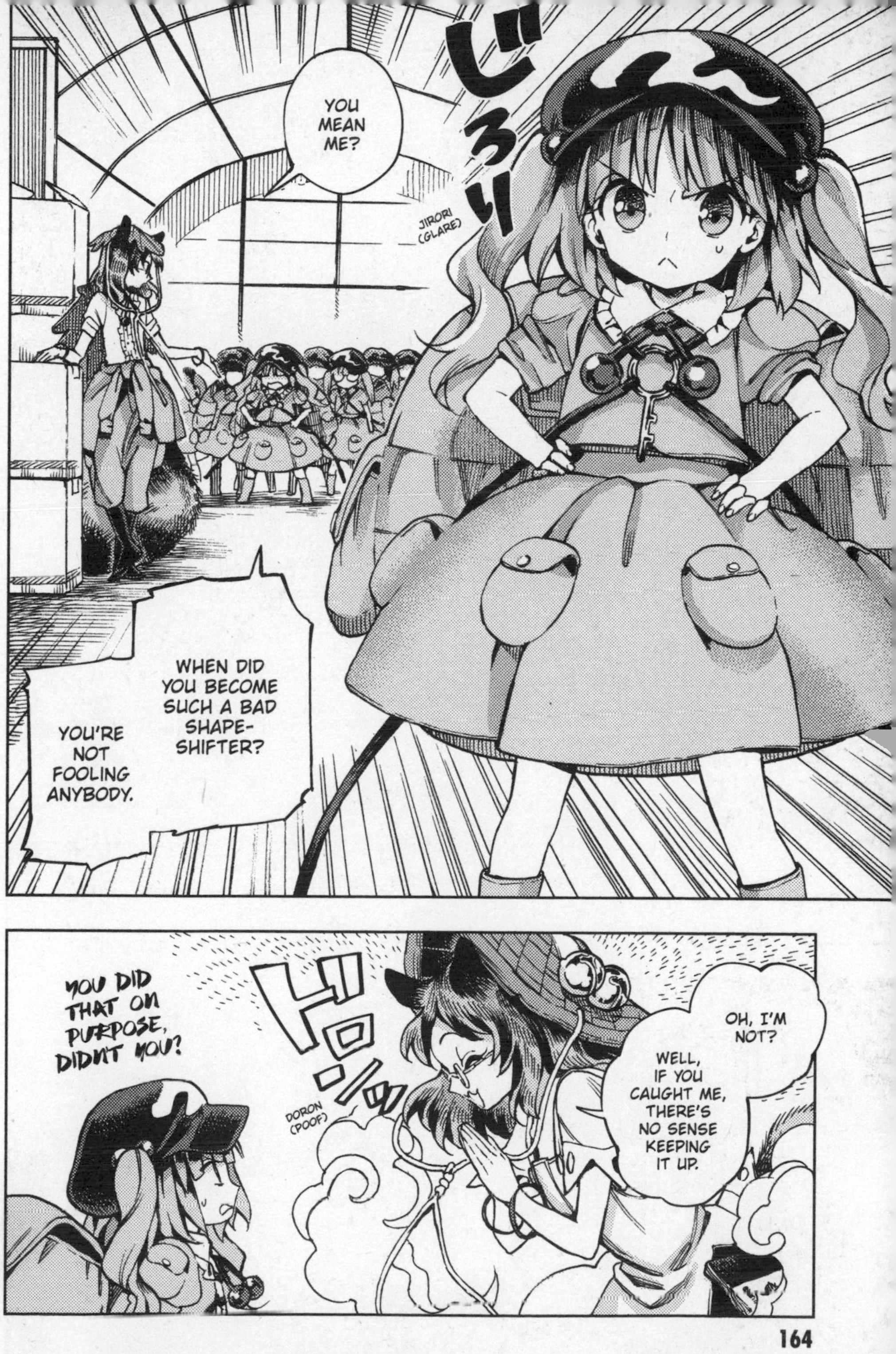
じろり
JIRORI (GLARE)
YOU MEAN ME?
WHEN DID YOU BECOME SUCH A BAD SHAPE-SHIFTER?
YOU'RE NOT FOOLING ANYBODY.
OH, I'M NOT?
WELL, IF YOU CAUGHT ME, THERE'S NO SENSE KEEPING IT UP.
ドロン
DORON (POOF)
YOU DID THAT ON PURPOSE, DIDN'T YOU?

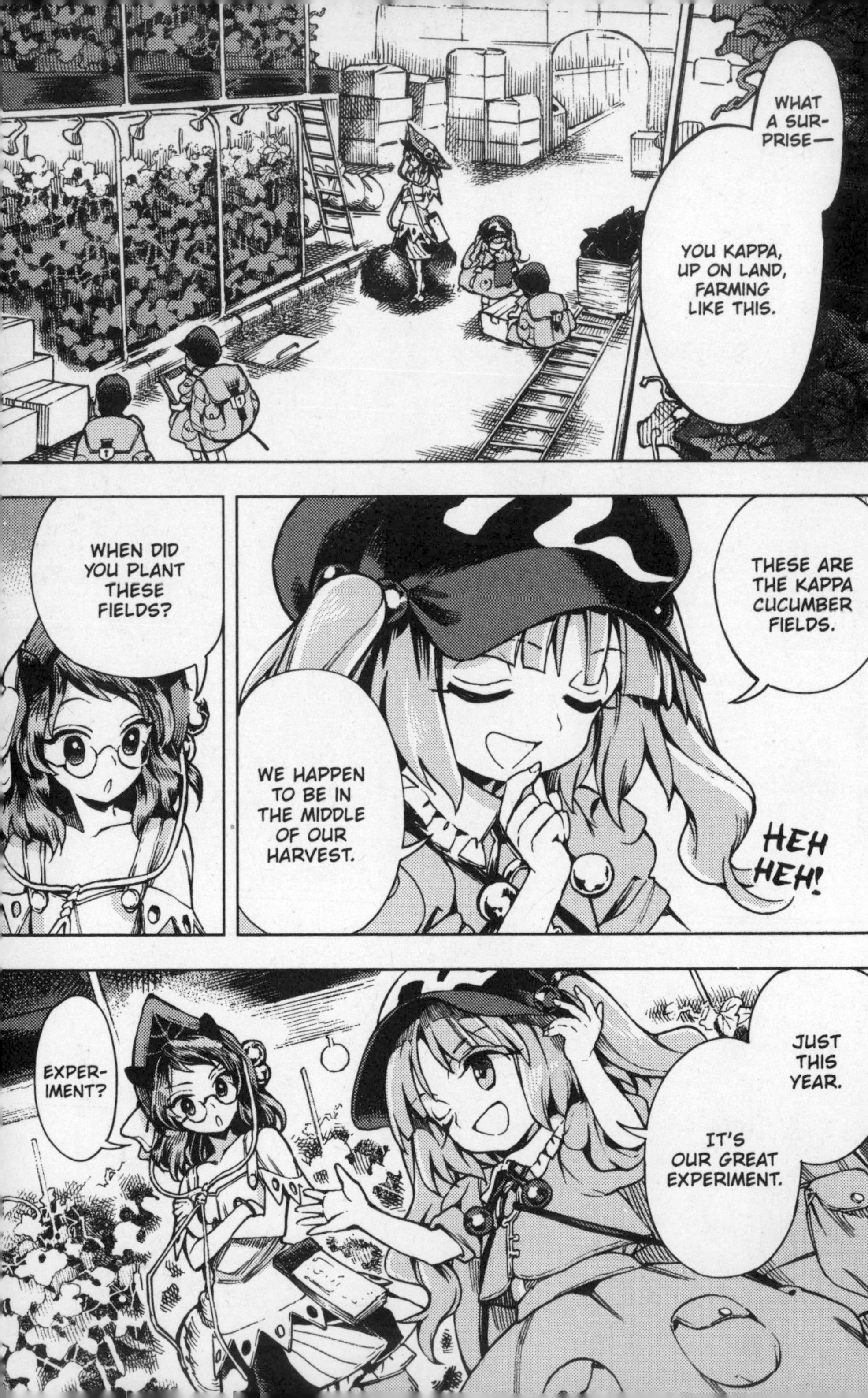
WHAT A SURPRISE—
YOU KAPPA, UP ON LAND, FARMING LIKE THIS.
THESE ARE THE KAPPA CUCUMBER FIELDS.
HEH HEH!
WE HAPPEN TO BE IN THE MIDDLE OF OUR HARVEST.
WHEN DID YOU PLANT THESE FIELDS?
JUST THIS YEAR.
IT'S OUR GREAT EXPERIMENT.
EXPERIMENT?

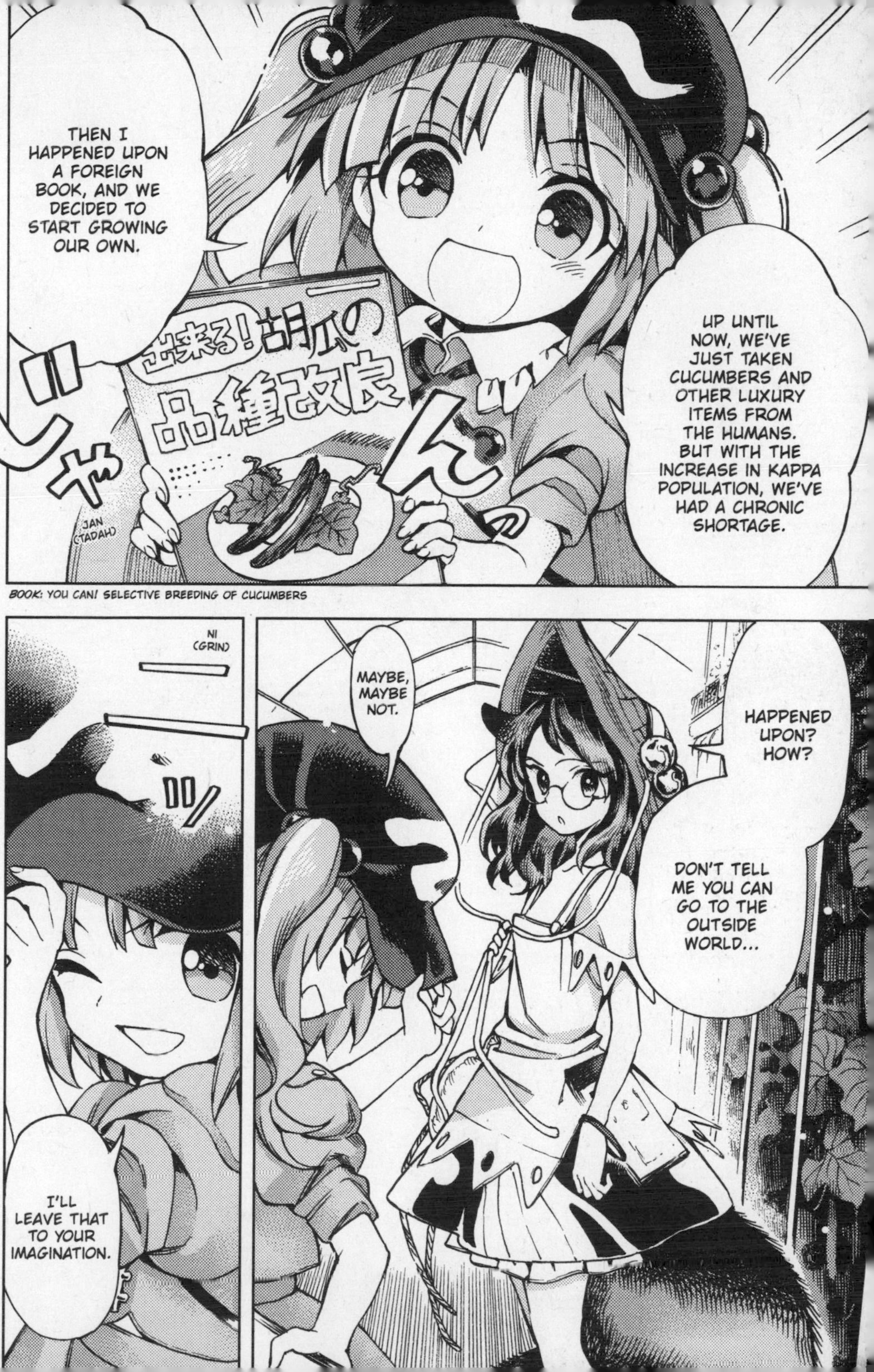
UP UNTIL NOW, WE'VE JUST TAKEN CUCUMBERS AND OTHER LUXURY ITEMS FROM THE HUMANS. BUT WITH THE INCREASE IN KAPPA POPULATION, WE'VE HAD A CHRONIC SHORTAGE.
THEN I HAPPENED UPON A FOREIGN BOOK, AND WE DECIDED TO START GROWING OUR OWN.
出来る！胡瓜の品種改良
じゃーん
JAN (TADAH)
BOOK: YOU CAN! SELECTIVE BREEDING OF CUCUMBERS
HAPPENED UPON? HOW?
DON'T TELL ME YOU CAN GO TO THE OUTSIDE WORLD...
MAYBE, MAYBE NOT.
NI (GRIN)
I'LL LEAVE THAT TO YOUR IMAGINATION.

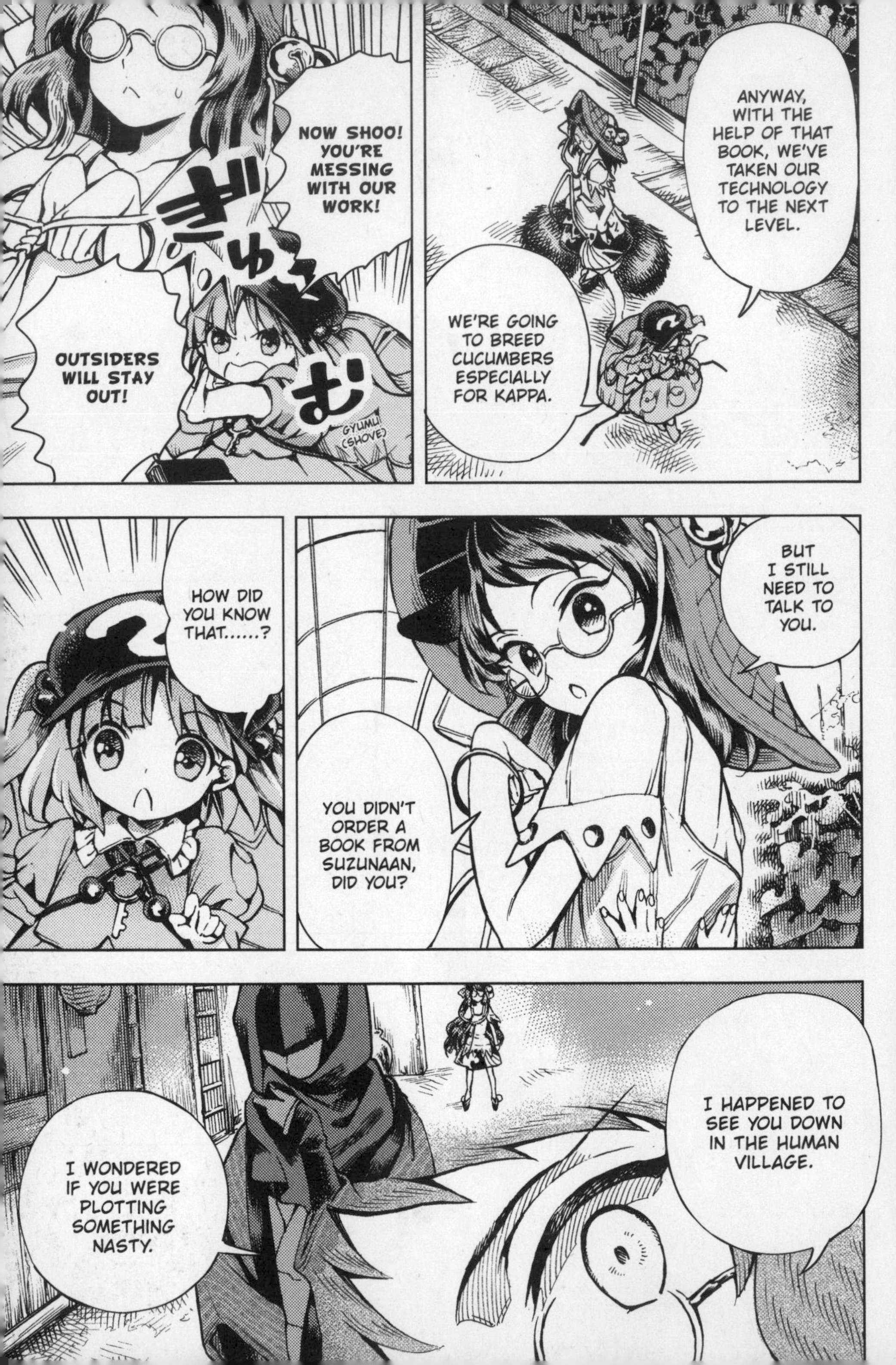
ANYWAY, WITH THE HELP OF THAT BOOK, WE'VE TAKEN OUR TECHNOLOGY TO THE NEXT LEVEL.
WE'RE GOING TO BREED CUCUMBERS ESPECIALLY FOR KAPPA.
NOW SHOO! YOU'RE MESSING WITH OUR WORK!
ぎゅむ
OUTSIDERS WILL STAY OUT!
GYUMU (SHOVE)
BUT I STILL NEED TO TALK TO YOU.
YOU DIDN'T ORDER A BOOK FROM SUZUNAAN, DID YOU?
HOW DID YOU KNOW THAT......?
I HAPPENED TO SEE YOU DOWN IN THE HUMAN VILLAGE.
I WONDERED IF YOU WERE PLOTTING SOMETHING NASTY.

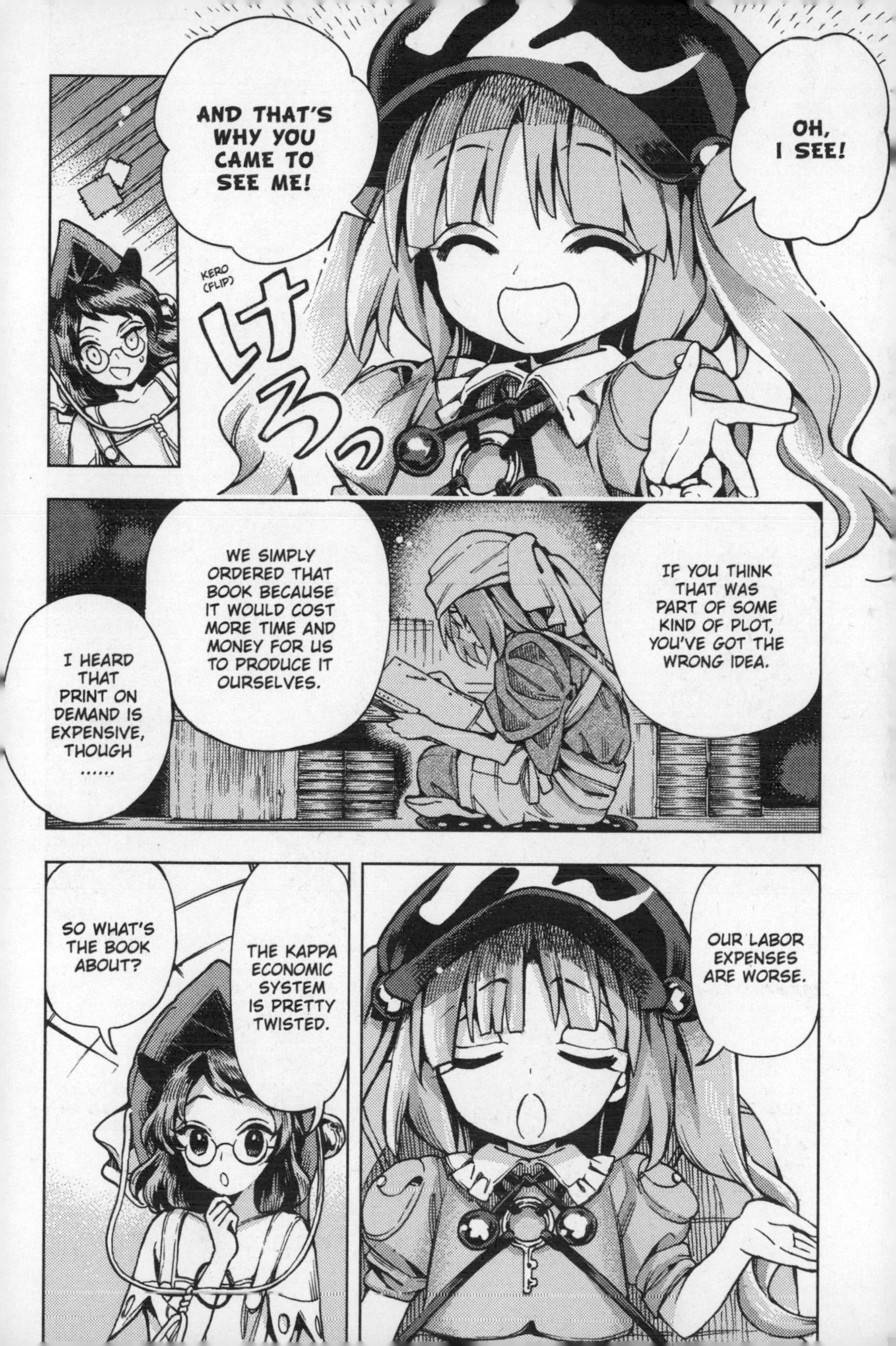
OH, I SEE!
AND THAT'S WHY YOU CAME TO SEE ME!
けろっ
KERO (FLIP)
IF YOU THINK THAT WAS PART OF SOME KIND OF PLOT, YOU'VE GOT THE WRONG IDEA.
WE SIMPLY ORDERED THAT BOOK BECAUSE IT WOULD COST MORE TIME AND MONEY FOR US TO PRODUCE IT OURSELVES.
I HEARD THAT PRINT ON DEMAND IS EXPENSIVE, THOUGH ......
OUR LABOR EXPENSES ARE WORSE.
THE KAPPA ECONOMIC SYSTEM IS PRETTY TWISTED.
SO WHAT'S THE BOOK ABOUT?

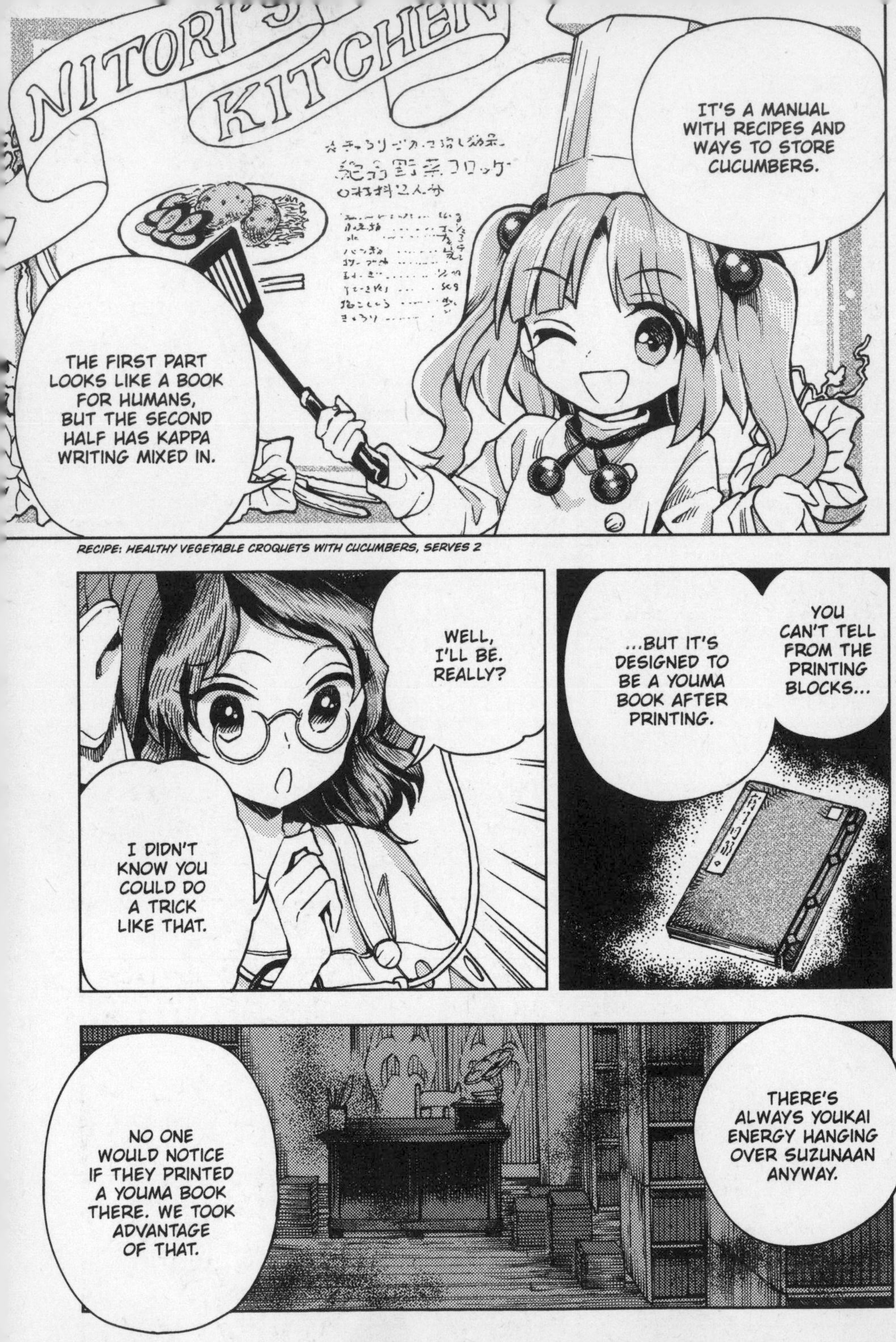
NITORI'S KITCHEN
IT'S A MANUAL WITH RECIPES AND WAYS TO STORE CUCUMBERS.
THE FIRST PART LOOKS LIKE A BOOK FOR HUMANS, BUT THE SECOND HALF HAS KAPPA WRITING MIXED IN.
RECIPE: HEALTHY VEGETABLE CROQUETS WITH CUCUMBERS, SERVES 2
YOU CAN'T TELL FROM THE PRINTING BLOCKS...
...BUT IT'S DESIGNED TO BE A YOUMA BOOK AFTER PRINTING.
WELL, I'LL BE. REALLY?
I DIDN'T KNOW YOU COULD DO A TRICK LIKE THAT.
THERE'S ALWAYS YOUKAI ENERGY HANGING OVER SUZUNAAN ANYWAY.
NO ONE WOULD NOTICE IF THEY PRINTED A YOUMA BOOK THERE. WE TOOK ADVANTAGE OF THAT.

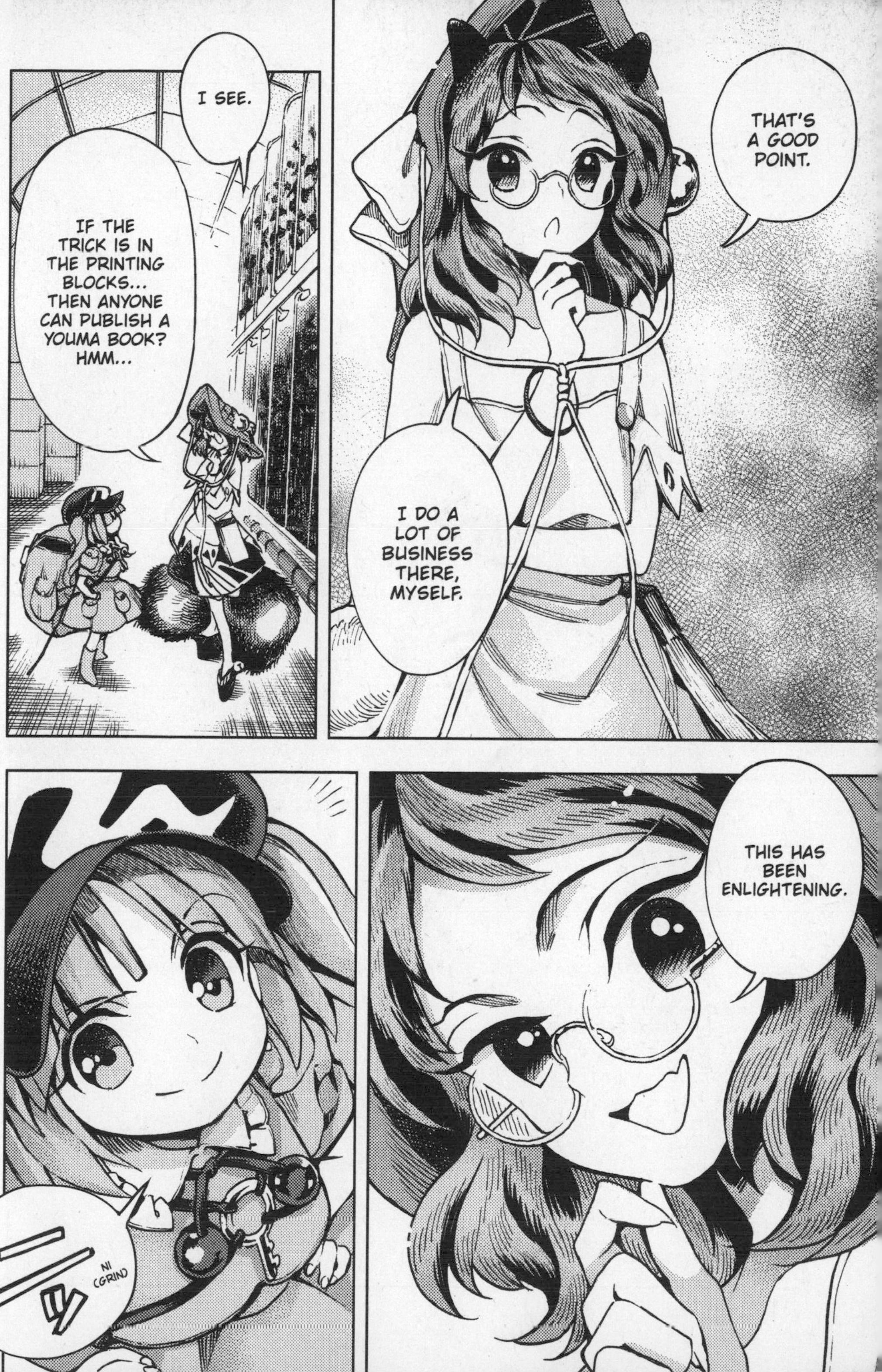
THAT'S A GOOD POINT.
I DO A LOT OF BUSINESS THERE, MYSELF.
I SEE.
IF THE TRICK IS IN THE PRINTING BLOCKS... THEN ANYONE CAN PUBLISH A YOUMA BOOK? HMM...
THIS HAS BEEN ENLIGHTENING.
NI (GRIN)

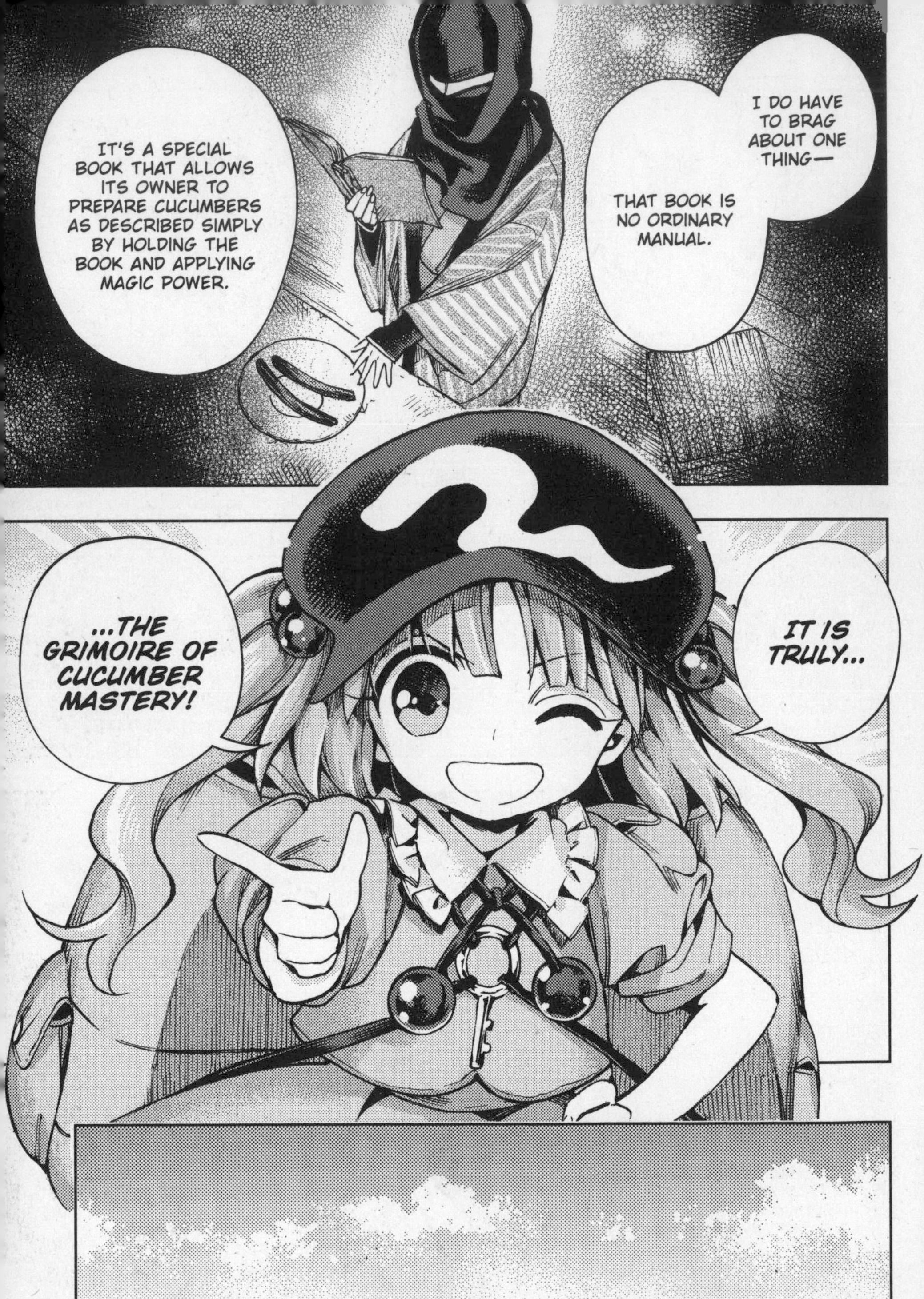
I DO HAVE TO BRAG ABOUT ONE THING—
THAT BOOK IS NO ORDINARY MANUAL.
IT'S A SPECIAL BOOK THAT ALLOWS ITS OWNER TO PREPARE CUCUMBERS AS DESCRIBED SIMPLY BY HOLDING THE BOOK AND APPLYING MAGIC POWER.
IT IS TRULY...
...THE GRIMOIRE OF CUCUMBER MASTERY!

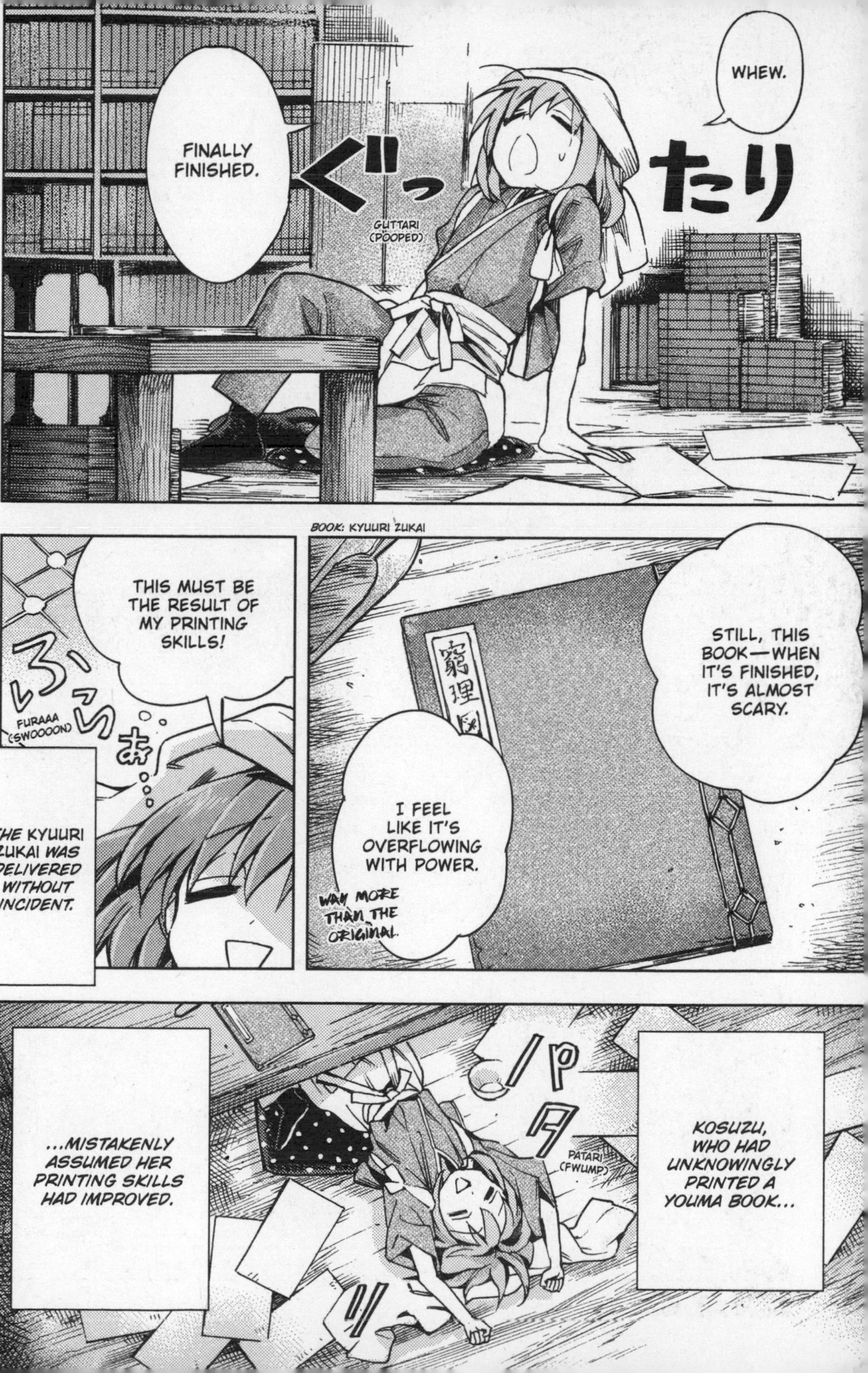
WHEW.
FINALLY FINISHED.
ぐったり
GUTTARI (POOPED)
BOOK: KYUURI ZUKAI
窮理図
STILL, THIS BOOK—WHEN IT'S FINISHED, IT'S ALMOST SCARY.
I FEEL LIKE IT'S OVERFLOWING WITH POWER.
WAY MORE THAN THE ORIGINAL.
THIS MUST BE THE RESULT OF MY PRINTING SKILLS!
ふらあ
FURAAA (SWOOOON)
THE KYUURI ZUKAI WAS DELIVERED WITHOUT INCIDENT.
KOSUZU, WHO HAD UNKNOWINGLY PRINTED A YOUMA BOOK...
パタリ
PATARI (FWUMP)
...MISTAKENLY ASSUMED HER PRINTING SKILLS HAD IMPROVED.

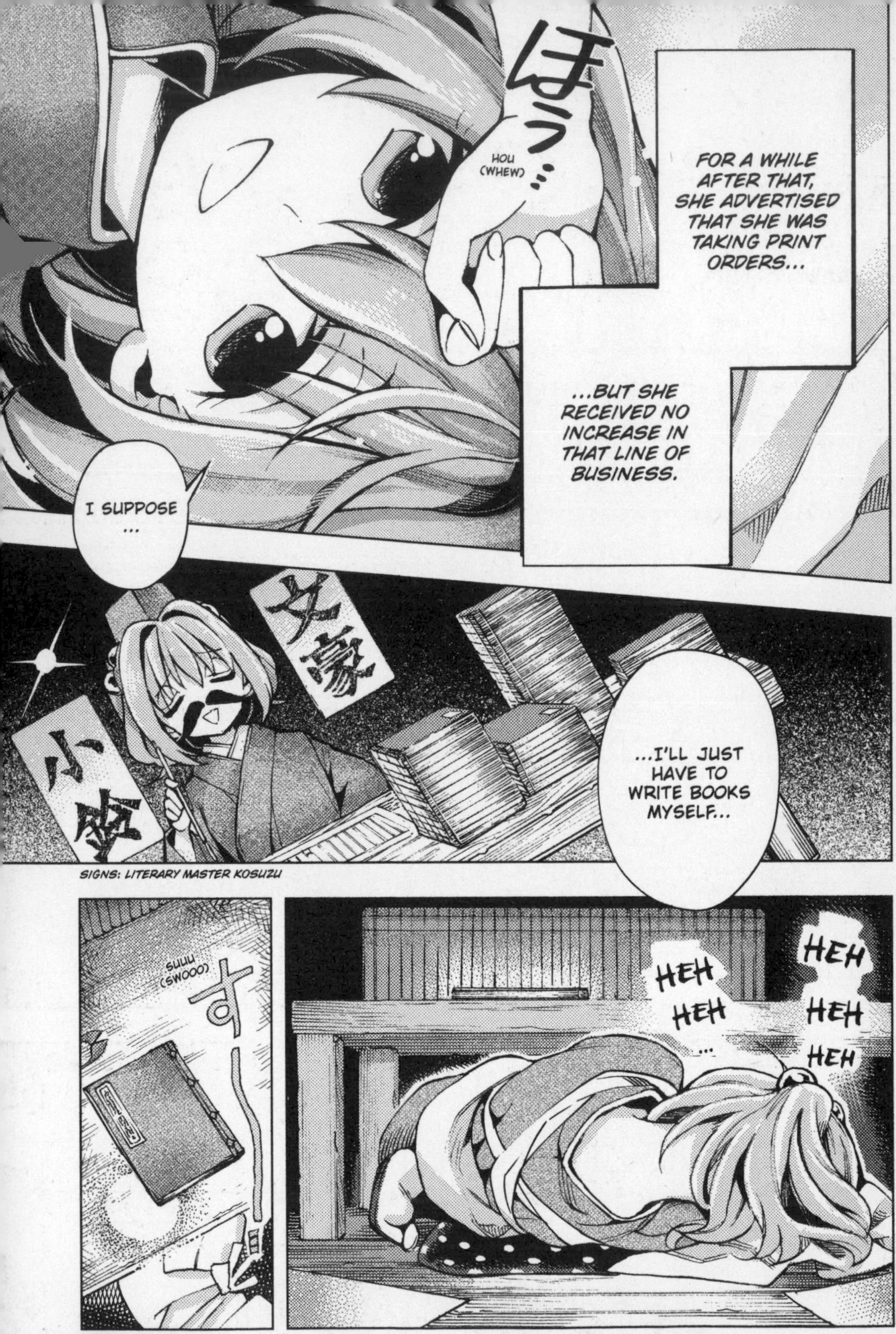

FOR A WHILE AFTER THAT, SHE ADVERTISED THAT SHE WAS TAKING PRINT ORDERS...
...BUT SHE RECEIVED NO INCREASE IN THAT LINE OF BUSINESS.
ほう
HOU (WHEW)
I SUPPOSE ...
...I'LL JUST HAVE TO WRITE BOOKS MYSELF...
文豪
小鈴
SIGNS: LITERARY MASTER KOSUZU
HEH HEH HEH
HEH HEH ...
す
SUUU (SWOOO)

Chapter 29 End

Forbidden Scrollery

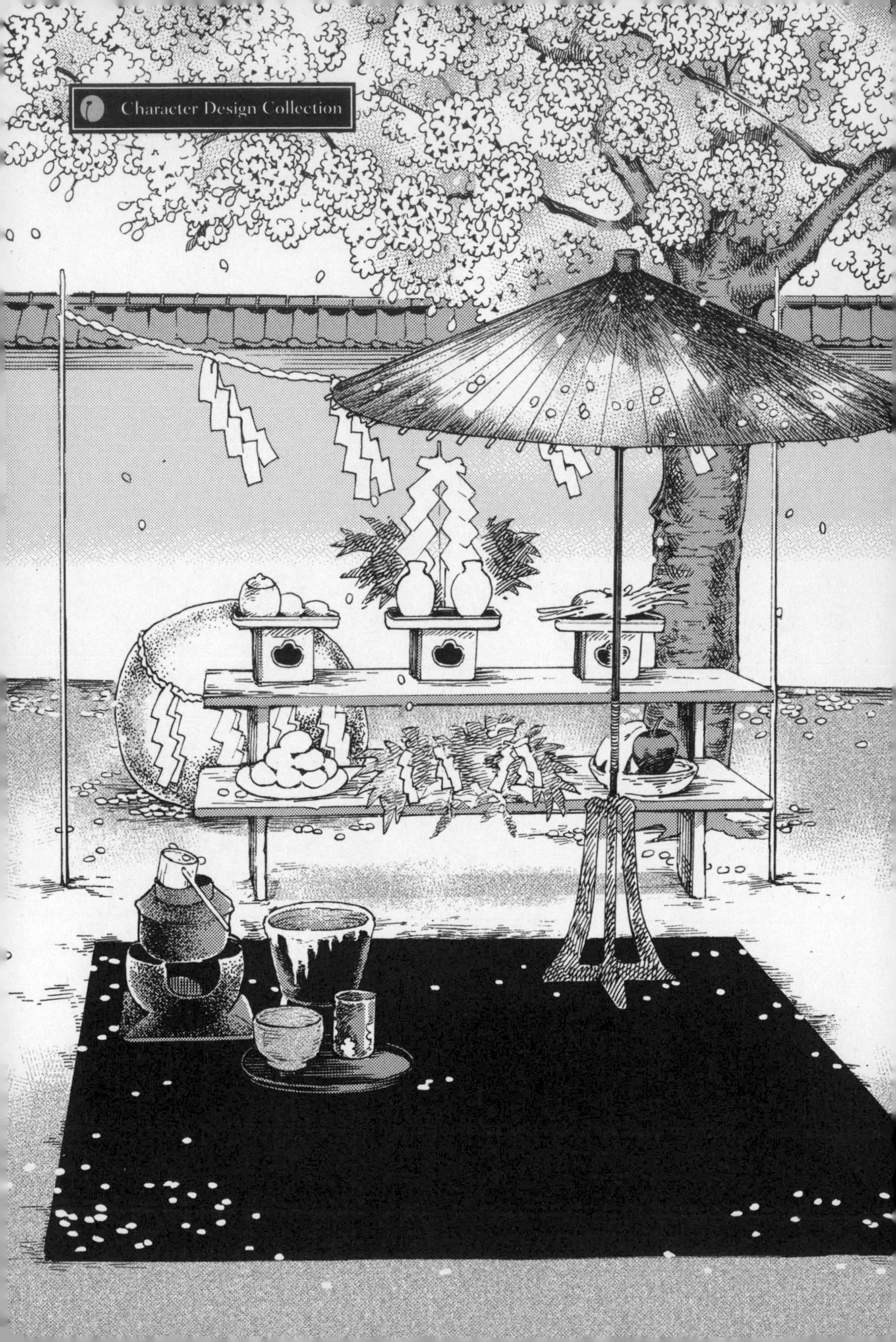
Character Design Collection

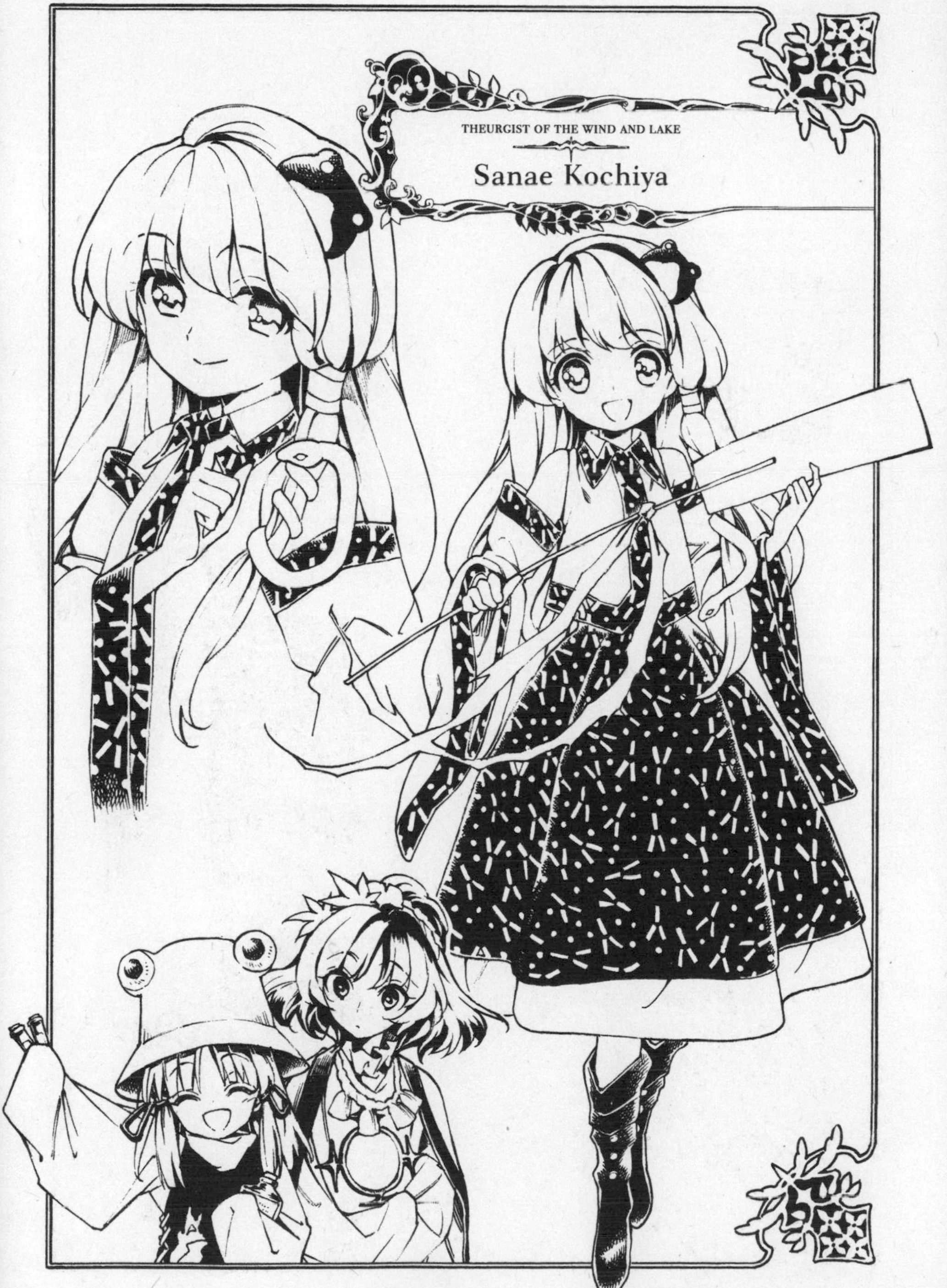THEURGIST OF THE WIND AND LAKE
Sanae Kochiya

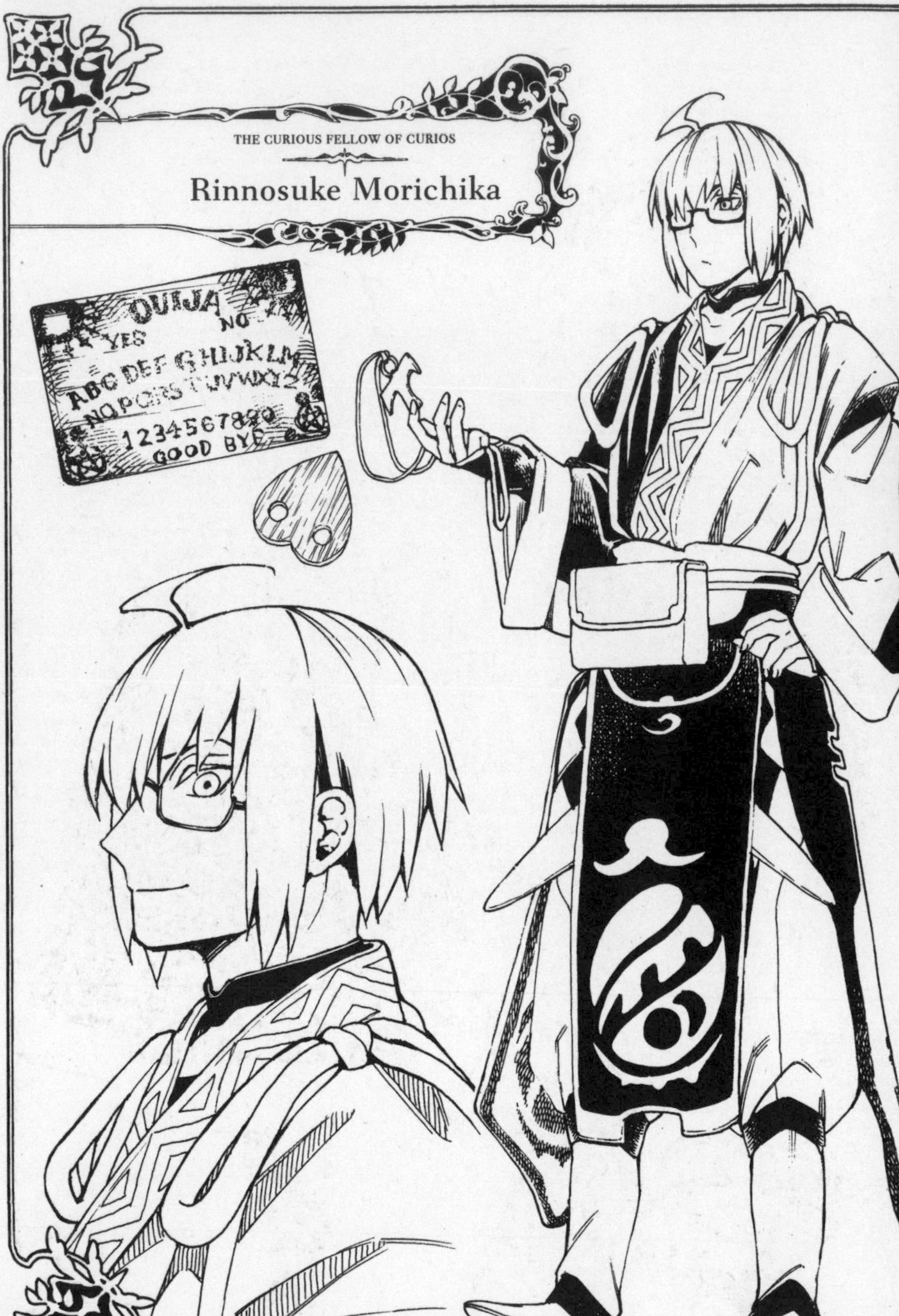
THE CURIOUS FELLOW OF CURIOS
Rinnosuke Morichika
OUIJA
YES
NO
1234567890
GOOD BYE

TRANSLATION NOTES

GENERAL

Certain character names, such as Akyu Hiedano, are also commonly rendered differently, i.e., Hieda-no-Akyu, literally "Akyu of the Hieda." This English edition renders names as given name first in order to avoid confusion.

The character names also frequently contain references or certain meanings due to how they're written in Japanese.

Sanae Kochiya: The surname "Kochiya" includes the kanji for "east wind," which most likely points to her role as a wind priestess in the Touhou universe. While "Sanae" in Japanese means "rice seedling," it is more probable the reference is to the seventy-eighth head of the real-life Moriya family, Sanae Moriya, as Sanae Kochiya is a priestess of the Moriya shrine.

Rinnosuke Morichika: "Morichika" means "near the forest," which is fitting, as that is where his shop, Kourindou, is located. "Rinnosuke" translated from the Japanese means something along the lines of "help for a long spell of rain."

PAGE 15

Red snake, come on!: Sanae is making a reference to Japanese pop culture with this phrase, which comes from a skit by the group Tokyo Comic Show. This skit is a snake-charming act by comedian Igari Chopin, involving a red snake hand puppet.

PAGE 35

Uwabami: Meaning "giant snake" or "giant serpent," this *youkai* is a shape-shifting creature that is a glutton and enjoys consuming alcohol. In Japan, *uwabami* is also a colloquial term used to call someone a heavy drinker.

PAGE 98

Human-faced dog: The *jinmenken*, or "human-faced dog," is a creature with, as may be expected, the body of a dog and the face of a human. The legend of the *jinmenken* was popular in the Edo era, and it is said they roam the streets at night. They are not supposed to be particularly harmful creatures but are seen as bad omens.

The foot-selling woman: The *ashiuribabaa*, or "foot-selling woman," is an old woman spirit who carries around a parcel of children's legs. She is said to haunt grammar schools, and she goes up to children, asking them if they want a leg. If they say no, she takes a leg from them, but if they say yes due to her persistence, she forces a third leg upon them.

PAGE 112

Torii: The symbol of Japanese Shintoism, a *torii* is a traditional gate found at the entrance of Shinto shrines to mark the boundary between earthly and sacred.

PAGE 153

Even the best swimmers drown: An adaptation of the original proverb *"kappa no kawanagare,"* it is equivalent to the English phrase "even Homer sometimes nods." This is to mean that even the best can slip up and make a mistake, but in Japanese the phrase literally translates to "even *kappa* can drown."

PAGE 159

Kyuuri Zukai: The title of the book Kosuzu gets a print order for, *Kyuuri Zukai* ("How to Use Cucumbers"), is a play on words from a book on natural law called *Kyuuri Zukai*. While they appear to have the same name, they are composed of different kanji characters.

ZUN

Hello, ZUN here. I feel like *Forbidden Scrollery* started only a little while ago, but here we are already at Volume 4 (the words of an old man).

This volume is full of *youkai* who quickly get beat up. Gensokyo seems peaceful, but deep at its roots, that peace is always threatened by unstable *youkai* and demons. That's why the Human Village, which can see only the surface world, is somehow always finding itself in a state of unrest.

In "Kokkuri-san Scatters with the Cherry Blossoms," there is some dialogue that suggests Akyu is fated to a short life. As far as her spirit is concerned, she will only be reincarnated and reborn as another person, but perhaps she still has some attachment to the current era. Well, anyone would. It's a fun era.

Well, I hope to see you again in Volume 5 or in *Comp Ace*.

Moe Harukawa

Hello. I am the artist, Harukawa.

Reimu, Akyu, Kosuzu... Each of the characters' motives come to light, and I feel like we're gradually starting to see the true essence of this series here in Volume 4. As a reader, I look forward to future developments.

To ZUN-san, who writes the story outline for me every month despite his busy schedule, my editor who deals with everything so quickly, and all of you who read this book, thank you very much.

I suspect that I'll worry a lot about the covers from Volume 5 on.

Forbidden Scrollery

4

STORY
ZUN

ART
Moe Harukawa

TRANSLATION: ALETHEA NIBLEY AND ATHENA NIBLEY
LETTERING: ALEXIS ECKERMAN

This book is a work of fiction. Names, characters, places, and incidents are the product of the author's imagination or are used fictitiously. Any resemblance to actual events, locales, or persons, living or dead, is coincidental.

TOUHOU SUZUNA AN ~Forbidden Scrollery. Vol. 4
© Team Shanghai Alice © Moe HARUKAWA 2015
First published in Japan in 2015 by KADOKAWA CORPORATION, Tokyo.
English translation rights arranged with KADOKAWA CORPORATION, Tokyo
through TUTTLE-MORI AGENCY, Inc., Tokyo.

English translation © 2018 by Yen Press, LLC

Yen Press, LLC supports the right to free expression and the value of copyright.
The purpose of copyright is to encourage writers and artists to produce the creative works that enrich our culture.

The scanning, uploading, and distribution of this book without permission is a theft of the author's intellectual property. If you would like permission to use material from the book (other than for review purposes), please contact the publisher. Thank you for your support of the author's rights.

Yen Press
1290 Avenue of the Americas
New York, NY 10104

VISIT US AT YENPRESS.COM

facebook.com/yenpress yenpress.tumblr.com
twitter.com/yenpress instagram.com/yenpress

First Yen Press Edition: August 2018

Yen Press is an imprint of Yen Press, LLC.
The Yen Press name and logo are trademarks of Yen Press, LLC.

The publisher is not responsible for websites (or their content) that are not owned by the publisher.

Library of Congress Control Number: 2017949553

ISBNs: 978-0-316-51194-0 (paperback)
978-0-316-51203-9 (ebook)

10 9 8 7 6 5 4 3 2 1

WOR

Printed in the United States of America